RELICS OF THE BUDDHA

BUDDHISMS:

A PRINCETON UNIVERSITY PRESS SERIES

EDITED BY STEPHEN F. TEISER

A list of titles in this series appears at the back of the book

RELICS OF THE BUDDHA

John S. Strong

PRINCETON UNIVERSITY PRESS · PRINCETON AND OXFORD

Published by Princeton University Press,
41 William Street, Princeton, New Jersey 08540
In the United Kingdom: Princeton University Press,
3 Market Place, Woodstock, Oxfordshire OX20 1SY

Library of Congress Cataloging-in-Publication Data

Strong, John, 1948–
Relics of the Buddha / John S. Strong.
p. cm. —(Buddhisms)
Includes bibliographical references and index.
ISBN: 0-691-11764-0 (cl : alk. paper)
1. Gautama Buddha—Relics—South Asia. 2. Gautama Buddha—Relics—Southeast Asia. 3. Buddhist shrines—South Asia. 4. Buddhist shrines—Asia, Southeastern. 5. Stupas—South Asia—History. 6. Stupas—Asia, Southeastern—History. I. Title. II. Series.

BQ924.S77 2004
294.3'63—dc22 2003065642

British Library Cataloging-in-Publication Data is available

This book has been composed in Sabon Typeface
Printed on acid-free paper. ∞
www.pupress.princeton.edu
Printed in the United States of America

3 5 7 9 10 8 6 4

ISBN-13: 978-0-691-11764-5
ISBN-10: 0-691-11764-0

For Anna and Aaron and Isaac

CONTENTS

TABLES

PREFACE

SOMETIME in the middle of the fifth century, the Chinese pilgrim Daorong set out for India on foot. When he and his companions arrived in what is now Afghanistan, they proceeded to visit various sites of pilgrimage, places that were, in one way or another, associated with the historical Buddha Śākyamuni. In Nagarahāra, they found "a piece of bone from the top of the Buddha's skull . . . , four inches long and beige in color" (Wang 1984: 243–44; text in *T.* 2092, 51:1021c). A bit further on, they visited a monastery, where the Buddha's staff was enshrined, and, in the city itself, they stopped at another sanctuary, where some teeth and hair of the Buddha were kept in a jeweled reliquary. Outside of town, they went to a famous cave, where they saw the "shadow" of the Buddha, an image he was said to have projected on a wall of the grotto.[1] Near the cave, they venerated a set of Buddha footprints imprinted on a rock, and, a bit further away, a spot where the Buddha had washed his robe. Beyond that was a large stūpa, said to have been built by the Tathāgata himself, which was gradually sinking into the ground; its final disappearance would mark the end of the Buddha's teaching. By the side of the stūpa was an inscription in Sanskrit reportedly written in the Buddha's own hand (*T.* 2092, 51:1021c–22a = Eng. trans., Wang 1984: 243–45; see also Chavannes 1903: 427–29).

Throughout the Buddhist world, pilgrims have long visited and venerated a great number and variety of buddha relics. Indeed, from Kandy to Kyoto, there was hardly a Buddhist site that did not enshrine some physical remains of the Buddha, some object that once belonged to him, some trace of his presence enlivened by association with his body, his teaching (dharma), or his community of followers (saṃgha). Simply put, buddha relics, broadly defined, were "everywhere." For hundreds of years, pilgrims to India commonly came across stūpas believed to have been built by the third-century B.C.E. emperor Aśoka, who was reputed to have enshrined relics of the Buddha in 84,000 places throughout his

[1] This "shadow cave" and its relic-like image were visited by many pilgrims besides Daorong. See *T.* 2087, 51:879a = Eng. trans., Li 1996: 67–68; *T.* 2085, 51:859a = Eng. trans., Li 2002: 173; and Petech 1966–74, 1:179–80. For legends about the cave and the nāga who dwelt there, see *T.* 643, 15:679b–81b = Fr. trans., Przyluski 1914: 565–68; *Avk.*, 2:338–40; and Soper 1949–50: 273–83. On the popularity of the Buddha's shadow in Chinese tradition and its reproduction on Mount Lu, see Shinohara 1999: 945–47; and Tsukamoto 1985, 2:885–89.

realm.[2] Shrines for hair relics (often associated with fingernail-clipping relics) were likewise numerous; a Southeast Asian tradition, for instance, asserts that, after the Buddha's parinirvāṇa, the gods distributed his 800,000 body hairs and 900,000 head hairs "throughout this universe of ours" (Halliday 1923: 46). In the seventh century, the pilgrim Xuanzang reported that, at the site in India where the Buddha was cremated, one could find any number of relics simply by praying earnestly (*T.* 2087, 51:904b = Eng. trans., Li 1996:190). In China, by the Tang dynasty, the proliferation of relics was so great that one scholar has spoken of it as a "hemorrhage of the sacred" (Faure 1996: 163). The same could be said of early medieval Japan, where relics were avidly collected by monks and aristocrats alike (see Ruppert 1997: appendix). Along with such proliferations went the assumption that relics were able to reproduce themselves, to grow, multiply, or appear miraculously (see Faure 1991: 138–39; Barrett 2001: 41; and Martin 1992). An eleventh-century Chinese author, for example, reports how once, when he was examining a buddha's tooth in a monastery, it suddenly started producing small relic pellets: "They wafted away in countless numbers, some flying up into the air and others falling to the ground. . . . They sparkled brightly, filling the eyes with light. When I arrived back at the capital they circulated among ranking officials there who passed them among themselves" (Kieschnick 2003: 51). Similar phenomena may be seen even in modern times. In 1970, for instance, buddha relics began to grow spontaneously out of the east side of the stūpa of Svayambhūnātha in Kathmandu. "There were thousands of them all over the ground," reported one observer, "and all the monastery, including the highest lama, who almost never left his room, were outside picking them up" (Allione 1984: 203–4; see also Martin 1994: 283).

In the Theravāda world, according to Buddhaghosa (fifth century), possession of a relic was one of the definitional criteria for what constituted a proper monastery (*AA.*, 4:186), and still today, relics of the Buddha are found in virtually every community, sometimes in very large numbers.[3] Richard Gombrich (1971: 106) remarks that, in all of his time in Sri Lanka, he "came across only one temple that did not claim to possess a relic," and he goes on to remind us of the routine nature of the phenomenon:

> Though they are of course handled with the greatest veneration, in a wider sense these relics are casually dealt with: I invariably asked after the origin

[2] For Aśoka stūpas visited by Chinese pilgrims in India, see Watters 1904: index, s.v. "Aśoka topes." On the legend of the 84,000 stūpas, see chapter 5 in this book.

[3] For instance, Wat Côm Ping in Northern Thailand claims to enshrine over 50,000 buddha relics. See Rhum 1994: 178.

> of a relic, but never got any reply more interesting than that it was inherited from the monk's teacher. . . . These village relics are indeed not very impressive objects: as a special favour I was shown those in Mīgala, precious casket removed to reveal precious casket, until the last tiny stūpa contained a couple of minute white balls of what I presume was bone. (106–7)

This is not to say that there are not famous relics of the Buddha, with impressive pedigrees and a full complement of myths attached to them. Indeed, in this book, I will primarily be considering traditions about such relics, but, in doing so, it is important to remember from the outset that these represent only the most visible and renowned parts of a heritage of relic veneration that was always, to some extent, extraordinary, but often routine and including common, generic objects of devotion.

I first became interested in Buddhist relics while working on a book on the legends of King Aśoka (Strong 1983). That interest then broadened into more general endeavors in the comparative study of relics (Strong 1987, 1995, and forthcoming) before narrowing once again to a "focus" on bodily relics of the Buddha. In the chapters that follow, I will be concerned primarily with South and Southeast Asian legendary and cultic traditions about relics of the Buddha's physical body, although I shall also pay some attention to "secondary" relics such as his footprints, his bowl, his robe, and his bodhi tree. Though not totally oblivious to questions of dating and historicity, I will not hesitate to mix together sources from the beginnings of the Buddhist record almost right up to the present, and representing a whole gamut of genres. Here, the stuff of legends, the stances of doctrine, the records of inscriptions, the makings of myth, the reports of pilgrims, even the comments of modern travelers, will all be combined in a "method" that I have called elsewhere "exegetical exploration" (Strong 1992: xii). In this approach, particular texts or particular issues are taken as focal points for presenting and discussing the problematics of a given tradition, and the effort to understand these texts and issues is further developed by the perspectives of different contexts and co-texts.

Since relics tell stories, much attention will be given to telling the stories of relics, and seeking to understand their significances and connotations. To a large extent, then, I shall proceed anecdotally, presenting and discussing a succession of stories about Buddhist relics, admitting that many of these texts are only partially representative of an overall tradition whose full complexity undermines generalizations. Nonetheless, it is my hope that, as Wendy Doniger ([O'Flaherty] 1988: 2) once put it, "stories reveal things that are not easily gleaned from the harder disciplines," especially if we can remember that "stories are not designed as arguments, nor should they be taken as arguments."

Throughout, I will try to make no judgments about the truth value of the traditions being explored. Some claims, made in some texts, may strike some readers as preposterous or absurd; others, as profound expressions of religious devotion or experience. In either case, it is important to remember that the Buddhist authors of many of the texts we will be considering sometimes experienced these same ambiguities themselves.[4]

Finally, it should be said that the Sanskrit and Pali words that are most commonly translated as "relic" have rather different connotations than their English counterpart (see Collins 1998: 277–78; Schopen 1998: 256). The Latin word for "relic," stemming from the verb *relinquere,* has the root meaning of "something left over or remaining behind." The Sanskrit *dhātu* (Pali: idem), however, means "constituent element of essential ingredient" (Monier-Williams 1899: 513). In this context, Buddhist relics may be seen not as the leftover but as the essence that is extracted from the dead, cremated body (Schopen 1998: 257; Gombrich 1971: 106), or, as we shall see, from the living person. The other relevant Sanskrit word, *śarīra* (Pali: *sarīra*) means "body," although, as Gregory Schopen (1998: 257) has pointed out, when it implies something like our notion of relic, it is usually used in the plural. In South Asian Buddhist sources, then, relics arise from a process of multiplication or addition rather than subtraction. They are products or sum totals of the body rather than remainders. How seriously all these diverging etymological connotations should be taken is another matter. It is important to note them, yet, as Schopen (1998: 257) further points out, though the meanings of the various terms may differ, the treatment of relics in both Christian and Buddhist traditions—"what is done for or to them, what is said about them, and what they themselves do"—is very often similar.[5]

Over the years, many individuals and institutions have helped me in the writing of this book, and I would like to express my gratitude to them here. First, I would like to thank participants in the American Academy of Religion Seminar on Buddhist Relic Veneration, which ran from 1994 to 1998. These include, in particular, David Germano and Kevin Trainor, who organized the seminar, and Yael Bentor, Bernard Faure, Charles Hallisey, Thomas Head, Jacob Kinnard, Suzanne Mrozic, Juliane Schober,

[4] See, for example, the story of Xuanzang's doubts about certain relics of extraordinary size that he saw in Bodhgaya in *T.* 2053, 50:244b = Eng. trans., Li 1995: 128–29. Alternatively, see the Tibetan story, recounted in Patrul 1994: 173–74, of the woman who had so much devotion that a fake relic (a dog's tooth) given to her by her son actually began to perform miracles.

[5] This is not to deny that there are also many real differences in the two traditions' treatment of relics. See Strong, forthcoming.

Gregory Schopen, Robert Sharf, and Donald Swearer, who, whether or not they realized it, helped me focus my thoughts as this project was getting started. In addition, I am grateful to the faculty and students of various institutions who gave me an opportunity to carry out research and to teach, over the years, a number of seminars on relics that also helped me develop my thoughts: as Numata Visiting Professor of Buddhist Studies at the Divinity School of the University of Chicago (Spring 1995), as Stewart Professor in the Department of Religion and the Council of the Humanities at Princeton University (Fall 1997), as Numata Visiting Professor of Buddhist Studies at Harvard University (Spring 2002), and as Visiting Professor in the Department of Religious Studies at Stanford University (Spring 2003).

Abbreviated versions of chapters one, two, and four were given as lectures: at the XIIth Conference of the International Association of Buddhist Studies in Lausanne (August 1999), at a symposium on relics entitled "Absence Made Tangible" at the University of California at Los Angeles (January 2001), and at a conference on "Death and Dying in Buddhism" held at Princeton University (May 2002). I would like to thank colleagues present on those occasions for their feedback, especially Richard Gombrich; James Benn, Robert Buswell, Jinhua Chen, Bryan Ruppert; and Phyllis Granoff.

Finally, I would like to express my gratitude to a number of other individuals who read all, or portions, of this work, and helpfully commented on it: Fred Appel, Johannes Bronkhorst, Benjamin Brose, Megan Bryson, George Clonos, John Holt, Sara Lerner, John Pang, Frank Reynolds, Kristin Scheible, Juliane Schober, Sarah Strong, Stephen Teiser, Donald Swearer, Kevin Trainor, Linda Truilo, and Zhaohua Yang.

NOTE AND ABBREVIATIONS

In citing Sanskrit and Pali sources, I have sought to provide references both to original language editions as well as to English, French, or German translations when available. In dealing with Chinese canonical works, I have been guided by existing translations in Western languages, but, for the convenience of scholars, I have also included references to the standard *Taishō* (*T.*) edition of the texts in question, even when those translations were based on originals found not in *T.* but in other earlier editions. In all cases, editions are cited by abbreviated title (as given below), and translations, marked off by an equals sign (=) and by the name of the translator plus the date (as listed in the bibliography). When I am directly quoting from someone else's translation, however, I cite the name of the translator first and indicate the original language source of the text second.

In discussions of texts and in references to names, I have generally used Sanskrit forms in preference to Pali ones, except in places where the context makes such a practice seem absurd. Thus, I speak of "nirvāṇa," "Gautama," and "Aśoka" (Sanskrit) rather than of "nibbāna," "Gotama," and "Asoka" (Pali). In references to Chinese Buddhist texts, I have used reconstructed Sanskrit titles when these are more or less reliable. In this, I have generally followed Lancaster 1979.

Abbreviations

(Full bibliographic information is given in the bibliography.)

A. = *Anguttara Nikāya*
AA. = *Manorathapūraṇī* [Commentary on *A.*]
AMMK. = *Ārya-Mañjuśrīmūlakalpa.* See edited text in Jayaswal 1934.
Ap. = *Apadāna*
ApA. = *Visuddhajanavilāsinī* [Commentary on *Ap.*]
Aśokāv. = *Aśokāvadāna*
Aṣṭa = *Aṣṭasāhasrikāprajñāramitā sūtra*
Avk. = *Avadānakalpalatā*
Avś. = *Avadānaśataka*
Bcar. = *Buddhacarita*

Brapaṃsukūla. = *Brapaṃsukūlānisaṃsam.* See edited text in Martini 1973.
Buv. = *Buddhavaṃsa*
BuvA. = *Madhuratthavilāsinī* [Commentary on *Buv.*]
Catuṣ. = *Catuṣpariṣatsūtra.* See edited text in Waldschmidt 1962.
Chak. = *Chakesadhātuvaṃsa*
Cūl. = *Cūḷavaṃsa*
D. = *Dīgha Nikāya*
DA. = *Sumangalavilāsinī* [Commentary on *D.*]
Dasab. = *Dasabodhisattuppattikathā.* See edited text in Saddhatissa 1975.
Dāṭh. = *Dāṭhāvaṃsa*
DhA. = *Dhammapadaṭṭhakathā.* In bibliography, see under *Commentary on the Dhammapada.*
Div. = *Divyāvadāna*
Dpv. = *Dīpavaṃsa.* See edited text in Oldenberg 1982.
ExtMhv. = *Extended Mahāvaṃsa*
GilgMss. = *Gilgit Manuscripts*
Hman-Nan-Y. = *Hman-Nan-Yazawindawgyi*
Itv. = *Itivuttaka*
JA. = *Jātakaṭṭhakathā.* In bibliography, see under *Jātaka Together with Its Commentary.*
Jin. = *Jinakālamālīpakaraṇam.*
Jinab. = *Jinabodhāvalī.* See edited text in Liyanaratne 1983.
Jināl. = *Jinālaṅkāra.* See edited text in Gray 1894.
JM. = *Jātakamālā*
KhpA. = *Paramatthajotikā I* [Commentary on *Khuddaka-Pāṭha*]. In bibliography, see under *Khuddaka-Pāṭha Together with Its Commentary.*
Lal. = *Lalitavistara*
LP = *Lokapaññatti.* See edited text in Denis 1977.
M. = *Majjhima Nikāya*
MA = *Papañcasūdanī* [Commentary on *M.*]
Mhv. = *Mahāvaṃsa*
Mil. = *Milindapañha.* In bibliography, see under *Milindapañho.*
MPS. = *Mahāparinirvāṇasūtra.* See edited text in Waldschmidt 1950–51.
Mtu. = *Mahāvastu*
Paññāsa-j = *Paññāsa-jātaka*
S. = *Samyutta Nikāya*
SA. = *Sāratthappakāsinī* [Commentary on *S.*]
Sanghbhv. = *Sanghabhedavastu.* See edited text in Gnoli 1978.
Sās. = *Sāsanavaṃsa*
Śayanās. = *Śayanāsanavastu.* See edited text in Gnoli 1978a.

Sdmp. = *Saddharmapuṇḍarīka Sūtra*
Skv. = *Samantakūṭavaṇṇanā*
Sn. = *Suttanipāta*
Suv. = *Suvarṇaprabhāsasūtra*
T. = *Taishō shinshū daizōkyō*. Citations refer to text number, volume and page number, and register (a, b, or c).

T. 1 *Dīrghāgama*
T. 5 *Mahāparinirvāṇa sūtra* (translated by Bo Fazu)
T. 6 *Mahāparinirvāṇa sūtra* (anonymous translation)
T. 7 *Mahāparinirvāṇa sūtra* (translated by Faxian)
T. 99 *Samyuktāgama*
T. 152 *Liu du ji jing*
T. 190 *Abhiniṣkramaṇa sūtra*
T. 192 *Buddhacarita*
T. 202 *Damamūkanidāna sūtra*
T. 203 *Za bao zang jing*
T. 262 *Saddharmapuṇḍarīka sūtra*
T. 384 *Pu sa chu tai jing*
T. 386 *Lian hua mian jing*
T. 392 *Fo mie du hou guan lian zang song jing*
T. 455 *Maitreyavyākaraṇa sūtra*
T. 456 *Mi le da cheng fo jing*
T. 643 *Buddhānusmṛtisamādhi sūtra*
T. 699 *Zao ta gong de jing*
T. 1421 *Mahīśāsaka vinaya*
T. 1425 *Mahāsāṃghika vinaya*
T. 1428 *Dharmaguptaka vinaya*
T. 1435 *Sarvāstivāda vinaya*
T. 1448 [*Mūlasarvāstivāda*] *Vinayavastu*
T. 1451 [*Mūlasarvāstivāda*] *Vinayakṣudrakavastu*
T. 1464 *Bi nai ye*
T. 1509 *Mahāprajñāpāramitā śāstra*
T. 1545 *Mahāvibhāṣa*
T. 2030 *Nandimitrāvadāna*
T. 2042 *Aśokarājāvadāna*
T. 2043 *Aśokarāja sūtra*
T. 2046 *Ma ming pu sa zhuan*
T. 2053 *Da ci en si san zang fa shi zhuan* [of Huili]
T. 2059 *Gao seng zhuan* [of Huijiao]
T. 2066 *Da tang xi yu qiu fa gao seng zhuan* [of Yijing]
T. 2085 *Gao seng fa xian zhuan* [of Faxian]
T. 2087 *Da tang xi yu ji* [of Xuanzang]

T. 2092 *Luo yang qie lan ji* [of Yang Xuanzhi]
T. 2122 *Fa yuan zhu lin* [of Daoshi]
T. 2125 *Nan hai ji gui nei fa zhuan* [of Yijing]

Thag. = *Thera and Therī-gāthā*

ThagA. = *Paramaṭṭha-dīpanī* [Commentary on *Thag.*]

Thūp. = *Thūpavaṃsa*. See edited text in Jayawickrama 1971.

VibhA. = *Sammohavinodanī* [Commentary on the *Vibhanga*]. In bibliography, see under Ñāṇamoli 1996.

Vin. = *Vinaya piṭakam*

VinA. = *Samantapāsādika* [Commentary on *Vin.*]. See also Jayawickrama 1962.

Vsm. = *Visuddhimagga*

RELICS OF THE BUDDHA

RELICS OF THE BUDDHA

In 1561, an interesting ceremony took place in the Portuguese enclave of Gõa, in Southwestern India. During a military operation in Sri Lanka, Portuguese troops had captured what "local idolaters" (i.e., Buddhists) claimed was the tooth of the Buddha, and had delivered it as a prize to their viceroy, Don Constantino da Bragança. The viceroy had hoped to hold it for ransom, but now the archbishop of Gõa, Don Gaspar, was insisting that it be destroyed. On a porch overlooking the river, in the presence of a great crowd of Christians and "pagans," he called for the tooth and "placed it in a mortar, and with his own hand reduced it to powder, and cast the pieces into a brazier which stood ready for the purpose; after which the ashes and the charcoal together were cast into the river, in sight of all those who were crowding the verandahs and windows which looked upon the water" (Tennent 1859, 2:215. See also chapter 7 in this book).

As benighted as such an action may seem to us today, it can at least be said that the Portuguese archbishop appreciated the nature of relics. Conscious of the power of holy objects from his own tradition, he felt that the tooth had to be utterly and permanently eradicated. In his mind, this was not just a piece of bone that he was destroying but a "relic of the devil" (*reliquia do demonio*) something alive that had to be killed (Tennent 1859, 2:214; text in De Couto 1783, 17:429).[1]

Rather different were the attitudes of some of Don Gaspar's Protestant contemporaries in Europe. John Calvin, to my knowledge, never said anything about Buddhist relics, but in 1543 he wrote a whole treatise on Roman Catholic ones (Calvin 1970). And although he too, given the chance, would probably have crushed the Buddha's tooth to bits, he would have done so for different reasons. For him, relics embodied no sacred or even demonic presence, and it was wrong and exploitative to pretend that they did. Relics were nothing but material things, as he pointed out when he got rid of what had been two of Geneva's prized relics—the arm of Saint Anthony and the brain of Saint Peter; the one, he proclaimed, was but the bone of a stag, and the other a piece of pumice (Calvin 1970: 53).[2]

[1] A similar view of this relic as possessed may be found in De Queyroz 1930, 1:365.

[2] Calvin's views were in line with those of earlier humanist and Reformation figures such

This is not the place to examine the varying influences of Roman Catholicism and Protestantism on the comparative study of material objects of devotion. Suffice it to say that Western scholarship on relics is heir to two rather different sets of prejudices, the one affirming the ongoing *presence* and power of the supernatural in objects, the other maintaining its ontological *absence* and seeing such objects as no more than material symbols or signifiers of a "divine" being or power whose locus is elsewhere or who died long ago.

During the nineteenth and early twentieth century, at least in certain circles, the second, or "Protestant," perspective came to predominate in the study of Buddhism. Championing the claim that the Buddha, after his final nirvāṇa, was totally removed from any relationship to this world, scholars tended to see Buddhist objects of devotion such as images and relics not as embodying the impossible presence of a deceased Master, but as mere mnemonic devices for recalling his teaching and his example. The Buddha was to be found primarily in his doctrine; to think of him as present elsewhere, in statues or relics, for instance, was an aberration to be condemned—as one missionary-scholar put it—as "mere material worship," akin to the Roman Catholic cults of "the [seamless] Garment of our Lord," of "the skulls of the Three Wise Men" in Cologne, and of the "exceedingly numerous" portions of the True Cross, all of which were "examples of a dark age" (Wylie [1897] 1966: 79–80).[3]

"True Buddhism," understood as the original teachings of the Buddha, was thought to have nothing to do with such things as relics. Thus, the American Monist Paul Carus, whose book, *The Gospel of Buddha,* achieved considerable popularity around the turn of the century, turned down the offer of a Buddha relic from a Sri Lankan monk, telling him, "The worship of relics, be they bones, hair, teeth, or any other substance of the body of a saint, is a mistake. . . . The soul of Buddha is not in his bones, but in his words, and I regard relic-worship as an incomplete development in which devotees have not as yet attained to full philosophical clearness" (Carus 1897: 123).[4] Along these lines, it was often assumed that those who had reached "full philosophical clearness" were the cultured monastic elite, while those who had not and worshiped relics and images were

---

as Erasmus, for whom "there could never be anything more disgusting than the cult of relics," and Martin Bucer, who declared that "bones are bones and not gods" (Eire 1986: 40, 91). See also Bentley 1985: 169–94.

[3] For Wylie, relics were "the surest symptom of decay" of a religion. For other examples of Protestant condemnations of Buddhist relics by comparing them to Roman Catholic ones, see Hardy 1850: 249; Smith 1918: 661; and Pratt 1928: 133n.

[4] For a fuller presentation of Carus's correspondence on relics with the monk Alutgama Sīlakkhandha, see Trainor 1997: 18–23.

the laity. The existence of relics in the Buddhist tradition, when it was recognized at all, was thus seen as a concession to the superstitious and devotional needs of the lay populace. Espoused by prominent scholars such as Hermann Oldenberg (1928: 377), this "two-tiered" view lingered well into the twentieth century and may, indeed, still be found.[5]

In more recent times, however, a pendulum swing away from such opinions has taken place in the study of Buddhism. Already in 1973, David Snellgrove declared that, although "there were certainly pure philosophical doctrines propounded during the early history of Buddhism, just as there have been ever since, . . . there is no such thing as pure Buddhism *per se* except perhaps the cult of Śākyamuni as a supramundane being and the cult of the relic *stūpa* (1973: 411). In more recent times, inspired by the emergence of sophisticated studies of Christian relics (e.g., Brown 1981, Geary 1978), religious images (Freedberg 1989), notions of the body (Bynum 1995, Dissanayake 1993) and death practices (Ariès 1982, Danforth 1982, Bloch and Parry 1982), buddhologists have developed a new seriousness about material culture in general and relics in particular. Thus today, as Robert Sharf (1999: 78) has pointed out,

> "[I]t is no longer acceptable to dismiss casually the worship of relics and images as aberrant or un-Buddhist, as a sop to the plebeian needs of the unlettered masses. Scholars now appreciate that, with few exceptions, the clerical elite found nothing objectionable in the worship of relics, but enthusiastically engaged in and promoted such activities themselves. There is thus little reason to believe that the display of relics contravenes either the letter or the spirit of Buddhist teachings."[6]

In questioning Protestant presuppositions in the field, buddhologists, in fact, have developed new perspectives of the tradition they study.[7] As Sharf (1999: 79), again, has commented, "Buddhism may no longer resemble European humanism, mysticism (the 'perennial philosophy'), or enlightened rationalism, but it has come to bear an uncanny resemblance to medieval Christianity . . . [with] its saints, relics, and miraculous images." In this process, certain views that attribute power and life and "presence" to the relics have reemerged. For instance, Gregory Schopen, who has eloquently critiqued Protestant prejudices in the study of Buddhism, has also explored the many ways in which the Buddha was thought to be

[5] See Bareau 1962: 269 and 1974b: 285; and Ling 1973: 167–74. For a discussion of Brown's (1981) "two-tiered" thesis in the study of Buddhism, see Ray 1994: 15–23.

[6] On the centrality of relics in the beliefs of both monastics and laypersons, see also Snellgrove 1973: 410; and Schopen 1997.

[7] On Protestant (and Orientalist) biases in the study of Buddhism, see Almond 1988; Gombrich and Obeyesekere 1988: 202–240; Lopez 1995; Schopen 1991.

"alive" in his relics: he / they had rights as a legal "person," or could own property; and destroying a stūpa containing relics was viewed as a capital offense, in other words, as the murder of a living person (Schopen 1997: 125ff. and 258ff., 1995, and 1996a). Alternatively, relics were seen as "saturated / invigorated / enlivened by morality, concentration, wisdom, emancipation, knowledge and vision," that is, "exactly the same spiritual forces and faculties that characterize, . . . constitute and animate the living Buddha" (Schopen 1997: 154). Elsewhere, Schopen declares that "there is no distinction between a living Buddha and a collection of relics—both make the sacred person equally present as an object of worship, and the presence of either makes available the same opportunity to make merit" (1997: 132).

As a number of scholars have pointed out, this comes very close to attributing to Buddhists a kind of Lévy-Bruhlian "prelogical mentality" that senses a "mystical participation" (Lévy-Bruhl 1926: 76–7) between the Buddha and his relics,[8] or a Robertson Smith–like view of objects being "instinct with divine life" or "embodiments of the presence of the deity" (Smith 1972: 173, 204).[9] I shall have more to say about Schopen's views of relics later. For now, suffice it to point out that, in the final analysis, he appears to shy away from an *ontological equation* of the Buddha and his relics and to assert rather their ritual and *functional equivalence.* The relics are alive, own property, perform miracles, inspire devotees, are filled with various buddha qualities, in exactly the same way that the Buddha is. This does not mean that they *are* the Buddha, that they make *him* present. Rather they are themselves present in the same way that he is, they can act like him, they are a substitute for him in his absence.

In between the poles of absence and presence, there is clearly a lot of room for positions that seek, in various ways, to combine the two views. Indeed, as more and more scholars have payed attention to Buddhist relics, a plethora of positions attempting to pin down this dialectical relationship have emerged. These cannot all be spelled out here. To put it succinctly, we now have open to us the possibility of viewing Buddhist relics as "indexical icons" (Tambiah 1984: 5, and 204, inspired by C. S. Peirce and Arthur Burks), "sedimentations of charisma" (Tambiah 1984: 335ff., developing Max Weber), products of the Buddhist "habitus" (Kinnard 1999: 9–11, 157–58, inspired by Pierre Bourdieu), "zero signifiers" (Ohnuki-Tierney 1994, inspired by Roman Jakobson and John Lotz, and Jacques Derrida), "chronotopes" (Eckel 1992: 62, inspired by Mikhail Bakhtin), "heterotopias" (Eckel 1992: 63, inspired by Michel Foucault),

[8] On this theme see Sharf 1999: 79, and, for a more general discussion of the persistence of Lévy-Bruhlianism, see Tambiah 1990: 84–110.

[9] On this theme, see Kinnard 1999: 4–5.

and places "where an absence is present" (Eckel 1992: 65, inspired by Nāgārjuna and Bhāvaviveka). They can also be seen as the manifest presence of an essence that acts as a "visible representation of the immortal nirvāṇa state," and that helps reconcile a contradiction between a "cognitive" understanding that the Buddha is dead, and a "psychological" or "affective" sense that he is living (Obeyesekere 1966: 8);[10] as "memory sites" that are "the ultimate embodiment of a commemorative consciousness" (Hallisey 1996: 7, inspired by Pierre Nora); as manifestations of the postmortem force of a buddha's resolutions (Trainor 1997: 136–88, inspired by Buddhaghosa); as "metamorphoses of the double" (Faure 1991: 132–47, inspired by Robert Hertz); as embodiments of "the sense of an ending" (Collins 1992: 233, inspired by Frank Kermode); as that "final and insensible scream that is the 'supreme affirmation of life'" (Sharf 1999: 90, inspired by Georges Bataille); as "instruments of magical power [and] kernels of pure *imaginaire*" (Faure 1999: 15, after Jacques LeGoff); as instances of "euphemization" (Ruppert 2000: 96, inspired by Pierre Bourdieu); as "hierophanies" (Schober 2001, following Mircea Eliade); as particular forms of buddha-emanation bodies (Bentor 1996, based on Tibetan nirmānakāya [*sprul-sku*] doctrine); as "blazing absences" (Germano 1994, based on Tibetan Nying ma sources); and probably in many other ways.

Relics and the Biographical Process

In this book, I would like to approach this whole question on a slightly different tack. I propose to view relics not as the embodiments of a transcendent or imminent or otherwise absent Buddha, nor just as functionally equivalent to the departed Master, but as *expressions and extensions of the Buddha's biographical process.* The same point has been made by others, especially with regard to buddha images. Juliane Schober (1997: 260–68), for instance, has shown how the relic-like Mahāmuni image of the Buddha in Mandalay was thought of as a continuator of the life story of the Buddha, to the extent that it was even deemed to have to suffer some of the unworked-out negative karma dating from the Buddha's previous lives. More generally, Donald Swearer (forthcoming) has demonstrated how image consecration ceremonies, at least in Northern Thailand, involve the ritual narrative infusion into the image of the whole life

[10] The same view was applied to Buddha images in Gombrich 1971: 4–10, 142. There are significant parallels between this and the views of Paul Mus, for whom the Buddha in nirvāṇa was treated as a "new kind of absence" that could be overcome not ontologically but through a ritual and magical process focused on relics (as well as stūpas and images) and based on the model of Brahmanical sacrifice. See Mus 1935, 1:74, 89–90, 190; and 1937: 91.

of the Buddha, especially of the event of his enlightenment. As he puts it elsewhere, "[T]he sacred biography takes a concrete, visual form in the very image of the *Tathāgata*" (1995: 268).

Much the same thing may be found in the practice of enshrining relics in the midst of architectural or artistic reminders of the Buddha's life story. I will examine a classic instance of this, in chapter 6, in the case of the relic chamber of King Duṭṭhagāmaṇī's "Great Stūpa" in Sri Lanka (first century B.C.E.). For now, suffice it to cite an example from Southeast Asia. In 1912, an earthquake in Northern Burma crumbled the corners of the Hlèdauk Pagoda, laying bare two of its relic chambers. Inside were found not only a vessel containing relics of the Buddha, but "many small figures in bronze representing the most important scenes in the life of [the] Buddha" (Duroiselle 1911–12: 149). These included representations of the first jātaka, the story of Sumedha prostrating himself at the feet of the past buddha Dīpaṃkara; images of all the other twenty-eight previous buddhas venerated by the Buddha in his past lives; figurines depicting the Buddha's mother, Mahāmāyā, giving birth to him; the seven steps he took immediately after he was born; the signs of the old man, sick man, dead man, and ascetic that prompted him to go forth on his "great departure"; scenes of him cutting off his hair with his sword and of Indra receiving that hair relic in heaven; statuettes showing his enlightenment and the events of each of the seven weeks following it; the first sermon he preached to his first five disciples; and various events from his teaching career, ending with the scene of his death and parinirvāṇa (Duroiselle 1911–12: 150–51).[11] Such "bioramas," as they may be called, are not uncommon,[12] and they testify to the importance of the life story of the Buddha in defining the nature of a relic.

It should be remembered that in Buddhism, it is biography that makes a buddha and not the Buddha who makes his biography. In other words, all buddhas, even in the Theravāda tradition, follow a biographical blueprint that defines them and makes them who they are (see Strong 2001: 10–14). At the most fundamental level, this biographical blueprint is the story of someone who comes and goes in the same way that other buddhas have come and gone. Another way of putting this is that it is the story of someone who becomes *present* as a buddha—who works toward buddhahood through his past lives and his quest for enlightenment, and manifests that buddhahood in his teaching—and who then becomes *absent* as a buddha, through his death and his parinirvāṇa. The great lesson of Buddhism is not that of impermanence, if, by impermanence is

[11] On all of these episodes in the life of the Buddha, see Strong 2001.

[12] For another instance, see Taw Sein Ko 1903–04: 154–56, and plates 51 and 52.

simply meant "nothing lasts forever." It is rather that of process—that things, beings, buddhas come into existence due to certain causes and go out of existence due to certain causes. Indeed, the one verse that best summarizes the whole teaching of the Buddha is the often-repeated and copied formula: "Ye dharmā hetuprabhavās teṣām hetum Tathāgata uvāca / teṣām ca yo nirodha evam vādī mahāśramaṇaḥ˙" ("The Tathāgata has explained the cause of those elements of reality (dharmas) that arise from a cause, and he, the Mahāśramaṇa [the "Great Recluse"], has also spoken of their cessation").

It is worth considering the implications of this for our study of relics. It is my contention that the Buddha himself, in his life story, exhibits the truth of this formula, in that his biography tells the causes of his final life and buddhahood as well as their cessation. His relics, in so far as they are *expressions* of the Buddha's biography, are thus also expressions of this process. In this regard, Buddhist relics (unlike Christian relics) do not make manifest some transcendent or immanent reality, but retell a tale; they sum up a biographical narrative; they embody the whole of the Buddha's coming and going, his life-and-death story; they reiterate both his provenance and his impermanence.[13] This is true, even when their immediate reference is only to one portion of that biography[14] for, as Steven Collins (1992: 241) has pointed out, "when an enshrined relic is venerated, the whole story is implicitly present." Though they are material objects, relics can thus help bring to mind and invite reflection on a whole narrative that is upheld and recognized by the community.

At the same time, however, relics are also *extensions* of the Buddha's biography. It is perhaps possible to think of this as an assertion of the ongoing "presence" of the Buddha, but it is preferable to think of it as the further development of a powerful narrative. Simply put, though the life of the Buddha stops with his parinirvāṇa, his biography goes on. (Similarly, though his life starts with his birth in Lumbinī, his biography begins much earlier than that with his previous lives). The Buddha's relics, as we shall see, do not just recall events from his life, but have adventures of their own. They travel to distant countries, to heavens and nāga worlds. They help legitimate empires here on earth and they further spread the dharma to places that the living Buddha never visited. Sometimes these adventures have been foretold, predestined, by the Buddha himself; at other times they have not. Sometimes they are aided and abetted by the actions of humans;

[13] Steven Collins's insight (1992: 232–35, and 1998: 242–49) that the life of the Buddha can be viewed either as non-repeatable or as repeatable, and that both nonrepetitive and repetitive time may be found in narrative (and ritual) contexts, is helpful in this regard.

[14] As we shall see, not all relics of the Buddha stem from his death and cremation. Some refer to earlier parts of his life, to his enlightenment, even to his previous births.

at other times, they take on a life of their own. Either way, the relics continue to do things the Buddha did, to fill the roles the Buddha filled; but they also do new things that the Buddha never did. They write new chapters in the Buddha's life story. Even so, the ultimate end of the story is not new, for like the Buddha's body before them, and like the Buddha's dharma after him, the relics are subject to dissolution. Indeed, as we shall see in chapter 8, the true end of the Buddha's biography comes only with the end of the relics, at that time still in the future in which all the relics will assemble again and undergo a parinirvāṇa (final extinction) of their own.

Types of Buddha Relics

I have, so far, been talking about Buddhist relics as though they were all a single sort of thing, but obviously that is not the case. In fact, various classification schemes dividing relics into different categories were developed by the Buddhist tradition. If we look again at the account with which we began the preface to this book, Daorong's description of what he found in Nagarahāra, it is easy to see that there were actual remains of parts of the Buddha's body (bones, teeth, and hair), objects that once belonged to the Buddha (the staff), things associated with the Buddha's teaching (the sinking stūpa and the inscription), and then a host of more ambiguous traces of the Buddha's former presence (his shadow image, his footprints, and the rock where he washed his robe). The first three of these items correspond pretty much to important Indian relic classification schemes that distinguish (1) body relics, (2) contact relics, that is, objects that the Buddha owned or used or with which he was closely associated, such as bowls, robes, bodhi trees (or in this case, his staff); and (3) dharma relics, by which was meant either whole sūtras, or a dharma verse (such as the "ye dharmā . . ." formula given earlier), or a dhāraṇī, or anything somehow recording the Buddha's teaching (see Bentor 1994: 16 and the sources quoted there).

Bones and Books

The inclusion of the Buddha's dharma—more literally of actual texts—in the category of relics is significant (see Wallis 2001). As is well known, when the Buddha, on his deathbed, was asked by his disciple Ānanda who should replace him after he was gone, his answer was his teachings, his dharma.[15] There was a sense, then, that the dharma could act as a substi-

[15] Often the dharma and the vinaya (or the prātimokṣa) are specified as the appointed successor of the Buddha. For the many variants of this story, see Bareau 1970–71, 2:136–37.

tute for the departed master, a claim that was taken quite literally in certain circles. "One who sees the dharma sees the Buddha" (*Mil.*, 71 = Eng. trans., Davids 1890–94, 1:110) went the assertion, and this was true regardless of whether the Buddha was alive or dead.[16] Similarly, other texts were to declare that "when the relics are seen, the Buddha is seen,"[17] a parallelism that should not go unnoticed. It comes as no surprise, then, to find that some later texts actually rewrote the Buddha's deathbed words to have him say that, after his death, the dharma, vinaya *and his bodily relics* will be his disciples' teacher (see *Jināl.*, 49 = Eng. trans., Gray 1894: 110).[18]

Not all Buddhists, however, were in agreement about the validity of this parallelism. In one of the Perfection of Wisdom sūtras, for instance, when it is asked which is better, the whole of "Jambudvīpa filled up to the top with [Buddha]-relics" or "a single written copy of this perfection of wisdom [sūtra]?" the answer is unequivocal: the perfection of wisdom scripture is preferable for the relics are subordinate to it; they are worshiped only because "they are pervaded by the perfection of wisdom" (Conze 1973: 116; text in *Aṣṭa.*, 48). And later, in the same text, the bodhisattva Dharmodgata proclaims that the Buddha "cannot be seen" from his physical body, but only from his dharma (Conze 1973: 291).[19]

Nevertheless, the fact remains that, in the context of the tradition broadly conceived, both dharma relics and body relics could be used in similar ways as stand-ins for the Buddha. For instance, stūpas and images and other objects that served as reminders of the Buddha were often consecrated or "enlivened" by the insertion within them of a body relic (e.g., a piece of bone), or of a textual dharma relic (e.g., a written verse from the Buddha's teaching), or of both. Thus, phenomenologically

---

As is well known, the earliest notion of the Buddha's "dharmakāya" was that of the corpus of his teaching. See Ohnuma 1998: 345–46; Lancaster 1974; Reynolds 1977: 377; Harrison 1992.

[16] See also *Itv.*, 91 = Eng. trans., Woodward 1948: 181; *S.*, 3:120 = Eng. trans., Davids and Woodward, 1917–30, 3:103; *Div.*, 23; and *Aśokāv.*, 23 = Eng. trans., Strong 1983: 192. In Mahāyāna literature, see the *Śālistamba sūtra* (text and translation in Reat 1993: 27).

[17] See, for example, *Mhv.*, 133 = Eng. trans., Geiger 1912: 116. Compare *VibhA.*, 431 = Eng. trans., Ñāṇamoli 1996, 2:179 ("while the relics endure, the enlightened ones endure"). For discussions, see Schopen 1997: 93 and Adikaram 1946: 137. *Thūp.*, 197 = Eng. trans., Jayawickrama 1971: 64 is a bit more ambiguous: "Even though [the Buddha] has passed away in perfect nibbāna, his bodily relics, however, remain."

[18] In Gandhāra, there are signs that efforts were made to include texts conceived of as dharma relics in the same reliquaries with bodily relics. See Salomon 1999: 68–86.

[19] The *Book of Zambasta* (see Emmerick 1968: 207) is even more emphatic, declaring that "the Dharmakāya of the Buddhas is where there are no bones," and *Suv.*, 9 = Eng. trans., Emmerick 1970:7 asks: "[H]ow [can] there be a relic in a body without bone and blood?" For other references and a discussion, see Boucher 1993: 2–3. A rather different polemic against relics may be found in the *Maitreyamahāsiṃhanāda sūtra* which, according to Schopen (1999), reflects a reactionary trend within the Mahāyāna.

speaking, "bones" and "books" could function in similar ways and accomplish some of the same things.

There was, in fact, an established practice of making "textual bodies" or "dharma relics" (Skt: *dharma-śarīra*) so as to embody the Buddha. When Xuanzang was in Rājagṛha, for instance, he heard of a pious layman who, whenever he preached, busied himself at the same time in the manufacture of such dharma-śarīra (Ch: *fa sheli*), miniature stūpas that he then further consecrated by inserting into the center of each of them a written verse from a sūtra (*T.* 2087, 51:920a = Eng. trans., Li 1996: 266).[20] Similarly, in the *Zao ta gong de jing,* a Chinese canonical work translated by Divākara in 680 C.E., a method is described for making small stūpas by inserting into a lump of clay the dharma verse par excellence "ye dharmā hetuprabhavās. . . ." In this context, this line is called the "dharma body" of the Buddha and is said to be just as effective in consecrating a stūpa as the insertion into it of a body relic of the Buddha such as a tooth, a hair, or a nail (*T.* 699, 16:800–801 = Eng. trans., Boucher 1993: 8–10). On the other hand, in Gandhāra, texts on birch bark were sometimes buried directly in clay pots very much like the pots used to inter the ashes and bones of deceased monks. Both have been found in the vicinity of larger stūpas (see Salomon 1999: 79–81).

Bones and Beads

In the case of body relics, it should be pointed out that distinctions came to be made between (a) relics that were actual physical remains of the body, such as bones, teeth, etc.,[21] and (b) transmogrified somatic substances that could be as small as mustard-seeds and appear as jewel-like beads (and which, in fact, in East Asia, eventually come to be associated with magical wish-granting gems [*cintāmaṇi*]).[22] These "very hard glittering particles" (Das 1902: 1182, s.v. *ring-bsrel*) exist in a variety of colors and sizes, and are usually found in the ashes of cremation fires. They can also appear, however, during a person's lifetime, by emanation, from their hands, or hair, or eyes, or clothes, or calligraphy brushes, or they can appear on altars, offering plates, other relics, or images, or by the

[20] For a bibliography of archaeological sites where such miniature stūpas and clay tablets have been found, see Boucher 1993: 6–8. See also Mitomo 1984: 1117. Much the same tradition is mentioned by Yijing (*T.* 2125, 54:226c = Eng. trans., Li 2000: 137). For similar practices in East Asia, see Hickman 1975; Hou 1984; Durt, Riboud, and Lai 1985; Yiengpruksawan 1987; Kidder 1992: 222; and Barrett 2001: 19ff.

[21] Sometimes, in these schemes, hair and nails were treated not as bodily relics, but as a form of contact-relic called "relics of the garb" (Tib.: *sku-bal*). See Bentor 1994: 16–17. On the special status of hair and nail relics, see also chapter 3 of this book.

[22] On this association, see Ruppert 1997: 189ff. See also *T.* 1509, 25:134a = Fr. trans., Lamotte 1949–80: 600.

side of stūpas, etc. (Faure 1991: 138ff.; Prip-Moller 1967: 172, 176; Kieschnick 2003: 34–35). The colors are said to reflect the part of the body or organ with which these particles were associated: white if they originated in bone, black if from the hair, red if from the flesh, etc. (*T.* 2122, 53:598c = Eng. trans., Ruppert 2000: 291; Faure, forthcoming). One Tibetan tradition even gives these relics different names and associates them with different "families" of buddhas: *Sharira* are white, the size of a pea, and come from the head; *barira* are blue, the size of a small pea, and come from the space between the ribs; *churira* are yellow, the size of a mustard seed, and come from the top of the liver; *serira* are red, also the size of a mustard seed, and come from the kidneys; finally *nyarira* are green, also the size of a mustard seed, and come from the lungs (Germano 1994).

Yet these particles, these colored crystalline "beads," are clearly to be distinguished from the organs or the bodily parts (e.g., bones) from which they are said to come. In Korea, for instance, when monks look for such relics in the cremated remains of saints and teachers, they at the same time pick out the unburnt bits of bone. These are specifically understood *not* to be relics, and are set aside to be pulverized and mixed with meal, formed into balls of dough that are then abandoned in the woods for animals to consume. The relics, if there are any, are carefully preserved and frequently distributed later to disciples or to lay patrons.[23] In Thailand, the unburnt bone fragments are similarly not considered to be relics, but they are often preserved because it is thought that they eventually may *become* relics, through a process of metamorphosis over time.[24]

These bead-like relics have their analog and precedent, perhaps, in the tradition reported by Buddhaghosa that the Buddha's own relics (*sarīra*) were of three types—"like jasmine buds, like washed pearls, and like (nuggets) of gold"—and came in three sizes, as big as mustard seeds, as broken grains of rice, and as split green peas (*DA.*, 2:603–4. See also *Thūp.*, 172 = Eng. trans., Jayawickrama 1971: 34; and *Jin.*, 37 = Eng.

[23] Robert Buswell, personal communication, Malibu, Calif., 27 January 2001. In Japan today, in one tradition, the bits of bone (recovered with a special pair of chopsticks) are placed in an urn, which is kept in the temple for forty-nine days and then buried (see Seidel 1983: 584–85). The practice of sifting through cremation ashes to extract the bones of a deceased person—either to destroy them or to preserve them—has a long history and many variants in Asia, and not just within Buddhism. For a Hindu example, see Oldenberg [1886] 1991: 245–46.

[24] On this process, see Taylor 1993: 175–77. The speed with which this transformation occurs may depend on how long the deceased has been an arhat; the longer he was enlightened, the faster the bones become relics (Thanissaro Bhikkhu, personal communication, Valley Center, Calif., 28 January 2001). The correlation between the salvational state of the deceased and the state of his or her bones is found in other cultures as well. See, for example, Danforth 1982.

trans., Jayawickrama 1968: 52–53). This is important because there has been a tendency among scholars looking at buddha-relics in India to think of them primarily as bones or ashes left over from the Buddha's cremation.[25] Given what we have just seen, however, we should be thinking of them also as "beads"—the results of a process of metamorphosis brought on not only by the fire of cremation but also by the perfections of the saint (in this case the Buddha) whose body they re-present. It is occasionally said that, physically speaking, such "beads" may result from the burning of the body under particular conditions at certain temperatures. From a cultural perspective, however, it is possible that such crystalized gem-like relics are a response to worries about pollution or further decay, especially in those cultures where handling—let alone venerating—the bones and ashes of the dead might be viewed as impure. On the other hand, the whole phenomenon may simply reflect a need to be able to distinguish between the relics ("beads") of the "special dead"[26] (such as saints and the Buddha) and the remains ("bones") of the "ordinary dead" who have no relics.

Relics, Bones, and Burial Practices in India and Beyond

Unfortunately, things are not as simple as this, if only because there were also bona fide bones among the Buddha's relics. Though this is not specified in the Pali text, the Sanskrit version of the *Mahāparinirvāṇa sūtra* refers to the Buddha's remains as *asthi* (bones) and specifies that they are collected and placed in a golden urn (*MPS.*, pp. 360, 432).[27] Moreover, as we shall see, the tradition in time came to feature, as relics, the teeth, collarbones, neckbone, forehead bone, breastbone, uṣṇīṣa bone, fingerbone, etc., of the Buddha, which clearly retained their osseous nature.[28] More immediately, however, such bits of calcined bone and ashes have been found in countless Buddhist reliquaries of various shapes and sizes made of various materials such as clay, stone, crystal, and precious metals.[29] Often, those reliquaries were placed in larger receptacles (or several

[25] For example, Davids (1899–1924, 2:186) and Walshe (1987: 275) both translate *sarīrāni* as "bones" in the Pali account of the Buddha's cremation.

[26] The word is borrowed from Brown 1981: 69ff.

[27] In this it departs from the Pali text which, as we have seen, refers to these remains as *sarīrāni*. On the similar collection of bones of the deceased and their placement in an urn in Brahmanical ritual, see Kane 1973: 240ff.

[28] Most of these relics will be considered in the chapters that follow. On the Buddha's *uṣṇīṣa* relic, see *T.* 2085, 51:858c = Eng. trans., Li 2002: 172; and *T.* 2087, 51:879b = Eng. trans., Li 1996: 69.

[29] For a good sampling of illustrations of such reliquaries, see Zwalf 1985: 28–30; and Subrahmanyam 1998: plates 33–62. For an unusual example of a wine goblet made into a reliquary, see Salomon 1996.

larger, nesting receptacles),[30] which, in turn were put into stūpas. For example, in a stūpa near Peshawar in Pakistan, the relics "consisted of some fragments of bone placed, with a little gold, inside a small round casket of schist stone; this in its turn was placed in a larger box of the same material, and the whole wedged tightly into a long narrow vessel of coarse earthenware, the space around being filled with hardened lime and earth" (Marshall 1902–3: 173). Sometimes the urns are specifically labeled with inscriptions identifying them as containing the remains of particular Buddhist saints or even of the Buddha;[31] alternatively, they remain anonymous. Usually, in addition to bits of bone, the reliquaries contain such things as beads, pearls, coral, semi-precious stones, jewelry, bits of gold, silver, coins, etc.[32]

Among the more famous relic finds in India are those made at Piprahwā, a site that some have identified with the Buddha's hometown of Kapilavastu;[33] at Vaiśālī, where relics were unearthed from what was possibly one of the original eight stūpas built over the Buddha's remains;[34] and near Peshawar, where a magnificently embossed gold reliquary was found in which there were three small fragments of bone that "are undoubtedly the original relics deposited in the stūpa by [King] Kanishka which [Xuanzang] tells us were relics of Gautama Buddha" (Spooner 1908–9: 49).[35] Lesser finds, however, are legion, and often stūpas of more modest dimensions, such as the so-called "votive" stūpas, may not contain any relics at all.[36]

This is not the place to embark on a full history of Buddhist funerary practices in India or other parts of South Asia. It is likely, however, that,

[30] On the terminology used for these receptacles, see Willis 2000: 17–21.

[31] For examples of reliquaries of different saints, see Cunningham 1854: 285–94; and Lüders [1912] 1973: no. 659–68. For examples of reliquaries labeled as being of the Buddha, see Marshall 1936: 55; Lüders [1912] 1973: no. 931; Solomon and Schopen 1984; Schopen 1997: 126; Stone 1994: 14; Subrahmanyam 1998: 85, 88; Roth 1987: 301; Konow [1929] 1991: 49.

[32] In general, see Subrahmanyam 1998. For specific examples, see Marshall 1902–3: 186, and 1910–11: 2, 15; Śāstri 1910–11: 64; Rea 1908–9: 88. In addition, various kinds of animal bones have been found in these remains. Some scholars (see Subrahmanyam 1998: 110) have speculated that these are meant to represent animal forms of the Buddha in his previous lives. See, however, Schopen 1995: 232–33.

[33] See Peppé 1898, Srivastava 1986: 8–44, and Nakamura 2000: 48–54. For an extensive bibliography on Piprahwā, see Kottkamp 1992: 70n. On the controversy involving the identification and location of Kapilavastu, the dating of the reliquary vase found at Piprahwā, and the rival claims of the site of Tilaurakot, see Härtel 1991: 70–80.

[34] See Altekar 1956 and Sinha and Roy 1969. For other references, see Kottkamp 1992: 20–21.

[35] For a bibliography on the so-called "Kanishka Casket," see Kottkamp 1992: 64–65.

[36] There has been much speculation about such "empty" stūpas. Schopen (1995: 222) suggests that they may be related to similar empty megalithic tombs. An intriguing argument by Debala Mitra (quoted in Subrahmanyam 1998: 56) has it that reliquaries devoid of ashes or bones belonged to non-Buddhist Brahmins.

in the context of Brahmanism, the Buddhist treatment of the dead was viewed with some dismay as culturally anomalous and aberrant, and that Buddhist monks, in particular, were not seen as taking sufficient measures against death pollution or to insure the well-being of ancestors. This is reflected in both Buddhist and Brahmanical sources. For instance, in a passage of the *Mūlasarvāstivāda Vinaya* that has been highlighted by Gregory Schopen (1997: 217–18), the Buddha is presented as instituting new measures to mollify Brahmanical objections about Buddhist funerary practices. At first, we are led to believe, when a monk died, his fellow monks simply abandoned his body by the side of the road. But this made the brahmins and householders criticize the new religion, declaring that this was what happened when people renounced the householder's life and joined the saṃgha; they no longer had anyone to perform funeral ceremonies for them! Accordingly, the Buddha told his monks that they should start carrying out funerals for their dead brethren. But they did not know what kind of funeral to perform, so the Buddha specified it should be a cremation by fire (except in certain instances when cremation was difficult, then immersion in water, or burial in the ground or abandonment in an isolated spot, was allowable). Further criticism arose, however, when monks, after handling a corpse at a cremation, failed to bathe and wash away the pollution. So the Buddha told those who handled corpses that they had to bathe.

The thrust of this story would appear to be corroborated in Brahmanical sources in which there were clear worries about various nonorthodox handlings of the dead. As early as the *Śatapatha Brāhmaṇa,* for instance, we hear of a particular type of funerary monument called the *śmasāna of the asuras* [demons], which is considered to be impure and is contrasted with the *śmasāna of the devas* [gods], which is deemed appropriate for those who accept the Vedas (Eggeling 1900, 5:423–24).[37] Some scholars have suggested that this *śmasāna of the asuras* (which predates Buddhism) is the prototype for the stūpa (Kottkamp 1992: 8–9; Sinha 1991: 1). It has also been identified with another funerary monument known as the *eḍūka,* or *elūka,* or *aiḍūka* which has likewise been associated with Buddhism as well as with Śaivism (Shah 1952: 280; De Marco 1987: 228; Allchin 1957: 1).[38] It was intended to be a place for memorializing the dead and preserving their ashes and bones. In the *Mahāvastu,*

[37] On the various Brahmanical rites for erecting mounds over the calcined bones of the dead, see Kane 1973: 251–53.

[38] The word is said to be of Dravidian origin. See [U. P.] Shah 1970. An extensive description of this monument occurs in the *Viṣṇudharmottarapurāṇa,* edited and studied in Pal 1971–72. On Buddhist influences on this text, see Sircar 1953.

for example, we find the case of a Buddhist girl of *kṣatriya* lineage, who is being threatened by some jilted suitors whom she has refused. Worried that they will murder her out of spite, she says to her mother, "If these nobles from far away kill me, then gather up my bones and burn them. And when you have burnt them, build a shrine (elūka) for my remains. And when you have built the shrine plant a *karṇikāra* tree there. Then when it blossoms in the springtime . . . , you will remember me, mother, and say 'such was the beauty of my daughter'" (*Mtu.*, 3:20 = Eng. trans., Jones 1949–56, 3:19).

In the *Mahābhārata,* however, the term appears in somewhat different light. There, in a passage that is commonly taken as a critique of Buddhist practices, *eḍūka* (which J.A.B. Van Buitenen translates as "charnel houses") are described as one of the signs of decline that will mark the end of the aeon (*kalpa*): "This world will be totally upside down: people will abandon the Gods and worship charnel houses (*eḍūka*) and the serfs [*śūdras*] will refuse to serve the twice-born. . . . The earth will be marked by charnel houses, not adorned by the houses of the Gods . . . and [all this] shall be the sign of the end of the Eon" (Van Buitenen 1973–75, 2:596).[39]

Given these oppositions, scholars such as André Bareau (1963: 122) have argued that Buddhists must have encountered considerable resistance to a cult of relics of the dead "in an India that has always been so attached to ritual purity." Similarly, Jean Przyluski (1935–36: 353–54) has declared, "Nothing [in India] prepared people's minds for the celebration of a cult of relics. The corpse was [generally considered to be] an impure, dangerous object, to be kept away from human habitations." The same sentiment was expressed more elaborately by Monier Monier-Williams ([1889] 1964: 495–96):

> Adoration of relics constitutes an important point of difference between Buddhism and Brāhmanism; for Brāhmanism and its offspring Hindūism are wholly opposed to the practice of preserving the ashes, bones, hair, or teeth of deceased persons, however much such individuals may have been revered during life. . . . Articles used by great religious teachers—as, for example, robes, wooden shoes and seats—are sometimes preserved and venerated after their death. All articles of this kind, however, must, of course, be removed from the body before actual decease; for it is well known that, in the minds of Hindūs, ideas of impurity are inseparably connected

[39] There is some debate as to whether the *Mahābhārata* here is referring specifically to Buddhist monuments, but see De Marco 1987: 228–29.

> with death, and contamination is supposed to result from contact with the corpses of even a man's dearest relatives. . . . Hence in the present day a corpse is burnt, and its ashes are generally scattered on the surface of sacred rivers or of the sea.[40]

Monier-Williams is probably overstating the case here, however. First of all, relics are only half connected to death.[41] As Bernard Faure (1991: 135) has put it, "[T]hey bring death into the world of the living, but they also assure the continuity of life into death, the regeneration of life through death, thereby contributing to blur the distinction." Indeed, a good argument can be made for seeing the enshrinement of relics as a "secondary burial," which, far from being concerned with the polluting aspects of death, seeks to end those by emphasizing the themes of purity, regeneration, and permanence (Bloch and Parry 1982: 11; see also Hertz 1960).

Secondly, it should be noted that within the Hindu tradition a distinction is also made between the ordinary dead and the special dead. Sannyāsins, great yogins, and other renunciants in India have long had funerary rituals that are radically different from those of householders. Their bodies are generally not cremated, and their places of burial (or entombment in a trance of *samādhi*) are often marked with monuments, "countless tumuli which dot the countryside all over India" (Goswamy 1980: 6). In fact, these burials mark for sannyāsins' their second funeral since their first was already ritually asserted at the time of their wandering forth. The Buddha and Buddhists in ancient India were not orthodox sannyāsins, but they were certainly renunciants, and it is perhaps no coincidence that ancient descriptions of the tumuli of sannyāsins, as well as extant modern ones, resemble stūpas in structure and shape (see Goswamy 1980: 10–11; De Marco 1987: 223, 225).

Bones and Bodies

Bones, however, served another purpose in Buddhism besides just memorializing the dead; they also provided opportunities for enlightenment. Buddhists advocated (or semi-advocated)[42] "cemetery meditations," a practice that further separated them from Brahmanical householders but tied them more closely to sannyāsins (renunciants) and other Hindu ascetics who, like them, had moved beyond certain social norms and so

[40] On the application of this practice to some unearthed buddha relics in Sarnath, see Duncan 1808. See also Kane 1973: 243–44.

[41] Schopen (1998: 261) argues that they are not connected to death at all , and hence they are not the object of any such fear of pollution.

[42] The cemetery meditations were not obligatory but could be undertaken as an optional ascetic practice. See Ray 1994: 293–323, esp. 301–2; and Tambiah 1984: 33–37.

were to some extent already dead to the world.[43] These practices consisted not only of being a *śmāśānika* (Pali: *sosānika*), that is, one who lives in a cemetery (or by a stūpa), but also of contemplating the various stages of decomposition of the corpse in order to realize the impurity and the impermanence of a person's physical form.[44]

Similar meditations were also advocated on the still living body. Overall, Buddhist views of the body have been shown to be somewhat ambiguous (see Collins 1997), but anyone reading the oft-repeated list of the thirty-two loathsome constituent parts of the body will have little doubt that they were not very hedonistic. According to this view, the body consists of hair of the head, hair of the body, nails, teeth, skin, flesh, sinews, bones, marrow, kidneys, heart, liver, pleura, spleen, lungs, colon, intestines, stomach, feces, bile, phlegm, pus, blood, sweat, fat, tears, lymph, saliva, snot, synovia, urine, and brain (*Mil.*, 26 = Eng. trans., Davids [1890–94], 1963. 1:42).[45]

Realizing the impermanence and impurity of the body was especially an activity undertaken by Buddhist monks and nuns. Even today, Theravāda monks, at their ordination, are supposed to contemplate the first five of Buddhaghosa's thirty-two parts of the body in a ritualized meditation on the impermanence and insubstantiality of the Self: "Kesa, lomā, nakhā, dantā, taco. . . ." they repeat, "hair of the head, hair of the body, nails, teeth, skin."[46] Bhikkhu Khantipālo (1980: 13; see also Wilson 1996: 47) has commented that all these things are actually dead matter. Hairs, nails, teeth, even skin, live only at their roots; the parts that we see are dead. One might also point out, however, that the first four of these "dead" things, when belonging to the Buddha or a Buddhist saint, can also be relics.

The question of the connection in Buddhism between the cult of relics, on the one hand, and cemetery meditations and other contemplations of the impurity and impermanence of the body, on the other, is interesting and rather complex. One of the complications is that relics, generally, were objects not of contemplation but of veneration. There is, moreover, a radical difference between the body of an ordinary person and the body of the Buddha, which, alive or dead, tends to be glorified. Indeed, Buddhist texts are filled with descriptions of the glorious nature of the

[43] For a recent example and discussion, see Parry 1982.

[44] On cemetery meditations and attendant views of the body, see Wilson 1996: 41–76; and Boisvert 1996. The *Vsm.* (1: 178–79 = Eng. trans., Ñyāṇamoli 1976, 1:185–86) lists ten stages of decomposition of the body. For other sources, see Lamotte 1949–80: 1312–14.

[45] Some sources (e.g., *M.* 1:57 = Eng. trans., Horner 1954–59, 1:74; *D.* 2:293 = Eng. trans., Walshe 1987: 337) omit the brain and so list only thirty-one parts. These lists, it should be noted, describe the *kāya*—a different term for body than *śarīra*. On the overlaps and divergences between *kāya* and *śarīra*, see the discussion in Williams 1997: 206–208.

[46] See Vajirañāṇavarorasa 1973: 23; Seneviratne 1973: 154; Bizot 1988: 26. See also the discussion in Hiltebeitel 1998: 3–4.

Buddha's physical form, and over against the thirty-two loathsome constituent parts of the (ordinary) body, were set the thirty-two physical marks of the "great man" (*mahāpuruṣa*).[47] Moreover, the Buddha's body was also thought to be pure, so much so that some texts went so far as to claim that at the Buddha's funeral, there was no need to wash his corpse (see Przyluski 1920: 179–80). Indeed, the Buddha had overcome death (and rebirth), and this was reflected in his remains. Relics of the Blessed One thus have little to do with cemetery meditations or the contemplation of the impermanence and impurity of the body. As André Grabar (1946, 2:39) put it in a different context: "The imagery of a [saint's] relics is never . . . an imagery of the *memento mori* [reminder of death]; rather it strives by all means in its power to proclaim the suppression of the fact of death."

And yet, as Peter Brown (1981: 75), who quotes Grabar, suggests, "[T]he dialectic continued at a deeper imaginative level." The Buddha's body, too, was impermanent, and his relics were a sign of that impermanence. Jack Goody (1997: 83) has pointed out that there is an "underlying paradox," a "structural ambiguity" in the veneration of relics, "for the concept of relics is characterized not only by attraction but also by repulsion, by an attachment to the dead as well as by a distancing from death which readily becomes associated with our death." It may well be, then, that relics of the Buddha are ultimately paradoxical and dialectic in nature: as pure symbols of impurity, ongoing representations of impermanence, signs of mortality enduring after death, embodiments of bodilessness; they are, as Lévi-Strauss said of myths, "good to think with." They are also, however, "good to worship," "good to possess," "good to rule with," and "good to tell stories about." In all these ways, as we shall see, relics become constitutive of communities; by means of narrative and ritual, they serve to link particular places and peoples to the life and times of the Buddha, or to the greater world of Buddhism; possessing sacred power and significance, they act as magnets for pilgrims and devotees, they enhance the prestige of their possessors, affording them magical power and protection, and they further and bolster the agendas of kings, monastics, and laypeople.

Relics and Images

It should be noted that none of the relic classification schemes mentioned so far has included in it "images" or other artistic representations of the Buddha. The same omission is found in another famous inventory of types

[47] For a listing of the thirty-two marks and a bibliography, see Lamotte 1949–80: 271–82.

of relics found in the *Questions of King Milinda*. There, the elder Nāgasena describes what he calls the "Blessed Buddha's bazaar"—a metaphoric general market toward which one can direct one's devotions to obtain "long life, good health . . . high birth, and nirvāṇa." In this market, there are four "shops": bodily relics, relics of use, the teachings of the Buddha, and members of the Saṃgha. No mention is made of buddha images here (*Mil.*, p. 341 = Eng. trans., Davids [1890–94] 1963, 2:230).

This dearth of references to images is significant for there has been a tendency in Western studies to lump together relics with images, as well as with stūpas and other things that denote or signify the Buddha, or are thought to embody his buddhahood (see Sharf 1999: 81). The roots of this tendency may perhaps be traced to an often cited late Theravāda classification of "relics," which distinguishes, in addition to bodily relic shrines (*sarīrikacetiya,* also called *dhātu[ka]cetiya)* such as stūpas, and shrines of use (*paribhogacetiya*) such as bodhi trees, a third category called commemorative or "indicative" shrines (*uddesikacetiya*) (*JA.*, 4:228 = Eng. trans., Cowell 1895–1907, 4:142; *KhpA.*, 221–22).[48] This latter class refers to objects that remind one of, or somehow point to or re-present, the Buddha, and includes, primarily, Buddha images.[49]

There are certain problems with this inclusion of images in the category of relics. First of all, it should be noted that the locus classicus of this scheme, the "Kalingabodhi jātaka," does not actually refer to relics (*dhātu*) but to various sorts of *cetiya* (Skt.: *caitya*; shrines or memorials) (*JA.*, 4: 228 = Eng. trans., Cowell 1895–1907, 4:142).[50] There is no doubt that all of these cetiya are in some ways "reminders" of the Buddha, but that does not necessarily make them all "relics." Indeed, the "Kalingabodhi jātaka" itself makes an important distinction between uddesikacetiya (e.g., images), and the other two types of memorials. The uddesikacetiya, it says, are "lacking in a foundation [*avatthuka*] by virtue of their being a matter of mind only [*manamattakena*]" (*JA.*, 4:228 = Eng. trans., Cowell 1895–1907, 4:142). In other words, unlike body relics and contact relics (relics of use), they do not have the basis of any

[48] In *DhA.*, 3:251 = Eng. trans., Burlingame 1921, 3:69, the order of categories 2 and 3 is reversed, and the latter is called *uddissa-cetiya.* There is another Theravāda scheme that, in addition to these three, includes "dharma relics" as a fourth category. See Damrong 1973: vi and Anuman Rajadhon, n.d.: 157ff.

[49] On the relation of this classification scheme to the structure of worship sites in Sri Lankan monasteries, see Trainor 1997: 89.

[50] The word *cetiya* (Skt.: caitya) is usually derived from the root √*ci* meaning "to pile up," and so is sometimes translated as "a mound" or "a tumulus" and likened to a stūpa. But a number of scholars have preferred a derivation from the root √*cit,* meaning "to think," "to contemplate," and so see a cetiya as anything that "reminds one" of the Buddha. See Bareau 1974b: 290–91 and Damrong 1973: v–vi. In this book, I shall not make a clean-cut

direct physical connection with the Buddha.[51] For this reason, perhaps, bodily (or textual) relics were sometimes used to "reinforce" an image's connection to the Buddha, and were inserted into images at the time of consecration. As Steven Collins (1992: 237) has put it, "[S]tatues of the Buddha, although allowing him to be 'seen' in a rather obvious way, in fact are usually thought only to mediate his presence in a stronger sense if they contain relics" (see also Collins 1998: 243).

On the other hand, there also exist qualitative distinctions between category 1—bodily shrines (sarīracetiya)—and category 2—shrines of use (paribhogacetiya) such as bodhi trees—although these distinctions are a bit more ambiguous. On the one hand, there are texts such as the devotionally inclined *Jinālaṅkāra* (p. 49 = Eng. trans., Gray 1894: 110) that claim that, just like the dharma and the vinaya, body relics *and* the bodhi tree (as well as the seat of enlightenment) can equally be viewed as the Buddha's successor. This would seem to indicate equivalence between them. On the other hand, there are more practically oriented sources such as the Pali commentary on the *Vibhanga,* which found itself having to resolve the issue of what to do when one kind of relic "encroached" on another. Thus, after admitting that an equal amount of negative karma may come from cutting down a bodhi tree or destroying a shrine that contains bodily relics, it goes on to qualify this statement by adding that it is permissible to cut a branch of a bodhi tree if it is pressing on a stūpa containing relics, or if birds roosting on it are dropping excrement on the stūpa. The reason given is that "the shrine [containing a part] of the body (sarīracetiya) is more important than a shrine [in commemoration] of what was made use of (paribhogacetiya)" (Ñāṇamoli 1996, 2:175; text in *VibhA.*, 427).

Limitations of This Study

Generally speaking, in this book, in light of these various hierarchical distinctions and differentiations among relics, I shall consider commemorative (*uddesika*) relics such as Buddha images hardly at all.[52] I will consider

---

distinction between stūpas and caityas. To be sure, there is a famous statement found in the *Mahāsaṃghika Vinaya* that "if there is a relic, it is a stūpa; if there is no relic, it is a caitya" (*T.* 1425, 33:498b = Fr. trans., Durt, n.d.: 12), but there is also a lot of contravening evidence (see, for instance, Schopen 1997: 90).

[51] There are, of course, some exceptions to this; certain images such as the "shadow of the Buddha" at Nagarahāra or the famous "Udrāyaṇa" sandalwood image of the Buddha may well qualify as contact relics of the Buddha.

[52] There is also a practical consideration at work here: the inclusion of Buddha images in this book would at least double its length.

relics of use (*paribhoga*), such as bodhi trees, the bowl of the Buddha, etc., to some extent, but my primary focus will remain on bodily (*sarīrika*) relics and the legendary and cultic traditions associated with them.

Secondly, I shall not be directly concerned with the cult of dharma relics. Although, as texts embodying the departed Buddha, these form, in some systems, an important category of relics, in others they are specifically distinguished from body relics, and are either praised as "purer" representations of the truth that is the Buddha's dharmakāya, or maligned as inferior symbols of the Buddha and not a remnant of his "real body." There may, in any case, be an important difference between the two genres. As Patrick Geary (1978: 5) has pointed out in a different context, unlike the text that "will always have some potential significance to anyone capable of reading it," the "bare relic—a bone or a bit of dust—carries no fixed code or sign of its meaning. . . . As a physical object, divorced from a specific milieu, [it] is entirely without significance." Geary's assertion, which is reiterated by Sharf (1999: 81) is not unproblematic, but it does point to the fact that what makes a body relic a relic is not so much its makeup as its context, both legendary, cultic, and physical (i.e., its reliquary).

Thirdly, as mentioned, I shall focus largely on relics associated with the Buddha, specifically the historical Buddha, Gautama Śākyamuni (although I will also deal with his predecessors, the so-called previous buddhas). I will not, however, occupy myself with relics of members of his *saṃgha*, whether they be his disciples or any of the subsequent saints of the Buddhist tradition—the great teachers, monks, nuns, and others who, throughout the ages, achieved some degree of sanctity either in life or in death. Their relics are even more common than the Buddha's—especially in East Asia and Tibet—but consideration of them would take us too far afield.[53] Nor will I deal with the possibility of seeing ordinary members of the saṃgha—either individuals or the community as a whole—as "living relics" of the Buddha, despite the indications of some texts that, as one of the three refuges, the jewel of the saṃgha might well qualify for inclusion in the conceptual category of relic.

Finally, it should be specified that I will primarily focus on traditions that developed in South and Southeast Asia—rather than in Tibet or East Asia. For the most part, then, I shall be having recourse to Pali and Sanskrit materials, or at least to traditions that were translated from Pali or Sanskrit materials or are ultimately based on them.

[53]On the cult of relics of disciples and saints, see Ray 1994: 179–212; Faure 1991: 132–79, and 1992; Daulton 1994; Sharf 1992; Schopen 1997: 165–203; and Kieschnick 2003: 34ff. On the lives and deaths of individual disciples, see Nyanaponika and Hecker 1997.

Outline

With these limitations in mind, I shall, in the chapters that follow, turn to an examination of a variety of traditions—mostly legends—associated with bodily relics of the Buddha. To give these stories some narrative continuity, and in line with my belief that relics embody the biography of the Buddha, I shall basically follow—through relic traditions—the biography of the Buddha himself. Accordingly, I will start not with an account of the Buddha's funeral and the division of his relics among various contending parties, but with a study (chapter one) of relics of previous buddhas, Śākyamuni's predecessors over the ages, under whom he first took the steps that eventually resulted in his buddhahood. Relics of previous buddhas often served to reinforce the pedigree of relics of Śākyamuni by giving to a particular site a greater depth of tradition and a truly cosmic sense of time. At the same time, as we shall see, these relics raise some interesting theoretical questions. For instance, it is commonly felt, at least in Theravāda Buddhism, that buddhas from different eras should not coexist. If buddhas of the past, however, are felt to be *present* in their relics, the question arises as to what happens to this "law" of nonsimultaneity of buddhas when the present Śākyamuni comes together with the relics of one of his predecessors. As we shall see, different texts have different solutions to this dilemma, depending on contextual considerations and on the particular school (Mainstream Buddhist or Mahāyāna) whose doctrine they reflect.

In chapter 2, I shall turn to a consideration of some of Śākyamuni's "bodhisattva relics," including both relics stemming from his past lives as a bodhisattva, and relics dating from his final life as Gautama but prior to his awakening at Bodhgaya. It is often thought that relics embody the qualities of someone who has transcended the processes of birth and death, that is, of a Buddhist "saint" who has attained enlightenment. The bodhisattva, because he is still working his way through saṃsāra and is still subject to rebirth, technically does not enter into that category. Yet, as we shall see, a number of texts feature relics that date back to Śākyamuni's previous lives. This not only makes possible interesting scenarios (such as the Buddha contemplating the bones of his former self), but it raises new definitional questions about the nature of a relic. The examples that I will look at suggest that these bodhisattva relics are really embodiments of one aspect of Śākyamuni's career—his determination to achieve enlightenment, and so may be thought of as "pre-presentations" of the Buddha rather than as "re-presentations" of him (something made possible in part by the fact that, at least etymologically, as we have seen, "relics" [dhātu, śarīra] are not necessarily "remains" of the Buddha).

Chapter 3 focuses on relics of the Buddha from the period *after* his enlightenment but before his parinirvāṇa. These relics of the "still living Buddha," which date from this period, obviously are not bones or ashes from the cremation fire but include such things as hairs, fingernails, and footprints, and form by themselves an important category. Among other things, in considering them, I will raise certain issues about the use of relics in spreading the dharma to persons who have never seen or heard the Buddha, and the function of relics as "markers" for the future conversion or conquest of countries.

In chapter 4, I shall finally reach the traditions surrounding the death and funeral of the Buddha, and the division of his relics that followed it. I will seek to read the account of the Buddha's parinirvāṇa from "a relic perspective," explaining certain enigmatic features of his cremation and of the treatment of his corpse as intended to produce relics. Relics are thus not just a by-product of the Buddha's cremation and funeral, they are the whole point of it. With this in mind, I will go on to consider the establishment of buddha relics as a precious commodity, intensely desired by local kings, to the point of their being willing to fight for them. This is the episode often called "the war of the relics," which results in the division and distribution of the Buddha's remains and their enshrinement in eight North Indian countries, in the so-called *droṇa stūpas."*

Chapter 5 will focus on a subsequent but equally important legendary event—the collection and redistribution of the Buddha's bodily relics by the Buddhist emperor of India, King Aśoka. Here a number of themes will come to the fore, including the use of relics to mark the kingship and kingdom of a Buddhist *cakravartin,* and the political / ideological use of relics to help unify the state and focus it, centripetally, on the king. In examining all these themes, I shall especially make use of some relatively late Pali and Burmese sources where they are most fully developed.

In chapter 6, I will consider the further extension of the Buddha's life in what I have called "predestined relics," that is, relics whose careers were foretold by the Buddha but did not come to pass until long after his final nirvāṇa. Here the focus will be on Sri Lankan traditions, and I will look at legends and cults surrounding the bodhi tree that was transplanted from Bodhgaya to Anurādhapura; the collarbone relic that was enshrined in the Thūpārāma in the same city; and the share of relics that ended up in the Mahāthūpa built by King Duṭṭhagāmaṇī.

In chapter 7, I will shift gears slightly to look at a number of traditions surrounding relics that were not subject to any prediction by the Buddha and that consequently long remained "on the move." In particular I shall focus on various tooth relics of the Buddha, paying most attention to the eye-tooth that came to be seen, along with the bowl of the Buddha, as the palladium of power in Sri Lanka. In addition, some consideration will be given to several other tooth relics that had varying fortunes in India and East Asia. I will then end with a consideration of the international tours that some of these relics have been sent on, in modern times, in what amounts to a kind of "relic diplomacy."

In chapter 8, I will turn to examine several eschatological traditions surrounding the Buddha's relics, laying out what is due to happen to them and, therefore, to the Buddha's life story. In particular, I will look at the Buddha's begging bowl, his robe, and the tradition of the parinirvāṇa of the relics.

In the conclusion, I will attempt to recapitulate the findings of the book as a whole and to make some summary comments on the nature of Buddhist relics.

Chapter One

RELICS OF PREVIOUS BUDDHAS

IT IS CUSTOMARY to start works on Buddhist relics with an account of the Buddha's parinirvāṇa and funeral, and the subsequent division of the remains of his body (see Altekar 1956; Benard 1988; Davids 1901; Fleet 1906–7; Heiler 1961: 1044; Wylie [1897] 1966). As mentioned, however, I shall delay my presentation of those events to look first at several less commonly considered preliminary topics, beginning, in this chapter, with the question of the relics of Gautama's predecessors, the so-called previous buddhas. It is impossible to cover here all of the various traditions about the precursors of the Buddha; some selection of topics and sources is necessary. Accordingly, I shall limit myself to (1) a brief introduction showing the connection between previous buddhas and the biography of Śākyamuni; (2) an investigation of the topic of previous buddhas and soteriology; (3) a study of traditions associated with the stūpa and the relics of the most recent previous buddha, Kāśyapa; and (4) an elucidation of the distinction between buddhas whose relics are "dispersed" and those whose relics are not. In this process, a number of important issues concerning the nature of buddha relics in general will be raised.

Śākyamuni and His Predecessors

As is well known, according to Buddhist tradition, Siddhārtha Gautama, or Śākyamuni, was but the most recent of a succession of buddhas who have appeared "at suitable intervals" (Conze 1959: 19) over the past aeons, and who will continue to do so in the future (see Nattier, forthcoming). In this context, although the Buddha himself is said to have reached enlightenment on his own in his final lifetime, the dharma that he found was not so much a brand-new doctrine as the rediscovery of an ancient truth. As he himself is supposed to have put it to his disciples, just as a man, traveling through the forest, may come across "an ancient path that was followed by men of ancient times," so too, the Tathāgata has found "the ancient path that was followed by former buddhas" (*S.*, 2:106 = Eng. trans., Davids and Woodward 1917–30, 2:74).

The notion of a multiplicity of buddhas existing in time appears very early in the history of Buddhism. Already in the third century B.C.E., King Aśoka recorded his visit to the stūpa of the past buddha Kanakamuni (Pali, Konāgamana). The pillar inscription that he left there is presently located at Nigalisagar (Nigliva), in what is now Southern Nepal. That, however, is a place where there are no traces of any ancient stūpas. Accordingly, it has been suspected that the broken pillar at Nigalisagar originally formed the top of a pillar stump at nearby Gotihawa, where there *are* the remains of an Aśokan era stūpa, and which some scholars consider to be the Kanakamuni stūpa in question (see Schopen 1995: 234; and Mitra 1971: 252). In any case, the inscription Aśoka had inscribed on the pillar reads as follows: "When King Devanampriya Priyadarshin [= Aśoka] had been anointed fourteen years, he enlarged the stupa of the Buddha Konakamana [= Kanakamuni] to the double [of its original size]. When he had been anointed [twenty] years he came himself and worshipped [this spot] and caused [a stone pillar to be set up]" (Bhattacharya 1960: 55; text in Bloch 1950: 158). Aśoka does not specify the exact nature of this stūpa of Kanakamuni, but, on the basis of Xuanzang's testimony, it is generally thought that it was his parinirvāṇa stūpa enshrining the remains of his body (*T.* 2087, 51:901b = Eng. trans., Li 1996: 176; see also Watters 1904, 2:5–6).

Aśoka's inscription is precious evidence of an early cult of the relics of a particular previous buddha. More generally, of course, Kanakamuni was but one of a whole series of buddhas who have appeared in the past and will continue to do so in the future.[1] In theory, the number of these predecessors and successors of Śākyamuni could be infinite, like time itself, but here and there in canonical sources, names and numbers are given, along with distinguishing traits. Especially important in this regard is the *Mahāvadāna-sūtra* (Pali: *Mahāpadāna-sutta*),[2] where the names of seven past buddhas are given, together with specifications as to when they lived, how long they lived, what their caste and clan were, what kind of tree their bodhi tree was, how many disciples they had, and what were the names of their two chief disciples, their personal attendant, their father, their mother, and their son, and their birthplace (Waldschmidt 1953–56: 68–8).[3] Thus Vipaśyin (Pali: Vipassin) lived ninety-one aeons

[1] André Bareau (1962: 261) has hypothesized that there must have been, in Aśoka's time, stūpas at least of Kāśyapa and probably of Krakucchanda as well, and that these were connected together by pilgrims. A cryptic reference in the *Aśokāv.* (124 = Eng. trans., Strong 1983: 286) mentions a king named Aśoka (presumably an ancient namesake of the Mauryan monarch) who built a stūpa for Krakucchanda made out of four kinds of jewels.

[2] For parallel editions of the Sanskrit and Pali texts, together with notes on Chinese versions, see Waldschmidt 1953–56. The Pali text may also be found in *D.* 2:1–54 = Eng. trans., Walshe 1987: 199–221.

[3] See also *Buv.*, 77–99 = Eng. trans., Horner 1975: 74–96. For other lists of various num-

ago and was a *kṣatriya*; Śikhin (Sikhin) and Viśvabhuj (Vessabhū) both lived thirty-one aeons ago and were likewise kṣatriyas; and Krakasunda or Kracucchanda (Kakusandha), Kanakamuni (Konāgamana), Kāśyapa (Kassapa), and Śākyamuni (Sakyamuni) all lived in our present "fortunate aeon" (*bhadrakalpa*), and were all brahmins except for our own Buddha Śākyamuni who was a kṣatriya (Waldschmidt 1953–56: 169–75; and Davids 1899–1924, 2:6–7).[4]

The rest of the *Mahāvadāna sūtra* goes on to spell out, in some detail, the life of the first of these buddhas, Vipaśyin, who lived ninety-one kalpas ago.[5] Its account of his life in virtually every way parallels the familiar legend of the Buddha Śākyamuni, and so has been seen as one of the early important textual building blocks in the development of the Buddha's sacred biography. It is clear to most scholars that the legend of Vipaśyin is here patterned on the life of Śākyamuni, whether that be understood historically or legendarily (see Gombrich 1980: 65; Nakamura 2000: 17). The thrust of the story itself, however, is to assert the opposite and to claim that Śākyamuni, in leading his life, was actually just following a preestablished biographical blueprint for buddhas, paradigmatically illustrated long ago by Vipaśyin. Reminders of this, in fact, constantly crop up in the telling of the Buddha's own life story. Thus, for example, when the bodhisattva first arrives at the bodhi tree in Bodhgaya, he tries out various sides of the tree as possible spots for his meditation seat; none of them is satisfactory until he finally settles down on the eastern side, realizing that that was the place where his predecessors, the previous buddhas, had all sat (*JA.*, 1:70–71 = Eng. trans., Jayawickrama 1990: 93–94).[6]

The tradition of an enlightened master having precursors or predecessors who set patterns for him was, of course, not exclusively a Buddhist one.

---

bers of previous buddhas, see *T.* 190, 3:672a = Eng. trans., Beal 1875:16; *Lal.*, 6 = Fr. trans., Foucaux 1884: 6–7); and *Mtu.*, 1:136–41 = Eng. trans., Jones 1949–56, 1:108–12. See also Yamada 1968, 1:125–26; Lamotte 1949–80: 248n.

[4] These seven correspond to buddhas nos. 19–25 on the longer list of previous buddhas given in table 1 below. It should be noted that in this tradition there are two types of aeons: empty ones (*śūnyakalpa*) that are devoid of buddhas, and non-empty (*aśūnya*) kalpas that are not. The latter are further divided into five types according to whether they have one, two, three, four, or five buddhas living in them. An aeon with five buddhas such as our own is an especially "fortunate" (*bhadra*) kalpa. See Horner 1975: xxvii; and Childers 1909: 185–86.

[5] On the significance of this number, see Strong 1992: 54–55, and La Vallée Poussin 1928.

[6] The site of the bodhi tree at Bodhgaya remains a constant for all buddhas, though the identity of their trees differs. See *JA.*, 4:233 = Eng. trans., Cowell 1895–1907, 4:146. Xuanzang reports the tradition that the bodhisattva first tried to attain enlightenment on the top of, and then in a cave on, Mount Prāgbodhi before realizing that the bodhi tree was the right spot that had been used by previous buddhas. See *T.* 2087, 51:915ab = Eng. trans., Li 1996: 243–44; Nakamura 2000: 148–50.

The Jains, as is well known, compiled a list of twenty-four *tīrthaṃkaras* ("ford-makers"), including their "founder," Mahāvīra (Stevenson 1915: 312–13). The Ājīvikas also had a tradition of twenty-four such departed masters, including their "founder" Maskarin Gośālīputra (Pali: Makkhali Gosāla) (Basham 1981: 27). It comes as no surprise then to find that the list of previous buddhas in the *Mahāvadāna sūtra* was soon extended to a set of twenty-four (twenty-five with Śākyamuni), which became the standard number in the Theravādin tradition (see table 1).[7] This list begins with the figure of the Buddha Dīpaṃkara, who is said to have lived over four incalculable ages ago (*Buv.*, 22–23 = Eng. trans., Horner 1975: 27–29).[8] It is in the presence of Dīpaṃkara that the bodhisattva, the future Śākyamuni who was then an ascetic named Sumedha, formally embarks on the path that will eventually result in his buddhahood. Seeing Dīpaṃkara approach a muddy section of the road, he prostrates himself in the mire at his feet so that the Buddha can pass over unsullied, by stepping on him (or on his spread out matted hair). He then resolves in his mind, and declares with his lips, his intention to become himself, some day, a fully enlightened Buddha (*JA.*, 1:2ff. = Eng. trans., Jayawickrama 1990: 3ff).[9] Dīpaṃkara then responds to this threefold expression of resolve (by body, speech, and mind) by making a prediction that Sumedha will indeed achieve his goal, ages and aeons hence, in a future lifetime, when he will attain enlightenment as Śākyamuni, under the bodhi tree at Bodhgaya. This basic scenario—of the bodhisattva expressing his determination to achieve his own buddhahood, and receiving in response from that buddha an assurance that he is on the path—is then reiterated under each of the subsequent twenty-three previous buddhas following Dīpaṃkara (see *Buv.* = Eng. trans., Horner 1975; and *JA.*, 1:2–47 = Eng. trans., Jayawickrama 1990: 3–61).

[7] On the presumed Jain influence here, see Gombrich 1980: 64. An account of these buddhas first appears in the Pali Canon in the *Buddhavaṃsa*. In an apparently later addition to that text (*Buv.*, 100 = Eng. trans., Horner 1975: 96), the number twenty-five is expanded to twenty-eight by the addition of three buddhas prior to Dīpaṃkara. See also *BuvA.*, 131 = Eng. trans., Horner 1978: 189; and *JA.*, 1:44 = Eng. trans., Jayawickrama 1990: 56. The twenty-eight are also featured in *Jinab.*, 65ff = Fr. trans., Liyanaratne 1983: 75ff; and in the "Aṭavisi pirita," on which see Saddhatissa 1975: 23–24 and DeSilva 1981: 11.

[8] In the Sanskrit tradition, the story of Dīpaṃkara is told at length in *Mtu*, 1:193–248 = Eng. trans., Jones 1949–56, 1:152–203. The cult of Dīpaṃkara is still popular today in parts of Nepal (see Vergati 1982). On its connection to messianism in China, see Lagerwey 1998: 92.

[9] In the Sanskrit tradition, Sumedha is variously known as Megha (see *Mtu.*, 1:232 = Eng. trans., Jones 1949–56, 1:188; and Bareau 1966–74), and Sumati (see *Div.*, 246 = Eng. trans., Strong 2002: 19). In other traditions, the origins of Śākyamuni's path are pushed back further. See Strong 2001: 19–27; and Lamotte 1949–80: 248–49.

TABLE 1

Relics of the twenty-five buddhas (based on *Thūpavaṃsa* and *Buddhavaṃsa*)

Buddha:	*Time period of life (in no. of incalculable* [asaṃkheyya] *ages + aeons* [kalpa] *ago)* *		*Lifespan (in years)*	*Relics: scattered or not?*	*Height of stūpa (in* yojanas)
1. Dīpaṃkara	4 ages + 100,000	aeons ago	100,000	not	36
2. Koṇḍañña	over 3	ages ago	100,000	not	7
3. Mangala	over 2	ages ago	90,000	not	30
4. Sumana	over 2	ages ago	90,000	not	4
5. Revata	over 2	ages ago	60,000	scattered	n/a
6. Sobhita	over 2	ages ago	90,000	scattered	n/a
7. Anomadassī	over 1	age ago	100,000	not	25
8. Paduma	over 1	age ago	100,000	scattered	n/a
9. Nārada	over 1	age ago	90,000	not	4
10. Padumuttara	100,000	aeons ago	100,000	not	12
11. Sumedha	70,000	aeons ago	90,000	scattered	n/a
12. Sujāta	70,000	aeons ago	90,000	not	3/4
13. Piyadassī	1,800	aeons ago	90,000	not	3
14. Atthadassī	1,800	aeons ago	100,000	scattered	n/a
15. Dhammadassī	1,800	aeons ago	100,000	not	3
16. Siddhattha	94	aeons ago	100,000	not	4
17. Tissa	92	aeons ago	100,000	not	3
18. Phussa	92	aeons ago	90,000	scattered	n/a
19. Vipassi	91	aeons ago	80,000	not	7
20. Sikhī	31	aeons ago	70,000	not	3
21. Vessabhū	31	aeons ago	60,000	scattered	n/a
22. Kakusandha	in the present	aeon	40,000	not	1/4
23. Konāgamana	in the present	aeon	30,000	scattered	n/a
24. Kassapa	in the present	aeon	20,000	not	1
25. Gotama	in the present	aeon	80	both	many stūpas

Note: Extra spaces separate buddhas who appeared in same aeon.

* The length of an "incalculable age" is usually left unspecified but is sometimes defined as 10^{140} years. A *kalpa,* or world cycle, is sometimes said to be 4,320 million years long.

Past Buddhas, Relics, and Soteriology

There is reflected in this a soteriological pattern that became well established in Buddhist literature. At its simplest, the Buddhist process of achieving enlightenment may be described as being marked by two crucial moments: (1) an embarkation on the path, which usually consists of a relatively simple act of devotion (such as Sumedha's) typically accompanied by the making of a vow (*praṇidhāna*) to attain enlightenment in the future; and (2) an arrival at the goal, that is, the actual attainment of enlightenment. In between these two moments, of course, there can be (and usually are) many many lifetimes of striving and merit-making, during which the initial act of embarkation may periodically be repeated and reaffirmed.

Various schools of Buddhist thought, however, differed on the question of how crucial it was to meet (or to have met) with a living buddha before being able to embark on the soteriological path. For instance, in telling the story of Śākyamuni's career, the *Jātaka-nidāna* (representing the Theravāda tradition) makes such a meeting one of the sine qua nons for embarkation on the bodhisattva path. There are, it proclaims, certain "right conditions" for the making of a vow for buddhahood: the person who does so must, inter alia, be a human being (and not a nāga or a deity), and must be of the male gender (and not a woman, eunuch, or hermaphrodite). He must be capable of attaining arhatship in the very same existence in which he makes the resolution (although he refrains from doing this and opts instead for the more difficult course of becoming a buddha).[10] Finally, and most interestingly for our purposes, his resolution must be made "in the presence of a living buddha"; it cannot be made "after the parinirvāṇa of a buddha, in front of a caitya, or at the foot of a bodhi tree." If it is, the vow will not bear fruit (*JA.*, 1:14 = Eng. trans., Jayawickrama 1990: 18–19).

It is not altogether clear, in the Theravāda, whether this injunction, made in the context of the bodhisattva embarking for *buddhahood,* should also be extended to persons embarking on the path to *arhatship.* Some scholars have suggested that it should. Peter Masefield, for example, though approaching the question from a somewhat different angle, has maintained that a person's first steps toward arhatship (as well as arhatship itself) can be occasioned only by the oral teaching of the dharma from a living buddha in person. Relics or stūpas will not do, for "the disappearance of the Buddha was at the same time the disappearance of [the] chance of salvation" (Masefield 1986: 141). In other words, it would seem to be impossible for anyone to embark on the road to enlightenment in this buddhaless time of ours.

[10] There is an interesting reflection, here in this Pali text, of the sentiment to be featured later on in the Mahāyāna, namely that the quest for buddhahood involves rejecting or moving beyond the attainment of arhatship. See Rahula 1974: 3.

Masefield's argument is made on the basis of Pali canonical texts, and, not surprisingly, certain Mahāyāna sources would radically disagree with it. Śāntideva, for example, devotes a whole chapter to the praise of the worship of stūpas in his *Śikṣāsamuccaya* (156–67 = Eng. trans., Bendall and Rouse [1902] 1971: 270–82), in which he quotes numerous sūtras all designed to show that even the smallest act of devotion towards the relic of a *tathāgata,* when accompanied by the proper mental resolve, can put one on the path to highest buddhahood. The *Lotus Sūtra,* similarly, asserts that of those who circumambulate a stūpa and venerate it, "some realise arhatship, others attain pratyekabuddhahood; and others . . . in immense numbers, raise their minds to supreme, perfect enlightenment [i.e., buddhahood]" (Kern 1884: 247; text in *Sdmp.,* 260).[11]

A third position may be seen in the Sarvāstivādin anthology of stories called the *Avadānaśataka.* The first several chapters—those dealing with persons on the path to buddhahood or pratyekabuddhahood—by and large confirm the Theravāda's assertion that the moment of embarkation for buddhahood necessitates a meeting with a buddha in person. The chapters that deal with arhatship, however, present a more mixed picture. To be sure, in many cases, the pattern is for an individual to encounter a buddha in a past life and be inspired to make a vow to attain arhatship under another buddha in a future life. In other words, both embarkation and arrival are done in the presence of a buddha. There is also, however, a whole chapter in the *Avadānaśataka* (155–74 = Fr. trans., Feer 1891: 233–58) featuring stories about arhats whose acts of embarkation are directed toward the stūpa enshrining the *relics* of the past buddha Vipaśyin. Story no. 62 is typical: in it, the arhatship of a young man named Sugandhi is explained by reference to a moment, ninety-one kalpas ago, when he made an offering of flowers and incense to the stūpa of the parinirvāṇized Vipaśyin, while at the same time making a praṇidhāna, vowing to attain arhatship (*Avś.,* 157–59 = Fr. trans., Feer 1891: 238–40).

The same pattern may be found in all the other stories of this chapter. In each of them, the text seems to go out of its way to make the point that what is being venerated here is not the living body of the buddha Vipaśyin but his stūpa, that is, his relics. Indeed, Vipaśyin is first introduced in terms that are stereotypical for the description of a buddha: "Ninety-one kalpas ago, O monks, in a time now gone by, there appeared in the world the altogether enlightened blessed buddha Vipaśyin, endowed with knowledge and good conduct, well-gone, unsurpassed, knower of the world, guide of those needing to be disciplined, teacher of humans and gods" (*Avś.,* 156 = Fr. trans., Feer 1891: 7). Then, however, we see this Vipaśyin—who, in the narrative, could very well have been venerated in

[11] See also Burnouf 1852:158, and, on stūpa worship in the *Lotus,* Hirakawa 1963: 85ff.

person—pass away and become a relic before our very eyes: "The altogether enlightened buddha Vipaśyin went and dwelt in the royal city of Bandhumatī. And when he had fulfilled the functions of a buddha, he parinirvāṇized without remainder, like a fire which has no more fuel. Then King Bandhumat performed the funeral ceremonies for the body of the Blessed One, and erected a stūpa made out of the four gems which was a league in circumference and a quarter-league in height" (*Avś.*, 156 = Fr. trans., Feer 1891: 7–8). It is toward this stūpa that the future arhats in these stories perform their initial acts of devotion. In the *Avadānaśataka,* then, both the enshrined relics of a past buddha (e.g. in the Vipaśyin chapter) or a past buddha in person (e.g. in other chapters) are equally effective in inspiring devotees on the way to arhatship.

This apparent functional equivalence of stūpa and buddha will, of course, come as no surprise to students of Buddhist relics for whom a stūpa "is" the living buddha, but its contextual importance should not go unnoticed. The authors of the *Avadānaśataka,* like Buddhists today, were living in post-parinirvāṇa times, in an age when there was no buddha present. The soteriological pattern they inherited and propounded was one that stressed the importance of meeting the Buddha in order to embark on the path to enlightenment. But meeting the Buddha in person is impossible in a buddhaless time. The solution that was adopted, then, was to leave open the possibility of meeting the Buddha in his relics, and being inspired by them. Thus, in the *Avadānaśataka,* relics, in the absence of a buddha, make soteriology possible, but they do not apparently open all soteriological paths; the relics are functionally equivalent to living buddhas in bringing individuals to future *arhatship,* but not in bringing them to future *buddhahood* (or pratyekabuddhahood). In this the *Avadānaśataka* differs from the *Lotus Sūtra,* and in this, it must be recognized, there lies a difference between buddhas and their relics, a difference occasioned by contextual considerations.

The Case of Kāśyapa and His Stūpa

Of the seven buddhas listed in the *Mahāvadāna sūtra,* the last three (i.e., Krakucchanda, Kanakamuni, and Kāśyapa) form a set of their own. They all appeared in our present "fortunate aeon" (bhadrakalpa) and, together with Śākyamuni who likewise came in the bhadrakalpa, they constitute a group of four buddhas, to which can also be added the future Buddha Maitreya, to make a set of five.[12]

[12] In later sources, the number of future buddhas (beyond Maitreya) in the bhadrakalpa was greatly expanded to as many as one thousand. For discussions of this move and bibliographies, see Nattier 1991: 23–24, and Yamada 1968, 1:136–39.

When the Chinese pilgrims Faxian (fifth-century) and Xuanzang (seventh-century) traveled about North-Central India, they routinely came across places where the first three buddhas of the bhadrakalpa were said to have sat, or walked up and down in meditation, or preached. Generally, these places were marked by stūpas, and usually, they were associated with another stūpa enshrining some physical remain of Śākyamuni, such as some of his hair or nails. The description of these is, in fact, utterly stereotypical, as Etienne Lamotte (1988: 338) has pointed out: "[I]t is always the same . . . formula that [comes] from Xuanzang's pen: 'An Aśoka stūpa on the spot where the Buddha had propounded his excellent doctrine . . . ; to one side, a stūpa where buddhas of the past had sat or walked; finally, a small stūpa containing relics of the Buddha's hair or nails.'"

There is very little indication that any of these memorials, except for the stūpas over the hair and nails of Śākyamuni, were anything but purely commemorative. They mark places, sites made sacred no doubt by the successive visits of various buddhas over the course of the aeon, but most likely not containing any bodily remains or personal possessions of the first three buddhas of the bhadrakalpa. Things are different, however, when the pilgrims reach the town of Toyikā (Pali: Todeyya), somewhere between Śrāvastī and Benares. There, Faxian reports seeing three stūpas marking different events in the life of the Buddha Kāśyapa, the last and largest of which, at the place of his parinirvāṇa, is said to enshrine "the entire relic of [his] whole body" (Legge 1886: 63; text in *T.* 2085, 51:861a; see also Li 2002: 185). Xuanzang tells us much the same thing, adding that this stūpa had been built by King Aśoka (*T.* 2087, 51:900c = Eng. trans., Li 1996: 173). Both pilgrims describe similar sets of three stūpas for the past buddhas Kanakamuni and Krakucchanda, a bit further on, in the region between Śrāvastī and Kapilavastu (*T.* 2085, 51:861a = Eng. trans., Li 2002: 185; and *T.* 2087, 51:901b = Eng. trans., Li 1996: 176), but the claim that Kāśyapa's stūpa contained the remains of his entire body is remarkable, and serves to distinguish his stūpa from those of the two other previous buddhas.

According to a tradition preserved in the Pali commentaries, the building of Kāśyapa's stūpa after his parinirvāṇa was a magnificent and costly enterprise; the bricks were solid blocks of gold, each one valued at a hundred thousand pieces of money, and the mortar was made of yellow orpiment and red arsenic mixed with sesame oil. The relic chamber was especially costly and the people, having run out of funds, had to raise a huge fortune to pay for it (*DhA.*, 3:29–30 = Eng. trans., Burlingame 1921, 2:280–81).[13] In the Sanskrit tradition, the stūpa of Kāśyapa is

[13] For an account of the fund raising for the relic chamber, see *DhA.*, 4:219–220 = Eng. trans., Burlingame 1921, 3:330. For other sources on the construction of the stūpa, see Malalasekera [1938] 1960, 1:544.

associated with the figure of King Kṛkin, who was responsible for its construction, and who ruled at the time in Benares (see *Avś.*, 207–8, 229–30 = Fr. trans., Feer 1891: 316, 359).[14]

By Śākyamuni's time, that ancient stūpa at Toyikā seems to have disappeared or, at least, gone underground.[15] The legend of Śākyamuni's visit to the site is recounted in similar stories contained in the *Dhammapada Commentary* (*Dh.A.*, 3:250–53 = Eng. trans., Burlingame 1921, 3:68–69), in the Vinayas of the Mahāsāṃghika, Mahīśāsaka, and Dharmaguptaka sects (*T.* 1425, 22:497–98 = Fr. trans., Bareau 1962: 257–59; *T.* 1421, 22:172–73 = Fr. trans., Bareau 1962: 259; *T.* 1428, 22:958 = Fr. trans., Bareau 1962: 259–60), and in a passage from the *Mūlasarvāstivāda Vinaya* (*GilgMss.* 3, 1:73–79; compare *Div.*, 465–69 and 76–80). Gregory Schopen, who has studied these sources, summarizes the story contained in the first four of these texts as follows:

> The Buddha is travelling in Kosala; he reaches a spot near a village called . . . Toyikā; he has an encounter with a man [always a brahmin] working in a nearby field as a result of which it becomes known that the stūpa of the Buddha Kāśyapa lays buried under this spot; the Buddha then makes the stūpa momentarily appear and after it disappears he and/or the monks construct a stūpa on that spot from mud . . . ; this then is followed—in one case preceded—by instructions on how a stūpa should be built and / or by verses praising the merit of building or worshipping stūpas. (1997: 28).

To this Schopen contrasts the story in the fifth text, the *Mūlasarvāstivāda Vinaya*. While it is basically the same in its outline, one of its distinguishing features, he argues, is that "it knows absolutely nothing about a stūpa at Toyikā or its construction. Here it is not a stūpa which the Buddha makes appear, but only 'the undivided mass of the relics of the Samyaksaṃbuddha Kāśyapa.'" This, he says, reflects the existence of an early stage of the relic cult "in which the stūpa did not yet have a part" (Schopen 1997: 29).

The exhibition of Kāśyapa's whole skeleton, apparently outside of its reliquary stūpa (if, in fact, it had one), is indeed noteworthy.[16] Most immediately, it calls to mind a story about the bones of a pratyekabuddha found in a Chinese Vinaya text not unconnected to the legend of Kāśyapa's

[14] See also *Div.* 22–24; *T.* 1425, 22:497–98 = Fr. trans., Bareau 1962: 258–59; *T.* 1421, 22:172–73 = Fr. trans., Bareau 1962: 259, 265–67; and Chavannes 1934, 2:349. See also Iwamoto 1968: 209–18. For further sources on Kṛkin, see Schopen 1997: 47n.31; and Hofinger 1954: 225n.

[15] On the theme of sinking stūpas, see Mus 1938.

[16] The fact that the skeleton is *whole* caused Vincent Smith (1918: 659) to speculate that, in ancient times (i.e., the time of the buddha Kāśyapa), Buddhists practiced burial rather than cremation.

stūpa at Toyikā. In this tale, King Prasenajit of Kosala goes to see the Buddha and sits down to listen to him preach, but he is distracted by a smell wafting through the assembly hall, a perfume so divine that he pays no attention to the Blessed One's sermon. Finally, he asks what is causing the wonderful odor, and the Buddha, reaching down into the earth, pulls up the sixty-foot skeleton of a former pratyekabuddha. The bones, still connected, rise up into the air, manifest miracles, and spread a pleasant odor everywhere. The king, naturally, is interested in the karmic history of this pratyekabuddha, and the Buddha launches into a lengthy *avadāna* about him: this pratyekabuddha had once been a young man who had stolen a flower blossom from the stūpa of the former Buddha Kāśyapa in order to give it to a courtesan. As a result, he developed a horrible abcess on his body, which, however, was cured when, repenting his ways, he offered some sandalwood to the stūpa and made a vow for pratyekabuddhahood (*T.* 1464, 24:897–98 = Fr. trans., Bareau 1982: 19–24; see also Bareau 1962: 264–65; Huber 1908: 355–61).[17]

The details of this karmic explanation are perhaps less interesting than some of the features of the tale itself. First of all, here too we have a case in which there is no mention of a stūpa and in which the pratyekabuddha's relics—his skeleton—seem very much alive; they smell good, they move about, they perform miracles. Secondly, because of the pratyekabuddha's sweet-smelling "presence," King Prasenajit is unable to pay attention to the Buddha and fails utterly to hear his sermon. Simply put, the two cannot coexist in his attention span. In this we have, perhaps, a distant metaphoric recall of the doctrine that buddhas (buddhas and pratyekabuddhas, or present and previous buddhas) are not supposed to overlap in time.[18] This, we shall see, is also an important feature of the Toyikā story. Thirdly, the divine perfume emanating from the body of the pratyekabuddha shows that these relics are more than just bones. This is not a cemetery meditation focusing on the corruption and rot of the human form, but a glorification of the incorruptability of bones-become-relics. Much the same can be said about Kāśyapa's bones at Toyikā. There is no hint of their decay or corruption, rather, they undergo an interesting metamorphosis in the text; when still buried underground, Kāśyapa's body is called an "undivided mass of bones [*asthi*]," that is, a skeleton (*GilgMss.*, 3, 1:74), but when the Buddha raises it up for all to see, it is

[17] The tradition associating a pratyekabuddha with Toyikā reappears in a strange way in a late Pali text about future buddhas beyond Maitreya. There a brahmin named Todeyya (=Toyikā) makes a vow for future buddhahood not in the presence of another Buddha, but in front of a pratyekabuddha, which is unusual, to say the least. See *Dasab.*, 149 = Eng. trans., Saddhatissa 1975: 81.

[18] Hence the stock expression "pratyekabuddhas arise in the world, when there are no buddhas." (*Div.*, 88). See also Wiltshire 1990: 303.

called an "undivided mass of relics [śarīra]," i.e., a body (*GilgMss.*, 3, 1:75). Generally speaking, in the mythic cosmology of buddhas, what is underground is what is past, while what is up (like Maitreya in Tuṣita Heaven) is what is future; thus the raising up and exposition of the underground relics of a buddha make him "present" in both the temporal and spatial senses of the word.

Schopen's claim that no stūpa appears or is constructed in the *Mūlasarvāstivāda Vinaya* version of the story needs some mitigating. While it is true that no mention is made of a buried stūpa of Kāśyapa in Toyikā, but only of his skeleton, the lay people of the area do end up building a stūpa there out of balls of mud or clay (*mṛttikāpiṇḍa*). A layman, acting on his own, places one ball of mud there as an offering—to mark the spot, so to speak—but when the Buddha proclaims that such an action is just as meritorious as offering hundreds of thousands of balls of gold, many hundreds of thousands of people, seeking to "cash in" merit-wise on the opportunity, follow his example and make a big pile of balls of mud there. In other words, a stūpa is born from the offerings to the spot (*GilgMss.*, 3, 1:76). This, to be sure, is a commemorative stūpa; its mode of construction makes it clear that the remains of Kāśyapa are not enshrined in it. But it is exactly the way in which the stūpa at Toyikā is built in the Dharmaguptaka, Mahīśāsaka, and Mahāsāṃghika Vinayas, except that in the latter, King Prasenajit eventually arrives with seven hundred carts filled with bricks and asks the Buddha for permission to "enlarge" (and obviously to reinforce) the dirt stūpa (see Bareau 1962: 257–60).[19] We shall encounter, in a later chapter, some more specific examples of the construction of stūpas over the relics of the Buddha. Suffice it to state here that the making of a stūpa out of clay, mud, or any other material, may be less a single act of commemoration than a result of ongoing communal acts of devotion toward a holy place (caitya), and that such stūpas do not necessarily contain any relics.

Two Buddhas at Once

Schopen (1987: 210) also wants to use the Toyikā story to reinforce the view that "there is no distinction between a living Buddha and a collection of [his] relics." This claim is particularly interesting since, if it is literally true, the story of the previous buddha Kāśyapa at Toyikā would appear to violate what might be called the principle of the nonsimultaneity of buddhas. As is well known, in Mainstream Buddhist traditions, though several (up to five) tathāgatas may appear in the same aeon, they

[19] This has an interesting correlation with archaeological finds at the ancient sites of Piprahwā and Vaiśālī where, according to some, the earliest layers show an original stūpa made of clay and then enlarged by a brick structure. See Sinha 1991: 1.

are not meant to coexist within that aeon. In Theravāda sources, the reason for this nonoverlap of buddhas is explained very simply: the Buddha is extraordinary, unique, one of a kind; "if two or four or eight or sixteen were to arise together, they would not be extraordinary" (*VibhA.* 433 = Eng. trans., Ñāṇamoli 1996, 2:181). Thus, if a relic *is* a living buddha, then Śākyamuni should not be handling the relics of Kāśyapa unless, of course, the text wishes to have him contradict the principle.

It comes as no surprise then to find, in certain canonical sources, stories apparently related to the Toyikā tale in which no bodily relic or stūpa of Kāśyapa is mentioned. In the Pali "Ghaṭīkāra sutta," for instance, we find that the Buddha, traveling in the land of Kosala, stops at an unidentified spot and smiles. Upon being asked why, he explains that, in former times, the monastic retreat (*ārāma*) of the Buddha Kasyapa had been in that place (*M.* 2:45–46 = Eng. trans., Horner 1954–59, 2:243). Similarly, in the *Mahāvastu,* the Buddha stops at a small town in Kosala, smiles and points out to Ānanda four pieces of ground *(pṛthivīpradeśa)*:[20] the sites of Kāśyapa's former monastic retreat (*ārāma*),[21] of his hut (*kuṭī*), of his meditation-walkway (*cankrama*), and his seat.[22] In neither of these texts is any mention made of Kāśyapa's stūpa or of his bodily relics, nor are any of the buildings or structures in question still extant, and in this way, perhaps, the problem of actual Buddha-overlap is avoided. To be sure, the memory of Kāśyapa's former presence adds mythological depth and sacrality to the site, but there is no question of the actual apparition of Kāśyapa here. Indeed, what makes the Buddha smile in the "Ghaṭīkāra sutta" is not the fact that two buddhas are being venerated at once (since they are not), but his own remembering of his reluctance, in a former life, as the brahmin Jotipāla, to venerate Kāśyapa (see *M.*, 2:47–49 = Eng. trans., Horner 1954–59, 2:244–46).

By way of contrast, in the Toyikā stories mentioned above, there appears to be a rather deliberate self-conscious proclamation that what makes the site an exceptional place is the possibility of worshiping two buddhas there simultaneously. The *Mūlasarvāstivāda Vinaya,* for instance, seems to go out of its way to make that point; the brahmin who fails to honor Śākyamuni properly is said to have made a mistake for, had he only drawn near, he could have venerated two buddhas at once—Śākyamuni, who is standing there, and Kāśyapa, whose bones lie under the earth at that spot. And Ānanda's response, when he finds this out, is to fold the Buddha's upper garment into a square, put it on the ground,

[20] On the importance of particular places and their connection to relics, see Schopen 1975.
[21] Reading "ārāma" for "āgama" as suggested by Jones 1949–56: 266, and by *M.*, 2:45.
[22] This was also the site of the seats of the previous buddhas Kanakamuni and Krakucchanda. Given this last revelation, Ānanda, of course, again has Śākyamuni promptly sit down there as well. See *Mtu.*, 1:318 = Eng. trans., Jones 1949–56, 1:266–67.

and tell the Tathāgata to "sit on this seat so that two buddhas will have enjoyed this piece of ground" (*Gilg.Mss.*, 3, 1:74; compare *Div.*, 76–77, 465). The *Mahāsāṃghika Vinaya* is similarly explicit in having the Buddha smile at the thought that the brahmin, in one act, is actually venerating two buddhas, though he does not realize it (*T.* 1425, 22:497b = Fr. trans., Bareau 1962: 257).

This potential "violation" of the principle of nonsimultaneity of buddhas is no oversight. It seems rather to be an intentional attempt to acknowledge a doctrine that was perhaps already being undermined. Indeed, the Toyikā story may be profitably compared and contrasted to one of the most popular chapters of the Mahāyāna's *Lotus Sūtra* , the one in which Śākyamuni and the past Buddha Prabhūtaratna are shown to coexist. Prabhūtaratna made a vow long ago, that, after his parinirvāṇa, the stūpa enshrining his entire body would appear, whenever and wherever the *Lotus* was preached. Prabhūtaratna's Buddha-field is located countless thousands of myriads of *koṭis* of worlds away, *underneath* the earth; like Kāśyapa's, therefore, it is out of the ground that his stūpa emerges, a voice heard within it singing the praises of Śākyamuni. When the Buddha actually opens the stūpa, the apparently still-living Prabhūtaratna continues to praise him and the *Lotus Sūtra,* and offers him half of his seat; the scene became a famous one, especially iconographically, and there could hardly be a more explicit assertion of the coexistence of two buddhas (*Sdmp.,* 239ff. = Eng. trans., Kern 1884: 228–37; see also Watson 1993: 171–75).

Like Kāśyapa in the Toyikā story, Prabhūtaratna "comes alive," and in both cases, both buddhas sit on the same spot, an event which in both traditions is presented as rather revolutionary.[23] Prabhūtaratna, however, seems somehow less skeletal—less of a relic—than Kāśyapa. Despite the fact that, at one point, his body is called a "relic form" (*dhātuvigraha*) (*Sdmp.*, p. 430 = Eng. trans., Kern 1884: 399), elsewhere his stūpa is said more ambiguously to enclose his "undivided [*ekaghana*] body [*ātmabhāva*]" (*Sdmp.*, 240 = Eng. trans., Kern 1884: 228).[24] More importantly, of course, the buddhological context here is the Mahāyāna one that proclaims the eternality (or at least the longevity) of all buddhas, a view reinforced by the fact that, in the *Lotus,* myriads of other living buddhas and emanations of buddhas all assemble to witness the occasion.

[23] The doctrine of the coexistence of buddhas was to become routine, however, and may perhaps best be seen iconographically in East Asian Buddhist temples not only in the representations of Śākyamuni sharing Prabhūtaratna's stūpa seat, but in the common depictions on altars of the buddhas of the three times—past, present, and future—sometimes identified with Kāśyapa, Śākyamuni, and Maitreya.

[24] Kern misleadingly renders *ekaghana* as "condensed." On the equation here of ātmabhāva and śarīra (body), see Edgerton 1953, s.v. "ātmabhāva."

We are left, then, with three distinct treatments of a theme that once again highlight the diversity of treatment of relics in different Buddhist milieux: At one end, we find the Pali "Ghaṭīkāra sutta" and similar texts in which there is no actual overlap between Śākyamuni and Kāśyapa because there are no bodily relics of the latter; at most, there are only secondary relics or traces of his former presence. In the middle, we find various versions of the Toyikā story in which the relics of the former buddha Kāśyapa do appear and in which the possibility of venerating two buddhas at once is proclaimed. Finally, at the other end of the spectrum, there is the *Lotus Sūtra* in which the overlap of buddhas of different times is fully proclaimed, and the distinctions between relics and living buddha become much more blurred.[25]

Relics and the Spread of the Tradition

The buddhological question of buddha overlap, however, is only one of the factors at work here. Another is the contextual question of why, in all versions of the story, Toyikā is presented as a village of brahmins, and why, in several of the versions, the Buddha's initial encounter there is with a brahmin who is tilling the soil. This brahmin, in fact, turns out to have an intimate association—a close kinship—with Kāśyapa's stūpa, which is located underneath his land. Thus, in the *Mahāsāṃghika Vinaya,* when the Buddha first reveals to his monks the underground stūpa of the former Buddha, the brahmin exclaims, "I belong to the Kāśyapa clan (*gotra*); this stūpa of Kāśyapa belongs to me!" (*T.* 1425, 22: 497 = Fr. trans., Bareau 1962: 258). Moreover, when the monks then make an above-ground stūpa to mark the spot, they do so with dirt taken from the brahmin's field, and this is what then inspires him to take refuge and become a Buddhist. What we have here, then, is the story of a conversion to Buddhism, but, importantly, it is the conversion not only of a person—the brahmin—but of a person's place—his "stūpa" (which he claims belongs to his clan) and his land (where that old stūpa was buried and whose earth was used to make a new one).

The same point is made even more explicitly in the *Dhammapada Commentary.* In that version of the story, the Buddha and his entourage, approaching the village of Todeyya (Skt: Toyikā), come to a shrine, a "god-place" (*devaṭṭhāna*) that is apparently dedicated to some local divinity. The Buddha sits down next to it and sends Ānanda to summon the brahmin who is plowing the nearby field. The brahmin comes but instead

[25]It might be thought that we have here a simple progression from Theravāda to other Mainstream Buddhist to Mahāyāna views, but, in fact, this is only partially true. The Pali *Ghaṭikāra sutta* finds a parallel in the Sanskrit *Mahāvastu,* and one of the versions of the Toyikā story is found in the *Dhammapada Commentary,* a Theravāda text.

of venerating the Buddha, he pays his respects only to the shrine. The Buddha then asks him about the place he has just venerated and the brahmin answers that that shrine, which he now calls a "caitya-place" (*cetiyaṭṭhāna*), has long been there and that worshiping it is an old custom of his people. The Buddha then reveals to him that this shrine is actually the site of the golden caitya of the Buddha Kāśyapa, a replica of which he then fashions in mid-air, using his supernatural powers. This is enough to convert the brahmin and his shrine to Buddhism (*DhA.*, 3:251–53 = Eng. trans., Burlingame 1921, 3:68–69).

The cooption and conversion of indigenous divinities and cults into Buddhism is a well-known phenomenon that has marked the advent of the religion wherever it has gone. Rather than proclaiming local gods and spirits to be antithetical to Buddhist belief, Buddhists commonly endeavored to incorporate them into the fold of the new religion by showing them to be in essence Buddhists themselves or, at least, supporters of Buddhism. The use of relics of Śākyamuni in this enterprise has been well documented and is a theme to which I shall return. The suggestion that emerges here, however, is the more limited one that the cult of the relics of previous buddhas may also have been used in this way.[26]

There is some evidence of the association of previous buddhas with pre-Buddhist divinities. Ernst Windisch, for instance, has argued that the seven buddhas of the past should, as a group, be homologized to the seven *ṛṣis* ("sages") of Vedic and Brahmanic tradition, not simply on the basis of their number but because of overlap between their gotra (clan) names and the gotra names of several previous buddhas (Kauṇḍinya, Kāśyapa, Gautama) (see Waldschmidt 1953–56: 72n.1, 169n.2; Bareau 1974:30). The ṛṣis were identified with the seven stars of the Big Dipper (Ursa Major) ,who themselves were deities (see Mitchiner 1982: 249–78), and in East Asia, at least, identifications were sometimes made directly between the seven buddhas and the stars of the dipper. Other scholars have suggested that the positioning of images of the previous buddhas above the doors to Buddhist sanctuaries recalls the parallel positioning of the seated figures of the *grahas* (planetary deities) that were often found over the doors of brahmanical temples (Vogel 1954: 810–11).[27] Finally, in a

[26] André Bareau (1974), agreeing for the most part with John Irwin (1973), attributes pre-Buddhist connections to most ancient caityas and many stūpas. Among other things, he argues that the theoretical restriction of stūpas to certain categories of extraordinary beings (including buddhas and cakravartins) meant that certain stūpas that were actually funerary mounds of ordinary persons were reassigned to past buddhas.

[27] Such astrological associations are given perhaps their greatest elaboration in von Simson 1981, where, by means of elaborate etymologizing, the seven buddhas are identified with the five planets + sun and moon, and so with the seven days of the week.

Sanskrit version of the "Ratana Paritta," the protection is invoked not of the buddhas of the past per se, but of the "deities [*devatā*] who believe in [the past buddhas] Vipaśyin, Viśvabhū, Krakucchanda," etc. (*Mtu.*, 1:294 = Eng. trans., Jones 1949–56, 1:244–45).[28]

It is important to remember that Buddhism, in India as elsewhere, was a missionary religion establishing itself—not always successfully—in a largely non-Buddhist milieu. In this context, it is noteworthy that many of the sites visited by the Chinese pilgrims, where there were stūpas marking the seat or meditation walkway of former buddhas, were located in the North central part of Madhyadeśa, to the west of the region where the Buddha spent most of his life. This was a region that was long a cradle of brahmanical civilization where, in Etienne Lamotte's (1988: 338) words,

> [T]he message of the Buddha had no hold on a population which was fiercely attached to its books and traditions, proud of its brahmins, faithful to its Devas and which punctually carried out ancestral sacrifices in which animals were immolated and the Soma flowed. Aśoka did indeed attempt to introduce his Dharma there, . . . but his efforts were powerless to change the population's mind. As for the Buddhist missionaries and propagandists of the Mauryan period, they did not even try to locate the great exploits of the Bodhisattva during his former existences in those unprofitable regions, but merely noted here and there the places which Śākyamuni had honored with his presence and where earlier buddhas had appeared.[29]

Lamotte takes the mythic claims about the former presence of previous buddhas in this region as a sign of a weak, almost desperate Buddhist missionizing effort. Be that as it may, they are also a sign of a propaganda strategy employed. The cult of previous buddhas, in fact, would seem to have been an ideal way for incorporating non-Buddhist, pre-Buddhist, or Brahmanical elements into the Buddhist fold. By identifying indigenous divinities and local sacred places with *past* buddhas, Buddhists could effectively "convert" them to Buddhism while still maintaining them at a distance. In this context, the injunction in some texts that previous buddhas (or their relics) cannot overlap or coexist with Gautama may take on a new significance as a convenient way of incorporating non-Buddhist elements and giving them an identity without allowing them too much of a presence. Much the same thing has been said about pratyekabuddhas who, also, are not supposed to overlap with buddhas (although they can coexist with one another). A number of scholars have argued that

[28] The "seven fully enlightened buddhas" are also invoked in a spell to ward off snake bites in *A.*, 2:73 = Eng. trans., Woodward and Hare 1932–36, 2:82.

[29] In this regard, it is noteworthy that some of the stories about the veneration of the past buddha Kāśyapa feature fierce opposition of brahmins. See Chavannes 1934, 2:343–49.

pratyekabuddhas were originally pre-Buddhist (and pre-Jain) figures who represented ascetic (*muni*) or recluse (*śramaṇa*) traditions that were incorporated in different ways into those two religions (Wiltshire 1990: 46–47, 117–18; Norman 1983; Kloppenborg 1974: 5–6). But while the cult of pratyekabuddhas may have been a way to incorporate non-Buddhist *śramanic* traditions into Buddhism, the cult of previous buddhas would seem to have focused on non-Buddhist *brahmanic* ones.[30] Indeed, it is not insignificant that Kāśyapa was a brahmin, as were his immediate predecessors Kanakamuni and Krakucchanda. Conversely, the brahmin of Toyikā was a "Kāśyapa" and, on that basis, claimed to "own" the stūpa on his land, up until, of course, his conversion to Buddhism.

If these associations are correct, then it becomes easier to understand why the cult of the previous buddhas should generally be carried out in conjunction with the cult of Śākyamuni. There are, in fact, a few hints in the tradition of the danger of divorcing the two. Faxian, for instance, makes, almost in passing, a very interesting and revealing statement. While traveling in the land of Kosala, he observes that "there are companies of the followers of Devadatta still existing. They regularly make offerings to the three previous buddhas, but not to Śākyamuni" (Legge 1886: 62; text in *T.* 2085, 51:861a; see also Li 2002: 184). This passage has usually been cited as evidence for the ongoing cult of Devadatta, the Buddha's cousin and archrival (see Bareau 1988–89: 544, 1989–90: 10, 1991: 123; and Mukherjee 1966: 104n), but it is also obviously informative for what it tells us about the cult of the previous buddhas. Unconnected to the worship of Śākyamuni, the making of offerings to his predecessors was something that was associated with the teachings of one of the great schismatics of Buddhist history, Devadatta. This is significant and points to the potential dangers of separating the worship of previous buddhas from that of Śākyamuni.

It also serves to put into new light an enigmatic passage in the *Dhammapada Commentary* version of the Toyikā story. After the conversion of the brahmin, the replica of Kāśyapa's golden shrine that the Buddha has created in mid-air remains poised there and is venerated by a great crowd of people. This veneration, it would seem, is directed toward Kāśyapa's stūpa alone and not toward the conjunction of Kāśyapa and Śākyamuni. In any case, after we are told that it was worshiped in various ways for a period of seven days, the text suddenly informs us that "thereupon, there arose the schism of the schismatics (*laddhika*), and by the power of the Buddha the [golden] caitya was returned to its former place," that is, it disappeared (*DhA.*, 3:253 = Eng. trans., Burlingame 1921, 3:69). We are

[30] In a somewhat different vein, Ray (1994: 239) has argued that pratyekabuddhas and former buddhas represent two categories of "proto-Buddhist saints."

not told who these schismatics were,[31] but an intriguing reference in Buddhaghosa's commentary on an Abhidharma text speaks of a schismatic group called the "white-robed recluses" (*setavattha-samaṇa*), whose claim to continue the order of the past Buddha Kāśyapa into and beyond that of Śākyamuni is questioned (*VibhA.*, 432 = Eng. trans., Ñāṇamoli 1996, 2:180–81).

If, however, the veneration of previous buddhas *apart* from Śākyamuni was potentially seen as schismatic, the cult of their relics *in conjunction* with that of Śākyamuni served to reinforce the latter and give it chronological depth. The Chinese pilgrims, as we have seen, visited many places in India where there were traces of the previous buddhas, stūpas marking spots where they had sat or walked in meditation. These stūpas were invariably associated with another one enshrining some actual relic (often a hair and / or nails) of the Buddha Śākyamuni. Together, then, they served to give layers of sacrality and antiquity to a particular site.

The establishment of such a pedigree for a given place of pilgrimage was not a phenomenon limited to Northern India. Throughout South and Southeast Asia, traditions developed that related the apocryphal visits of the buddhas of the bhadrakalpa to countries and sacred spots far and wide. Thus, the earliest chronicle of the island of Sri Lanka, the *Dīpavaṃsa*, develops an elaborate scenario according to which Kakusandha, Konāgamana, Kassapa, and Gotama, each in turn, travel to Sri Lanka, and, in various places, leave various personal relics (water pot, monastic belt, bathing cloth, and corporeal relics). In other places, they plant branches of their various bodhi trees (*sirīsa, udumbara, nigrodha,* and *assattha*) (*Dpv.*, 88–93 = Eng. trans., Oldenberg 1982: 196–201). A similar story is told with reference to the Shwe Dagon pagoda in Burma. According to an oral tradition recorded over a century ago by Shway Yoe (1882: 179), at the end of the last kalpa, five lotus blossoms appeared on Singuttara Hill (the actual site of the Shwe Dagon in Rangoon). In these lotus blossoms were five monastic robes. A large bird came to the hill and layed an egg. From that egg, Garuḍa was born, and taking hold of the five robes, he flew away with them to the heavens, where they escaped the destruction of the world that took place at the end of the kalpa. Those five robes, of course, presaged the coming to Singuttara Hill of the five buddhas of the next kalpa, our own fortunate bhadrakalpa, and of their leaving relics there.[32]

[31] In *JA.*, 1:373 = Eng. trans., Cowell 1895–1907, 1:216, the same term, *laddhika*, is applied to a brahmin who objects to Gautama using clothes from the cremation ground.

[32] The same pattern may be found at many other sites throughout Southeast Asia. See, for example, Pruess 1976a: 177. The story of the large egg-laying bird here recalls the very widespread Southeast Asian myth of the Mother Crow who gives birth to the five brothers, each of whom becomes one of the buddhas of the bhadrakalpa; see Martini 1969: 125–44; and Swearer, forthcoming.

It is noteworthy that, in these places, unlike most of the sites visited by the Chinese pilgrims in India, the past buddhas actually leave relics of themselves. These relics, however, (except for those of Śākyamuni) are not bodily relics, and in this they are unlike the remains of Kāśyapa in the stūpa at Toyikā. They are instead relics of use. It may be that we have here another reflection of the principle of nonsimultaneity of buddhas and its concomitant doctrine of the parinirvāṇa of the relics, and the resultant hesitancy to assert the survival of bodily relics from one Buddha to the next. For, although Sri Lankan tradition sometimes asserts that all images of the Buddha (along with his bodily relics) will also disappear at the time of the parinirvāṇa of the relics (see Gombrich 1971: 292), there are some indications that certain relics of use can make the transition from one Buddha to the next, as we shall see in chapter eight. Such a notion may have been significant in the choice of secondary relics to represent the presence of these previous buddhas here. Yet the thrust of these stories is not so much to make a point about different types of relics, as to give antiquity and a pedigree to a particular site. Such legends, as Lamotte (1988: 124) has put it, "must have been elaborated at a time when regions which had only embraced the Buddhist faith belatedly attempted to consider themselves holy lands by claiming that the buddhas had trodden their soil."

Relics Dispersed and Not Dispersed

There is one more tradition relative to the relics of previous buddhas that needs to be considered here. That is the distinction between relics that are "dispersed" or "scattered" (*vikiṇṇa* or *vippakiṇṇa*) and relics that are not. Something like this distinction first appears in the Pali Canon in the *Buddhavaṃsa*. In the course of describing the different characteristics of each of the twenty-four previous buddhas, this text differentiates between those buddhas whose biographies end with "their relics being spread far and wide [*dhātuvitthārika*]" and those for whom single stūpas are built (see table 1). Typical of the former is the past Buddha Revata (no. 5 on the list), whose mini-biography ends as follows:

> Having demonstrated the power of a Buddha, he explicated deathlessness in the world, and, no longer burning [with desire to be reborn], he nirvāṇized like a fire whose fuel has been consumed. His gem-like body and his uncommon dharma—all have vanished. Truly, all karmic constituents are void [*ritta*]. That great sage, the renowned Buddha Revata, nirvāṇized and his relics were spread far and wide to various regions. (*Buv.*, 36–37 = Eng. trans., Horner 1975: 40–41)

Besides Revata, there are seven other previous buddhas in the *Buddhavaṃsa* whose relics are said to have been dispersed. They are Sobhita (no. 6), Paduma (no. 8), Sumedha (no. 11), Atthadassī (no. 14), Phussa (no. 18), Vessabhū (no. 21), and Konāgamana (no. 23). For the other sixteen buddhas in the text, no mention is made specifically of the dispersal of their relics; instead, the focus is on the construction and on the dimensions of the single stūpas of the buddhas in question. Typical in this regard is the case of Dīpaṃkara (no. 1), whose mini-biography ends as follows:

> Having elucidated the Good Dharma and brought the people across to the other shore, blazing like a mass of flames, he nirvāṇized, in the company of his disciples. His supernatural powers, and his entourage, and the precious wheel marks on his feet—all have vanished. Truly, all karmic constituents are void. Dīpaṃkara, the Victorious One, the teacher, nirvāṇized in Nandārāma, and there, a victor's stūpa [was built] for him that was thirty-six yojanas high. (*Buv.*, 23 = Eng. trans., Horner 1975: 28–29)

No specific mention is made here of Dīpaṃkara's relics, but the fact that a single stūpa was built for him implies that his body (or skeleton or relics) remained together in an undifferentiated whole. That, in fact, is stated explicitly in a number of texts, with regard to other previous buddhas. In the *Apadāna*, for instance, some gods who wish to build a stūpa of their own (in heaven) over the relics of the Buddha Padumuttara (no. 10) are told that, for that tathāgata "there are no separate relics, his body remained in a single agglomeration" (*Ap.* 1: 71. See also Konow 1941: 41). Similarly, in the *Buddhavaṃsa Commentary*, we are told explicitly with regard to the Buddha Koṇḍañña (no. 2), that "the relics of this teacher were not dispersed but remained in one single compact mass, like an image made of gold" (*BuvA.*, 141 = Eng. trans., Horner 1978: 202).[33]

It is therefore possible to conclude that, in terms of relics, there are two basic types of previous buddhas: those whose bodily relics are scattered to various regions, and those whose relics (bodies) are kept together and enshrined in a single stūpa.[34] Much the same polarity may be seen in the traditions dealing with the relics of the Buddha's chief disciples. The first "master of the Dharma," the elder Mahākāśyapa, for example, is not

[33] Much the same thing is stated, in the *Lotus Sūtra*, with regard to the relics of the future buddha Devarāja (*Sdmp.*, 259 = Eng. trans., Kern 1884: 247) and of the past buddha Prabhūtaratna (*Sdmp.*, 240 = Eng. trans., Kern 1884: 229). See also, however, Gjertson 1989: 190–91.

[34] The same bifurcation may be found in East Asia where a distinction is made between teachers whose bodies are cremated and produce multiple relics and those who are mummified and kept whole. On the latter, see Faure 1991: 148–69 and Sharf 1992. On the differentiation between "dispersed" or "smashed" relics (Jpn: *saishin shari*) and "whole-body relics" (*zenshin shari*), see Ruppert 2000: 291n.1.

even cremated after he parinirvāṇizes. Instead, his entire body (or alternatively, his whole skeleton [*asthisaṃghāta*]) is enshrined intact underneath the mountain Kukkuṭapāda, where it will remain until the advent of the next Buddha Maitreya (*T.* 1451, 24:409 = Fr. trans., Przyluski 1914: 527–28; *Div.*, 61). His successor, however, the second master of the Dharma, the elder Ānanda, parinirvāṇizes in mid-air over the Ganges; his body is autocremated, and his relics, of themselves, divide into four shares that fall to the people of Rājagṛha, the kingdom of Vaiśālī, the nāgas, and the gods (*T.* 2042, 50:115–16 = Fr. trans., Przyluski 1923: 337–40; see also Strong 1992: 66).

This polarity, as we shall see, is of some significance in the traditions surrounding the relics of Śākyamuni, who is presented, at least in one tradition, as unique in that his relics are said to be both scattered and not scattered. On the one hand, as we shall see in chapters 4 and 5, Śākyamuni Buddha's relics are "spread far and wide to various regions," first, right after his death, to the eight north Indian kingdoms that claimed a share of him, and, then later, by King Aśoka to the 84,000 stūpas throughout Jambudvīpa. On the other hand, it should be remembered that such a division and distribution of relics were not part of the specification for the funeral of a cakravartin king, which was supposed to serve as the model for the Buddha's obsequies. The remains of a cakravartin, the Buddha tells Ānanda in the *Mahāparinirvāṇa sūtra,* should be enshrined in a single stūpa erected at a crossroads (see *D.*, 2:141–42 = Eng. trans., Walshe 1987: 264; Waldschmidt 1944–48: 213–16). No explanation is given for why this does not happen in the case of the Buddha, but the contradiction remains, perhaps, as a witness to the ambiguity on this issue.

A rather different treatment of this whole question emerges in the *Thūpavaṃsa,* a relatively late but important Pali text. There, we are told that Śākyamuni's relics, apparently unlike those of his predecessors, are actually of two kinds: "[If it is asked] how many of his relics were dispersed and how many were not dispersed, [the answer is]: the four canine teeth, the two collarbones, and the *uṣṇīṣa*—these seven relics were not dispersed, but the remainder were dispersed" (*Thūp.*, 172 = Eng. trans., Jayawickrama 1971: 34). Here, it would seem that "not dispersed" does not really mean "not spread far and wide to various regions" (since the *Thūpavaṃsa* itself later recounts the dispersal of several of these seven relics). Rather, "not dispersed" in this context appears to connote something like "not disintegrated" or "still together enough to be identifiable" as a specific bone or body part. These are all notable relics, what the Roman Catholic Church might call "reliquiae insignes" (see Dooley 1931: 4, 65–66). By way of contrast, the other relics mentioned in the *Thūpavaṃsa,* the remaining ones that *were* dispersed, are no longer thought to be body-part specific, or individually notable. They are instead described generically as rather small "relics" (*dhātu*) that are said to come in three sizes—the smallest like mustard-seeds, the middling ones the size of grains of rice broken in two, and the biggest ones the size of split peas.[35] They are intended to be distributed—not to different kings and countries—but to the multitude of people who are to take them, make shrines (cetiya) for them, and worship them, in their own individual dwelling places (vasanaṭṭhāna) (*Thūp.*, 172 = Eng. trans., Jayawickrama 1971: 34).

This is not to say that the*Thūpavaṃsa* does not know the tradition of the division of the Buddha's relics among the eight contesting kings; it does and it recounts it. Nevertheless, in this particular passage, we seem to have a different vision of things—one that sees "dispersed" relics as minute objects of the kind that could be personal possessions venerated in people's homes, to be distinguished from more identifiable bones and body parts, enshrined in major communal places of worship.[36]

Relics and Compassion

None of this, however, responds to a more fundamental question: why (apart from history and legend) are some buddhas' relics dispersed and others not? The very last line of the *Buddhavaṃsa* seeks to address this issue. It states simply that, according to ancient tradition, the dispersal of the relics of a buddha is "out of compassion for living beings" (*Buv.*, 102 = Eng. trans., Horner 1975: 99). This makes good sense. The relics not only offer protection to kings, nations, and /or ordinary people, but also give them occasions to make merit, and, perhaps, to embark on the path to arhatship. The more widely they are distributed, the greater are these chances.

This vision of things, however, raises the specter of having some previous buddhas (i.e., those who disperse their relics) being thought of as somehow more compassionate than others (those who do not). Buddhaghosa, in his commentary on the *Dīgha Nikāya,* was not blind to this problem. He distinguishes between buddhas who have enjoyed a very long final lifespan and those whose terminal life on earth has been much shorter. The former, he claims, are the ones whose body (sarīra) is not dispersed, but remains compact in a single mass. They have essentially had the time to accomplish everything they were going to do, to spread their teaching as far as it was going to spread. The latter, however, because their lifespans were shorter, still have work to do, and so count on their

[35] The same point is made in *Jin.*, 36–37 = Eng. trans., Jayawickrama 1968:52. The Catholic Church might call them *reliquiae non-insignes.*

[36] Bareau (1974a: 34), following a somewhat different tack, likewise argues that the dispersed relics (i.e., those distributed to the eight stūpas) should be thought of as the private property of the faithful inhabiting a given region, whereas relics at the major places of pilgrimage (caitya) were public, and belonged to all Buddhists.

relics to continue their careers, to be available to many people so that those who make a cetiya with a relic even as small as a mustard seed, may reap the rewards thereof (*DA.*, 2:603–604).[37] Much the same point is made in the *Thūpavaṃsa,* where, after resolving to have most of his own relics dispersed, Śākyamuni points out his reason for doing so: "I will parinirvāṇize without having been a long time [here on earth]; my Teaching is not yet widely spread everywhere (*Thūp.*, 172 = Eng. trans., Jayawickrama 1971: 34).

Conclusion

I have, in this chapter, examined a number of different topics relating to relics of previous buddhas; it remains to spell out how these can help us better understand the relics of the Buddha, Śākyamuni, on which I shall be focusing during the remainder of this book. First of all, it should be said that many of the stories dealing with relics of previous buddhas are equally applicable to the present post-parinirvāṇa situation in which devotees deal with relics of the "present" Buddha Śākyamuni. Secondly, it is clear in these stories that a text's understanding of the nature of relics (e.g., whether or not a relic "is" the Buddha) varies contextually according to its buddhology and doctrinal stance. In the section dealing with relics and soteriology, for instance, we encountered a whole spectrum of positions: from the claim of some Theravādins that relics (compared to a living buddha) are ineffectual in getting a person started on the path to buddhahood, to the stance of some Mahāyānists that relics are just as good as living buddhas; passing through the middle position of certain Sanskrit Mainstream Buddhist texts (e.g., the *Avadānaśataka*) that relics can help persons embark on the path to arhatship, but not on that to buddhahood. Similarly, there was a spectrum of traditions with regard to the question of whether or not a buddha (e.g., Śākyamuni) could overlap with the relics of a past buddha (e.g., Kāśyapa), with the Toyikā story this time representing a middle position between the extremes of the Pali "Ghaṭīkāra sutta" (which shied away from actual overlap) and the *Lotus Sūtra* (which fully affirmed it).

[37]Another pattern may perhaps be detected in the fact that there seems to be an unstated formula at work whereby the number of buddhas in a given kalpa that do not scatter their relics is always half or one more than half of the total number of buddhas in that kalpa. Thus, in kalpas when only one Buddha appears, that Buddha does not scatter his relics; in kalpas when two buddhas appear, one scatters his relics, the other does not; in kalpas with three buddhas, one scatters his relics and two do not; in kalpas with four buddhas, two scatter and two do not; in the only kalpa listed with five buddhas (our present bhadrakalpa), the exact ratio is not yet clear since Maitreya is yet to come.

Thirdly, despite the question of buddha overlap, or perhaps because of it, there was a sense that relics of buddhas of the past should be venerated only in conjunction with the present Buddha Śākyamuni. In part, this was to make clear the Buddhist nature of their affiliation (in cases where previous buddhas may have incorporated pre-Buddhist or non-Buddhist elements); in part it was to add mythological depth to certain sites or scenarios that could now be associated with a whole series of buddhas throughout the ages. But within these conjunctions, a certain hierarchical relationship is nonetheless maintained between Śākyamuni and the previous buddhas. For instance, when Śākyamuni is alive (as in the Toyikā tradition), he may relate to the *bodily relics* of previous buddhas (e.g., Kāśyapa or Prabhūtaratna); but when Śākyamuni is dead and is himself a relic (as in the case of the Shwe Dagon tradition), his bodily relics relate to secondary *relics of use* of previous buddhas. In other words, though there seem to be different ways of asserting relative degrees of presence in these traditions, Śākyamuni, the Buddha of the "present" is always being given more "presence" than buddhas of the past, whether he himself appears in person or as a relic. Formulaically, this might be expressed by the following equation. Living Śākyamuni : bodily relics of previous buddhas :: parinirvāṇized Śākyamuni : relics of use of previous buddhas.

Finally, there is an important distinction to be made between buddhas whose relics are divided and dispersed throughout various regions, and buddhas whose bodies are kept together integrally in a single stūpa. We shall see that this fundamental polarity not only distinguishes different buddhas of the past from each other, but it also informs the whole saga of Śākyamuni's own relics, which are dispersed and brought together again a number of times during their history in a variety of literal and symbolic ways. Ultimately the theme of dispersal and nondispersal is connected to the equally important questions of center and periphery, of attainment and continued teaching, of wisdom and compassion.

Chapter Two

RELICS OF THE BODHISATTVA

IT IS SOMETIMES maintained that Buddhist relics embody, more than anything, the quality and power of one who has transcended the processes of birth and death, of someone who, like the Buddha, has attained enlightenment (see Kieschnick 2003: 34–35). According to this view, relics, almost by definition, stem from the remains of saints—whether arhats, pratyekabuddhas, buddhas, or other enlightened beings. They thus mark, as Steven Collins (1992: 233) has pointed out, "the sense of an ending,"[1] in this case, the terminal point of the person's life in *saṃsāra*. Much the same point is made by Robert Sharf (1999: 87). He suggests that relics should not be viewed as embodiments of something transcendent, but as marking the final end-point of a life process that has reached changelessness. In doing this, he invokes the notion of a "secondary treatment" of the corpse, "when the dried bones or fully dessicated corpse are moved to their final resting place," something that ritually marks the terminal point of the person's life cycle, and brings to an end the process of rebirth.[2]

In this light, we should not expect to find any relics of the Buddha while he was still a bodhisattva, working his way through saṃsāra; the remains of Śākyamuni should all "date" from what might be called his "terminal time," from after the endpoint of his parinirvāṇa, or at least from after the time of his nirvāṇa—his enlightenment at Bodhgaya—when he first realized an end to rebirth. Nonetheless, as we shall see in this chapter, there is evidence that there did exist stūpas and relics—both remains and reminders—that recall events in the Buddha's life from periods *prior* to his enlightenment, when he was still a bodhisattva. These may basically be said to be of two kinds: relics stemming from his previous lives (*jātakas*), and relics stemming from the first thirty-five years of his final life as Gautama, that is, after his birth at Lumbinī but before he became the Buddha at Bodhgaya.

[1] See also Collins 1998: 280–81. The term is borrowed from Frank Kermode.

[2] See also Faure 1991: 136. This view of the death process owes much to Van Gennep 1960 and to Hertz 1960.

Relics and the Jātakas

Tales of the Buddha's previous lives (jātakas) were and continue to be popularly recounted for both the entertainment and the edification of the faithful throughout Asia. They also form a significant part of the overall biography of the Buddha, and are intimately involved in the recounting of his whole life story. As is well known, it is during the Buddha's previous lives, through the practice of various perfections, that he works his way toward buddhahood, karmically building the physical body (*rūpakāya*), that he is to have as Gautama.[3] This is chiefly characterized as a body endowed with the thirty-two major and eighty minor marks of the "great man" (*mahāpuruṣa*), and indeed, in some texts, particular jātakas are said to feature the practice of particular perfections (pāramitās) and to lead to the attainment of particular physiognomic signs of the mahāpuruṣa (*D.*, 3:145ff = Eng. trans., Davids 1899–1924, 3:139ff. See also Makransky 1997: 120; Conze 1975: 659–61; Lamotte 1949–80: 668). Thus, during all those previous lives, the bodhisattva is not so much striving for enlightenment, understood as a realization of the truth of the dharma, as he is building a buddha body.[4]

This somatic scenario may help us understand better the close connection between jātaka tales and buddha relics: both have to do with the buddha body, the one in working toward its formation, the other in asserting its ongoing presence. This was true not only textually, but iconographically and ritually as well. Mention need hardly be made of the extensive use of depictions of jātakas, both in sculpture and painting, in the adornment of stūpas and other Buddhist monuments containing relics.[5] At the Mahāthūpa in Sri Lanka, for instance, all 550 jātaka tales were said to be represented inside the reliquary chamber itself (*Thūp.*, 234 = Eng. trans., Jayawickrama 1971: 116), and, in East Asia, the sides of small reliquaries were often beautifully embossed with illustrations of previous life tales (see Soper 1940: 641, 647, 654; Ruppert 2000: 69–72).

Taken individually, such jātakas might be construed as morally edifying or awe-inspiring. Taken together, they can be seen as building up the buddha body, or perhaps more accurately, as creating a "biorama" in which the Buddha can be present. The same pattern may be detected, perhaps,

[3] For this same reason, the consecration of Buddha images (*buddharūpa*) involves imbuing them with the various perfections (see Bizot 1994: 101).

[4] As *JA.*, 1:14 = Eng. trans., Jayawickrama 1990: 18 makes clear, the bodhisattva could have attained enlightenment (i.e., arhatship) at the moment of his embarkation on the path under Dīpaṃkara.

[5] For various examples, see Duroiselle 1920–21; Bryner 1956; Lüders 1963: 120–63; Wray, Rosenfield, and Bailey 1972; Fontein 1981; Cummings 1982: 15–104; Brown 1997.

in ritual processions of relics (or of images), which can involve references to the jātakas. For instance, the Chinese pilgrim Faxian, who witnessed the festival of the Buddha's tooth relic in Sri Lanka in the early fifth century, tells us that, for ten days ahead of time, a man dressed in royal robes rode an elephant through the streets, extolling in a stentorian voice the sacrifices made by the Buddha in his previous lives: "The bodhisattva practiced for the incalculably long time of three *asaṃkhyeya* (immeasurable) *kalpas*. . . . He gave up his kingdom, his wife, and his child. He even tore out his eyes to give them to others. He cut his own flesh to ransom a dove, gave his head as alms, offered his body to feed a famished tigress, and did not begrudge his marrow and brain" (Li 2002: 206; text in *T.* 2085, 51:865b). And on the day of the procession itself, the road was lined with statues depicting the five hundred previous lives of the Buddha "true to life . . . painted in colors and richly adorned," and through this double hedgerow, the tooth relic was brought in procession as if passing in review all of his previous lives (Li 2002: 206; text in *T.* 2085, 51:865b).

The stories given special mention here by Faxian are among the most famous in the jātaka repertoire. In what follows, I would like to discuss their connections to relic traditions, as well as those of other tales, under three topics: (1) stūpas marking the sites of jātaka events in North India; (2) traditions concerning the bodhisattva's matted hair, which, in his former life as the ascetic Sumedha, he spread at the feet of the previous Buddha Dīpaṃkara; and (3) legends about the enshrinement of the bones of the bodhisattva—all that was left of him after he sacrificed his body to assuage the hunger of a tigress.

Jātaka Stūpas in North India

When Faxian and various other Chinese pilgrims visited Northern India, starting in the fourth century, they all came across stūpas commemorating previous lives of the Buddha. Xuanzang, for instance, reports seeing stūpas marking the following sites: in Puṣkarāvatī, the place where, as Śyāma, the bodhisattva fulfilled his filial duties toward his blind parents; nearby, the place where, as the young ascetic Ekaśṛnga, he was seduced by a beautiful woman; in Mangalura, the place where, as Kṣāntivādin, he submitted patiently to mutilation by a king; at Haḍḍa Mountain, the place where, as a young brahmin, he sacrificed himself for the sake of learning a half verse of the dharma; in Mahāvana, the place where, as Sarvadatta, he sold himself for ransom in order to make offerings to a brahmin, etc. (*T.* 2087, 51:881b, 881b, 882b, 882c, 883a = Eng. trans., Li 1996: 78, 79, 84, 86). For the most part, such stūpas, as David Snellgrove (1987: 311) has pointed out, are located in Northwest India, in Gandhāra, "where the faithful could not claim . . . possession of actual historical sites connected with his final life on earth." The implication here is that local Buddhists, given the dearth in this region of sites immediately associated with the Buddha's final life as Gautama, turned to the jātakas to find pedigrees for their own local places of pilgrimage.[6]

Stūpas of the bodhisattva were thus very important in this region. Most famous, perhaps, were a set of monuments commemorating jātaka stories that were renowned as the "four great stūpas" of Northern India, and which Faxian describes as being large and magnificently adorned with precious substances (*T.* 2085, 51:858b = Eng. trans., Li 2002: 170). The stūpas in question marked the sites (a) where the bodhisattva as King Śibi sacrificed his flesh to ransom a dove from a hawk;[7] (b) where he willingly gave up his eyes when asked for them;[8] (c) where he lay down his body to feed a hungry tigress;[9] and (d) where, as King Candraprabha, he cut off his head as a gift to a brahmin.[10]

It is noteworthy that each of these stūpas commemorates a jātaka tale in which the bodhisattva sacrificed part or all of his body. Reiko Ohnuma (1998: 359) has emphasized the importance of such "gifts of the body" (*dehadāna*) in the overall context of the jātakas. More specifically, she shows how such acts are both symbolic of the Buddha's later gift of the dharma and transformative of the bodhisattva into a knower and giver of dharma (see also Parlier 1991; Durt 1998 and 2000). It is clear, then, that these events form an important part of the conceptualization of the bodhisattva path, or the practice of the perfections, and it is for this reason, perhaps, that they were venerated by pilgrims to the region. It is clear also, as we shall see, that such tales inspired offerings to relics, in gratitude for the bodhisattva's self sacrifice (see Ruppert 2000: 71), and emulation by devotees who might sacrifice a part of their body (a finger, a toe, an arm, even a life) in front of a stūpa containing relics.[11]

[6] See also Shinohara 2003.

[7] For a bibliography on this jātaka, see Lamotte 1949–80: 255–56, to which should be added Parlier 1991. The same site was visited by Songyun (*T.* 2092, 51:1021 = Eng. trans., Wang 1984: 243), and by Xuanzang (*T.* 2087, 51:883a = Eng. trans., Li 1996: 86).

[8] For a bibliography on this jātaka, see Lamotte 1949–80: 144. The stūpa is also mentioned by Xuanzang (*T.* 2087, 51:881a = Eng. trans., Li 1996: 78; see also Watters [1904] 1961, 1:215).

[9] A discussion of this jātaka, appears later in this chapter. The site was also visited by Songyun (*T.* 2092:1020 = Eng. trans., Wang 1984: 232) and by Xuanzang (*T.* 2087, 51:885c = Eng. trans., Li 1996: 99).

[10] For a bibliography on this jātaka, see Lamotte 1949–80: 144. The site was also visited by Xuanzang (*T.* 2087, 51:884c = Eng. trans., Li 1996: 95).

[11] The locus classicus for this is the *Lotus Sūtra*'s chapter on Bhaiṣajyarāja in *T.* 262, 9:54a = Eng. trans., Hurvitz 1976: 298; see also Kern 1884: 385. On such practices in China see Benn 1998 and Kieschnick 1997: 35–50. For Buddhist objections to it, see *T.* 2125, 54:231b = Eng. trans., Li 2000: 163–65.

Jātakas featuring "gifts of the body" were not the only previous lives commemorated in the Northwest, however. The penultimate life of the bodhisattva as Prince Viśvantara (Pali: Vessantara) was also honored by a set of memorial mounds not far from the "four great stūpas." The story of Viśvantara is well known. It recounts the utter generosity of the bodhisattva who, as son of a king, gives away the state white elephant, an act that causes the people of his kingdom to become angry and banish him. This does not stop him, however, from making further gifts before his departure and even as he proceeds into exile with his wife and two children. On the road and later in his place of exile, his generosity continues and he successively gives away his horses, his chariot, and eventually his children and his wife. In this way, alone in his hermitage, having abandoned his family, he becomes, as it were, monk-like, while still remaining a layman. There are different versions of the jātaka and different endings to the tale, but it would not be wrong to state that it has long been and remains today, in its poignancy and implications, the most popular story in the whole of Buddhism.[12] It comes as no surprise, then, to find it identified with pilgrimage sites. According to Xuanzang, at Varṣapura, in Northwestern India, there were stūpas, said to have been erected by Aśoka, at the place where Viśvantara was forced to leave his city after giving away the state elephant; the place where he gave away his children as slaves to the brahmin who requested them; the place where he resided as a hermit; and the place where his children ran around a tree trying to escape from the brahmin who beat them until their blood flowed on the ground (*T.* 2087, 51:881b = Eng. trans., Li 1996: 78–79). It is clear from this that pilgrims in the region were able to retrace the whole route taken by Viśvantara as he went into exile.

For the most part, in these pilgrims' accounts, the stūpas at these sites seem to be purely commemorative; they mark the place where a jātaka event is supposed to have occured, but no hint is given of their actually enshrining the remains of the bodhisattva. Occasionally, some naturally occuring phenomenon in the region may have given rise to a slightly more somatic connection. Thus, Xuanzang describes a particular stone at one site that exuded some damp viscous matter. This was identified as the place where the bodhisattva, as the ascetic Utpala, had broken off one of his bones to use it as a pen to write down a teaching (using his blood as ink and a parchment made of his skin). The marrow that had spilled from the broken bone, was supposed to be this viscous substance on the stone (*T.* 2092, 51:1020 = Eng. trans., Wang 1984: 232).[13] Alternatively, the

[12] For a bibliography on Viśvantara, see Lamotte 1949–80: 713–14, 2251; to which should be added Cone and Gombrich 1977; Schlingloff 1987: 146ff; Durt 1999 and 2000a.
[13] For a bibliography on this jātaka, see Lamotte 1949–80: 144–45.

vegetation or earth in a given spot is reddish in color, and this is attributed to the spilling of the bodhisattva's blood at that place (*T.* 2087, 51:885c = Eng. trans., Li 1996: 99). But there is no indication that the stūpas themselves contain any remains and that we should be speaking properly here of bodily relics of the bodhisattva.

Sumedha's Hair

The same is true of the pilgrims' account of a stūpa that marked the spot of yet another famous jātaka. Near Nagarahāra, in what is now Afghanistan, both Faxian and Xuanzang visited the place where the bodhisattva, countless aeons ago, made his vow for future buddhahood at the feet of the past Buddha Dīpaṃkara (*T.* 2085, 51:858c = Eng. trans., Li 2002: 193; and *T.* 2087, 51:878c = Eng. trans., Li 1996:66). According to his biographer, Xuanzang was surprised to see a stūpa here, and asked a local monk how it was that this place had survived the repeated destruction of the cosmos at the end of the many kalpas since Dīpaṃkara's time. The monk replied that "when the world was destroyed, this spot was also destroyed, but when the world was reconstructed, the spot also reappeared at its original place where it was before. . . . As this is a holy place, why should it not have the potency to emerge again?" (Li 1995: 54; text in *T.* 2053, 50:229). Here, it is quite clear that what is being commemorated is the place—or even more abstractly, the space—where an event happened, but there is no question of the bodhisattva's hair or deerskin garb still being there.

This picture changes, however, when we move to consider literary sources. The story of Dīpaṃkara and Sumedha (who is also known, in the Sanskrit tradition, as Megha or Sumati) is found in many different texts. The precise manner in which Sumedha honors Dīpaṃkara before making his vow, however, varies somewhat. In some sources, he offers some flower blossoms to the Blessed One. More famously, as we have seen in chapter one, he unties his long hair and lies down in the mire on the roadway in front of the Buddha so that Dīpaṃkara can avoid sullying his feet by stepping on his hair (and/or his body, and/or his deer skin garment), as he passes.

A study of the many versions of this legend is not possible here. From the perspective of the study of relics, however, what is interesting are the ultimate status and fate of Sumedha's hair, and, in this connection, it is possible to distinguish three different layers of tradition. First, there are relic-less tales where no further mention of the hair is made; after his act of homage, Sumedha simply gets up, rejoicing at having received his prediction of future buddhahood. Examples here would include the Pali *Jātaka nidāna* (*JA* 1:10–14 = Eng. trans., Jayawickrama 1990: 14–18), and the Sanskrit *Mahāvastu* (1:2231–48 = Eng. trans., Jones 1949–56, 1:188–203).[14] Secondly, there is a story such as that found in the *Dharmaguptaka Vinaya,* in which Megha (=Sumedha), as soon as he receives the prediction of his future buddhahood, springs up in the air to a height of seven tāla trees, but *his hair remains spread on the ground,* detached from his body. Dīpaṃkara then tells his disciples not to tread on that hair, for "it is the hair of a bodhisattva, and no śrāvaka or pratyekabuddha should step on it." Hundreds of thousands of persons then come and make offerings of flowers and perfumes to the hair on the spot but no mention is made of a stūpa or of its being enshrined (*T.* 1428, 22:785 = Fr. trans., Bareau 1966–74: 15).[15] Finally, there is a story such as that preserved in the *Divyāvadāna,* in which Sumati (=Sumedha) likewise springs up into the air to a height of seven tāla trees as soon as he receives the prediction of his buddhahood, but as he does so, his hair falls out and is replaced by "even better hair." King Dīpa then gathers up the bodhisattva's fallen hair and gives it to his friend, King Vāsava, who counts out 80,000 strands of it. His ministers each request one of those strands, wishing to have something to venerate. King Vāsava gives them each one hair, and they, variously going home to their own districts, set up caityas in which to enshrine them (*Div.,* 252–53 = Ger. trans., Zimmer 1925: 57–58).

In comparing these three versions of the jātaka, it is not hard to imagine a "progression" similar to that which we found in the case of the relics of the previous buddha Kāśyapa, and that seems to mark a gradual development in the cult of this relic of the bodhisattva. We move from a scenario in which Sumedha's hair is not thought of as a relic at all, to a tradition in which his hair is honored, undispersed and in situ, but not put in a stūpa, to a final outcome in which the hairs are divided up, dispersed, and enshrined as bona fide relics in stūpas in different regions. "Progression" is perhaps not the right term here; all of these versions of the story are from Mainstream Buddhist sources, and though it may be possible to arrange them chronologically in terms of layers of tradition, it may be wiser to speak here of "variations" on a theme that reflect different attitudes toward relics in general and toward relics of the bodhisattva in particular.

The Bodhisattva's Bones

Much the same pattern can be detected in an analysis of different versions of the well-known jātaka tale in which the bodhisattva, seeing a

[14] Here again, as in the case of the previous buddha Kāśyapa, we find a curious alliance of a Theravāda and Lokottaravāda text, both resisting an emphasis on relics, although for different reasons.

[15] It should be noted that Megha's loss of hair here symbolically recalls or looks forward to ordination.

hungry tigress who is unable to feed her cubs and is in fact considering eating them, sacrifices his own body by lying down in front of her. She is too weak to attack him; thus (at least in some versions of the story) he cuts his own throat so that she can drink his blood and gain enough strength to devour him.[16] She does so and, satiated and now able to feed her cubs, she goes away, leaving behind his bare bones.[17]

Again, there are many versions of this story, and I cannot analyze them all here. It is possible, however, to distinguish between several different ways in which the bones of the bodhisattva, not consumed by the tigress, are treated. First, there are those sources that simply recount the bodhisattva's sacrifice and make no mention of his remains or of a marker to honor them (see *T.* 152, 3:2 = Fr. trans., Chavannes 1934, 1:15–17; *Avk.*, 2:317–19 = Eng. trans., Das 1893: 4–6; *Avk.*, 2:437–38; and *Jin.*, 4 = Eng. trans., Jayawickrama 1968: 5–6). This is the stūpa-less, relic-less phase. Secondly, there is a tradition in which the bones are found by the bodhisattva's companions or family. This is best exemplified, perhaps, by the end of *Jātakamālā* version of the story, in which the bodhisattva's disciples, looking for him, come across his remains. Figuring out what must have happened, they are amazed and stricken with admiration for his deed, along with gods, *gandharvas, yakṣas,* and *nāgas.* And together this multitude of beings then "cover the earth which held his precious bones, with showers of garlands, garments, ornaments, and sandalwood powder" (*JM.*, 6 = Eng. trans., Khoroche 1989: 9). Here no mention is made of a stūpa, but instead, honor is paid directly to the remains of the bodhisattva, which seem to be conceived of as simply buried in or lying on the ground.[18]

Finally, there are stories that variously emphasize the actual enshrinement of the bodhisattva's relics. Two examples of this may be given. The first is found in the *Damamūkanidāna sūtra (Sūtra on the Wise Man and the Fool),* a collection of tales that became popular in many parts of the Buddhist world. Here, we are told that it is the bodhisattva's parents who gather up his bones and put them in a seven-jeweled casket over which they erect a stūpa (*T.* 202, 4: 252–53; see also Schmidt 1843: 21–26; Frye 1981: 12–16). The second much more elaborate version is in the eighteenth chapter of the well-known Mahāyānist *Suvarṇaprabhāsa sūtra (Sūtra of*

[16] In one version of the story (*Div.*, 477–78), the bodhisattva must go to considerable lengths to convince the tigress to eat him since she is worried about the karmic repercussions of such an action. As James Benn (2002) has pointed out, Chinese devotees seeking to emulate this bodhisattva's action likewise sometimes found it difficult to get tigers to eat them.

[17] For a bibliography on the jātaka, see Lamotte 1949–80: 243–44; Dantinne 1983: 138–39; Khoroche 1989: 257. See also Schlingloff 1987: 195.

[18] The absence of a stūpa in this tale is also mentioned by Schopen 1997: 48n.37.

Golden Light). There, we are told that the Buddha himself, traveling through the land of Pañcāla, in Northwest India, comes to a resting spot where he desires to preach a sermon. He sits down on a seat prepared for him by Ānanda and asks the monks whether or not they would like to see "the relics [śarīra] of bodhisattvas who have done what is difficult to do?" (*Suv.* , 106 = Eng. trans., Emmerick 1970: 85; see also Nobel 1958, 1:333). The offer comes as a bit of a surprise considering the same text's earlier broadside attack on relics (dhātu) of the Buddha as having no ultimate reality whatsoever (*Suv.,* 7–9 = Eng. trans., Emmerick 1970: 6–7), but perhaps they are seen here as just an "expedient means" (*upāya*) of teaching, or perhaps, the text's antagonism to relics of the *Buddha* does not extend to relics of the *bodhisattva.* In any case, the monks affirm their eagerness to see the relics, and the Buddha strikes the earth at that spot with his hand, and, instantly, a bejewelled stūpa emerges. The Blessed One asks Ānanda to open it, and inside he finds a golden container that is actually only the outermost of seven reliquaries. Ānanda opens all of them and in the innermost he finds relics, which are now called "bones" (*asthi*), and are described as being as white as snow or water lilies. The Buddha then asks Ānanda to take out the relics (which are now qualified as being "bones of a *mahāpuruṣa*") and to give them to him. Then, in an extraordinary gesture, the Buddha takes the bones, praises them, places them in front of the assembly, and says: "Worship, monks, the bodhisattva's relics [which are now again called śarīra], which are fragrant with morality and virtue, which are extremely difficult to behold, and which have become fields of merit" (Emmerick 1970: 86; text in *Suv.,* 106–7. See also Nobel 1958, 1:334). All present venerate the relics. Ānanda, however, is puzzled by something. "The Tathāgata," he declares, "has surpassed the whole world and is venerated by all beings; how is it that he venerates these bones?" And the Buddha replies, "It is because of these bones, Ānanda, that I quickly achieved unsurpassed total enlightenment." And then he goes on to recount the jātaka of the hungry tigress, ending with an account of how his parents, at that time long ago, found these very bones that the tigress had left behind, honored them, and buried them at that very spot (*Suv.,* 107 = Eng. trans., Emmerick 1970: 87; see also Nobel 1958, 1:335f).

The importance of this *Suvarṇaprabhāsa* story cannot be overemphasized. In all the other sources we have looked at so far, the relics of the bodhisattva, if they were featured at all, remained in the "tale of the past." Here, however, they are seen to be in the "tale of the present" and to coexist with the Buddha whose bones, in fact, they once were. In the last chapter, we encountered the question of the simultaneous presence of two buddhas—of the past and the present—when one of them overlaps with the relics of another, and we saw how different traditions treated that problem in different ways. Here the question is taken one step further: the overlap is not between two buddhas, but between a buddha and a bodhisattva, between the Buddha and the relics of his former self. What is more, the Buddha is shown as venerating his own former self by his honoring of the relics.

It is possible, of course, that the *Suvarṇaprabhāsa,* a boldly Mahāyānist sūtra, is playing here with notions of time and identity to make a point about the utter transcendence and eternity of the Buddha, or to show how a bodhisattva in a past life is really just another *nirmāṇakāya,* a projection of the eternally enlightened Buddha, and no different in this docetic context from any other manifestation of the Buddha, including the final body he adopted as Śākyamuni. Even so, I would suggest that the scenario raises some important questions about the nature of relics. What do the relics of the bodhisattva here actually represent? Is their relationship to the bodhisattva the same as that of buddha relics to the Buddha?

The answer to these questions may be found in the text itself. As the Buddha puts it to Ānanda, it is the effectiveness of those relics in having brought him to final enlightenment that makes them worthy of veneration. The bones of the bodhisattva are said to be "fragrant" or "perfumed" (*vāsita*) with the virtue of morality (*śīlaguṇa*), as well as with many other practices of one who "has continually acted more and more with his mind [set] on full enlightenment" (*Suv.*, 107 = Eng. trans., Emmerick 1970: 86; see also Nobel 1958, 1:335). The language here recalls inscriptions and texts in which the relics of the Buddha are similarly said to be "infused" or "invigorated" (*paribhāvita*) with various perfections of the bodhisattva path. Gregory Schopen, who has presented and studied these references, takes them as further evidence of the conception of relics as "living entities," "impregnated with the qualities that animated and defined the living Buddha" (Schopen 1987: 205).

In this light, the bones of the bodhisattva do not signify so much the person whose bones they *were* (i.e., the son of King Mahāratha), as the person whose bones they *became* (i.e., the enlightened Buddha). If relics generally make the past present, here they appear to make the future present (at least retrospectively). In other words, bodhisattva relics are not so much re-presentations of the particular hero of a jātaka tale as "pre-presentations" of the Buddha himself.[19]

There is an important difference, however, between these bodhisattva relics that pre-present the Buddha, and the buddha relics we shall be considering that re-present him. The bones of the bodhisattva in our story are not only relics of the dead, they are "dead relics." Unlike the relics of the

[19] In this light, it should also be remembered that, unlike the English word "relic," the Sanskrit words for *dhātu* and *śarīra* do not necessarily imply something that was "left behind."

past buddhas Kāśyapa or Prabhūtaratna considered in chapter one—relics which, in an analogous situation, proceeded to "come alive" by rising up into the air or in some way manifesting miraculous behavior—these relics of the bodhisattva remain inert. They commemorate a moment of the past and recapture perhaps some of its emotions, but they do not really make the past person present. The reason for this, of course, should be clear. The "past person" (i.e., the bodhisattva) is not "present" in the relics but remains in the past. The person who is "present" in these relics is the future Buddha whom he became.

Bodhisattva Relics in the Final Birth as Gautama

It has been remarked, at least since the time of Paul Mus ([1935] 1998: 65), that there is a curious discrepancy, an asynchronism between the achievement of the Buddha's physical body, his rūpakāya, and his attainment of enlightenment. In other words, while the Buddha's understanding of the truth—what might be called his "dharmalogical realization"— does not occur until his experience at Bodhgaya, the achievement of his buddha body—what might be called his "rupalogical realization"—takes place at the moment of his birth in Lumbinī. He is thus born with the thirty-two marks of the mahāpuruṣa—physical signs that occasion the soothsayer Asita's prediction that he will become a buddha. Put simply, the bodhisattva becomes a buddha in body before he becomes a buddha in mind.

The situation, however, is somewhat more complicated than this; when one reads the biographies of the Buddha, it becomes obvious that Gautama's possession of the buddha body—in so far as it can be defined as the presence of the physical marks of the mahāpuruṣa—is something that is emphasized more at certain times of his life than at others. In fact, for great portions of Gautama's pre-enlightenment life in the palace and during his quest, the glorious marks on his buddha body would seem to be hidden, obscured by his princely garments, his layman's hair, or his ornaments, or unseen because of his fasting and extreme austerities.[20]

Only at a few specific points are the signs of the mahāpuruṣa emphasized during this period of his life. The first of these points has already been mentioned: at the time of his birth, the bodhisattva is said to be in possession of the auspicious marks that make clear his status as a great being. The second is the time of his famous departure from the palace when he cuts his hair with his sword (*JA.*, 1:64 = Eng. trans., Jayawickrama 1990: 86); the inch-long hair left on his head is said to curl to the

[20] In a different context, Mus (1928: 168) has shown how the signs of the mahāpuruṣa cannot be seen on a bodhisattva because they are obscured by his ornaments.

right (one of the signs of the great man) (see Burnouf 1852: 560), and his discarding of his princely garments in favor of a monastic robe further makes clear his other physiognomic features. He loses these signs, however, when he starts practicing his austerities. As one text puts it, "as a result of his fasting," his "body which was once golden in colour turned black [and] the thirty-two characteristics of a Great Being were obliterated" (Jayawickrama 1990: 89; text in *JA.*, 1:67). This sets up the third point in his pre-enlightenment biography when his buddha body becomes most evident: when he gives up his austerities and resumes eating, the signs of the great man are said to reappear and his body regains its golden hue (*JA.*, 1:67 = Eng. trans., Jayawickrama 1990: 90).

It need hardly be pointed out that these biographical moments when possession of the physical signs of buddhahood is most emphasized are also soteriologically significant moments—times of passage when the bodhisattva's turn toward his future enlightenment is made most clear. Thus, at the moment of his birth, he takes seven steps and declares that this is his final life (i.e., that he will attain nirvāṇa), and that he himself is the foremost being in the world. This certainty and declaration then seem to be forgotten as he moves into his life as a young prince. His departure from the palace, however, again makes clear his opting for the life of renunciation that will lead him, for sure, to buddhahood, only to have him struggle to find a teacher and embark on the wrong path of asceticism. Finally, by ending his fasting, he discovers the middle way between asceticism and hedonism and this, at last, leads him to buddhahood.

Interestingly, these same three soteriologically significant moments are also the times of the early biography of the Buddha that are most clearly associated with bodhisattva relics. Indeed, if one looks at pilgrimage accounts of visits to sites associated with the early life of Gautama, one notes that there is a curious lack of relics—at least bodily relics—recalling the bodhisattva's growing up, the "life in the palace" that he abandoned. Only those moments that are soteriologically significant times of passage are so marked. For instance, in the *Aśokāvadāna*'s account of Aśoka and Upagupta's pilgrimage tour, the king is said ritually to mark, with the building of a caitya and the making of an offering, only two pre-enlightenment sites: the aśoka tree at Lumbinī, under which the Buddha was born, and the spot near Bodhgaya where he meets the nāga king Kālika (who was closely connected to the episode featuring the Buddha's acceptance of the offering of milk rice, his resumption of eating just prior to his enlightenment) (*Aśokāv.*, 81–83, 86 = Eng. trans., Strong 1983: 244–46, 249).

This aśoka tree at Lumbinī is clearly a "relic of use" (*pāribhogika*) like the bodhi tree at Bodhgaya. In the legend, it "comes alive" for Aśoka, through the intermediary of its tree spirit, whom he asks to recall the moment of the bodhisattva's birth, but the description of this moment emphasizes not the infant but his status as a great being and the certainty of his achievement (*Aśokāv.,* 82–83 = Eng. trans., Strong 1983: 246). Much the same thing happens in the case of the nāga king Kālika, near Bodhgaya, who similarly recounts meeting the Buddha and makes the glories of his body come alive: "[H]is complexion [was] like blazing gold, his face like the autumn moon . . . [he] shone on the world of men . . . surpassing the sun in splendor" (*Aśokāv.,* 86 = Eng. trans., Strong 1983: 249–50).

In between these two transfigurational sites, Aśoka and Upagupta visit many other places associated with the early life of the Buddha. In the city of Kapilavastu, for example, they see the spots where the bodhisattva was nourished by his stepmother, Mahāprajāpatī; where he learned to write; where he mastered the arts of riding an elephant, a horse, a chariot; of shooting a bow, grasping a javelin, using an elephant hook; where, in his harem, he pursued pleasure with sixty thousand concubines, surrounded by a hundred thousand deities. In none of these places, however, are there any relics, nor is any mention made of a caitya or a stūpa (*Aśokāv.,* 82–84 = Eng. trans., Strong 1983: 245–47; see also Bareau 1974). Somewhat the same thing can be seen in the account of the Chinese pilgrim Xuanzang, who describes many of the sites he visits in Kapilavastu as being marked not by stūpas but by small "temples" (*jingshe*), in which are featured not relics but images depicting the event that took place there (*T.* 2087, 51:901 = Eng. trans., Li 1996: 174–76; see also Watters 1961, 2:2).

The reasons for this comparative dearth of relics are complex, but it would seem, once again, that bodhisattva relics are intended to be prepresentations of the Buddha. They are not supposed to glorify the person that the bodhisattva *was* (in this instance, the prince Gautama), but the person that the bodhisattva *became,* that is, the fully enlightened one. This does not mean that there was not great appreciation for the great accomplishments of the young Gautama and for the magnificence of his youth in the palace. Clearly both the biographies and the pilgrimage tours dwell on these things, but Buddhist relics did not become channels for expressing that appreciation. Relics were meant to signify things that pointed the bodhisattva toward buddhahood.

With this in mind, I would now like to turn to traditions about some of the relics that *were* associated with this early period of the bodhisattva's career, and that did point to his later accomplishment—relics that featured the moments of his birth, of his great departure, and of his final embarkation on the Middle Path.

The Embryo in the Relic or the Relic as Embryo

It is not without cause that Maurice Winternitz ([1933] 1972, 2:251) once remarked that "with regard to the legends of the conception and birth of the Buddha, the *Lalitavistara* differs very conspicuously from the accounts of the other schools." Here, in what is perhaps one of the most embellished of the Buddha's biographies, not only does the bodhisattva have the marks of the mahāpuruṣa at birth, he already possesses them in his mother's womb. Moreover, that womb itself is rather extraordinary, for, implanted in it (or rather, implanted into Queen Mahāmāyā's right side) is a bejewelled palace-like structure called a *ratnavyūha* in which the Buddha spends his ten uterine months sitting on a couch that is soft as Benares silk. Part of the thrust of the episode, of course, is to make it very clear that the Buddha is unsullied by any contact with the impurities that are normally characteristic of the womb and the birth canal (see Hara 1980). But significantly, for our purposes, the ratnavyūha that makes this possible is also treated as though it were a relic. Indeed, it is consistently called an "object of enjoyment or use" (paribhoga) of the bodhisattva, and, as we shall see, it is enshrined in a stūpa after Mahāmāyā's parturition.

It should be said that, in the *Lalitavistara,* the Buddha for the most part narrates his own life story, which he tells to his monks. When he gets to an account of his own conception, he pauses and asks his disciple Ānanda whether or not he would like to see the actual ratnavyūha in which he had dwelt while in his mother's womb? Ānanda indicates that he would, and so the Buddha summons the god Brahmā, for Brahmā is the one who, soon after the bodhisattva's birth at Lumbinī, acquired the no-longer needed ratnavyūha and took it to his Brahmā heaven where he enshrined it in a caitya. The Buddha now requests him to go and fetch it. Brahmā, however, is hardly discrete about this; on his way back to his heaven, he lets it be known to all the divine hosts that an exhibition of the bodhisattva's ratnavyūha is going to take place, and by the time he comes back with the relic, myriads of *koṭis* of divinities have assembled (*Lal.*, 60–62 = Eng. trans., Mitra 1881: 98–100 = Fr. trans., Foucaux 1884: 60–61).

They have come with good reason, for the structure is extraordinary. Made of gold and bejewelled, it has three turrets (*kūṭāgara*) that are set one within the other. Inside the innermost one, which is said to be made of perfumes (*gandhamaya*), is set the couch of the bodhisattva. The whole structure is indestructible, as hard as *vajra,* but also soft to the touch so that it in no way disturbs Queen Māyā in whose right side it has been set (*Lal.,* 63–64 = Eng. trans., Mitra 1881:101 = Fr. trans., Foucaux 1884:

62–63). According to the *Lalitavistara,* it was in this palace-like abode, on this seat, that the bodhisattva spent his ten months in the womb.[21] Later, when he was born, painlessly, from his mother's side, unsullied by the pollution of birth, the ratnavyūha, like a kind of pure placenta, came out too, and Brahmā carried it off to his heaven where a caitya was built for it and it was honored by the gods (*Lal.*, 83 = Eng. trans., Mitra 1881: 124 = Fr. trans., Foucaux 1884: 77–78). This clearly, then, was the very first relic from the Buddha's last life as Śākyamuni, even though it did not get enshrined here on earth but was transported away to the heavens.

In analyzing this account, it is sometimes difficult to decide what is the relic and what is the reliquary. As mentioned, the ratnavyūha is said to be a "paribhoga," an object "enjoyed" by the bodhisattva, and as such it seems to belong to the category of relics of use or enjoyment (*pāribhogika dhātu*)—a fact confirmed by its enshrinement in a caitya. At times, however, the ratnavyūha—bejewelled and golden, with its nesting turrets—seems more like a reliquary than a relic, with the difference that, in the innermost chamber, where one would expect to find the relic of the Buddha, one finds the embryonic bodhisattva. The embryonic imagery here recalls the notion of the *tathāgatagarbha,* a doctrinal expression, perhaps, of some of the same ambiguities. The tathāgatagarbha, as is well known, can be seen both as the "seed" of buddhahood in all beings, and as such associated with notions such as the Buddha nature within, or, alternatively, as the matrix or womb of buddhahood, the environment in which enlightenment is manifest. In both cases, what is emphasized is what might be called the "realized potentiality" of buddhahood (see Ruegg 1969 and Grosnick, forthcoming). The same would seem to be the case with the ratnavyūha relic: it is both a re-presentation and a pre-presentation of Gautama's buddhahood. At the same time, however, we should not be blind to the nature of the ratnavyūha as a bejewelled pavilion/throne. This structure represents a palace, a divine abode, a heavenly dwelling, and as such it symbolizes what the bodhisattva leaves behind—first, when he comes down from heaven to enter this world; second, when he leaves the womb at birth; and third, when he wanders forth from his princely life in the palace to search for enlightenment. In this light, it is perhaps not surprising that it gets enshrined not on earth but in Brahmā's heaven.

[21] For his intra-uterine activities, see *Lal.,* 65–72 = Eng. trans., Mitra 1881: 104–8 = Fr. trans., Foucaux 1884: 63–70.

The Relic of the Bodhisattva's Hairknot

Much the same thing can be said about a somewhat more down-to-earth bodhisattva relic, the hair that he cuts off at the time of his great departure. After telling the tale of the bodhisattva's ratnavyūha, the *Lalitavistara* proceeds with equally elaborate descriptions of his infancy, his life in the palace, his marriage, and his princely achievements. The next mention of a relic or reliquary, however, does not come until fifteen chapters later in the account of the bodhisattva's departure from the palace. That in itself is a magnificent occasion, marked by all kinds of miracles, but the text soon passes to a description of the bodhisattva's sending his groom, Chandaka, and his horse, Kaṇṭhaka, back to Kapilavastu, and then his cutting of his own hair with his sword. This episode becomes the focus of a relic tradition. Having severed his hairknot (*cūḍā*), the bodhisattva throws it up into the air, where it is caught by the gods of the Trāyastriṃśa Heaven. They take it to their heaven where they enshrine it in a stūpa called the Cūḍāpratigrahaṇa "Receipt of the topknot" Caitya, and where a festival (called the *cūḍāmaha*) is instituted (*Lal.*, 225 = Fr. trans., Foucaux 1884: 197 = Eng. trans., Bays 1983: 339).[22] Much the same event is featured in other biographies of the Buddha. In the Theravāda tradition, for instance, we learn that the bodhisattva cuts off his hairknot along with his crest jewel, and throws it up into the air saying, "If I am to become a Buddha, let it remain in the sky; if not, let it fall to the ground" (*JA.*, 1:65 = Eng. trans., Jayawickrama 1990: 86). The hairknot becomes stationary in mid-air at the height of one league, and there, Sakka (Indra), the king of the gods, receives it in a jeweled casket and establishes the Cūḷāmaṇi (Crest Gem) Shrine for its worship in his Trāyastriṃśa heaven (see also *BuvA.*, 283–84 = Eng. trans., Horner 1978: 406–7; and *Thūp.*, 165–66 = Eng. trans., Jayawickrama 1971: 25).[23] Much the same sequence of events is related in the *Mūlasarvāstivāda Vinaya* and other Sanskrit texts (*Sanghbhv.*, 1:91 = Eng. trans., Strong 2002: 12; *Mtu.*, 2:165–66 = Eng. trans., Jones 1949–56, 2:161; and *Bcar.*, 65–66 = Eng. trans., Johnston [1936] 1972: 89–90).

The same texts then go on to recount the bodhisattva's "receipt of his robes." Here the traditions vary somewhat, and the story gets a little bit more elaborate because it is caught up in customs involved in the giving and finding of "monastic robes." In some texts, no mention of a reliquary is made for the princely robes that the bodhisattva discards. Instead, a divinity named Ghaṭikāra, said to have been a friend of the bodhisattva's

[22] For an early representation of the shrine at Bharhut, see Cunningham 1879: pl. 16(a).

[23] For a traditional Thai depiction of Indra waiting to catch the bodhisattva's hairknot as he cuts it off, see Leksukhum 2000: 174.

during the time of the previous buddha Kāśyapa, comes down from heaven and provides Gautama not only with a set of monastic robes but with the other "requisites" of a monk (bowl, razor, girdle, needle, and water-strainer) (*JA.*, 65 = Eng. trans., Jayawickrama 1990: 87; see also *BuvA.*, 234 = Eng. trans., Horner 1978: 297). Here, clearly, the bodhisattva's receipt of his robes is associated (as is the tonsuring of his head) with monastic ordination ceremonies. In other traditions, the divinity who comes down disguises himself as a hunter wearing ochre-colored robes, and the bodhisattva, seeing him and thinking his own garments of Benares silk are inappropriate for one who has wandered forth, asks to exchange clothes with this "hunter." The trade being accomplished, the "hunter" then goes back to heaven, where, according to at least one version of the story, he establishes a caitya for the bodhisattva's royal robes (*Lal.*, 226 = Fr. trans., Foucaux 1884: 197 = Eng. trans., Bays 1983: 339).[24] In the *Mūlasarvāstivāda Vinaya,* the bodhisattva's new robes are given a pedigree that associates them with the tradition of "finding" discarded "dust-heap" robes (*pāṃśukūla*), the wearing of which is specifically associated with ascetic practices. Such robes, presumably, were once made from rags or shrouds found in such places as cremation grounds, but, as their acquisition became ritualized, they were actually hung on trees by laypersons and left there for monks to "happen" to find (see Martini 1973). In any case, it is to this tradition that the *Mūlasarvāstivāda Vinaya* makes initial reference. It tells a story of ten brothers who, long ago in Kapilavastu, all became pratyekabuddhas and received hempen robes from their mother. When they were about to parinirvāṇize, they told their mother that they soon would no longer have need of these robes, but that eventually a king named Śuddhodana would have a son named Śākyamuni, and these robes should be passed on to him. The robes were then kept in the mother's family. When she died, she passed them on to her daughter, who, in turn about to succumb to death, hung them on a tree, asking the tree spirit to guard them and deliver them to the son of Śuddhodana. At this point, the god Indra decides to intervene. Taking on the guise of a hunter, he takes the robes from the tree and waits for the bodhisattva to happen by, and gives them to him in exchange for his garments of Benares silk. These he then takes up to heaven, where he enshrines them

[24] There is some confusion concerning this caitya. In *Lal.,* it is called the Kāṣāyagrahaṇa Caitya, i.e., the "Receipt of the Monastic Robes Shrine," but the robes it contains are the bodhisattva's princely garb! It may be that this was the name of a stūpa on earth marking the spot where the bodhisattva acquired his monastic robes. At least that is the case in *Sanghbhv.,* 1:93. In *Bcar.,* 66 = Eng. trans., Johnston [1936] 1971: 90, no mention is made of a caitya connected to these robes, either in heaven or on earth. In *Thūp.,* 166 = Eng. trans., Jayawickrama 1971: 26, it is called the "Dussacetiya" (the "Caitya of the Clothes").

and establishes among the gods a celebration called the "Festival of the Garments of Benares Silk" (*kāśikāmaha*) (*Sanghbhv.,* 1:93 = Eng. trans., Strong 2002: 13).

It is noteworthy that the actual relics here (the cut hair and exchanged robes), like the ratnavyūha, do not remain on earth but are taken to heaven, where they are worshiped by the gods. To be sure, the *Mūlasarvāstivāda Vinaya* does specify that at the sites at which the topknot was cut and the robes were received, here on earth, commemorative caityas were built, and these are "still venerated by monks" (*Sanghbhv.,* 1:91 = Eng. trans., Strong 2002: 12). In fact they were visited by Xuanzang (*T.* 2087, 51:903a = Eng. trans., Li 1996: 183–84). But the relics themselves are in a shrine in heaven, and the festival in their honor is something carried out by the gods. This curious "removal" of relics from this period of the bodhisattva's life requires some explanation.

It may be argued that, narratively, the story of the bodhisattva's cutting his own hair demands a resolution to the question: what then happened to the hair? And likewise that the story of his divestment of his royal robes poses a similar question: what happened to them? Indra's heaven would seem an appropriate place for their storage because of their inherent involvement, as objects, in royal/divine symbolism. Moreover, as we shall see, the gods, sometimes, are viewed as caretakers of relics who venerate them until it is time for their enshrinement back on earth. Similar functions are sometimes fulfilled by nāgas who are often thought to be enthusiastic collectors, guardians, and worshippers of relics.[25] These bodhisattva relics, however, are not among those that return to earth, except briefly as in the case of the placental palace. Their permanent place is in heaven, and this requires some explanation. In fact, these relics appear to be Janus-like symbols. On the one hand, as we have seen, they mark a significant soteriological moment when the bodhisattva's advance to buddhahood is clear, and they look forward to that event. On the other hand, like all the other objects from this period of the bodhisattva's life, they embody what gets left behind, and help devotees look back at what is abandoned. And it is, perhaps, in this capacity, as markers that capture the sentiment of sacrifice, that it will not do for them to make present here on earth those very objects that were abandoned. Still, the sentiment and the moment are important and should be preserved and recalled somewhere. Hence the solution of having these relics permanently enshrined "elsewhere," in heaven.

[25] On this theme in East Asia, see Faure 1999a: 274ff.

Relics and the Certainty of Buddhahood

After the his great departure and the establishment of his hairknot relic and robes relic in heaven, the bodhisattva proceeds, in his quest, to study with the sages Ārāḍa and Udraka, and then to undertake austerities for several years. No relics appear to mark these soteriological detours. Eventually, however, the bodhisattva realizes that extreme fasting is a wrong path, and he decides to resume taking food and adopt a middle way between the extremes of asceticism and hedonism. This decision is epitomized in his acceptance of the offering of milkrice presented to him by the laywoman Sujātā (who in the Sanskrit tradition is sometimes replaced by the sisters Nandā and Nandabalā). And here another relic is generated: the bowl in which he receives the milkrice offering and which he later sets afloat on the Nairañjanā river.[26] In the *Jātaka nidāna,* this bowl is made to act as yet another omen of the bodhisattva's imminent enlightenment. "If," he declares, "I [am to] succeed in becoming a Buddha this day, let this bowl go upstream; if not let it go down with the current" (Jayawickrama 1990: 93; text in *JA,* 1:70).[27] The bowl, of course, miraculously floats upstream and then sinks down to the nāga Kāla's abode where it comes to rest on the bowls of the three previous buddhas of the aeon.[28]

No mention is here made of the bowl being worshipped by the nāgas or treated as a relic, but in the *Lalitavistara,* its status as such is made clear. Indeed, in that text, almost everything associated with this episode is enshrined as a relic of use. Accepting the milkrice from Sujātā, the bodhisattva goes to the river, and, thinking he should bathe before eating, he leaves the bowl and his clothes on the bank, and enters the water. Immediately, hundreds of thousands of divinities perfume the river water with sandalwood and aloes and flower blossoms. And when the bodhisattva finishes his ablutions, they each take portions of his bathwater away with them and, in their various divine abodes, build caityas for them. Apparently, while bathing, the bodhisattva also trimmed (or washed) his hair and beard, for, as soon as the gods have made off with the bathwater, Sujātā herself gathers up some hairs from his head and some facial hair, and takes them away to her home to build a caitya as well. The bodhisattva, having gotten out of the water, wants to find a place to sit down to eat.

[26] Not all sources agree that this bowl was received from Sujātā or that the bodhisattva, having eaten from it, got rid of it. According to a late Chinese tradition, he received this bowl from a mountain god and kept it for most of his career. See Wang-Toutain 1994: 78–79; and chapter 8 in this book.

[27] On the different versions of this episode, see Nakamura 2000: 142–46.

[28] For a Thai depiction of the moment, see Fickle 1979: pl. 15.

Immediately the nāga maidens, coming out of the earth, offer him a throne. He sits on that, consumes the milkrice, and having no more need for the bowl, tosses it into the river. There, the nāga king immediately takes it, thinking the vessel worthy of veneration. However, Indra, who also wants the bowl, takes on the form of a *garuḍa* bird and tries to steal it from the nāga. Failing in this, he resumes his own form as Indra and asks for it courteously. The nāga king then willingly gives up the bowl, and Indra takes it to the Trāyastriṃśa heaven, where he builds a caitya for it, and where he institutes a regular annual "festival of the vessel" (*pātrīmaha*). The nāga maidens, lest they be left with nothing, wait until the bodhisattva gets up from the throne they had given him, and then cart that away and enshrine it in a caitya in their kingdom (*Lal.*, 267–68 = Fr. trans., Foucaux 1884: 230–32).[29]

Conclusion

This profusion of relics of the bodhisattva marking events just prior to the Buddha's enlightenment is interesting. It is almost as though the closer one gets to his buddhahood, the greater the demand for relics. This should not surprise us. From what we have seen in this chapter, relics of the bodhisattva, whether from his previous lives or from his early life as Gautama, are all in someway precursive signals of his final enlightenment. Thus Sumedha's hair recalls the first step made by the bodhisattva on the path, when, aeons ago, at the feet of the previous Buddha Dīpaṃkara, he took his initial vow for buddhahood. Similarly, the bones of the bodhisattva left by the tigress are a further reaffirmation of that vow and a reconfirmation of the path. As we have seen, the Buddha himself proclaims, "It is because of these bones, Ānanda, that I quickly achieved unsurpassed total enlightenment."[30] Finally, the few relics associated with the early part of his life as Gautama—relics that act as markers for the soteriologically significant moments of his birth, his great departure, and his finding the Middle Path—all serve to point to his buddhahood as well.

And yet, there is a certain ambivalence surrounding these relics. They pre-present the bodhisattva's buddhahood, but they cannot re-present him lest they make him present as a bodhisattva rather than as a buddha.

[29] In later Chinese tradition, the Vinaya master Daoxuan maintained that the Buddha kept the bowl he used for the milkrice and that it had been given to him by a local mountain god who had received it from the previous Buddha Kāśyapa. See *T.* 2122, 53:1008a = Fr. trans., Wang-Toutain 1994: 78. See also Shinohara 2003.

[30] In other traditions, it is said that the zeal exhibited here by the bodhisattva is what resulted in his moving ahead of Maitreya in their "race" toward buddhahood. See La Vallée Poussin 1928.

Hence there is a certain reticence about the relic status of Sumedha's hair or of the bodhisattva's bones from the jātaka of the tigress. And indeed, the latter, as we have seen, remain bones in that they fail to "come alive" and perform miracles. Similarly, the relics from the bodhisattva's birth, youth, and pre-enlightenment days are enshrined "elsewhere" in heaven, or in the realm of the nāgas, a move that gets around, perhaps, the problem of presence.

Finally, it is noteworthy that all of these relics are what might be called "episodic" relics—in that they are directly connected to particular events in the life of the bodhisattva. They recall specific moments when the bodhisattva's determination to become a buddha was most manifest, and only secondarily do they recollect the undifferentiated figure of the Buddha as a whole.

Chapter Three

RELICS OF THE STILL-LIVING BUDDHA: HAIRS AND FOOTPRINTS

THE *Jātaka-nidāna,* one of the most influential of the Theravādin biographies of the Buddha, divides the life of Śākyamuni into three major sections: (1) the "distant epoch," which recounts the career of the bodhisattva throughout his previous lives from his birth as Sumedha, at the time of the Buddha Dīpaṃkara, to his birth as Jotipāla, at the time of Kāśyapa, the last of the previous buddhas; (2) the "intermediate epoch," which deals with his early life as Gautama—the period from his birth at Lumbinī to his enlightenment at Bodhgaya; and (3) the "recent epoch," which covers his career as a bonafide buddha from his enlightenment at Bodhgaya until his death and parinirvāṇa (*JA.*, 95 = Eng. trans., Jayawickrama 1990: 127). In the last chapter, I considered relics from the first and second of these epochs. In this chapter, I shall turn to relics from the third. In so doing, of course, I will no longer be dealing with relics of the *bodhisattva,* but relics of a being who, having reached enlightenment at Bodhgaya, is now a fully awakened *buddha.*

Obviously, relics from this period of the Buddha's life, since he is still alive, cannot be bones or body parts or crematory ashes that could emerge only after his death. Indeed, many of them are secondary contact relics, that is, relics of use (*pāribhogika*), which are often still episodically based, and which are connected to pilgrimage traditions. For instance, there are rocks where the Buddha washed his clothes, and shadows he projected on walls, and forests grown from his discarded toothsticks, and a whole series of places where he sat and where he walked up and down (*T.* 2087, 51:875b, 879a, 898c, 915b = Eng. trans., Li 1996: 47, 68, 163, 243–44. See also *T.* 2085, 51:860b = Eng. trans., Li 2002: 180).

As fascinating as such traditions might be, in this chapter, I will not try to cover this plethora of pāribhogika relics dating from this period of the Buddha's life. Instead, I shall focus on the presentation and analysis of two important traditions that concern relics that might be thought of as coming closer to the category of bodily (sarīrika) relics: (1) various hair relics (and nail parings) of the Buddha, in particular the hairs given by him to the laymen Trapuṣa and Bhallika; and (2) various footprints of the Buddha imprinted by him in different parts of the world. As we shall see, these two types of relics are classificatorily ambiguous, that is, they fall somewhere in between the categories of bodily relics and contact relics. Hairs and nails are technically part of the Buddha's body, but they are detachable parts, and, as such, they were sometimes viewed as sarīrika, and sometimes as being in the same category as the Buddha's clothes (see Bentor 1994: 17).[1] Likewise, footprints ended up being classified in a variety of ways. Some were clearly *uddesika*—representational relics. Others were seen as pāribhogika—relics of use, or rather, more specifically, relics of contact (Damrong 1973: vi). And occasionally they have even been classified as sarīrika, as though they were not just footprints but buddha feet (see Snellgrove 1978: 44 and Quagliotti 1998: 140–41).[2]

Hair and Nail Relics

Stūpas supposedly enshrining hairs and nail parings of the Buddha were "everywhere" in ancient India. Xuanzang mentions having visited over twenty such sites (see Wylie [1897] 1966: 71–73). A Southeast Asian tradition, less hampered by factuality perhaps, proclaims that the gods distributed 800,000 of the Buddha's body hairs and 900,000 of the hairs from his head "throughout this universe of ours" (Halliday 1923: 46; see also *Jin.*, 37 = Eng. trans., Jayawickrama 1968: 53). Sanskrit texts often refer to "hair-and-nail stūpas" (*keśanakhastūpa*) almost in passing, as though they were perfectly ordinary monuments (see Schopen 1997: 196n. 34). Indeed, we are told that "it is the norm" for all buddhas to have hair-and-nail stūpas while they are still alive (*Div.*, 196), and various texts feature hair and nail relics of previous buddhas such as Kāśyapa and Vipāśyi (*Avś.*, 56, 205 = Fr. trans., Feer 1891: 95, 312; and *Śayanās.*, 28). It seems that these stūpas were intended to make the veneration of the Buddha possible when it was otherwise difficult. For example, in one story, the women of King Bimbisāra's harem find that although the king takes them to visit the Buddha in his monastery in the evening, they often cannot see him during the day. Accordingly, they ask the king to establish, in the harem, a hair-and-nail stūpa of the Tathāgatha where they can "at any time, venerate him with flowers, perfumes, garlands, unguents, umbrellas, flags, and banners" (*Avś.*, 136 = Fr. trans., Feer 1891: 210). Bimbisāra relays their message to the Buddha, who complies by giving him some hairs from his head and nail clippings that the king can enshrine in his gynaeceum. In a different story, it is specified that monks at the Jetavana monastery were in the habit of venerating a hair-and-nail

[1] In a similar category, perhaps, we might find the Buddha's excrement and his snot, enshrined in different sanctuaries in Northern Thailand. See Swearer, forthcoming A.

[2] On the classificatory ambiguity of footprints, see also Kinnard 2000: 39–45.

stūpa whenever the Buddha withdrew for the purpose of a meditational retreat. The merit earned by a certain monk who repeatedly prostrated himself before this relic is said to have been rebirth as a *cakravartin* king as many times as there were grains of sand in the ground covered by the stūpa, extending downward to a distance of 80,000 leagues (*Div.*, 197; see also *Śikṣ.*, 82 = Eng. trans., Bendall [1902] 1971: 147–48).

Trapuṣa and Bhallika

The most famous hair relics, however, are those that were given by the Buddha, shortly after his enlightenment, to two merchants named Trapuṣa (Pali: Tapassu) and Bhallika (Pali: Bhallika). The story can be summarized as follows: For seven weeks after his enlightenment, the Buddha remained in the vicinity of the bodhi tree at Bodhgaya. Then, in the eighth week, he dwellt under the tree called Rājāyatana. While he was sitting there, two merchants, Trapuṣa and Bhallika, happened to be traveling by with a caravan of five hundred ox carts. At the urging of a local divinity, who in fact had been their mother in a previous existence, they were convinced to stop and make an offering of food to the Blessed One. This was the first meal to be given to the Buddha after his enlightenment, and the first food to be consumed by him for over seven weeks since the time of the milkrice offering by Sujātā. To receive the food, however, the Buddha first needed to acquire a bowl, since he had thrown the bowl he had used for the milkrice into the Nairañjana River. Thus, there is usually inserted into the story at this point the legend of how the Buddha received four bowls from the four heavenly kings and then squeezed them together to make them into a single monk's bowl.[3] This done, the Buddha then used his new bowl to accept Trapuṣa and Bhallika's offering of sweets and rice, ate it, and then gave them a few words of dharma in return. The brothers responded by taking "double refuge" in the Buddha and in the dharma (there being as yet no saṃgha).[4] In this way, they became the first lay disciples of the Blessed One. Then, wishing to take their leave, they asked the Buddha for something by which they could remember and honor him in his absence. Accordingly, the Buddha stroked his head with his hand and gave them eight hairs as relics. They made golden caskets for the relics and took them to their own city where they enshrined them in

[3] On this event, see chapter 8 in this book, and *Catuṣ.*, 84ff = Eng. trans., Kloppenborg 1973: 9. See also Wang-Toutain 1994: 60; Kuwayama 1990: 954–55; and Lamotte 1949–80: 1676–79).

[4] This "double-refuge" is usual in Pali versions of the tale, Rhys Davids's indication (1880: 110) otherwise being a faulty translation. See also, however, *Mtu.*, 3:310 = Eng. trans., Jones 1949–56, 3:297; *Sanghbhv.*, 1:124 = Eng. trans., Kloppenborg 1973: 10; and, more generally, Nakamura 2000: 225–26.

a stūpa, by the city gate. On each festival day, we are told, a blue ray of light still issues forth from this shrine.[5]

Xuanzang, who recounts this tale as well, adds that Trapuṣa and Bhallika's was the very first stūpa to be built and that the Buddha had first to instruct them in how to erect it by folding his three robes into squares, piling them up, and then topping them off with his inverted bowl (*T.* 2087, 51:873a = Eng. trans., Li 1996: 36). We thus have an important tradition here that brings together several "firsts": first lay disciples of the Buddha to take refuge in him and his teaching; first meritorious food offering to the Buddha after his enlightenment; first Buddhist monk's bowl; first words of dharma given by the Blessed One; first relics of Gautama after his attainment of buddhahood; and first stūpa of the Buddha here on earth.[6]

The symbolic significance of hair—on or off the head—is, of course, a much discussed topic, from the perspective of both psychology and anthropology.[7] More specifically, in Brahmanical circles in India, cut hair tended to be viewed as impure and the business of outcaste barbers. Patrick Olivelle (1998: 28), in his elucidation of this subject, cites several Sanskrit sources in which hair is seen to be equal to bodily waste. The same could be true in Buddhistic circles: there is a "Sinhala belief that hair and nails are made from the impure waste produced in the process of digesting food, and that cutting hair and nails is similar to voiding excrement" (Olivelle 1998: 28).[8] More generally, in Buddhism, hair of the head became a sort of symbol of the body in its impermanence and nonself. In mindfulness meditations and in ordination rituals (e.g., *M.*, 1:56 = Eng. trans., Horner 1954–59, 1:71), it consistently tops the list of the thirty-two loathsome constituent parts of the body, where, as Alf Hiltebeitel (1998: 3) has put it, it is "a synecdoche for the whole body and a metonym for the whole meditation."

Given these connotations, it may at first seem strange that hairs should come to be venerated as precious relics, signs of the Buddha himself. Indeed, in one variant version of our story, Trapuṣa and Bhallika are initially disgusted by the hair relics (and nail parings) given them by the Buddha. "These are things which people in this world despise and throw away,"

[5] This summary generally follows *AA.*, 1:382–84, but there are many variants. Other sources of interest include *JA.*, 1:80–81 = Eng. trans., Jayawickrama 1990: 107–8); *VinA.*, 5:959–61; *ThagA.*, 1:49–51; *ApA.*, 85; *Mtu.*, 3:302–11 = Eng. trans., Jones 1949–56, 3:290–98); and *T.* 1428, 22:78–85 = Fr. trans., Bareau 1963: 107–09). See also Nakamura 2000: 457–58n.18.

[6] As we have seen in chapter 2, stūpas had already been erected for various relics of the bodhisattva by the gods in their heavens.

[7] See Berg 1951; Leach 1958; Lang 1995; and the bibliography in Hallpike 1987: 157, to which should be added Obeyesekere 1981: part 1.

[8] See also Seneviratne 1992: 181. Leach (1958: 157) has also pointed to a number of Sinhalese puns that associated baldness with the buttocks, and head hair with urine.

they declare, "why does the Blessed One wish us to make offerings to this?" And it is only after the Buddha narrates to them the whole jātaka story of Sumedha laying out his *hair* at the feet of Dīpaṃkara that he manages to convince them that worshiping such things would be meritorious (see *T.* 1428, 22:781–85 = Fr. trans., Bareau 1963: 107–9; and Bareau 1966–74, 1:1–16). This, then, amounts to a karmic justification of hair veneration, one which asserts that the bodhisattva's hair is worthy of worship because it once served an important soteriological function.

A similar story occurs a bit further on in the same vinaya. There, we are told that once, in Rājagṛha, the Buddha needed to have his hair cut. None of the monks, however, was willing to do it, until finally the novice Upāli, a member of the barber caste but still a young boy, was asked to undertake the task.[9] As he began shaving the Buddha's head, Upāli's nervous parents, present in the room, kept asking the Blessed One whether or not their son was doing a good job. "Yes," the Buddha would answer, "but he is leaning over too much." Or again, "Yes, but he is holding his head too high." And, "Yes, but he is breathing irregularly." Young Upāli, overhearing all these comments, made efforts to control his posture and his breathing to such an extent that he entered into the fourth level of trance (*dhyāna*). Fortunately, Ānanda, ever on the *qui vive,* saw what was happening and was able to take the razor from Upāli's hand in time. The haircut had come to an end but, with the barber in *samādhi,* a problem had arisen: what to do with the cut hair? And here, Ānanda's initial reaction is very interesting: he thought the hair was an impure thing, put it in an old broken pot, and was about to throw it in the trash, when the Buddha reprimanded him, and told him to put the hair in a new pot and give it, as a relic, to a general named Gopalī, who took it into battle where he was victorious (*T.* 1428, 22:957a-b = Fr. trans., Bareau 1962: 262. See also Demiéville 1934: 170).

Edmund Leach (1958: 158), in the context of a broader discussion, has proposed that we see buddha hair (and tooth) relics not only as symbols of a beneficial deity but as objects of magical power. More specifically, the success of hairs as relics would seem to involve several other contextual considerations. First of all, just as the body of the Buddha was different from that of most people, so too the hair of the Buddha was not the same as the hair of ordinary persons. For one thing, once cut short at the time of the Buddha's great departure, it no longer grew; it thereby achieved a sort of permanence and freedom from growth and decay (*saṃsāra*) that is not unlike that of relics, which by definition are beyond death.[10] Secondly, though the veneration of the Buddha was in many

[9] Clearly, in India, the impurity of hair is also connected to the question of caste.

[10] As we have just seen in the tale of the Buddha's haircut, not all traditions accepted the

ways different from that of Hindu gods, the bhaktic assertion—that the most impure part of a divinity or great being (such as their feet or left-overs, or, in this case, their cut hair or nail parings) was still purer than the purest part of their worshipers (their heads)—was pan-Indian in nature and may have gotten applied here to the Buddha. Thirdly, and perhaps in contradiction to these two points, there is a sense in which the Buddha's plucking of a hair from his head repeats the cutting of his hair that symbolically made him a monk, a buddha, and asserted his purity. The veneration of the *cut* hair of the Buddha is thus a veneration of one of the things that made the bodhisattva into a buddha and so makes it worthy of worship. Finally, there was probably a very practical consideration in the use of hairs as relics, namely their removability and movability. Simply put, hairs made good relics, especially while the Buddha was still alive. As detachable parts of his body, they could be taken away and venerated in his absence anywhere.[11]

It is understandable, then, that in time several elaborations on the story of Trapuṣa and Bhallika's hair relics arose, as well as several traditions rival to it. In what follows, I want to look at some South and Southeast Asian examples. I shall start with the tradition that claims that hair relics of the Buddha were enshrined in the Shwe Dagon Pagoda in Myanmar, then I shall consider a number of Sri Lankan traditions about hair relics, before moving to a Pali chronicle, the *Chakesadhātu-vaṃsa,* which recounts the enshrinement of hair relics in a variety of places.

The Hair Relics at the Shwe Dagon Pagoda

The best-known elaboration of the Trapuṣa and Bhallika tale is the Southeast Asian tradition which asserts that these two brothers were actually Mon merchants from Lower Burma, named Tapu and Tabaw, who were responsible for bringing the hair relics back to their home country and enshrining them in what is today one of the most magnificent monuments in the Buddhist world, the Shwe Dagon Pagoda in Rangoon.

The legend of the enshrinement of the Buddha's hair relics there is a relatively late one, probably not appearing in its present form until the fifteenth century, but it can be seen as a local elaboration of certain themes that appear in older Pali materials. Three kinds of sources are useful in reconstructing it: (1) Mon and Burmese inscriptions, most notably those

---

premise that the Buddha's hair stopped growing. The view that the hairs and nails of living liberated beings did stop growing, however, is also found in Jainism. See, on this, Olivelle 1998: 22 and 44n.30.

[11] On the portability of relics in Christianity, see also Brown 1981: 89; in Buddhism, see Shinohara 2001.

at the pagoda itself (see Forchhammer 1883; Pe Maung Tin 1934: 8–33; Singer 1995: ch. 1); (2) literary chronicles of the legend in Mon and Burmese;[12] and (3) oral accounts preserved in various books over the past one-hundred-and-fifty years (e.g., Shway Yoe 1882: 179–83 and Halliday 1917: 86–88). I will, in what follows, put together a number of these sources.

The first part of the story basically follows the Pali account given in the previous section. Hearing that there is a famine in a land in India, two Mon merchants named Tapu ("dove") and Tabaw ("plentiful") load a ship with rice and other foodstuffs (honey, molasses, etc.), and set out across the sea. Upon arrival, they transfer their cargo to bullock carts, and proceed inland until they meet a nat (a divine spirit), who had been their mother in a previous existence. She tells them that the Buddha, having just attained enlightenment, happens to be dwelling, right then, at the foot of a nearby tree, and that if they wish to attain benefit for themselves they should pay homage to him. The brothers do so and offer him sweetened rice cakes. There follows the story of the Buddha getting a bowl from the four regent nats of the four directions.

After his meal, the Buddha asks the two merchants where they are from, and, upon learning that they are natives of of Ukkalā in lower Burma, he tells them a story about their native place and how it got its name.[13] He then goes on to explain the names of a number of other localities in lower Burma, focussing especially on Mount Singuttara, the hill in Ukkalā on which the present- day Shwe Dagon Pagoda is located.[14] Singuttara is so-called because, ages ago, a giant centipede or scorpion used to devour elephants on the hill and piled up their tusks (Pali: *singa*) in a pile that was very high (*uttara*).[15] Alternatively, it is known as Tikumbha, meaning "Three Hills," because the mountain originally had three summits.[16] Yet another theory connects Tikumbha to the Mon word *takun* supposed to be at the origin of the *dagon* of Shwe Dagon (Forchhammer 1883: 17). *Takun* (dagon) is said to mean a tree trunk placed athwart something—a popular etymology that lies, perhaps, at the root of the story that Trapuṣa and Bhallika will know they have found the mountain

[12] These include the *Shwe Dagon Thamaing Athit* = Eng. trans., Pearn 1939: 1–8; the *Lik Wan Dhāt Kyak Lagun, Lik Wan Dhāt, Slapat Taphussa Bhallika,* and *Slapan Wan Dhāt Kyak Ceti Lagun,* passages of which are edited and translated in Pe Maung Tin 1934: 33–57, 65–91; and the *Slapat Rājāwan Datow Smin Ron,* edited and translated in Halliday 1923.

[13] For this amusing (and somewhat lengthy) tale featuring a deer, gooseberries, a hare, a tiger, and a monkey, see Pe Maung Tin 1934: 37–38; and Strong 1998: 84–85.

[14] For other traditions concerning Mount Singuttara, see Swearer, forthcoming: ch. 8.

[15] This tale is much developed in the oral tradition recorded by Shway Yoe (1882: 179–80).

[16] Literally *kumbha* means "elephant head" or "pot" but the word is used to designate any rounded hillock. For other names for the hill, see Pe Maung Tin 1934: 41 and Singer 1995: 12.

on which they are to enshrine the hair relics when they see a tree trunk perfectly balanced on top of a peak in such a way that neither end of it touches the ground (Shway Yoe 1882: 181–82).

Whatever the etymologies of its names, Mount Singuttara is much praised by the Buddha as a special place, for it was visited and honored in times past by the previous buddhas; Krakucchandha left his water pot to be enshrined there, Kanakamuni his staff, and Kāśyapa his bathing cloth.[17] Having said this, the Buddha then reveals to Trapuṣa and Bhallika that he himself is due to have some hairs of his head enshrined at the same spot, and that the task of enshrining them there on the mountain will be theirs. And he gives them eight hairs from his head, enjoining them to return with them to their own land (Pe Maung Tin 1934: 41–42).

In this tradition, then, Trapuṣa and Bhallika do not actually ask for the hairs; they are, rather, *given* them, with a specific mission in mind. The brothers therefore quickly abandon their plans to sell their goods in India and immediately set out for their home country, bearing the relics that are now housed in an emerald casket. According to the Mon and Burmese tellings of the tale, their way is embellished and made easy by the god Sakka (Indra) and by his divine engineer Viśvakarman, who provides them first with five hundred newly fashioned divine carts, and then with a great ship befitting their mission.

This does not prevent them, however, from having certain adventures and encountering certain mishaps en route. Sailing aboard the ship they first come to a land called Ajettha, and there the local king, in an excess of piety leading to attachment, takes two of the relics from them and decides to keep them for himself. Trapuṣa and Bhallika are very upset by this, but there is nothing they can do about it and, in the end, they have to resign themselves to sail on with only six hair relics. In due time, they round Cape Negrais (Nāgaraj Point) and drop anchor at a place that is just above the underwater palace of a nāga king called Jayasena. Attracted by six rays of light emanating from the relics, the nāga boards the boat at night, opens the casket and steals two more of the Buddha's hairs, which he takes down to his palace to worship. Unable to do anything about this theft either, the two brothers sail on their way with just four hair relics left (Pe Maung Tin 1934: 42–45).

The logic of the story seems to imply that further mishaps will occur and that they will lose some more relics before getting home. However, nothing of the sort happens; instead, there follow a series of positive encounters in which various beings profit from the passage of the brothers'

[17] There is considerable variation in the identity of these relics and which buddha they belonged to. In Halliday 1923: 41, each previous buddha leaves two relics on the hill.

ship as an occasion for venerating the relics and making offerings to them (Pe Maung Tin 1934: 45; see also Pearn 1939: 3).

Finally, Trapuṣa and Bhallika reach their home where they tell their king about their journey. When they relate to him how the Buddha gave them *eight* hairs to be enshrined on Mount Singuttara in their own kingdom, he becomes ecstatic, thinking this makes him uniquely honored, more glorious than all the other monarchs in the world. He immediately wishes to view the relics and is about to open the casket, when the brothers, realizing that they must forewarn him, quickly complete their story and admit that, though the Buddha gave them *eight* hair relics originally, there are now only four of them left, since King Ajettha took two of them and the nāga king Jayasena stole another pair. The king is very upset by this news, and angry with the brothers, but his fury is forestalled when they undertake an act of truth, stating, "If it be true that the Omniscient Buddha vouchsafed us to enshrine the eight hairs on Mount Singuttara, let the missing four hairs return so that we may have the full eight hairs" (Pe Maung Tin 1934: 46–48).[18] The miracle happens, and when King Ukkalapa opens the casket, all eight hairs are there.[19]

They still need, however, to locate "Singuttara Hill" where they are meant to enshrine the relics, and here there ensues a second saga, in which, for a period of more than three years, the brothers search for the hill. Success comes only with the intervention of the god Indra who, as a *deus ex machina,* comes down from heaven and clears the whole mountain top of trees and vegetation, thus revealing its location (Pe Maung Tin, 1934: 48–49; see also Halliday 1923: 41 and Pearn 1939: 4). Indra, however cannot help them find the exact place on the mountain where the relics of the former buddhas—Krakucchanda, Kanakamuni, and Kāśyapa—were enshrined, for he is only thirty-six million years old and that is not old enough to remember the visits of those former buddhas. Thus, they turn to the five great nats of Rangoon. The oldest of these is the Sule Nat (associated with the Sule Pagoda not far from the Shwe Dagon). He, it turns out, remembers Krakucchanda well, for, in fact, he once tried to eat that former buddha (he then suffered from ogreish tendencies). But Krakucchanda had converted him to Buddhism instead, and had given him his water pot, which Sule Nat then enshrined on Singuttara hill (Pearn 1939: 6; see also Pe Maung Tin 1934: 51).[20]

[18] On the effectiveness of the Act of Truth, see Brown 1968.

[19] It should be specified, however, that there is, in both the Burmese and the Mon Shwe Dagon inscriptions, a consistent tradition, not found in the later chronicles, that only six hair relics of the Buddha were enshrined. See Pe Maung Tin 1934: 18–19, 29–30.

[20] The chronicles also recount similar stories about the meetings of two other Rangoon nats with the two other previous buddhas, Kanakamuni and Kāśyapa, who recall the enshrine-

With some effort, Sule Nat is able to point out the location of the hill. He is so old that his eyelids droop down over his eyes, and Trapuṣa and Bhallika have to prop them up with palm trees so that he can see. The next day, however, the identity of the site is confirmed when they cut down a tree on the summit and it remains perfectly balanced, "a trunk lying across" (dagon) the mountain top, just as the Buddha had predicted. And they enshrine the relics there (Shway Yoe 1882: 181–82).

Sri Lankan Traditions

The Shwe Dagon legend does not end with this but goes on to describe the building of the relic chamber, the construction and later aggrandizement of the pagoda (see Strong 1998: 90–92). We cannot follow the story here, but need to turn instead to other elaborations on the Trapuṣa and Bhallika legend. In Sri Lanka, several variant traditions arose. One of these, recorded in an eighth-century inscription as well as in the thirteenth-century collection of stories, the *Pūjāvaliya* (see Paranavitana 1934–43: 154; Goonasekere 1966: 686; Rahula 1956: 241n.5), maintains that Trapuṣa and Bhallika themselves actually visited Sri Lanka in person, and brought one of their hair relics with them, in a golden reliquary.[21] At a place called Girihaṇḍu,[22] they put it down on a rock while they prepared their meal. When they got ready to go on, they found to their surprise that they could no longer move the reliquary. They concluded that this was a sign that this was the place for its enshrinement and they built a stūpa over it (Fernando 1970: 91–93).[23]

A second Sri Lankan tradition is somewhat more elaborate. It picks up on the Burmese/Mon tradition that Trapuṣa and Bhallika lost at least some of their hair relics to the nāga king Jayasena on their way home. Jayasena took the hairs down to his palace in the bottom of the ocean where he worshipped them. Centuries later, King Kākavaṇṇa Tissa of Sri Lanka (father of the heroic ruler Duṭṭhagāmaṇī) came into possession of

---

ment of their relics (the staff and bathing cloth) at the same spot, and they further imply that the two remaining nats (of the five great nats of Rangoon) should be associated with the relics of the two remaining buddhas of our era, Gautama and Maitreya. The traditions about all of these nats, however, are somewhat confused. For variants, see Pearn 1939: 6–7; Pe Maung Tin 1934: 51–52; Singer 1995: 15; and Halliday 1923: 41.

[21] As mentioned, the Burmese inscription at the Shwe Dagon (see Pe Maung Tin 1934: 29) indicates that Trapuṣa and Bhallika, in fact, did not enshrine all of the hairs in the pagoda.

[22] There is some debate as to the location of Girihaṇḍu. Paranavitana (1934–43: 156) is inclined toward locating it at a site north of Trincomalee; others have proposed placing it at Ambalantota on the South Coast.

[23] For another miracle associated with this site, see *Vsm.*, 143–44 = Eng. trans., Ñyāṇamoli 1976, 1:150. Fernando (1970) includes an account of a modern-day pilgrimage to the site.

the forehead bone relic of the Buddha. This relic had originally been acquired by the Mallas at the time of the Buddha's parinirvāṇa, and then was appropriated by Mahākāśyapa, and passed on, within monastic circles, from elder to elder and monastery to monastery in India. Eventually, it was transmitted to Southern Sri Lanka (Rohaṇa), where it was preserved within royal circles until the time of Kākavaṇṇa, who was destined to put an end to its peregrinations by permanently enshrining it at a place called Sēruvila.[24] In doing so, Kākavaṇṇa wished to coif this headbone relic with some actual Buddha hairs. These, he had learned, could be found in the land of the nāgas. Accordingly, he summoned the saṃgha and asked for its help in obtaining them. The elders promptly despatched a monk with magical powers, named Siva, to the kingdom of the nāgas to get the relics. The nāga king Jayasena, knowing why Siva was coming, quickly swallowed the hairs in their casket in an attempt to hide them, but Siva, stretching out his arm and making it very thin and long, reached down into Jayasena's stomach, grabbed the relics, and returned to Sri Lanka with them.[25] The elder Siva then delivered the hair relics to the king, who enshrined them on the forehead bone of the Buddha as planned, despite the protestations of the nāgas, who claimed the relics had been stolen from them (see Pe Maung Tin 1934: 63–64).

These two Sri Lankan traditions are connected to the Trapuṣa and Bhallika story in that they still feature those two merchants as direct or indirect intermediaries in the delivery of the Buddha's hair relics to Sri Lanka. Other Sri Lankan traditions, however, were to bypass Trapuṣa and Bhallika altogether. Thus, in the very first chapter of the *Mahāvaṃsa,* we learn that the Buddha himself, during his first "apocryphal" visit to the island, just nine months after his enlightenment, gave some hair relics to Mahāsumana, the god of Adam's Peak.[26] The latter (just like Trapuṣa and Bhallika) had requested some memento by which he could worship the Blessed One after his return to India, and the Buddha obliged him with a handful of hairs from his head. These Mahāsumana placed in a golden urn on a bed of variegated jewels, and had the whole thing enshrined in a magnificent stūpa at Mahiyangana. After the Buddha's death, this first stūpa at Mahiyangana was then covered over by an even larger monument, which also enshrined the neckbone relic (*gīvaṭṭhi*) of the Blessed One (*Mhv.* 1.33–36 = Eng. trans., Geiger 1912: 5; see also

[24] This tradition, recorded in the fourteenth-century *Dhātuvaṃsa* and elsewhere, has been studied by Trainor 1997. See also *Jin.*, 52–56 = Eng. trans., Jayawickrama 1968: 71–78; and Pe Maung Tin 1934: 32–33. On the present-day importance of Sēruvila, see Kemper 1991: 149–60.

[25] This method of acquiring the relics is very much akin to the way in which the relics for Duṭṭhagāmaṇi's Mahāthūpa get stolen from the nāgas at Rāmagāma. See chapter 6.

[26] On the god of Adam's peak, see Paranavitane 1958 and Aksland 2001: 56–65.

Thūp., 209–10 = Eng. trans., Jayawickrama 1971: 80; and *Skv.*, 46 = Eng. trans., Hazlewood 1986: 61).

The continuation of the *Mahāvaṃsa,* the so-called *Cūḷavaṃsa,* tells yet another story. Citing a no-longer extant text called the *Kesadhātuvaṃsa* (*Chronicle of the Hair Relic*),[27] it tells of a certain man named Silākāla, who went into exile to India with King Moggallāna (r. 496–513) and became a novice at a monastery in Bodhgaya. There, he obtained a hair relic of the Buddha, which he eventually brought back with him to Sri Lanka. Moggallāna had it enshrined in a crystal casket, and had it housed in a building depicting scenes from the life of the past Buddha Dīpaṃkara (at whose feet the Buddha, in his past life, had spread his hair). He furthermore instituted a regular festival in honor of the hair, and endowed Silākāla, who apparently by then had returned to lay life, with the rank of "sword-bearer" (*asiggāha*) and the duties of keeper of the relic (*Cūl.*, 1:36–37 = Eng. trans., Geiger 1929, 1:48–49).

The Chronicle of the Six Hair Relics

Finally, there is one other hair-relic tradition that needs to be referred to here. The just mentioned *Kesadhātuvaṃsa* should not be confused with the still extant *Chakesadhātuvaṃsa* or *Chronicle of the Six Hair Relics of the Buddha* (see *Chak.* = Eng. trans., Law 1960–61; see also Das 1994). Written in Burma by an anonymous author, this relatively late Pali text tells the history of six hairs given by the Buddha—not to Trapuṣa and Bhallika—but to six of his disciples, while he was residing at the Veṇuvana in Rājagṛha. The Buddha's motive in providing them with these hair relics is one with which we are already familiar: the disciples, all of them arhats, announce that they are going to a distant border country where the inhabitants have never had a chance to venerate the Buddha in person.[28] Could he not, therefore, provide for them some sort of memento that could act as a substitute for his person, and be enshrined in those countries?

The six arhats making this request comprise both famous and virtually unknown disciples. Having received the hair relics from the Buddha, they fly off together to the border country, and then proceed, each in turn, to find a total of six donors willing to build stūpas—one for each of the separate hairs. Anuruddha asks the god Indra (Sakka) to undertake the

[27] In 1928, Malalasekera claimed that this text was "extremely rare" (1928: 227). In 1938, he stated it was "not now available" ([1938] 1960, 1:668).

[28] The identity of this country, later called "Kesavatī" ("Endowed with hair [relics]"), is not exactly clear. The *Chak.* was composed in Burma, however, and a Mon legend (see Shorto 1970: 17) knows an alternative tradition in which six arhats bring six hairs of the Buddha to Burma.

construction of the first stūpa. This done, the six arhats worship it, and proceed in a southerly direction where Sobhita asks the deity (*devaputta*) Pajjuna to build a second stūpa for the second hair relic. They then go west[?] to the shore of the ocean, where Padumuttara asks the goddess (*devadhītā* of the sea, Maṇimekhalā, to build a third stūpa. At first she is reluctant, saying that she is a woman, so how can she undertake such a project, but eventually she is convinced to enlist the help of the local inhabitants. The arhats then proceed to the north, and there they meet a spirit (*devatā*) dwelling in a banyan tree. Guṇasāgara is the arhat who negotiates with her and gets her to agree to become the protective divinity of a fourth stūpa, which a passing sailor actually builds by her banyan tree. The arhats then go east where, on the banks of a river, they find a propitious spot, and the elder Ñānapaṇḍita calls on the nāga king Varuṇa to build the fifth stūpa. Finally, going to the north again, the arhats come to a place frequented by travelers, and there they meet some Tamil merchants and sailors who arrive in seven boats. They are said to have faith in the Buddha, but some doubts arise in them as to the powers of the last remaining hair relic. Accordingly, it then performs a miracle, and, their doubts allayed, the Tamils agree to the elder Revata's request that they build the final, sixth stūpa in that place. On account of all these hair relic stūpas, we are told, the whole country came to be known as "Kesavatī" (*Chak.*, 7–16; Law 1960–61: 33–42).

TABLE 2.
Distribution of hair relics in the *Chakesadhātuvaṃsa.*

Hair Relic #	*Disciple responsible for the relic*	*Location of the stūpa*	*Being who is in charge of stūpa construction*
1	Anuruddha	Center? (Zenith?)	Indra, king of gods
2	Sobhita	South	Pajjuna, god of rain
3	Padumuttara	West (?) (by ocean)	Maṇimekhalā, sea goddess
4	Guṇasāgara	North	Tree spirit
5	Ñānapaṇḍita	East	Nāga
6	Revata	North (Nadir?)	Humans (Tamil merchants)

Two patterns of relic distribution seem to be at work here (see table 2). The one, imperfectly developed, is a directional one, spreading the six stūpas out to at least three, and probably all four, of the cardinal points. It seems to hint at a circumambulation scheme whereby the relics are established on a tour of the whole country. We shall encounter such patterns again in subsequent relic traditions featuring King Aśoka. The other distribution scheme involves a hierarchy of beings. Each of the hair relics and each of the stūpas is associated with a different type of being in a more-or-less descending cosmological order. The first is enshrined by Indra, king of the gods. There is no surprise here; Indra often intervenes in the affairs of humans and is specifically said to play special roles in the enshrinement of relics. The second stūpa is built by Pajjuna, a deva subordinate to Indra who is often invoked as the god of rain (*Mhv.*, 21.31 = Eng. trans., Geiger 1912: 144; and *JA.*, 1:330 = Eng. trans., Cowell 1895–1907, 1:183). He is said to inhabit the heaven of the four kings (Cātummahārājika) and, indeed, in the text is called a *mahārāja* (*Chak.*, 9). The third stūpa takes us further down the hierarchy to Maṇimekhalā, the goddess of the sea, who is assigned the role of protecting shipwrecked sailors by the four heavenly mahārājas (See *JA.*, 4:17 and 6:35 = Eng. trans., Cowell 1895–1907, 4:11 and 6:22).[29] Her cult was especially popular among sea-goers in Lower Burma (see Strong 1992: 345), and, appropriately, her stūpa here is located on cliffs by the seashore. The involvement of sailors continues in the case of the next stūpa commissioned by Guṇasāgara, but at the same time, we move lower in the hierarchy of divine beings, for the appointed guardian of this fourth stūpa is, for the first time, a local divinity—a tree spirit (*rukkhadevatā*)—the equivalent of a nat associated with a banyan tree. With the fifth stūpa we find yet a different kind of divine being—a nāga, or snake divinity—in the person of the nāga king Varuṇa. There were at least two different nāgas named Varuṇa in the Pali canon (see Malalasekera 1960, 2:836–37), but nāga kings more generally are famous for their involvement with relics. Finally, with the sixth and last stūpa, we enter the human realm, but a human realm of a special type, featuring Tamil sailors and merchants who have to be convinced by a miracle to become the donors of the stūpa.

It becomes apparent from the *Chakesadhātuvaṃsa,* as well as from the Sri Lankan and Mon (Shwedagon) traditions we have considered, that one of the themes of the Buddha's hair relics centers around the concepts of "distribution and dispersal." I have already mentioned the tradition that the Buddha's thousands of body hairs and head hairs were spread "throughout the universe." Here, it would seem, we have a more specific and concrete instance of this; these hairs of the Buddha are meant to be spread, far and wide, to foreign countries (Burma, Sri Lanka), and to many different realms (the land of the nāgas, of the gods, and of the various types of beings just specified in the *Chakesadhātuvaṃsa*). In these various settings, these hairs are to act as substitutes for the Buddha in his absence, for persons (such as Trapuṣa and Bhallika and the God of Adam's Peak) who will no longer be able to see him, or for persons (such as the inhabitants of border lands or of other realms such as the world of the

[29] On Maṇimekhalā, see also Lévi 1930; Richman 1988: 12–15; Monius 2001: 11–13.

nāgas) who will never get a chance to see him. In these traditions, for the most part, the absence of the Buddha, which these relics are meant to remedy, is physical—geographical rather than temporal. Simply put, the Buddha's hairs are able to go and stay where the Buddha cannot. At the same time, of course, it is clear that these same hairs were able to remain as relics long after the Buddha's more metaphysical absence in parinirvāṇa.

FOOTPRINTS

The veneration of the feet of great beings such as the Buddha was commonplace in ancient India. Indeed, one of the most routine ritual gestures in Buddhist texts, described countless times in formulaic terms, consists of a person approaching the Buddha and prostrating him or herself fully at his feet, sometimes touching them with the head or hands or mouth, before getting up and sitting down to one side to ask the Buddha a question.[30] The logic of this kind of prostration is well known and is much the same as that of venerating the cut hairs of a great being. By placing the purest part of one's self (one's head) at or under the most impure part of another person (their feet), one makes a declaration of hierarchy, affirming the absolute superiority and complete purity of the venerated one, as well as one's total submission and devotion.[31] The extension of this logic to footprints of the Buddha, in the absence of his actual feet, was an easy step, especially in the context of the similar veneration, in Hinduism, of stone imprints of the feet of the god Viṣṇu (Viṣṇupad), or of veneration of the footprints impressed on a piece of cloth of a departed guru (see Bakker 1991: 25).[32]

Within Buddhism, the veneration of footprints of the Buddha seems to have started quite early. Sculpted depictions of the Buddha's footprints were featured already during the so-called aniconic phase of Buddhist art, at Sāñcī, Bhārhut, and elsewhere (see Snellgrove 1978: 27, 30, 38, 43; Niwa 1992: pl. 66–72; Cunningham 1879 pls. 16 and 17, and Brown 1990: 96–98). Some of these representations may have been meant to signify events in the life of the Buddha, but, as Susan Huntington (1990: 404) has suggested, others may actually have been depictions of persons

[30] For a pan-Buddhist study of the practice, see Durt 1979. On the significance of prostration with specific reference to Buddhism in China, see Reinders 1997.

[31] It comes as no surprise, then, to find—for example in Pagan—footprints of the Buddha commonly depicted on the ceiling vaults of entryways to temples. See Pichard 1993: 97–98; Strachan 1989: 101, 136; Shorto 1971: 80.

[32] The connection with Viṣṇu became especially strong at Gaya and Bodhgaya (see Mitra 1972: 126–27; Kinnard 2000). The Buddha, of course, was deemed to be an avatar of Viṣṇu.

worshiping at footprint shrines.[33] Paul Mus, on the other hand, has argued that in India footprints were "the very type of magical object which enables one to act at a distance on people related to it." In this light, he considers the "aniconic" footprints to be superior sorts of representations of the Buddha than fully bodied images. Footprints are not "a defect of plastic art, but the triumph of a magical art" (Mus 1998: 67).

Robert Brown (1990: 73–96) has spoken eloquently of the importance of walking in the life story of the Buddha and of the connection of footprints to that theme. More specifically, the footprints help mark the Buddha's first presence in this world, when, just born, the young Gautama takes seven steps in the four directions, "the soles of his feet resting evenly upon the ground," and leaving footprints that, as one text puts it, "remained bright as seven stars" (Beal 1883: 3–4; text in *T.* 192, 4:1b).[34] At the same time, however, footprints could serve to emphasize the Buddha's absence, being traces of where he had once been. In this light, it is noteworthy that a number of scholars have connected the worship of buddhapāda to Mahākāśyapa's veneration of the Buddha's feet, which, just prior to his cremation, miraculously stick out from the coffin of their own accord (see Perera 1971: 450 and chapter four of this book). The Buddha's feet thus serve to mark both his coming into and his going from this world.

Like hair relics, footprints of the Buddha abound throughout the Buddhist world and throughout the ages. Anna Maria Quagliotti (1998) has catalogued multiple examples of isolated sculpted footprints of the Buddha in the art of ancient India and Southeast Asia, and has discussed also those seen by various Chinese pilgrims.[35] Motoji Niwa (1992: 10), an enthusiast who spent years tracking down buddha footprints throughout Asia, estimates that he found over 3,000 such "relics," dating from various periods. In China, during the Tang Dynasty, the discovery of a very large footprint in Chengzhou actually caused the Empress Wu Zetian to institute a new reign name in that year (701 C.E.) and initiate the Dazu ("Big Foot") era (Jan 1966: 47; Barrett 2001: 41).[36] In Japan, not long thereafter, a sculpted footprint of Śākyamuni at the Yakushiji temple in

[33] For a discussion of Huntington's view, see Dehejia 1991. See also Huntington 1992.

[34] Here the footprints of the infant bodhisattva are apparently likened to the stars of the Dipper, or to the five planets and the sun and the moon. In other texts, the seven steps are marked by lotus blossoms or by footprints on a cloth held by gods (see Stone 1994: pl. 172; and Snellgrove 1978: 27). On the seven steps, see also Mus 1935, 2:473–576. For their possible connection to Vedic rites, see Auboyer 1987: 126–27.

[35] One of these, seen by Faxian and Xuanzang in Northwestern India, was said to vary in size depending on the merit of the devotee (*T.* 2085, 51:858a = Eng. trans., Li 2002: 169; *T.* 2087, 51:882c = Eng. trans., Li 1996: 85). See also *T.* 2087, 51:870b, 882c, 883a, 911c = Eng. trans., Li 1996: 23, 85, 86, 226.

[36] On a contemporary footprint at Wutai shan, see Hummel 1971.

Nara gave rise to a set of twenty-one devotional poems, the *bussokusekika* ("Buddha footstone poems"), which remain an important example of early Japanese verse (see Mills 1960; Miller 1975). In Myanmar, "one or two of Buddha's foot-prints can be found in monasteries or temples or on pagoda platforms in almost every town or village" (Mya 1936: 321). In Sri Lanka, a recent survey estimates that there are perhaps two thousand footprints on the island (Sailer 1994: 65), and in Thailand, they have also been popular in large numbers since at least the fourteenth century (Lorillard 2000).[37]

Many of these, of course, are acknowledged not to be actual footprints of the Buddha, but replicas or representations of them, which, if they are thought to be relics at all, should be considered to be uddesika relics, in the same category as Buddha images (Damrong 1973: vi).[38] Indeed, in some cases, they are really parts of Buddha images, the "prints" being actually on the bottoms of the feet of large Buddha statues, usually lying down in the outstretched parinirvāṇa posture, in such a way that their soles are visible (see Quagliotti 1998: 46–49, 62). In such instances, the Buddha's feet are usually engraved with various symbols—from the simple representation of a single wheel (one of the signs of the mahāpuruṣa is that the soles of his feet were marked with a *cakra*), to an elaborate charting of as many as 108 auspicious signs (*buddhapādamangala*).[39]

There are also, however, a certain number of footprints, "stamped on mountain-top and river-bank" (Damrong 1973: vi), that are thought to be the actual impressions left in a place by the Buddha in person.[40] These are counted as pāribhogika relics of contact, and it is on these that I wish to focus here. As François Bizot (1971: 421) has pointed out, these "natural relics," whether partially sculpted out or not, are always treated differently from the more common fabricated uddesika prints. Footprints, in fact, are not accidental everyday markers of the Buddha's passage but

[37] Although an earlier footprint, dating from the seventh to the eighth centuries, has been found at Sa Morakot (see Brown 1990: 106). For a survey of types of footprints in Cambodia, see also Leclère 1899: 481–95; Bizot 1971.

[38] Some are, in fact, replicas of other famous footprints, such as that at Adam's Peak. See Fournereau 1895, 1:242–54; and Griswold 1967: 54.

[39] For various studies of these auspicious marks on the bottom of buddha feet, see Burnouf 1852: 622–47; Alabaster 1871: 286–310; Leclère 1899: 488–91; Mya 1936: 323ff.; Perera 1971: 451–53; Bizot 1971: 411–19; Karunaratne 1976; Skilling 1992, 1996; Quagliotti 1998: 79–107; Lorillard 2000: 33–37. Such marks could be read by persons knowledgeable in signs. A Pali legend, for instance, tells the story of a brahmin woman who realized, from her examination of his footprints, that the Buddha was one who had given up lust and forsaken the world and so was not a suitable match for her daughter (*DhA.*, 1:201 = Eng. trans., Burlingame 1921: 775–76; see also Obeyesekere 2001: 54).

[40] Vogel (1925:17) refers to these as "svayambhu" ("self-born") footprints. For cases of the Buddha leaving his footprints in different places during a tour of Northeastern Thailand, see Pruess 1976:18–22.

exist only when the Buddha deliberately wills them to. According to a number of Pali commentaries, the Buddha only leaves tracks when he consciously wants to do so for the sake of other beings; ordinarily his footprints cannot be perceived (*DhA.*, 3:194 = Eng. trans., Burlingame 1921, 3:32; *AA.*, 3:77–78; see also Brown 1990: 95–96). A Sinhalese tradition specifies that the Buddha's foot generally brushes the ground as though it were cotton wool; it leaves no impression, and, if it did, people following the Buddha would want to stop and venerate it and this would impede their progression (Hardy [1853] 1995: 367). A Khmer text on the worship of the Buddha's prints makes much the same point, only more elaborately. It indicates that, generally speaking, the Buddha leaves no footprints, since golden lotuses spring up from the ground wherever he walks. These lotuses disappear as soon as the Buddha moves on or sits down. Occasionally, however, the lotuses fail to appear, and traces in the sand can be seen. But when this happens, a wind immediately arises and blows the footprints away. The reason for this obliteration is to avoid having people inadvertantly step upon the Holy Footprints of the Buddha, an act of desecration that would entail grave demerit, and possibly immediate disaster. Footprints that are left, therefore, are special and intended to be recognizable objects of cult, and these, nothing can obliterate (Bizot 1971: 413; see also Perera 1971: 457).

Perhaps for this reason, these footprints are, for the most part, far larger than a normal human foot.[41] Sometimes they show some of the auspicious signs said to be on the soles of the Buddha's feet, but usually they are not much more than very weathered depressions in some natural rock formation, with few, if any, discernible marks on them. Indeed, some of them, at least, would hardly be recognized as footprints at all were it not for pilgrimage traditions centered around them, or nearby inscriptions pointing them out. "It requires a great deal of imagination to trace it out," said Lieutenant Malcolm of the footprint on Adam's Peak in 1815 (see Skeen 1870: 339).[42] "Likeness to foot there is none," said Henry Alabaster (1871: 284) of the Phrabat in Saraburi, Thailand, in the late nineteenth century.[43] "All that is visible," said Charles DeFacieu of the footprint in Minbu District in Burma, is "an egg-shaped depression . . . [that] does not bear the faintest resemblance to the human foot. It has

[41] The argument is sometimes made that the size of the footprints reflects the giant stature of the Buddha, said to be sixteen feet tall. But even such a great being would not have feet so large. Charpentier (1918: 1) connects the size to the disease, elephantiasis (Skt: *ślīpada*; Pali: *sīpada*), a word he associates with the oversized footprint on Śrīpāda—Adam's Peak [!]

[42] Fournereau (1895, 1:243) called the same print "a shapeless cavity, dug into the rock, without any visible sculpture; it may be that it is just a natural phenomenon."

[43] For an interesting account of a pilgrimage to the Phrabat by the Thai king and a Dutch party, see Van den Heuvel 1997: 11–50.

neither heel nor toes. It is covered with thin gold leaves, which pilgrims stick on it annually." (see Mya 1936: 321).[44]

The number of these pāribhogika footprints is hard to estimate, and may indeed fluctuate as the location of certain prints is either rediscovered or forgotten (Bizot 1971: 421–22). Certain Theravāda traditions, however, have tended to limit the number of famous ones to just a few. Thus Guy Tachard ([1688] 1981: 298), a European ambassador to the Thai court in the late seventeenth century, was told that people "from all parts" go on pilgrimage and honor the footprints left by the Buddha in "three different places, in the Kingdom of Siam [i.e., the Phrabat, in Saraburi Province], the Kingdom of Pegu [i.e., in Minbu in Burma], and the Isle of Ceylon [i.e., on Adam's Peak]." Similarly, Burmese children, at least those of a couple of generations ago, were taught to say nightly bedtime "prayers" in honor of three footprints, that the Buddha had left on earth before his parinirvāṇa. One of these was said to be in Sri Lanka (i.e., at Adam's Peak); the other two were located in Burma (in Minbu District) (Mya 1936: 320–21). In Sri Lanka itself, an oral tradition preserved by monks cites four footprints, which it tends to situate in the four cardinal directions—on Adam's Peak, in Yonakapura, in the Nammadā River, and on Mount Saccabandha (Wirz 1948: 62–63; see also Lorillard 2000: 24; Aksland 2001: 107; Perera 1971: 451).

More standardly, perhaps, a Khmer source, reflecting a Pali mnemonic verse still learned by Theravāda monks today, specifies that there are *five* places in the world with most excellent genuine footprints that are worthy of worship: Suvaṇṇamāli, Suvaṇṇapabbata, Sumanakūṭa, the Nammadā River, and Mount Saccabandha (Bizot 1971: 413). Sumanakūṭa, as we shall see, is one of the names for Adam's Peak in South Central Sri Lanka, and the footprint there is well known. But the location and identity of the other sites are not always evident and tend to fluctuate from one tradition to the next. Suvaṇṇamāli is one of the names for the Mahāthūpa, the great stūpa at the Sri Lankan capital of Anurādhapura (*Mhv.* 27.3 = Eng. trans., Geiger 1912: 182), but there is no known tradition of a famous footprint there today or in Sri Lankan sources. Nonetheless, the Chinese pilgrim Faxian mentions a tradition in which it is thought that the Buddha, when visiting Sri Lanka, stood with one foot on top of Adam's Peak, and the other "north of the royal city [i.e., Anurādhapura]" and that over that footprint the king built "a great stūpa four hundred feet tall . . . of gold and silver and . . . decorated with . . . various kinds of jewels" (Li 2002: 204; text in *T.* 2085, 51:864c).[45] The identity

[44] Even more formless are the "footprints" in the Straits of Malacca studied most recently by Caldwell and Hazlewood 1994.

[45] An even more extraordinary claim made in Sinhala folklore, but clearly reflecting Muslim influence, is that the Buddha stood with one foot on Adam's Peak and the other in the sands

of Suvaṇṇapabbata (the "golden mountain") is equally uncertain, but in Thai tradition, it refers to the place of the footprint (Phrabat) in Saraburi, and, by legend, is associated with the story of Mount Saccabandha (Manowattanan 1995: 6).[46] The Nammadā River is, on the basis of Pali materials, said to be located in Sunāparanta, and is commonly identified with the Nerbudda River, in Western India (Malalasekera [1938] 1960, 2:1211). Burmese tradition, however, transfers the whole of Sunāparanta to Middle Burma, and identifies the Nammadā with a small stream in Sagu township in the district of Minbu (Duroiselle 1905: 167; Mya 1936: 321). Thai and Khmer sources generally place it in Northern Thailand, in the region called Yonakaraṭṭha (Yonok) (see Porée-Maspero 1962–69, 2:365n.2 and 3:733).[47] The footprint on Mount Saccabandha is often closely connected, in legend, with the Nammadā relic (Malalasekera 1960, 2:1211). Accordingly, Burmese and Cambodian and Thai traditions have also transposed it to locations in Southeast Asia (see Mya 1936; Law 1952: 61; Alabaster 1871: 245–310).[48]

It is not possible to consider here the whole history and cult of each of these footprints. I shall, rather, concern myself primarily with the stories of their origin—of the Buddha's visits to these lands and his leaving his footprints on them. In what follows, I shall consider, first, together, stories of the footprints on Mount Saccabandha and on the bed of the Nammadā River, and then the legend of Adam's Peak (Sumanakūṭa).

The Saccabandha and Nammadā Footprints

The tale of these two relics is associated with the Pali legend of Puṇṇa (Skt.: Pūrṇa), a disciple of the Buddha who is said to have been born in the land of Sunāparanta.[49] After becoming ordained, Puṇṇa goes back to his native land where he soon becomes enlightened. Realizing that his fellow countrymen have never had a chance to see the Buddha and that they

---

of Mecca, where, rumor had it, there was a great stūpa enshrining the relic (the Makkama Mahāvihāra). Accordingly, the Buddha was sometimes called "the sage of Mecca" (Makkama Muni). See Obeyesekere 1984: 135–36, 307.

[46] For this reason, perhaps, Thai Pali listings of the five footprints do not include Saccabandha. Instead, they mention Yonakapura, in Northern Thailand. See Bidyalankarana 1935: 1. On the Saraburi shrine, see Van den Heuvel 1997.

[47] The Yonaka country is sometimes (see Malalasekera 1960, 2:699) located in Northwest India. On its identity in Northern Thailand, see Law 1952: 54–58; Vickery 1976: 362.

[48] More generally, on this kind of geographical transposition of Indian sites to Southeast Asia, see Duroiselle 1905; and Aung-Thwin 1981.

[49] On the legend of Puṇṇa, see *SA* 2:373ff = Fr. trans., Duroiselle 1905: 161–66; *MA* 5:85–92 = Eng. trans., Tatelman 2000: 180–87. The Sanskrit version, the *Pūrṇāvadāna,* is found in *Div.,* 24–55 = Eng. trans., Tatelman 2000: 46–95, as well as in *Avk.* 1:233–38 = Eng. trans., Tatelman 2000: 192–99, but it makes no mention of the footprint relics.

are eager to do so, he uses his newly acquired supernatural powers to fly to Śrāvastī, where he formally invites the Blessed One to pay a visit to his homeland. The Buddha agrees, and the next day, together with 499 disciples, he flies through the air to Sunāparanta. Along the way they stop at the mountain called Saccabandha, where they meet a heretic teacher of the same name, who has been leading people astray with his false doctrines. The Buddha preaches the dharma to him, and immediately Saccabandha not only attains arhatship but finds himself transformed into a monk, his layclothes magically replaced by monastic robes, his head suddenly shaven, and his hands carrying a bowl. Thus "ordained," he joins the Buddha's party, and, together, the group proceeds on its way. In Sunāparanta, they are cordially received by Puṇṇa and the entire population, and the Buddha preaches there for seven days, converting thousands of people. On his way home, he stops on the banks of the Nammadā River, where he is welcomed by a nāga king who is a devout Buddhist, and who invites him into his home. When it comes time for the Buddha to leave, the nāga king asks him for some sort of memento by which he can continue to honor him after his departure, and the Buddha obliges him by leaving the mark of his footprint (*pādaceṭiya*) on the riverbank. Depending on the height of the water, we are told, this relic is sometimes visible and sometimes not, but greatly venerated in any case, by humans and nāgas alike (*MA.*, 5:86–92 = Eng. trans., Tatelman 2000: 180–85; see also Duroiselle 1905: 161–66).[50] Leaving the Nammadā River, the Buddha and his entourage then stop again at the mountain, where they leave Saccabandha, who, in bidding farewell to the Buddha, also asks for a relic that he can use as an object of veneration. Once again, the Blessed One obliges by impressing his footprint in the solid rock of the mountain, as though it were soft mud (*MA.*, 5:92 = Eng. trans., Tatelman 2000: 186).

The Pali commentaries that recount this story assume that Mount Saccabandha and the Nammadā are located not far from one another in Western India. However, in Thai and Burmese sources, as we have seen, the story has been transfered to Southeast Asia. Both these vernacular traditions, moreover, suggest that these original sites, established by the Buddha, were lost and forgotten (in some cases, several times) until they were more definitely "rediscovered" and "reconnected" to the parent tradition. Thus, it was not until the early seventeenth century that a passing hunter, following a wounded deer, happened across the Saccabandha footprint, in the Saraburi region of Thailand, not too far from the capital of Ayutthya. Upon being told the news, the king "sent a number of learned monks to examine it, and compare it with the description of the

[50] There are many other traditions of the Buddha leaving a footprint on the bed of a river. For two examples, see Porée-Maspero 1962–69, 2:365n; and Archaimbault 1966: 15, 28n.2.

Buddha's foot in the sacred books," and the place soon became the Phrabat—"the great Siamese memorial of Buddha"(Alabaster 1871: 253–54; see also Van den Heuvel 1997: 84–85; Wood 1924: 170).

Similarly, the Burmese footprint in Minbu was "rediscovered" under "quasi-miraculous" circumstances at more or less the same time. The story goes that the king of Ava, having heard one day the tale of the relic as contained in the Pali commentaries, made inquiries about it. He then sent some monks (along with an army of five thousand men to protect them against the Chins and the Karens) to search for it. The monks sailed down the Irrawady as far as Minbu, where they stopped for the night. This was the region thought to be the Sunāparanta of the Pali Commentaries, and that night, the head monk dreamt he met a man who told him that, if he wished to find the prints left by the Buddha, he should follow a black dog. The next day, the search party set out, and, as they were about to enter a woods, they met the black dog. It led them as far as a stream, which turned out to be the "Nammadā river." There they eventually found the sacred footprint, guided by the light it emitted. Nearby was a mountain, where they were led to the exact spot of the "Saccabandha" footprint by a black crow, an incarnation of the protective deity of the hill. In time, a cetiya was built over the footprint and each year, thousands of pilgrims come to visit it from all over Burma (Alabaster 1871: 253–54).

The Footprint on Adam's Peak

If the traditions about the Mount Saccabandha and Nammadā footprints are mixed and fluctuating, those about the "most famous" footprint of the Buddha—the one on Sumanakūṭa (aka Samantakūṭa, aka Sri Pāda, aka Adam's Peak) in South Central Sri Lanka—are relatively more stable. We have already seen how, on his first apocryphal visit to Sri Lanka, the Buddha is said to have given some hair relics to Mahā Sumana, the god of Adam's Peak, which were then enshrined at Mahiyangana. According to the *Mahāvaṃsa,* on his *third* visit to the island, in the eighth year after his enlightenment, the Buddha went first to Kelaniya, where he was entertained by a nāga king, Maṇiakkhika. Then, after he had preached the dharma there, "he rose . . . and left his foot[print] on Sumanakūṭa" (*Mhv.,* 10 = Eng. trans., Geiger 1912: 8). That is all that the chronicle tells us.

In time, however, Adam's Peak became one of the sixteen major pilgrimage sites in Sri Lanka (see Gombrich 1971: 109–10), but it is quite likely that it too was "forgotten" or at least not developed as a center of worship for a number of centuries.[51] Despite an oral tradition that claims

[51] For an account of a modern day pilgrimage, see Aksland 2001: 66–107.

that King Vaṭṭagāmaṇī Abhaya (c. 100 B.C.E.) was led to the footprint by a deer he was hunting (Skeen 1870: 16–17), we have to wait until the time of King Vijayabāhu I (1059–1114 C.E.) for more solid historical references. In 1111 C.E., he left an inscription at Ambagamuva, not far from the mountain, in which he declares that he made offerings of various sorts (including his own crown) to the footprint at "Samanoḷa rock" (Adam's Peak), which the previous buddhas of this aeon had also visited. The inscription goes on to specify that he built rest-stations and alms houses for pilgrims, both lay and monastic, and that he dedicated a number of properties in villages in the surrounding area to the service of the footprint, and that on the mountain itself, he enclosed the upper terrace with a wall and two gates, and constructed below it a lower terrace from which low caste people could worship the relic (Wickremasinghe 1928: 217–18). Clearly, it was at this time (early twelfth century) that the tradition of pilgrimage to the mountain must have begun in earnest.

By the thirteenth century, the footprint on Adam's peak was the focus of a long eulogistic poem in Pali by Vedeha Thera, a forest-dweller monk who may have lived not far from the mountain. His panegyric, the *Samantakūṭavaṇṇanā,* begins by recalling the whole life of the Buddha, including his first two visits to Sri Lanka before climaxing with an account of his third. At the invitation of the nāga king Maṇiakkhika, the Buddha flies to Kelaniya, where he and his retinue are honored by the nāgas, and where he also meets Sumana, the god of Adam's Peak. The latter invites the Buddha to come to his mountain and to "make a pure mark there with the rays of his foot" (*Skv.,* 721 = Eng. trans., Hazlewood 1986: 86).[52] "O Chief of Sages," he declares, "you made an imprint of your foot on the bank of the River Nammadā at the meeting of the river with the ocean—may this compassion of yours be towards me also! Invited by the ascetic Saccaka, you made an imprint of your foot on Mount Saccakabandha for the good of the world—may that favour of yours be towards me also!" (Hazlewood 1986: 93–94, slightly altered; text in *Skv.,* 72–73).[53] And the Buddha obliges him by making an imprint there with his left foot, the way a ruler might mark a piece of wax with his signet ring. Instantly, a cloud comes up and rains down upon the footprint a shower not only of water but of jewels, flowers, and gold (*Skv.,* 73 = Eng. trans., Hazlewood 1986: 94).

[52] The auspicious marks on the sole of the foot—most of them symbols of sovereignty—are then described at some length.

[53] In the *Saddharmaratnakāra,* a fifteenth-century Sinhala text, the Buddha's visit to Sri Pāda is actually prefaced with the story of his trip to Sunāparanta, and he is described as coming to the island directly *from* Mount Saccabandha. He is also said to leave a footprint in the bed of the river at Kelaniya for the nāgas. See Hardy [1853] 1995: 209–212.

It is not possible to trace here the further traditions about this footprint.[54] It should be pointed out, however, that it was an object of devotion for more than just Buddhists. Indeed, it came to be thought of also as the footprint of Adam (by Muslims, as well as some Christians—see Rosenthal 1989: 292; Hussein 1976: 222–23; Skeen 1870: 58), of Thomas the Apostle (by other Christians—see Tennent 1859, 2:138; Ludowyk 1958: 19), of Śiva (by some Tamil Hindus—see Paranavitana 1958: 21; Skeen 1870: 9–10), of the eunuch of Candace, Queen of Ethiopia (by some Portuguese—see Smith 1918), of Pangu (by the fifteenth-century Chinese Ma Huan—see Paranavitana 1958: 21). Starting in the sixteenth century, a number of Portuguese adventurers visited the peak (see Pieris 1909: 168–70; De Queyroz 1930, 1:37–42), and Robert Knox, who lived in the Kandyan Kingdom in the seventeenth century, often mentions it as a popular place of pilgrimage (Knox 1958: 136). The first Englishman to have climbed the peak seems to have been Lieutenant Malcolm of the 1st Ceylon Rifles. He made it to the top in April 1815 only weeks after the British conquest of the Kandyan kingdom. He reports the belief that the footprint was that of Adam. Lacking a Union Jack (which he had hoped to hoist on the peak to spite the priest who had told him that no white man could ever ascend the mountain), he fired three volleys instead, to the surprise of the Buddhist and Hindu pilgrims who were there (see Skeen 1870: 337–40).

Conclusion

It is a long way from the Buddha's apocryphal visits to Burma, Thailand and Sri Lanka to Lieutenant Malcolm's conquest of Sri Pāda, and we have by no means exhausted, even for South Asia, the traditions relating to footprints (and hair relics). Enough has been said, however, to allow for some conclusions about these relics of the still-living Buddha. Hair relics and footprints serve, as we have seen, to make the Buddha present where he is not, both during and after his lifetime. Not being a product of his dead body, they bear a slightly different symbolic thrust than bones, ashes, and teeth taken from the cremation fire. If the latter hearken back to the event of the Buddha's decease and parinirvāṇa, his hairs and footprints recall, for the most part, encounters with or visits of the living, preaching, still-in-this-world Buddha. They are, or were initially, substi-

[54] The *Cūḷ.* contains many references to kings who gifted villages to the footprint, built or repaired structures there, erected resthouses, improved the staircase access, or made pilgrimages and offerings there. See Geiger 1929, 1:221, 2:128, 170, 172, 186, 221–22, 240, 241–42, 253, 292. For a survey of reports by visitors to the mountain over the years, see Charpentier 1918 and Aksland 2001: 41–55, 118–40.

tutes for a Buddha who could not physically be present or remain everywhere. Typically, they are given to devotees who request them as an ongoing object of devotion or as a safeguard against backsliding, at the time of the Buddha's departure, when they realize that he cannot stay with them always. They are thus extensions of the Buddha's own physical self rather than metamorphoses of his body.

A number of themes can be discerned in the various traditions about hair relics and buddha footprints, and it may be useful to spell these out here. First of all, they were clearly early means of expressing or asserting the spread of the dharma to a given area, especially a place that had not known Buddhism before. In this regard, it is significant that Sunāparanta, Sri Lanka, Burma, Thailand, were all non-Buddhist and rather remote areas when the Buddha supposedly visited them. As in Christianity, relics in Buddhism often served the missionizing purpose of extending and establishing the religion in regions where it was previously unknown or to which it was just spreading (see Brown 1981). In this, they were almost inevitably related to politics and the state.

Formally putting one's foot down on or in a country or place is, of course, a symbolic assertion of sovereignty and dominance. The traditional markings thought to be on the sole of the Buddha's foot, and replicated on at least some of the footprints, further iterate that symbolism. For the most part these signs, whether they number 108 or not, are symbols of the cosmos and of the sovereignty of a cakravartin king. The most common of these emblems—the wheel—in fact directly recalls the Dharma Wheel, by which a cakravartin conquers the cosmos (see *D.*, 3:58ff. = Eng. trans., Walshe 1987: 395ff.), and the other symbols—of Mount Meru, the continents, the emblems of sovereignty, etc.—reinforce that message. As François Bizot (1971: 438) has put it, "[T]he sacred footprint takes on the character of an ideal microcosm, a replica of the universe governed according to the Dharma. . . . The Buddha, and the Wheel which he puts in motion, preside over the structural and temporal order of the world." The impressing of a buddha footprint thus represents an imposition of Buddhist Order on a land.

The same symbolism of cosmic conquest and order—obvious in the case of footprints— may perhaps also be found in some traditions about hair relics. Thus, in a sequel to the story of the Buddha's haircut by Upāli given earlier, the Buddha's hair clippings, once enshrined in a new vase, are given to the son of a king, a general named Gopāli. Being careful to treat the hair relics with respect (they are transported in caskets on elephant back or on the heads of soldiers), Gopāli takes them with him on his military campaigns in Western India, and, thanks to their magical efficacy, he is always victorious, establishing the rule of dharma wherever he goes. He then returns to his capital, where he builds a large stūpa for the hairs (*T.* 1428, 22:957a–b = Fr. trans., Bareau 1962: 262. See also Demiéville 1934: 170). In this story, then, the hair relics function much as would a cakravartin's wheel: they make possible the conquest of new lands.

The cosmic dimensions of this spread are reinforced by the notion that the relics are to be extended to all realms of the cosmos. This can be expressed horizontally, as in the Mon assertion that the hundreds of thousands of hairs of the Buddha's head and body were distributed "throughout this universe," or, as in the *Chronicle of the Six Hair Relics,* where the hairs are taken to the various directions for enshrinement. Or it can be expressed vertically, as in the same text's assertion that the six hair relics were enshrined by a whole hierarchy of divinities, from Indra at the top to local spirits and nāgas at the bottom. Much the same verticality is implicit in traditions about footprints that are impressed either on mountain tops (Adam's Peak, Saccabandha) or on river bottoms (the Nammadā). Mountains (beginning with Mount Meru) are commonly, in Buddhism, the abode of the gods, Adam's Peak being no exception. There, the footprint was both for pilgrims who made the ascent, but also for the divinity Sumana.[55] Similarly, the footprint on the bed of the Nammadā was both for humans and for the nāgas, a duality reinforced by the fact that, depending on the height of the water, it was sometimes visible and sometimes covered. It was thus in the interest of the nāgas periodically to "bring on the rains" so as to be able to submerge the footprint and reclaim it for worship.[56] The intermediate position of these relics points to their liminal status as commodities of communication and control between human beings and other realms. Viewed in this way, the footprints of the Buddha (and perhaps relics in general) may be seen as meeting points between worlds, as places where humans and deities, or humans and nāgas, may encounter each other. At the same time, the periodic visibility and invisibility of the Nammadā relic—its submergence and resurfacing—reinforces the notion that buddhas come and go, that they become present and are then absent.

Finally, it is important to note that all of these footprints and hair relics are being impressed on and enshrined in new lands with the cooperation and consent of indigenous forces. In virtually all of the stories we have looked at, the Buddha is invited to these new lands by locals. Sometimes, these locals are humans (Trapuṣa and Bhallika, the ascetic Saccabandha),

[55] This theme was also iterated in Muslim traditions about the peak; according to al-Ṭabarī (Rosenthal 1989: 292–93), the mountain was so close to heaven (and Adam was so tall) that, though he was standing on the ground, he could hear the angels in paradise.

[56] On this theme of the relation of relics and other rituals to climatic cycles in "monsoon Asia," see Porée-Maspero 1962–69: 730ff; and Archaimbault 1972: 88ff. On the use of Buddhist relics in rainmaking, see chapter seven of this book. For East Asia, see Ruppert 2002a: 157–58.

on other occasions, they are divinities and spirits (the nats of Rangoon, the god of Adam's Peak, the nāga of the Nammadā River, the various gods and spirits in the *Chakesadhātuvaṃsa*). The presence (or at least the future presence) of the Buddha and his relics in these lands, therefore, is presented as something that is requested or agreed to, not imposed. The hair relics and footprints, however, do not always signify the immediate conversion of these new lands, for there is a sense in which they, and especially the footprints, may be thought to lay latent for a while, until the land is ready for the actual teaching of the dharma. Donald Swearer has spoken eloquently of the ways in which relics of the Buddha—at least in the Southeast Asian tradition—may be seen as seeds that are planted in new soil only to emerge and be cultivated at a later date (Swearer and Sommai 1998: 25). The visits of the Buddha thus prepare the land for future growth. Here, obviously, the theme of the discovery or "rediscovery" of the site of these relics comes to the fore, and, with it, the notion that this discovery is intended, and brought on by local protective forces, often symbolized by the animals—deer, crow, dog—who typically reveal the site of the relic, or by some other type of "miracle"—the relic itself refusing to move on (as at Girihaṇḍu in Sri Lanka).

Chapter Four

THE PARINIRVĀṆA OF THE BUDDHA

THE *Mahāparinirvāṇa-sūtra,* in its many versions, is one of the most studied of Buddhist texts, as well as one of the earliest substantial fragments of a buddha biography.[1] It recounts the last days of the Buddha's life and contains many fascinating episodes and important teachings—the final sermons and advice of the Blessed One to his disciples, his last conversions and concerns. It is of special interest to us here, however, because it recounts also the funeral ceremonies undertaken for the Buddha at Kuśinagarī,[2] in the land of the Mallas, where he died between the twin śāla trees, and it details the treatment and preparation of his body, its cremation, and the subsequent collection and distribution of his relics.

It is, of course, impossible to do justice here to the whole of the *Mahāparinirvāṇa-sūtra,* so I shall enter the narrative at a point just slightly before the actual death of the Buddha, when the Buddha tells his disciple Ānanda about the proper treatment of a tathāgata's corpse. I will then follow the course of events, pausing to consider various features of the Buddha's funeral and instances of the post-mortem but pre-cremation veneration of his body. Finally, I will deal with the immolation of that body, and the post-cremation dispute over and distribution of the Buddha's bodily relics to no fewer than eight monarchs. Throughout, the theme of this chapter will be a simple one: the *Mahāparinirvāṇa-sūtra* ends and culminates with the distribution of the Buddha's relics. Far from being a postscript, these relics are, in fact, the governing motif that helps determine the whole shape and format of the Buddha's obsequies up to and including his cremation; the Buddha's funeral rites thus have less to

[1] On the place of the *MPS.* in the gradual development of the Buddha's biography, see Lamotte 1988: 650–51 and Reynolds 1976. The text itself exists in multiple renditions. For the Sanskrit, see *MPS.*, 102–453; for the Pali, see *D.*, 2:71–168 = Eng. trans., Davids 1899–1924, 2:78–191, and Walshe 1987: 231–77; for Chinese versions, see *T.* 1, 1:11–30 = Ger. trans., Weller 1939–40; *T.* 5, 1:160–75; *T.* 6, 1:176–190; *T.* 7, 1:193–207, and *T.* 1451, 24:382–402 = Ger. trans., Waldschmidt 1950–51: 103–496. For the Tibetan *Mūlasarvāstivāda Vinaya* version, see Waldschmidt 1950–51: 103–496 = Eng. trans., Rockhill 1907: 122–47 (see also Obermiller 1931–32, 2:56–67). For studies of these sources, see Przyluski 1920, Waldschmidt 1944–48, and Bareau 1970–71, 1975, and 1979.

[2] In Pali texts, this town is called Kusinārā. I have opted to use the Sanskrit Kuśinagarī, which is the form used in the *MPS.* The name Kuśigrāmaka is also found.

do with the treatment of his body and the mourning of his passing than they have to do with the preparation of his relics.

The Duties to the Corpse

In the Pali version of the text (the "Mahāparinibbāna-sutta," which is part of the *Dīgha Nikāya*), the Buddha's disciple Ānanda, as part of a whole series of requests for last-minute instructions and admonitions from his master, asks what should be done with the Blessed One's body (sarīra) after his death? The Buddha, at least initially, answers, "Do not worry yourselves about the funeral arrangements, Ānanda. You should strive for the highest goal, devote yourselves to the highest goal, and dwell with your minds tirelessly, zealously devoted to the highest goal. There are wise Khattiyas [Skt.: kṣatriyas], Brahmins and householders who are devoted to the Tathāgata: they will take care of the funeral" (Walshe 1987: 264; text in *D.*, 2:141. See also Waldschmidt 1944–48: 213–16; and Bareau 1970–71, 2:36).

The word that Maurice Walshe translates here as "funeral arrangements" is *sarīrapūjā* (Skt.: *śarīrapūjā*). It has sometimes been taken to mean "the worship of relics," and the passage has been interpreted as an indication that monks are not to concern themselves with such things—that the cult of relics is something that lies entirely in the provenance of the laity (see Hirakawa 1963: 102; Bareau 1970–71, 2:37). Gregory Schopen, however, has convincingly argued that such an interpretation is wrong (1997: 99–113). On the one hand, there is plenty of evidence for the involvement of monks in relic worship. On the other, *śarīra* is here intended as a singular, and when used in that way, it means "body" rather than "relics" (Schopen 1997: 101–2; see also Norman 1990–92, 2:250–68). *Śarīra-pūjā* thus does not appear to focus on the post-mortem cult of a person's enshrined relics as much as it does on the preparation of the body for cremation and commemoration. As such, it means "the worship of the body," or, less literally, "the funeral arrangements," and, as Schopen (1997: 99ff.) points out, Ānanda is essentially being told here not to worry about the whole business of carrying out the Buddha's obsequies.

More specifically, a śarīra-pūjā would seem to involve a particular sequence of ritual acts. In the very next paragraph of the Pali text (*D.*, 2:141–42 = Eng. trans., Walshe 1987: 264), Ānanda—although he has just been told not to worry about the whole business—still wants to know what should be done with the body of the Tathāgata.[3] And this time, the

[3] In *MPS.*, 358, Ānanda repeats his question so that he can later tell the brahmins and householders how they should carry out the ceremonies. For studies of parallel versions of this episode, see Waldschmidt 1944–48: 213–16 and Bareau 1970–71, 2:35ff.

Buddha answers him. The body of a tathāgatha, he says, should be (a) treated in the same manner as that of a cakravartin king.[4] This means that it should be (b) wrapped in alternating layers of new cloth and teased cotton wool (five hundred pieces of each)[5] and (c) placed in a sort of sarcophagus made of an iron vessel (Pali: *doṇī,* Skt.: *droṇī*) filled with oil (Pali: *tela,* Skt.: *taila*), which is then to be covered with another iron oil vessel.[6] Throughout this period, implicit in the very notion of śarīra-pūjā (though not explicitly mentioned by the Buddha here) are (d) various ritual forms of veneration (pūjā) of the Buddha's body which I shall examine as a sort of excursus. Returning to the list, we then find the injunction that (e) the Tathāgata's body be cremated on a fire made with all sorts of odoriferous woods, (f) that his relics / remains be collected,[7] and (g) that a stūpa be erected for him at a crossroads.[8] In what follows, I want to comment on each one of these points.

The Funeral of a Cakravartin

The introductory injunction that the Buddha's śarīra-pūjā should be like that of a cakravartin king may be dealt with rather quickly. In the *Mahāparinirvāṇa-sūtra,* the theme is reinforced by the argument that the site of the Buddha's death and funeral was itself once the capital of a great cakravartin king. Indeed, upon arrival at Kuśinagarī, Ānanda calls the place a "miserable little town of wattle-and-daub" in the middle of nowhere, and asks the Buddha why he has chosen to die in it rather than in some more grandiose and famous city (*D.,* 2:146 = Eng. trans., Walshe 1987: 266; *MPS.,* 304–5). The Buddha responds by extolling the past glories of the town—once called Kuśavatī—and reveals that he himself once, in a former life, dwellt there as the great king Mahāsudarśana, and passed away there, being given the funeral of a wheel-turning monarch. This then is

[4] Though the Pali text uses *sarīra* here to describe the body of a cakravartin, the Sanskrit (*MPS.,* 360) uses *kāya,* a point that Roth (1987: 293) seeks to make much of.

[5] *T.* 1, 1:20 = Ger. trans., Weller 1939–40: 434 adds that the body should first be washed in warm, perfumed water. The same specification occasionally appears elsewhere (see Waldschmidt 1944–48: 296). In most texts, however, no mention is made of washing the Buddha's corpse, it being considered to be inherently pure. See Waldschmidt 1944–48: 213; and Schopen 1994: 38–39.

[6] For a bas-relief, in the Gandhāran style, of the Buddha's coffin, see Foucher 1987: 305.

[7] Schopen (1997: 103, 107) resists the idea that the śarīra pūjā has anything to do, even preliminarily, with the relics. However, though the collection of relics (śarīra) is not specified in the Buddha's instructions in the Pali text, it is in other versions of the story (see Waldschmidt 1944–48: 214–15, and Bareau, 1970–71, 2:46).

[8] At one point, Schopen also seeks to divorce the erection of a stūpa from the funeral ceremony, but later corrects that view (see Schopen 1994: 39).

not the first time he will be dying in this town as a cakravartin—although it will be the last.[9]

This is not the place to examine the origin of the cakravartin ideal and its influence on the legend of the Buddha. Suffice it to say that the parallelism between the Buddha's funeral and that of a cakravartin continues a theme already implied in the doctrine of the twin careers of a mahāpuruṣa. It is sometimes argued that this association with great kingship was intended to enhance the prestige of the Buddha as a figure of great distinction. At the same time, however, it is important to see one of the more specific implications of this. Jean Przyluski, who has looked to Northwest Indian, Hellenistic, and, ultimately, Ancient Near Eastern traditions as sources of at least parts of the cakravartin mythology, has argued that we should look in the same direction for the origins of relic worship in India. He points out that Alexander the Great was divinized and that a dispute erupted over his body, which the Macedonians felt would bring happiness and prosperity to the land where it was kept (Przyluski 1927 and 1935–36: 354–55). Even more specificially, he cites the case of King Menander, whose ashes (according to Plutarch) were divided among the cities of Northwest India, which erected *mnêmeia* [memorials, i.e., caityas] over each portion (Przyluski 1935–36: 354; see also Foucher 1943: 2). For Przyluski, then, the veneration of a great being's remains was intimately linked to the nascent cult of the cakravartin and both were imported ideologies. This is important because, if it is true, the fact that the Buddha's body is to be treated as though it were that of a great king may not simply be intended to "glorify" or "divinize" him. More basically, it may be related to the injunction that his *relics* be preserved, and that his body not be handled like those of ordinary beings or of other sannyāsins, whose remains were not preserved (see Kane 1973: 229–31). This is a theme to which I shall return.

The Corpse's Clothing

The first substantial instance of what a cakravartin's (and hence a tathāgata's) funeral consists of is the specification that his body should be wrapped in five hundred pairs of shrouds or pieces of cloth and then placed in a sort of iron coffin filled with oil. This intriguing injunction has caused much scholarly ink to flow. Alfred Foucher (1987: 318) bemoans

[9] In *D.*, 2:169–200 = Eng. trans., Walshe 1987: 279–90, the *Mahāsuddassana sutta* forms a separate sūtra immediately following the *Mahāparinibbāna sutta*. In all other sources, however, it is incorporated as a whole into the account of the Buddha's parinirvāṇa. See Waldschmidt 1950–51: 304–55.

the difficulty of imagining the Buddha's body as "an enormous mummy, enshrouded in a thousand cotton sheets," and wonders how his disciples could possibly have gotten it into a sarcophagus approaching anything like normal size. André Bareau (1970–71, 2:39), always seeking to demythologize, clearly prefers the one Chinese textual variant that puts the number of shrouds at ten rather than five hundred. Jean Przyluski (1920: 143) is willing to go further, arguing that the number five hundred can be dismissed as hyperbole; what is important here is the notion of a *pair* of cloths, which he sees as garments rather than as shrouds. Charlotte Vaudeville (1964: 84–85), in a study of the description of the Buddha's parinirvāṇa found in the *Avadānaśataka* (260–63 = Fr. trans., Feer 1891: 430–36), is guilty perhaps of "remythologizing" the question. She suggests that the five hundred pairs of "shrouds" referred originally to five hundred layers of flowers that two divinities, resident in the two śāla trees, rained down upon the deceased Buddha. Finally, Ernst Waldschmidt (1944–48: 264) is convinced that the multiple shrouds were intended to help preserve the body from decay in the seven days it had to wait before cremation.

All of our textual sources are agreed that the fabric out of which the shrouds were made (or at least one of the fabrics when two types of cloth are specified) was cotton (see Bareau 1970–71, 2:39–41). In the Pali text, a distinction is made between alternating layers of cotton that is "torn," or "beaten" (*vihata*), and cotton that is "untorn," or "unbeaten" (*ahata*) (*D.*, 2:141–42). Waldschmidt's conclusion (1944–48: 211), as well as Walshe's (1987: 264), is that the former represents some sort of cotton wool, and the latter some sort of new, "unbeaten," that is, never washed, cotton cloth.

It has been suggested, at least since the time of Buddhaghosa, that these kinds of cloth—especially the teased cotton wool—were chosen because they would better absorb the oil in the iron vessel (*DA.*, 2:583).[10] Apparently it was hoped that the oil-soaked cotton would make the body burn better. More specifically, the description of the wrapping of the Buddha's body suggests that he—or rather it—was being made into a sort of human torch or oil lamp. The metaphor is not without significance. At one level, it recalls the old likening of final nirvāṇa (i.e., "extinction") to a fire or lamp going out when all its fuel has been spent, when there is no remainder.[11] In fact, this image is invoked in the Pali account of the Buddha's own cremation, when, we are told, after being completely burned, his body left no ash or soot, "just as an oil or butter [lamp] leaves none when it is burned" (*D.*, 2:164 = Eng. trans., Walshe 1987: 275). At an-

[10] *T.* 5, 1:169 = Fr. trans., Bareau 1970–71, 2:43 likewise specifies that the cotton is to be sprinkled with oil and fat.

[11] See, for a graphic example, *Thag.*, 134–35 = Eng. trans., Norman 1969–71, 2:14–15.

other level, however, the wrapping of the Buddha's body in cotton and the soaking of it in oil recalls (or prefigures) other examples in which kings or great Buddhist devotees transform their bodies into lamps or torches and set them on fire as self-sacrificial expressions of devotion.[12] Thus, the past Buddha Mangala, in one of his previous existences, is said to have "wrapped his whole body in the manner of making a torch" and to have set it ablaze along with a golden thousand-wick butter lamp, as an offering to the caitya of another Buddha (*JA.*, 1:31 = Eng. trans., Jayawickrama 1990: 40. See also *BuvA.*, 143–44 = Eng. trans., Horner 1978: 206–207).[13] Similarly, in a famous passage of the *Lotus sūtra,* we read of the bodhisattva Sarvasattvapriyadarśana, who ate resins and drank oil for twelve years and then wrapped his body in garments and bathed in oil before setting himself ablaze in honor of a Buddha; he burned, we are told, for twelve thousand years (*Sdmp.,* 405–8 = Eng. trans., Kern 1884: 377–80). Sarvasattvapriyadarśana's name suspiciously recalls that of King Aśoka (Priyadarśa), as does his act of building 84,000 stūpas. Thus, it is not surprising to find that Aśoka (at least in one tradition) is also said to have honored the relics of the Buddha by setting himself on fire after "having his own body wrapped in cotton . . . and having himself soaked with five hundred pots of scented oil" (*LP.*, 174 = Fr. trans., Denis 1977, 2:152; see also chapter five of this book).

In China, these self-immolations were sometimes called by one of the terms used for cremation (*shao shen*) (see Benn 1998: 296), and became paradigms for all sorts of related devotional practices, such as suicides by fire or the burning off of fingers or arms.[14] It has long been recognized (Gernet 1960: 542–43; Jan 1964) that virtually all of these autocremations—whole or partial—were done in honor of buddha relics.[15] More recently, however, John Kieschnick has shown (1997: 44) that these practices were also intimately related to the funeral of the Buddha—that they were seen not only as sacrifices, but also as acts of imitation and appropriation, attempts to repeat the Buddha's own cremation and creation of relics.

In this connection, it may be good to recall that, in most accounts of the Buddha's parinirvāṇa, his cremation is actually an autocremation,

[12] On such suicides, in addition to the sources cited later in this paragraph, see La Vallée Poussin 1919, Filliozat 1963, Lingat 1965, Lamotte 1965, and Kieschnick 1997: 37–39. For Yijing's protest against such practices, see *T.* 2125, 54: 231a–b = Eng.trans., Li 2000: 163–65.

[13] A similar tale is told about Śākyamuni in a former life (see Lamotte 1949–80: 688–89).

[14] In *Mil.,* 1:197 = Eng. trans., Davids [1890–94] 1963, 1:276, however, making a torch of the hand or wrapping the arms in oiled clothes and setting them ablaze appear in a long list of painful punishments inflicted on prisoners.

[15] Most famous, perhaps, are the accounts of persons burning off fingers or limbs as offerings to the finger-bone relic in Chang'an during the Tang Dynasty. See Dubs 1946: 11-12; Ch'en 1973: 268–70; Benn 1998: 307n.; Huang 1998.

since his funeral pyre, sometimes after a number of false starts, is said to light itself, spontaneously irrupting into flames through the supernatural power of the Buddha (Bareau 1970–71: 255). I shall return to this theme when we examine the traditions related to Aśoka's stūpa festival in the next chapter. Suffice it to say for now that the wrapping of the Buddha's body in layers of cotton and the soaking of it in oil may be connected to cremation practices that were intended to produce relics.

There is another complication to the question of the Buddha's multiple shrouds, however. That is the cryptic declaration, in most of our sources, that, after the Buddha's cremation, all the envelopping cloths were burnt, except for two of them—the innermost and the outermost ones.[16] Bareau (1970–71, 2:261) finds the texts' emphasis on this rather mysterious, but limits himself to suggesting that we may have, here, evidence of a monastic prudery that felt the need to safeguard the Buddha's decency by covering his "nudity" (even when his body had been reduced to nothing but calcified bones). He may have a point; as we shall see, the issue of the "exposure" of the Buddha's body after death was not uncontroversial, especially when it is believed that the Blessed One was still somehow alive and present in his relics. However, this does not explain why *two* shrouds—the innermost and the outermost—remained unburnt. Vaudeville (1964: 84–85), seeking to address this question, suggests, rather esoterically, that this miracle is somehow symbolic of the progress of the *dual* fire that consumed the body of the Buddha: the flames of the funeral pyre, and the inner heat (*tejas*) of his spontaneous combustion.[17] Jean Przyluski (1920: 102–67, especially, 145–46) takes a rather different tack. As mentioned, he considers these two layers of cloth to be garments rather than shrouds, and, after a long study of a host of sources concerning robes of kings and robes of monks in ancient India, he concludes that this two-layered garb replicated an ancient tradition about the clothing of cakravartin kings.[18] The Buddha was thus cremated dressed not as a monk but as a cakravartin (see Foucher 1987: 318).

There are certain problems with this conclusion, however, as Przyluski himself admits. For one thing, in the Sanskrit and Tibetan versions of the *Mahāparinirvāṇa-sūtra* (*MPS.*, 430–31; Snellgrove 1973: 407n.), the two layers of generic cotton cloth that are left unburned at the end of the cremation are suddenly given a rather specific name: they are called *cīvara*

[16] The Pali text, however, indicates the opposite: that of the thousand layers of cloth, *only* the inner and the outer were consumed. Przyluski (1920: 38n) suspects that, due to a copyist's error, a negative participle disappeared from the text here, but see also Waldschmidt 1944–48: 306n.

[17] Vaudeville's argument works best when considering the Pali version of the story that states that *only* the innermost and the outermost layers were burnt.

[18] Przyluski (1920: 152ff) further wants to relate the Buddha's funerary dress to the two pieces of golden fabric given to him by Putkasa (see Bareau 1970–71, 1:282–99).

(Tib.: *chos gos*), that is, monastic robes.[19] Przyluski (1920: 39) sees in this, evidence of a lost earlier tradition in which the Buddha is cremated in his monastic robes, a tradition whose memory, he thinks, was abolished in certain sects (e.g., the Theravādins) but lingered on in others (e.g., the Mūlasarvāstivādins). Przyluski, however, is probably reading both too much and not enough into the texts here; rather than look for layers of traditions, we may detect here a symbolic transformation in the overall story of the Buddha's cremation. Simply put, the Buddha's cremation makes a monk out of a monarch; it changes his dress from a thousand-layered princely garment (prescribed as one of the marks of the funeral of a cakravartin) to just two monastic robes (cīvara), made of unburnt shrouds from a cremation ground.

It is often pointed out that the Buddha's funeral is modeled on that of a cakravartin, but it is seldom asked wherein it departs from it. This notion that the unburnt shrouds are monastic robes would seem to be such a point. In this, the Buddha's cremation can be viewed as an ordination, as a repetition of his great departure, for, like his great departure, it changes him from being a cakravartin king to being a buddha. Just as Gautama (or any candidate for ordination), at the time of his wandering forth from home, gives up his princely garb in exchange for the robes of an ascetic, and thereby becomes a monk, so too here, in death, his cremation fire chooses the buddha option for the "great man" over that of the great king.

The two monastic robes, however, are not just the dress of the Buddha; they are also the dress of his relics, for we know from at least one version of the story that, after the extinction of the pyre, the relics were found enveloped in the two unburnt shrouds. Thus prepackaged, they were placed in a golden casket and put on a litter (*T.* 7, 1:207a = Fr. trans., Przyluski 1920: 38).[20] As we shall see, this may reflect the need to keep the relics distinct from the ashes of the fire (something that the non-burning of the two shrouds accomplishes neatly), but it also serves further to establish a clear homology between the body of the Buddha and the body of his relics. Like the Buddha's body, the relics are dressed in a double robe made of two pieces of cloth. Like him, they are placed in a golden casket and then carried off in procession. In other words, as Bareau (1970–71, 2:262) has pointed out, the relics here are being treated, and "re-encoffined" in very much the same way as the Buddha's body had been.

[19] The same word is used in *Avś.*, 261 = Fr. trans., Feer 1891: 432). Elsewhere, Waldschmidt (1944–48: 306, 310) claims that *cīvara* means simply a "piece of cloth." See also Bareau 1970–71, 2:259.

[20] In *T.* 1435, 23:436a (see Waldschmidt 1944–48: 312), they are wrapped in the cloths before being put in the urn. Archaeologists have occasionally found relics still wrapped in cloth inside their reliquaries.

The Iron Coffin

I have suggested so far that some of the details of the Buddha's funeral ceremonies can be understood not so much as having to do with his body, as having to do, anticipatorily, with his relics. The same conclusion may be found in the case of the iron oil-vessel (Pali: *tela-doṇī,* Skt.: *taila-droṇī*) that functions as the Buddha's coffin. It too has been the subject of much perplexity. Bareau (1970–71, 2:43) points out that the Indian custom—to this day—is for corpses to be placed directly on the cremation fire, at most on a bier, and he resists the image conveyed by the iron sarcophagus, which leads one to think of the Buddha's body as being baked or deep-fat fried "like a fish."[21] Thus, he would prefer to see the vessel in question as being made of wood rather than of iron; in this way, as the wood burned, the oil would leak out of it and further feed the fire. Since the original implication of the word *doṇa* [Skt.: *droṇa*] is that it is a wooden vessel or box, Bareau (1970–71, 2:43–44) speculates that the vessel came to be seen as made of iron only because, at the time of the composition of the text, iron was a new precious, prestigious metal in the area. Later, when iron was dethroned from its position of preeminent value, the coffin was said to be made of silver or gold.

Ernst Waldschmidt (1944–48: 263–64), on the other hand, sees the vessel full of oil as a means of preserving the body, either because it needed to be transported some distance, or simply to preserve it because of the one-week delay in cremation resulting from the absence of Mahākāśyapa. In support of this theory, he cites the case of King Daśaratha in the *Rāmāyaṇa* (see Pollock 1986: 213) whose body was kept from decaying in a vat of oil (Skt.: taila-droṇī) while awaiting the arrival of his son, whose participation in the funeral was ritually essential. Mahākāśyapa, as the Buddha's chief disciple, would be the monastic equivalent of his eldest son, and, as we shall see, he is similarly late in getting to the site of the Buddha's cremation.

A somewhat different interpretive tack is taken by Jean Przyluski (1920: 185). He too cites Indian instances of an oil vessel being used to preserve a corpse, especially when death has occurred on a journey, far from home, and the body must be transported some distance. This is significant in view of the fact that Kuśinagarī was admittedly an out-of-the

[21] Upon being asked what would happen if a corpse were to be cremated in such a container as the taila-droṇī, the director of a local crematorium in Auburn, Maine, said that, with the top on, there would be a risk of explosion, and with the top off, the corpse would basically get boiled in oil, which would result in "a gross mess" (described as rendered fat with bones floating in it). Personal communication, Gracelawn Memorial Park, Auburn, Maine, 9 June 1999.

way place visited by the Blessed One while on tour far away from his hometown of Kapilavastu or from his usual monastic centers. Przyluski adds, however, that one of the meanings of the word *doṇī* is a trough-shaped canoe,[22] and, with this in mind, he proposes that the place to which the Buddha's body needed to be transported was the Ganges River. He reinforces this thesis with a reminder of the importance of the Ganges as a place for the disposal of the dead—whether of their bodies or their ashes—and of the fact that renunciants, in ancient India, were commonly immersed, or buried in the beds or banks of rivers. He then (1935–36: 345) cites a less-common funeral custom mentioned by Xuanzang in which decrepit persons are put in a simple boat, towed to the middle of the Ganges, and set adrift to float downstream and drown in the river (*T.* 2087, 51:878a = Eng. trans., Li 1996: 62).

This, Przyluski (1935–36: 347–49) affirms, is the paradigm that was followed (metaphorically) in the case of the Buddha's disciple Ānanda, who was not cremated but passed into parinirvāṇa in the middle of the Ganges (see Strong 1992: 65–66), and he proposes that we apply it, at least contextually, to the original form of the funeral of the Buddha. Summing up, Przyluski then concludes,

> In the Buddha's day, part of India remained attached to the custom of obsequies by immersion. Sometimes, the whole body was consigned to the river; sometimes, only the ashes were. In other cases, especially for ascetics, the body was simply buried in the banks of a river that flowed to the sea. We do not know which of these rites was chosen by the disciples of Śākyamuni; it is permitted to suppose that, not many years after the event, contradictory information began to circulate. The use of the double *doṇī* to preserve the body is explained by the necessity to transport it all the way to the Ganges, and this coffin in the form of a canoe did not go without recalling the voyage to the land of the dead. (1935–36: 365–66).

Przyluski's suggestions are imaginative and intriguing, but his views, as well as those of Waldschmidt, run into certain difficulties. It is true that there is non-Buddhist evidence (e.g., the case of Daśaratha in the *Rāmāyaṇa*) for the use of an iron oil-vessel as a means of preserving a corpse in India.[23] The only other *Buddhist* instance of this that I am aware of, however, is the case of Bhaddā, the wife of King Muṇḍa of Magadha.

[22] He cites apparently cognate words in a host of non-Indo-European South Asian languages and suggests a possible indigenous origin to some of the customs surrounding the Buddha's funeral (see Przyluski 1935–36: 341–42). According to *Hobson-Jobson,* the word "dinghy" may be related to *droṇa.* See Yule and Burnell [1903] 1994: 318.

[23] Outside of India, however, one might note Zoroastrian opposition to the use of an iron cauldron for cremating the dead. See Darmesteter 1880: 110–111. I would like to thank Phyllis Granoff for this reference.

When she died, her husband, in despair, sought to preserve her corpse so he could continue to see her body a while longer. Accordingly, he instructed his minister to place her "in an oil vessel (tela-doṇī) made of iron and covered with another iron vessel" (Woodward and Hare 1932–36, 3:48; text in *A.*, 3:58). His minister was willing to do this but thought it a bad idea. He therefore arranged for the elder Nārada to visit the king and preach to him on the impermanence of the body and the need to accept death. King Muṇḍa, seeing the light, then had Bhaddā's body cremated and a stūpa built for her (*A.*, 3:57–62 = Eng. trans., Woodward and Hare 1932–36, 3:48–51). This story is instructive for, in language that exactly recalls the story of the Buddha's parinirvāṇa, it shows Buddhist opposition to the very notion of the preservation of a body in an iron oil-vessel. Given this, and given other Buddhist tales that emphasize acceptance of the fact of death, and given the call in all accounts of the Buddha's own funeral for a cessation of lamentations and an acceptance of his death (Bareau 1970–71, 2:171–74), it seems a little strange to think of such a procedure being advocated, even for a valid reason.

More importantly, however, within the *Mahāparinirvāṇa sūtra* itself, there is a contextual problem with Przyluski's and Waldschmidt's assumption that the purpose of the oil vessel was either to preserve the Buddha's body until the arrival of Mahākāśyapa or to transport it elsewhere. As Waldschmidt (1944–48: 273) himself admits, in all versions of the tale, the body of the Buddha is not actually put in the oil vessel until *seven days* after his death, i.e., just prior to his cremation. Such timing simply makes no sense if the purpose of the action was preservation. Moreover, in virtually all of the sources where the issue is clear, this belated encoffining of the Buddha takes place only *after* he is transported, in procession, from the śāla grove where he died to the site of his cremation (Bareau 1970–71, 2:193). The oil vessel, then, was apparently not used for transportation either.

Przyluski (1920: 184) tries to explain the delay in placing the Buddha's body in the taila-droṇī as being due to the difficulty in finding, in a small town like Kuśinagarī, not only such a coffin, but a thousand shrouds in which to envelop the corpse. Waldschmidt (1944–48: 273), on the other hand, suggests that the non-use of the oil vessel was due to the unwillingness of the authors or redactors of the text to accept the notion that the Buddha's body might actually have decayed. It seems easier to admit, however, that the purpose of the iron oil vessel had not to do with the preservation or transportation of the corpse but with its cremation.

One of the difficulties that can arise in cremations in which the body is placed, uncovered or in a wooden casket, on an open pyre, is the potential mixing that may occur of the remains of the person (i.e., the relics) and the ashes of the fire.[24] The *Mahāparinirvāṇa-sūtra* itself shows signs of this concern. As we shall see, later on, at the time of the actual distribution of the Buddha's relics, the tradition is quite careful to differentiate between bodily remains (śarīra) and "embers from the fire" (*jvalanasya angāra*) in such a way as to imply that these could be kept separate (*MPS.*, 448). There must, therefore, have been some way of keeping the Buddha's relics apart from the remains of the fire, especially when the latter gets extinguished by a rain shower, or a spontaneously appearing flood of water (or of milk).[25] We have already seen how, in some sources, one of the possible functions of the unburnt top and bottom shrouds enveloping the Buddha's body was for them to serve also as an envelope for the relics. It may be that the iron vessel was intended to serve the same purpose. We are not told, in our sources, what happens to the taila-droṇī during and immediately after the Buddha's cremation, but presumably, being made of iron, it would not be consumed by the flames, and so could serve as a means for keeping the relics separate from the fire.

This suggestion, already made by Foucher (1987:318), may put, however, too much emphasis on the burning process and not enough on the symbolic, precursorial, role of the taila-droṇī. It surely is not without significance that the word *droṇī*—meaning "vessel"—is also the name of the brahmin, Doṇa (Skt.: Droṇa) who, as we shall see, effects the division of the relics.[26] It is often thought that the name derives from his using a "droṇa"—a wooden box or bucket used as a measure for grain—to apportion out the Buddha's relics (see Foucher 1987: 379n.321), and indeed, in the final verses of both the Sanskrit and the Pali texts, that word or its Pali equivalent is used to indicate the measure of the portion of relics received by each of the kings (*D.*, 2:167 = Eng. trans., Davids 1899–1924, 2:191; *MPS.*, 450). The actual receptacle, however, that was used by Droṇa to divide the relics is called in both traditions a *kumbha*—a clay pot or jar (*D.*, 2:166 = Eng. trans., Davids 1899–1924, 2:189; *MPS.*, 442). In the Sanskrit text (*MPS.*, 432), a gold kumbha is used by the Mallas as the first receptacle for the relics of the Buddha, and the same word, of course, comes to designate the part of the stūpa that may contain the relics (Kottkamp 1992: 74; see also Harvey 1984: 72–73). If the kumbha and the droṇī are homologizable, then there is further evidence here that the latter was intended less as a sarcophagus than as a

[24] In the Brahmanical tradition (see Kane 1973: 241), a winnowing basket is sometimes used to separate bones from ash.

[25] On the different ways in which the cremation fire is extinguished, see Waldschmidt 1944–48: 307–8 and Bareau 1970–71, 2:261–62.

[26] In the Sanskrit tradition (see *MPS.*, 442), he is also called Dhūmrasagotra, although he is said to come from Droṇa-village.

receptacle for relics. Moreover, some of the descriptions of the droṇī in which the Buddha is encoffined recall reliquaries in another way. Thus, in one text (*T.* 1, 1:20a = Ger. trans., Weller 1939–40: 435), his body is actually put in a gold casket, which is placed in the iron droṇī, which, in turn, is put in a sandalwood coffin. In another, the innermost gold coffin is placed in a silver one, which is put in a copper one, which is put in an iron one (*T.* 7, 1:199c = Fr. trans., Bareau 1970–71, 2:41). Such accounts of multiple coffins inevitably remind one of the sets of nested boxes, often of different metals or woods, commonly used to enshrine relics.[27]

The Veneration of the Buddha's Body

There is another aspect of the Buddha's funeral that needs to be considered. Throughout the sequence of ceremonies, various devotees are also, of course, performing different acts of veneration, paying *pūjā* to the body of the Blessed One. The first to mourn are the Buddha's disciples and the gods who are present at the master's deathbed. The verses they utter on this occasion, mostly expressive of sorrow and of impermanence, have been extensively studied by Przyluski (1920: 5–46) and others (Waldschmidt 1944–48: 254–60; Bareau 1970–71, 2:161–71) and need not be recapitulated here. Their lamentations are brought to an end by a prominent monk (either Ānanda or Anuruddha), who exhorts them to be still and to realize that all composite things are indeed subject to dissolution (*MPS.*, 402–4; Bareau 1970–71, 2:171–74).

We need to focus, however, on subsequent events that mark the period in between the Buddha's death and his cremation. During these seven days, prior to being put in the taila-droṇī, the Buddha's body "lies in state" and is the object of much veneration and celebration by the Mallas of Kuśinagarī. Informed of his passing, they approach the Buddha's body between the twin śāla trees, and make traditional offerings to it of garlands of flowers, cloth, perfumes, music, dance, lights, etc., rituals that, we shall see, may be considered as precursors to later relic venerations. The seven-day delay in cremating the Buddha's corpse is, in fact, intimately linked to these celebrations (and not, as might be thought, to the need to await the arrival of Mahākāśyapa). In the Pali tradition, for instance, the Mallas each day get so intent on and caught up in their devotional offerings to the Buddha's body, that, by the time it occurs to them that they ought now to proceed with his cremation, they realize that "it is too late to cremate the Lord's body today. We shall do so tomor-

[27] For a good picture of such a set, see Zhang 1990: 73–74.

row" (Walshe 1987: 273; text in *D.,* 2:159). The next day (and the next and the next), however, exactly the same thing happens, until a whole week has passed. On the seventh day, when they actually do resolve in time to transport the Buddha's body to the cremation ground, they find they cannot lift it; that is because the gods have in mind a different route for the funeral procession than do the Mallas, and not until the latter acquiesce to the plans of the former, are they able to move the body (*D.,* 2:160 = Eng. trans., Walshe 1987: 273).[28] In other texts, there are other reasons given for the delay, but whatever the excuse, during all this time, the celebrations of dance, song, music, garlands, perfumes, continue nonstop (see Bareau 1970–71, 2:187–92).

Such, of course, is not the usual way of conducting a funeral in India, where it is rarely delayed (see Kane 1973: 212ff.). Some of the Buddha's disciples may have shown extreme sorrow at the passing of the Blessed One, but the Mallas appear to use the occasion for merit making and celebration. As Alfred Foucher (1987: 317) has remarked, we seem here to be dealing with something resembling a village fair, and "we must understand that, over the course of time, the Buddha's obsequies were no longer conceived of as being funereal; they had rather been transformed . . . into a festival of the sort that was to be celebrated in honor of the relics of the Blessed One."

In the midst of this fête, however, one scene is noteworthy for its mournful emotionality, as well as for the controversy it later created. Reflecting on the singular appearance of buddhas in the world, and on the rare opportunity presented by the chance to make offerings to a buddha at the time of his parinirvāṇa, the Buddha's disciple Ānanda decides that he will first give the Malla women a chance to come forward and venerate the Buddha, figuring that they might not otherwise manage to push their way to the front. In many ways, here, Ānanda continues to act as the Buddha's chief protocol officer, in death as in life. At his invitation, the Malla women approach the body of the Blessed One. There, they break into lamentations, circumambulate it, and make all sorts of offerings, except for one old widow who, having nothing to give at all, is carried away with emotion; she bursts out crying and her tears run down

[28] On the various routes proposed for the funeral cortege, see Waldschmidt 1944–48: 273–85 and Bareau 1970–71, 2:195–96. In *T.* 5, 1:173 = Fr. trans., Bareau 1970–71, 2:205, the gods want to participate in the cortege itself but are told that they cannot because the Buddha said brahmins and householders were to take care of the funeral arrangements. The gods therefore "freeze" the Buddha's bier, preventing its removal until a compromise is agreed to whereby the body will be carried by gods (Śakra and Brahmā) on the right, and humans (Ānanda and the Malla king) on the left. Schopen (1998: 261) argues that the route chosen by the gods (*into* the city) shows that the Buddha's body was not thought of as polluting (because it was not thought of as dead).

and wet the Buddha's feet (Waldschmidt 1944–48: 267–70; Bareau 1970–71, 2:185–86).[29]

Ānanda's willingness to espouse the cause of women in the saṃgha is well known.[30] Here, however, it seems to be set in the context of an opposition between himself and the Buddha's disciple Mahākāśyapa. As we shall see, when the latter subsequently venerates the feet of the Buddha himself, he notices that they are spotted and discolored, and that the mark of the wheel on them has been sullied. "The Buddha's body was golden-colored," he declares, "why are his feet now different?" (*T.* 1, 1:28–29 = Ger. trans., Weller 1939–40: 197). Ānanda then explains that the stains and discoloration are due to this old woman crying on them, and Mahākāśyapa reprimands him for neglect of duty (see also Bareau 1970–71, 2:249–51; and *Mtu.*, 1:68 = Eng. trans., Jones 1949–56, 1:55).

Later, in traditions featuring the so-called trial of Ānanda, at the First Council of Rājagṛha, Mahākāśyapa brings up the same episode again as one of a series of faults committed by Ānanda. At the same time, the severity of the particular charge against him is increased. Thus, in addition to being accused of encouraging the Buddha to ordain women (thereby reducing the duration of the dharma); of being faulted for failing to get the Buddha water when he asked for some at the time of his parinirvāṇa; of being reprimanded for failing to ask the Buddha to extend his life until the end of the aeon when he had a chance to; and of being blamed for once treading on the robe of the Buddha when he was washing it;[31] Ānanda is also accused of showing the women who approached the Buddha's body after his parinirvāṇa his "sheath-encased penis." The Buddha's peculiar male organ was one of the thirty-two marks of the Great Man, and Ānanda seeks to justify his action by explaining how he hoped that the women, upon seeing the Buddha's penis, would be ashamed of their female bodies and moved to plant roots of merit so as to be reborn as men (see *T.* 1509, 25:68b = Fr. trans., Lamotte 1949–80, 1:96; *T.* 2043, 50:152b = Eng. trans., Li 1993:104; *T.* 2042, 50:114a = Fr. trans., Przyluski 1923:325).[32]

The rivalry between Ānanda and Mahākāśyapa is given yet another expression in the final story of the veneration of the Buddha's body prior

[29] In Brahmanical ritual it is sometime specified that the corpse should be wrapped in such a way that the feet are left exposed. See Kane 1973: 202.

[30] Most famously, it is Ānanda who helps Mahāprajāpatī convince the Buddha to institute the order of nuns. On Ānanda in general, see Nyanaponika and Hecker 1997: 137–210.

[31] For accounts of all these and bibliographies, see Lamotte 1949–80, 1:94–96n.

[32] See also Przyluski 1926: 15, 233; and Rockhill 1907: 154. In other sources dealing with the First Council, no mention is made of the Buddha's sheath-encased organ; instead, Ānanda is simply accused of having authorized the women to be the first to venerate the body of the Buddha, and to have sullied it with their tears. See Przyluski 1926: 153, 157, 186.

to his cremation: Mahākāśyapa's worship of his feet. The story is well known (see Waldschmidt 1944–48: 185–89; Bareau 1970–71, 2:215–22). Mahākāśyapa, who will play a presiding role in the saṃgha at the First Council, is not present at the time of the Buddha's parinirvāṇa and does not find out about it until a week after it occurs. In the meantime, back in Kuśinagarī, the Mallas have enshrouded the Buddha's body in a thousand layers of cloth and encoffined it in its taila-droṇī, but they find they are unable to light the cremation pyre. This is explained as being due to the gods, who do not want the fire to be lit until the coming of Mahākāśyapa (*MPS.*, 424–27). Fortunately, the latter, having learned on the road of his master's demise, does not tarry long in coming. Upon arrival, he first wants to be able to see the body of Buddha so as to venerate it one last time, before consigning it to the flames. At this point, various sources differ in their accounts of what happens. In the Pali text (*D.*, 2:163 = Eng. trans., Walshe 1987: 275), Mahākāśyapa merely uncovers the Buddha's feet and venerates them before proceeding with the cremation. In the Sanskrit, he proceeds to open the coffin and unwrap the whole of the Buddha's body in order to venerate it. Then he rewraps and re-encoffins it, and lights the cremation fire (*MPS.*, 428). In a number of Chinese accounts of the episode, Mahākāśyapa asks Ānanda for permission to view the Buddha's body, but Ānanda refuses, saying that to do so would be too difficult due to the iron sarcophagus being closed and already on top of the pyre, and to the thousand shrouds enveloping the corpse (Bareau 1970–71, 2:243; *T.* 1, 1:28c = Ger. trans., Weller 1939–40: 197; and *T.* 2087, 51:904b = Eng. trans., Li 1996: 191). This scene, as Waldschmidt (1944–48: 300) has pointed out, once again serves to underline the rivalry between Ānanda and Mahākāśyapa, but it also helps magnify the later miracle of the appearance of the Buddha's feet. And indeed, in these and the remainder of our sources, either in some unexplained way, or through the intervention of the gods, or by miraculous action of the Buddha himself, the Tathāgata's feet emerge from the coffin so that Mahākāśyapa is able to venerate them (Bareau 1970–71, 2:241–42).

The miracle of the feet, moving of their own accord after the Buddha's death, is significant because it is the first graphic example of the Buddha's ongoing magical powers (*ṛddhi*) after his parinirvāṇa (Bareau 1970–71, 2:247–48). As such, it foreshadows similar magical movements, which, as we shall see, will commonly be exhibited by the Buddha's relics. In fact, it may be argued that the Buddha's feet here, though attached to his body, are relics, and that Mahākāśyapa's action is a precursor to the cult of the Buddha's footprints, which, as we have seen, was an important and early form of relic worship in Buddhism (see Cunningham 1879: 112–13).

As the Buddhist tradition developed, however, it was not content with this single miraculous manifestation at the Tathāgata's deathbed. Thus, when Xuanzang visits Kuśinagarī, he refers to stūpas commemorating *three* post-mortem appearances of the Buddha while he was in his coffin. In addition to the time when his feet appeared to Mahākāśyapa, there was also the time when he stuck out his hand to ask Ānanda a question, and the occasion on which he sat up in his coffin to preach the dharma to his mother (*T.* 2087, 51:904b–c = Eng. trans., Li 1996: 191; see also*T.* 2053, 50:235b = Eng. trans., Li 1995: 84). The second of these episodes is relatively obscure,[33] but the third is much more developed. Xuanzang's retelling of it appears to be based on the *Mahāmāyāsūtra* (*T.* 383, 12:1012–14 = Fr. trans., Durt n.d.: 1–4; see also Durt 1996), and may be summarized as follows: As soon as the Blessed One has been encoffined, Anuruddha goes up to Tuṣita Heaven, where the Buddha's mother was reborn, and informs her of the death of her son. As soon as she hears the news, she comes down to the place of the coffin. Seeing it from a distance, she faints from emotion. Revived by her attendant divine maidens, she then approaches the coffin, and loudly laments her son's death, while fingering his robe, his bowl, and his staff, relics and reminders of him that are lying nearby, or hanging on a tree.[34] It is at this point in the story that the miracle occurs: the lid of the Buddha's coffin opens, and the Blessed One himself sits up. Joining his two hands together, he turns to his mother and tells her not to be overwhelmed by grief, that his passing away is in harmony with the law of all things, and that even after the extinction of a buddha, there are still the refuges of the dharma and the saṃgha. This comforts Mahāmāyā to some extent, but the Buddha's always practical disciple, Ānanda, witnessing this scene, wants to know how to interpret it, and the Buddha tells him, "You may say that after the Buddha's Nirvāṇa, his compassionate mother came down from the heavenly palace to the Twin Trees. As a lesson to unfilial people, the Tathāgata sat up in the golden coffin and preached the Dharma [for his mother] with his hands joined palm to palm" (Li 1996: 190; text in *T.* 2087, 51:904b).[35] The lesson here, then, is not only one of accepting impermanence but of observing filial piety (see Durt 1996: 19).

[33] As Hubert Durt (n.d.:1) has pointed out, it appears to be connected to the theme of the rivalry between Mahākāśyapa and Ānanda; just as the feet of the Buddha appeared to the former, so, here, his hand appears to the latter.

[34] On this episode, see Durt 1996: 16–17.

[35] See also Baochong's Ming Dynasty biography of the Buddha (text and translation in Wieger 1913: 246–53), where the story is retold in some detail and a woodblock illustrating the scene is reproduced. The scene became a common one in Chinese and Central Asian Buddhist art (see Soper 1959a). On possible parallels between this and the *Mahābhārata* stories of Gangā mourning her son Bhīṣma and of Kuntī mourning Karṇa, see Przyluski 1920: 176–78.

Cremation

In the *Mahāparinirvāṇa-sūtra,* Mahākāśyapa's worship of the Buddha's feet is the last act prior to the igniting of the funeral pyre. This occurs spontaneously in most versions of the story, although in some the action is undertaken by the Mallas, or alternatively by Mahākāśyapa, acting as the Buddha's eldest "son" (see Bareau 1970–71, 2:254ff.; and Waldschmidt 1944–48: 305ff.). Cremation was the normative Buddhist way of disposing of bodies, at least the bodies of monks, in ancient India, although other forms were also recognized. According to the *Mūlasarvāstivāda Vinaya,* for example, immersion in a river, and burial or exposure in a deserted place were also allowable under certain circumstances, although cremation was preferable to all of them (*T.* 1451, 24:286c–287a = Fr. trans., Seidel 1983: 578; see also Schopen 1997: 217–19).[36]

Cremation, of course, has also long been (and remains today) the usual means of dealing with the corpse in Hindu India, but that parallelism should not mislead us. On the one hand, the symbolism of cremation for Buddhist monks and cremation for ordinary Hindus is rather different. The former is a ritual hopefully productive of relics; the latter is a sacrificial rite intended to insure rebirth and generally resulting in the eradication of all bodily remains (see Parry 1994: 187–88).[37] On the other hand, the important point about the cremation of the Buddha (and of his monks) is that it ritually differentiates him (and them) from orthodox brahmanical ascetics and renunciants who were typically *not* cremated. Because they have essentially already performed their own mortuary rite at the time of their wandering forth, and because they have abandoned the family and hence no longer recognize any relatives who might perform their cremations, and because they have given up their sacrificial fires needed to kindle the cremation pyre, Hindu sannyāsins are generally not cremated, but buried in sand or abandoned in a river (see Kane 1973: 229–31; and Parry 1994: 184). We come here to the flipside of the injunction on how to conduct the funeral of a tathāgata; not only is he to be cremated *like* a cakravartin king, but he is is also to be cremated *unlike* a sannyāsin.[38]

[36] According to Xuanzang (*T.* 2087, 51:877c = Eng. trans., Li 1996: 62), there were three methods of dealing with dead bodies in ancient India—cremation, immersion, and exposure.
[37] The symbolism of cremation in the Jain tradition is yet different again, and was a topic of some controversy with Hinduism. See Jaini 1979: 297, 302–4.
[38] This departure from the orthodox norm is noteworthy, but it is also, of course, perfectly in line with countless other examples in which Buddhists sought to differentiate themselves from the Hindu renunciant tradition.

Ever since the work of Robert Hertz (1960) and of Arnold Van Gennep (1960: 146–65), it has been customary to think of death as at least a two-stage process of passage ending in a final stable state—for the body, the soul, and the mourners. In some cultures, this final resolution takes place with a secondary burial, or its equivalent.[39] In this context, cremation may be seen as a rite that accelerates the process of passage, and the relics as a sign of attaining that new state. Just how this "new state" is to be understood in the case of the Buddha is, of course, a question replete with difficulties. As Nāgārjuna, refusing any attempt at hypostatization, put it, in Stephan Beyer's (1974: 213–14) memorable translation, "[A]fter his final cessation, the Blessed One isnt is (isnt isnt) isnt is & isnt, isnt isnt is & isnt." In the Sanskrit version of the *Mahāparinirvāṇa-sūtra,* however, we are somewhat cryptically told that, as a result of his cremation, the Buddha has gone to the world of Brahmā (brahmaloka) (*MPS.,* 430 = Ger. trans., Waldschmidt 1944–48: 306 = Fr. trans., Bareau 1970–71, 2:258).[40] André Bareau (1970–71, 2:258), seeking to explain this away, suggests that this is just a metaphor reflecting the way the flames engulf-ing the Buddha's body mount up and disappear into the highest sky.

Bareau might well have considered, however, the traditional Upaniṣadic understanding of the brahmaloka as a place to which those who have escaped from rebirth go at death. Indeed, the *Bṛhadāraṇyaka Upaniṣad* makes it clear that this transcendence of the sage, this liberation, occurs at the time of cremation, when the flames lead the deceased higher and higher until finally "these exalted people" dwell in the worlds of Brahmā (brahmaloka) from which "they do not return" (Olivelle 1996: 84). In this light, a passage in Aśvaghoṣa's *Buddhacarita,* quoted by Gregory Schopen (1997: 127) in another context, may also be significant. There we are told that the relics of the Buddha cannot be destroyed at the end of the kalpa, just like the sphere (*dhātu*) of Brahmā in heaven (see also Johnston 1937: 276).

Collection, Dispute, and Distribution: The "War of the Relics"

However we interpret the Buddha's cremation, it is clear that here below on earth it produces relics. We come here to a crucial moment in the story of the Buddha's bodily remains, the start of the episode with which the *Mahāparinirvāṇa-sūtra* culminates and ends. Just what were these relics

[39] See also the helpful discussion in Danforth 1982: 35–69. For the relevance of this scheme to Buddhism, see Faure 1991: 134.

[40] The same thing is said in *Avś.,* 261 = Fr. trans., Feer 1891: 432, but does not appear in the Pali text.

that were found when the cremation fire went out? According to the Pali tradition, nothing was left after the Buddha's body burned—neither "skin, under-skin, flesh, sinew, or joint-fluid" . . . nor even ashes or soot—nothing at all except for the sarīra (*D.*, 2:164 = Eng. trans., Walshe 1987: 275).[41] Walshe (1987: 275), Rhys Davids (1899–1924, 2:186), and Bareau (1970–71, 2:260) all translate *sarīra* here as "bones," although Buddhaghosa's description of them in his commentary as being like jasmine buds, washed pearls, and nuggets of gold, and as coming in three sizes (as big as mustard seeds, broken grains of rice, and split green peas), suggests that something more generic and less osseous than bones or teeth may be meant here (*DA.*, 2:603–4). If these sarīra are bones, they are bones that have been transformed into something much more akin to the relic beads or "jewels" that are looked for and found still today in the cremation ashes of great masters. Moreover, the texts that do go on to refer to "teeth" and other identifiable bones of the Buddha are careful to distinguish those teeth from these śarīra, which are treated rather differently (see *Thūp.*, 172 = Eng. trans., Jayawickrama 1971: 34; and *Jin.*, 37–38 = Eng. trans., Jayawickrama 1968: 53–54). In any case it is these śarīra (relics) and these only that are the subject of the dispute—the so-called "war of the relics" among the eight kingdoms—that forms the next episode of the story.

Our sources agree, for the most part, that the Mallas of Kuśinagarī first collect the Buddha's relics. They put them in a casket (usually made of gold), put the casket on a litter, and transport it to the center of their city, where they enshrine the relics in a place that is variously described as a great building, a high tower, or their own assembly hall (see Waldschmidt 1944–48: 309; Rockhill 1907:145).[42] What seems to be emphasized here is the defensive posture of the setting. This is clear from the Pali text's specification that once the relics were placed inside the Mallas' assembly hall, they were surrounded by "a lattice-work of spears," and encircled by a "wall of bows" (Walshe 1987: 275; text in *D.*, 2:164). Later texts were to elaborate on these defenses and specify that the relics were surrounded by concentric circles of elephants (standing so close together that their heads touched), horses (whose necks touched), chariots (whose axle heads touched), soldiers (whose arms touched), and archers (whose bows touched) (see*Thūp.*, 174 = Eng. trans., Jayawickrama 1971: 36). These preparations make sense in view of the "war" over the relics that threatens to follow, but it may be that these "cages of spears" (*satti-pañjara*) are

[41] The Sanskrit text (*MPS.*, 432) does refer to what is left as bones (asthi).

[42] In *T.* 5, 1:174b, the Mallas first wash the relics before putting them in a golden urn. In *T.* 1435, 23:436a, Mahākāśyapa actually collects the relics, wraps them in a woolen cloth, and gives them to the Mallas. See Bareau 1970–71, 2:262–63.

intended not only to ward off humans but also malignant spirits, in particular Māra, who, as we shall see, later figures as an important threat to relic worship.

In any case, the news of the Buddha's cremation and of the Mallas' possession of his relics spreads quickly through Northern India and is greeted with strong emotions. Just how strong is hinted at in a striking story preserved in Buddhaghosa's *Commentary on the Dīgha Nikāya,* a relatively late Pali source. We are told that when the news reached the capital of Magadha, King Ajātaśatru's ministers, knowing their sovereign would react emotionally to the event of the Buddha's death, took certain precautions before informing him. The episode, interestingly, features three golden vessels (doṇī), perhaps here best translated as "troughs." The ministers fill these troughs with a sweet syrupy mixture of four "cool" ingredients: ghee, froth-of-ghee, honey, and sugarcane juice. They invite Ajātaśatru to lie down in one of these troughs so that he is completely immersed in the mixture. Then, one of the ministers breaks the news: "Sire, the Blessed One has passed away into parinirvāṇa at Kuśinagarī." Hearing this, Ajātaśatru faints and the mixture in the trough begins to heat up from the discharged emotion of the king. The ministers quickly take him out and put him in the second trough. He regains consciousness, and again, they announce to him the news: "Sire, the Blessed One has passed into parinirvāṇa." Again he faints, again his bath gets hot, and they transfer him to the third trough. This time, he manages to sustain the news (*DA.*, 2:605–6; see also*Thūp.*, 74–75 = Eng. trans., Jayawickrama 1971: 36–38).[43] Fully recovered, Ajātaśatru now becomes the man of action that befits his status. Declaring "nothing will be gained by lamentation," he resolves to have the Buddha's relics brought to his kingdom, and sends a message to the Mallas peremptorily asking for them. Suspecting, however, that his request might well be turned down, he backs it up by equipping a fourfold army and setting out himself to Kuśinagarī (*Thūp.*, 175 = Eng. trans., Jayawickrama 1971: 38).

Much the same sequence of emotions and events is recounted in most canonical accounts of the parinirvāṇa, albeit in less colorful and more abbreviated terms. In addition to Ajātaśatru, no fewer than six other kings join into the contention. The lists of these vary slightly in names and order, but in general, there is agreement that the peoples and countries involved, besides the Mallas of Kuśinagarī and Ajātaśatru of Magadha, are as follows: the Licchavis of Vaiśālī, the Śākyas of Kapilavastu, the Mallas of Pāvā, the Bulakas of Calakalpa, the Krauḍyas of Rāmagrāma, and the brahmins of Viṣṇudvīpa (see Waldschmidt 1944–48: 314 and 1967;

[43] In the *Mahāsampiṇḍanidāna,* Ajātaśatru needs seven troughs to revive him when the elder Mahākāśyapa passes away, years later (see Saddhatissa 1975: 44).

Couvreur 1967: 168, 173).[44] All of these groups want to have a share in the Buddha's relics and either send messages to that effect to the Mallas of Kuśinagarī, or raise troops and declare themselves ready to take the relics by force (Bareau 1970–71, 2:284–85). The Mallas themselves variously respond by reaffirming their claim to the relics, refusing outright to consider surrendering them, and, in some texts, by beginning to teach their women, young girls, and boys the art of archery, hoping thus to add warriors to their ranks in order to overcome their inferiority in numbers (*MPS.*, 440–41; see also Waldschmidt 1944–48: 320n; Bareau 1970–71, 2:284).[45]

In the depiction of these events on two friezes appearing on architraves on the Southern and Western gateways of the great stūpa at Sāñcī, it seems that the armies are engaging in combat and that the "War of the Relics" actually took place (see Marshall 1955: 53, and pl. 4; Srivastava 1983: 99 and pl. xv–svi). In the texts, however, hostilities never quite break out, and instead the matter is resolved by the arbitration of the brahmin Dhūmrasagotra, also known as Doṇa (Skt.: Droṇa). Droṇa goes about his task in an apparently equitable and satisfactory fashion, dividing the relics of the Buddha into eight equal shares, each one of which will be taken away to be enshrined in a stūpa in the recipient's home country (Waldschmidt 1944–48: 321–24; Bareau 1970–71, 2:288–303). When this process is finished, Droṇa asks the assembled kings for the urn (*kumbha*), in which he measured out the relics, and he is accorded that. He resolves to build a stūpa over it. Finally, to close the episode, a young brahmin of Pippalāyana arrives belatedly;[46] realizing (or being told) that all the relics have been distributed, he has to settle for the embers of the cremation fire, which he takes away to enshrine in a stūpa as well (Waldschmidt 1944–48: 324–28; Bareau 1970–71, 303–8). There is thus an initial division of the relics here into ten portions.

Phyllis Granoff has suggested that this move to a total of ten shares of relics may be informed by Brahmanical / Hindu navaśraddha rituals in which ten rice balls (piṇḍa) are formed and layed out over a period of ten days after death in order to build a new body for the deceased and help prevent him from becoming a *preta* (malignant departed spirit) (see Kane 1973: 262). Indeed, some Gandharan depictions of Droṇa's dividing of

[44] In Pali: the Licchavis of Vesāli, the Sakyas of Kapilavatthu, the Mallas of Pāvā, the Bulis of Allakappa, the Koliyas of Rāmagāma, and the brahmins of Veṭhadīpa.

[45] *Thūp.*, 176 = Eng. trans., Jayawickrama 1971: 39 adds that the gods were on the Mallas' side so that they would have won had a peaceful repartition of the relics not taken place. See, however, Waldschmidt 1967, in which it is the Buddha himself who predicts this distribution of his relics.

[46] In the Pali text, the Moriyas of Pipphalivana.

the relics show him shaping the śarīra as though they were balls of rice.[47] Be this as it may, the theme of late-comers or others besides the eight peoples getting relics was to give rise to a host of traditions. Xuanzang, for instance, tells the story of King Uttarasena of Udyāna, who comes late to Kuśinagarī but who declares that, while he was alive, the Tathāgata said that he should be given a portion of his bones. This claim is apparently verified by some monks, because Uttarasena is then given a share of relics, although Xuanzang (*T.* 2087, 51:883b = Eng. trans., Li 1996: 87) adds that, because of being granted his request, he was greatly resented by the other kings. A more radical variant on this theme is found in another tale, this one featuring divine claims. In this story, once all eight kings agree to divide the relics equally among themselves, the god Indra comes and says that the gods too have rights to a share of the relics. He is followed by three nāga kings who say "Don't forget about us!" and who indicate in no uncertain terms that they are stronger than the combined kings. Droṇa then resolves this new quarrel by proposing to divide the relics into three portions—one for the gods, one for the nāgas, and one for humans—something that everyone agrees to (*T.* 2087, 51:904c = Eng. trans., Li 1996:192).[48] Presumably, then, the eight countries have to content themselves with divying up only one third of the Buddha relics.[49]

In all these stories, the brahmin Droṇa is presented as an arbitrator, but in subsequent traditions, he himself is not immune from suspicion. Thus one tale, also recounted by Xuanzang (*T.* 2087, 51:908a = Eng. trans., Li 1996: 209), portrays him as smearing the inside of the urn that he used to measure out the relics with honey, so that a portion of the relics would stick to the container that he then asked for and received as the payment for his arbitration.[50] Another story has it that Droṇa secreted the right eye-tooth of the Buddha in his turban, thinking to save it for himself. Unfortunately for the brahmin, the god Indra, seeing the tooth from up above in his heaven, then came down and stole it away in turn.[51] Droṇa, busy dividing up the rest of the relics, did not even notice his loss until it

[47] Phyllis Granoff, oral communication, Princeton, N.J., 18 May 2002.

[48] The same division is found in *T.* 384, 12:1057c–58a; and *T.* 2122, 53:599b = Eng. trans., Ruppert 2000: 290. Phyllis Granoff (oral communication) has further likened this tripartide division of the relics to the Hindu sapindīkaraṇa ceremony in which the body of the deceased, represented by a ball of rice (the pretapiṇḍa), is divided and then conjoined with others to make three piṇḍas representing three generations of male ancestors. See Kane 1973: 520–23.

[49] See also Faure 1999a: 174 who cites a tradition according to which the humans get eight shares of the relics, the gods three, and the nāgas twelve.

[50] Droṇa's use of honey is also found in *T.* 2122, 53: 599b = Eng. trans., Ruppert 2000:290–91.

[51] For a traditional Thai depiction of Indra in the act of taking the tooth from Droṇa, see Leksukhum 2000: 180.

was too late (*Thūp.*, 177 = Eng. trans., Jayawickrama 1971: 41). A later Pali tradition, studied by Kevin Trainor (1997: 132, and 1992), expands this scenario, and portrays Droṇa as stealing *three* teeth of the Buddha at this time, hiding one in his turban, one between his toes, and one in his clothing. Indra then steals the first one, the nāga king Jayasena takes the second, and a human being from Gandhāra takes the third. Here we would seem to have nicely replicated the tripartide division hinted at earlier by Xuanzang. In any case, we have once more a reflection of a theme that we have already seen and that we shall encounter again, namely the distribution—the spread—of the Buddha's relics in a cosmic scheme that includes both humans and nonhumans.

The Construction of the Stūpas

It will be recalled that the last point in the Buddha's instructions to Ānanda, concerning a cakravartin's (and his own) funeral, was that the relics, once collected, were to be enshrined in a single stūpa at a crossroads. The defensive tower in which the Mallas initially housed the relics, whether conceived to be at a "crossroads" or not, was not a stūpa, and the subsequent division of the relics and their distribution to eight kingdoms make it legitimate to wonder whether or not, here at last, there has been a "violation" of the Buddha's prescriptions for his funeral.

There are some indications of possible concerns about this issue. André Bareau (1970–71, 2:314–20), for instance, has detected in one of the Chinese versions of the *Mahāparinirvāṇa-sūtra* traces of a tradition of a single sepulcher for the relics, which may have been built at a village near Kuśinagarī ninety days after the cremation. Jean Przyluski (1935–36: 353) has argued, on rather different grounds, that the most ancient tradition was that of a single stūpa. Moreover, as we shall see in the next chapter, a later Theravāda tradition was similarly inclined to affirm that, even after the construction of the various stūpas, Mahākāśyapa decided to enshrine the bulk of the relics in one place, leaving only token amounts for the eight countries. For the most part, however, the tradition of a single sepulcher did not hold sway, and instead we find the common affirmation of the construction of ten stūpas—one in each of the eight countries that took a share of the relics, one built over the urn used by Droṇa, and one over the embers from the cremation fire (see Bareau 1970–71, 2:311; and Waldschmidt 1944–48: 329–30).[52]

[52]*T.* 1, 1:30a = Ger. trans., Weller 1939–40: 205 mentions, cryptically, an eleventh stūpa: the "hair stūpa from the time of his birth." As Weller (205n.1111) legitimately asks, "What stūpa is this?" The reference may be intended simply to smooth the transition to the next passage.

The various versions of the *Mahāparinirvāṇa-sūtra* are rather terse about the transportation of the different shares of relics to their respective countries and their enshrinement there. For details on this we have to turn to later traditions. Perhaps one of the most extraordinary of these is found in the *Commentary on the Dīgha Nikāya,* where the focus is on the share of relics kept by the king of Magadha, Ajātaśatru. He first has the twenty-five leagues (yojana) of road between Kuśinagarī and his capital of Rājagṛha leveled and embellished, and, all along the route, bazaars set up for the delight of the people. The relics themselves are transported in a golden casket (doṇī), and the procession stops wherever there are lots of flowers. At such places, the casket is put down, in an enclosure of spears, and the relics are worshiped by the people until all the flowers are exhausted. This turns out to be a very slow process for, according to the text, after seven years, seven months, and seven days, the procession has still not reached Rājagṛha. Worse, nonbelievers along the way are beginning to complain about being forced to join in the sacred festivities and pay homage to the relics, and because of their grumblings, thousands of them are reborn in hell. Worried that the whole situation is about to backfire, the elders try to convince the king to speed up the procession. He is reluctant, but, by use of good means, they eventually get him to agree to take the relics directly to the city where he promptly has them enshrined in a stūpa. Exactly the same thing, the text implies, happens in the case of the seven other shares of relics, as well as Droṇa's measuring urn and the embers of the fire (*DA.*, 2:610; see also*Thūp.*, 178–79 = Eng. trans., Jayawickrama 1971: 42–43).

Conclusion

There are many ways to read the *Mahāparinirvāṇa-sūtra.* It is sometimes seen as an important early segment of the Buddha's sacred biography. It is sometimes examined for its depiction of how the early Buddhists dealt with the crisis presented at this critical moment in their history, that is, the passing away of their founder. It is sometimes examined for its doctrinal statements. In this chapter, I have sought to look at it from the perspective of relic traditions and have interpreted several of its features in that light. Thus, we have seen that virtually all of the steps in the prescribed funeral rituals for a buddha or a cakravartin—his *śarīra-pūjā* or worship of the body—have in mind the production and preservation of his relics.

This centrality of relics is, in fact, well brought out in the addendum that has been attached to the very end of the sūtra. Buddhaghosa who, in his commentary, does not deal with these final verses, says that they were "added by elders in Sri Lanka" (*DA.*, 2:615). The same verses, however, are also to be found in the Sanskrit and Tibetan texts (see *MPS.*, 450; Obermiller 1931–32, 2:66; and Rockhill 1907: 147). They summarize once more the fact that eight measures of relics have been enshrined in stūpas. They make no mention of the stūpa over Droṇa's measuring box (the *kumbha-thūpa*) or of that over the embers (the *angāra-thūpa*), but they do include, this time, a list of the four tooth-relics of the Buddha. And then, the Pali text at least adds a parting recommendation: "Because of the glory of his [relics], this great earth is embellished by excellent offerings. Thus the all-seing Buddha's relics [sarīra] are well honored by those who are most honored; they are worshipped by the lord of gods, the lord of nāgas, and the lord of men. . . . Bow down with folded hands, for it is difficult indeed to meet a buddha through hundreds of aeons" (*D.*, 2:167–68 = Eng. trans., Davids 1899–1924, 2:191).[53] And with this injunction to venerate the remains of the Buddha's body, the *Mahāparinirvāṇa-sūtra* finally ends.

[53] These very final lines are not found in the Sanskrit text but, as Bareau (1970–71, 2:337n.) points out, they are contained in the Chinese and Tibetan.

Chapter Five

AŚOKA AND THE BUDDHA RELICS

After reporting the distribution of the Buddha's bodily relics and their enshrinement in the eight "droṇa stūpas,"[1] as well as the establishment of the two additional stūpas over the measuring box and the embers from the cremation fire, the Pali text of the *Mahāparinibbāna-sutta* sums things up with a noteworthy phrase: "That," it declares, "is how it was in the old days" (Walshe 1987: 27, text in *D.*, 2:167). Implicit in this statement is a recognition that, already at the time of the redaction of the sūtra, a number of changes were thought to have taken place in the situation of the buddha relics. The purpose of this chapter is to consider these changes and their repercussions. More specifically, I shall focus on traditions featuring or connected to the third-century B.C.E. Mauryan ruler of India, King Aśoka.

Recapitulating in a nutshell the reign of Aśoka, the historically unreliable but often interesting eighth-century ritual manual, the *Ārya-mañjuśrīmūlakalpa,* says: "he lived for a hundred years and ruled in peace; for eighty-seven years he venerated relics" (*AMMK.*, 28). Indeed, whatever he may have been historically, in Buddhist legend, Aśoka was seen as a relic venerator. His most famous legendary deed was his redistribution of the buddha relics from the droṇa reliquaries into 84,000 stūpas, which he had constructed throughout the southern continent of Jambudvīpa. As a result, for generations, Buddhist pilgrims, coming across ancient stūpas, have thought of them as "Aśokan stūpas," and seen them as part of the original 84,000. This has been true not only in India, but elsewhere in South and East Asia.[2] For example, in China, such monuments necessitated perhaps a redefinition of what was meant by "Jambudvīpa," but were commonplace nonetheless, and certain Aśoka stūpas there, such as that at the Ayuwang si (King Aśoka Monastery), became famous and important centers.[3] The tradition as a whole also gave

[1] The *MPS.* does not actually call them *droṇa stūpas* but the term is found in the *Aśokāv.*, 52 = Eng. trans., Strong 1983: 219, and is a convenient designation.

[2] For India, see *T.* 2087, 51:911b = Eng. trans., Li 1996: 224–25; for Nepal, Wiesner 1977; Allchin 1980; Lewis 1994: 11; for Korea, Durt 1987; Lee 1969: 24; for Southeast Asia, Lafont 1957: 43; for China, Zürcher [1959] 1972: 277–80; Campany 1995: 49ff; Shinohara 1988; Nishiwaki 1992; Barrett 2001: 21; Huang 1998; Faure 2002: 36–38.

[3] On the gradual development of the legends of Aśokan stūpas, see Huang 1998: 486ff. On those visited by various Japanese monks in China, see Ruppert 1997: 94–95. On the

rise to notions of miraculous images associated with Aśoka (see Shinohara 1992: 201–18), to tales of apocryphal visits of Aśoka or his sons to distant lands,[4] and to legends about Aśoka's daughters.[5] Moreover, it also served to inspire various Buddhist rulers throughout East Asia who sought to emulate Aśoka's paradigm for generations to come.[6]

More immediately, however, the legend of Aśoka's involvement with relics can be presented under a number of different topics. In what follows, I shall examine (1) traditions surrounding Aśoka's collection of all (or at least of a significant part) of the Buddha's śarīra, (2) the "event" of his building of the 84,000 stūpas, and (3) the transformative dedicatory festival Aśoka celebrates in honor of the relics.

The Collection of the Relics

According to a well-established Sanskrit legend, when approaching the end of his life, the Buddha's disciple Mahākāśyapa decides to go on a sort of cosmic tour and visit all the relics of the Buddha, one last time, before passing into final nirvāṇa. Making use of his supernatural powers, he travels, first, to the four sites of pilgrimage specified by the Buddha in the *Mahāparinirvāṇa-sūtra*—the places where the Tathāgata was born, where he became enlightened, where he preached his first sermon, and where he passed away (see Bareau 1970–71, 2:29–32; and Waldschmidt 1944–48: 244–46). Technically speaking, these sites do not house any actual bodily relics of the Buddha, but, after visiting them, Mahākāśyapa goes on to venerate the "eight great relic stūpas," that is, the droṇa stūpas,

---

reported nineteen Aśoka stūpas on Mount Wutai, see Pelliot 1907: 504. On the Ayuwang si, see Tamura 1967; Tsukamoto 1985, 1:391–92; Maspero 1914: 44–60; Soper 1949–50: 669–78; Vetch 1981: 137–48; Ruppert 2000: 233–35; Faure 2002: 36–38.

[4] For Khotan, see the references in Lamotte 1988: 257–59; for Yunnan, see Sainson 1904: 24–61, Chapin and Soper 1971: 38; for Southeast Asia, see Archaimbault 1966: 5.

[5] On the relations of Aśoka's daughter Cārumatī to Nepal, see Lamotte 1988: 256. On the Buddha image made by Aśoka's ugly fourth daughter, see the sources in Shinohara 1988: 219.

[6] On the Aśoka-inspired reign of Emperor Wu of the Liang (r. 502–49), see Ch'en 1964: 124–28. On the Renshou-era (601–604) relic-distribution campaigns of the Emperor Wendi, see Chen 2002: 51–108; Kieschnick 2003: 40–42; Wright 1957. On the Empress Wu Zetian's ambition to outdo Aśoka, and her use and veneration of relics, see Barrett 2001: 33–36; Chen 2002a: 48–61 and 2002: 109–48. On the once-per-reign-offering of Buddha relics to Shintō shrines throughout the nation carried out by most Japanese emperors from the ninth to the thirteen centuries, see Ruppert 2000: 43–101. On the Japanese Empress Shōtoku's distribution of 1,000,000 miniature stūpas, see Hickman 1975 and Yiegpruksawan 1987. On various Kamakura shoguns sponsoring the making of 84,000 miniature reliquaries, in conscious emulation of Aśoka, see Ruppert 2001: 236–40. On such miniature stūpas in China, see Durt, Riboud, and Lai 1985; in Korea, see Ch'ŏn 1972: 7.

which clearly do. He then proceeds to the underwater nāga kingdom, where he makes offerings to the Buddha's tooth, and on to Indra's Trāyastriṃśa Heaven, where he worships another tooth, as well as the Buddha's hair, his crest-jewel, and his almsbowl. Finally, he returns to Rājagṛha (*T.* 2043, 50:153b = Eng. trans., Li 1993: 110; *T.* 2042, 50:114b = Fr. trans., Przyluski 1923: 329; *T.* 1451, 24:408c = Fr. trans., Przyluski 1914: 523).

In this account, brief as it is, we have a sort of inventory of immediate post-parinirvāṇa remains of the Buddha.[7] What is interesting here is that we have a glimpse of a layer of tradition in which, except for a few references to relics located in heaven and in the nāga kingdom, the chief relics here on earth are those in the eight droṇa stūpas and these, moreover, are all assumed to be accessible to pilgrims. Much the same picture may be found in what is perhaps one of the earliest versions of the tale of Aśoka's collecting the relics from the droṇa stūpas. This story, preserved in the *Saṃyuktāgama,* simply presents the Mauryan monarch going to each of the stūpas, including that at Rāmagrāma (which, as we shall see shortly, is significant), demanding to be given the relics so that he can pay homage to them, and then returning with them to his capital (*T.* 99, 2:165a = Eng. trans., Lamotte 1988: 242). As a consequence, his subsequent redistribution of the Buddha's bodily relics into 84,000 stūpas is a *total* redistribution, with the exception, of course, of the various tooth and other relics that came to be treated in a categorically different manner.

The Relics at Rāmagrāma

This situation was to change, however, when at least one of the droṇa stūpas—that at Rāmagrāma—was thought to have passed out of the strictly human world and into the realm and control of the nāgas, and so no longer to be readily accessible. According to at least some versions of the Aśoka legend, when Aśoka sets out to gather all the buddha relics, he goes first to the droṇa stūpa built by Ajātaśatru in Magadha. Breaking it open, he takes out the bulk of the śarīra there, and then rebuilds the stūpa, leaving a token portion of relics for continued worship at the site.[8] He then does the same with the next six droṇa stūpas—those at Vaiśālī, Kapilavastu, Pāvā, Calakalpa, Viṣṇudvīpa and Kuśinagarī—but, when he

[7] Later, as we shall see, such lists were considerably expanded. See, for example, *Buv.,* 102–3 = Eng. trans., Horner 1975: 98–99; *Jin.,* 37–38 = Eng. trans., Jayawickrama 1968: 53–54; and Lafont 1957: 49n.

[8] Leaving a small number of relics behind is a standard indication in many of these stories. This action, along with reclosing the stūpa, not only serves to mitigate local outrage but also lessens the chance of being accused of being a *stūpa-bhedaka* (a breaker of stūpas—often paired with being a *saṃgha-bhedaka*—a breaker of the community). See Davids 1901: 399–400.

comes to the last droṇa stūpa, at Rāmagrāma, he finds that it is now underwater in the palace of the nāgas. This in itself does not stop the great Mauryan monarch; he asks the nāga king to take him down to his abode to show him the relics, but, once there, Aśoka realizes that the nāgas are worshiping the relics in a much more fervent and grandiose way than he could ever hope to emulate, and so he decides to let them keep their relics. Accordingly, he returns to his capital with śarīra from only seven of the eight droṇa stūpas (Aśokāv., 52 = Eng. trans., Strong 1983: 219; *T.* 2042, 50:102a = Fr. trans., Przyluski 1923: 292; *T.* 2085, 51:861b = Eng. trans., Li 2002: 86–87; *T.* 2087, 51:902b–c = Eng. trans., Li 1996: 181).[9] Much the same notion is found repeated in a Sanskrit verse that states:

> Today in Rāmagrāma the eighth stūpa stands
> for in those days the nāgas guarded it with devotion.
> The king did not take the relics from there,
> but left them alone and, full of faith, withdrew.
> (*Aśokāv.*, 52–53 = Eng. trans., Strong 1983: 219).

The Sri Lankan chronicle, the *Mahāvaṃsa,* seeks to give a naturalistic explanation to this situation. It claims that the droṇa stūpa, originally built on the shores of the Ganges at Rāmagrāma, was carried away in a flood, as a result of which the urn containing the relics sank to the bottom of the ocean, where it was recovered and kept by the nāgas. However, in this text, when Aśoka tries to get the relics from the nāgas, he refrains from doing so not because the nāgas are doing a fine job taking care of the relics, but because some ascetic arhats tell him that those relics are, in fact, destined for later enshrinement in Sri Lanka by the future king Duṭṭhagāmaṇī (*Mhv.,* 247 = Eng. trans., Geiger 1912: 211). I shall consider, in chapter 6, the whole saga of the capture of these Rāmagrāma relics from the nāgas by the arhat Soṇuttara and of their enshrinement in Sri Lanka. For now, suffice it to point out that the grounds for Aśoka's failure to retrieve this eighth portion of the droṇa relics are rather different in the Sanskrit legends and the Sri Lankan Pali tradition.

The Underground Chamber of Mahākāśyapa and Ajātaśatru

It should also be realized, however, that Aśoka does not always seek to collect the buddha relics directly from the droṇa stūpas. According to an alternative scenario, it is the Buddha's disciple, Mahākāśyapa, who first gathers the relics from the droṇa stūpas, about twenty years after the Buddha's parinirvāṇa. He then enshrines them in a new single underground

[9] On the Sāñcī and Amarāvatī reliefs depicting these scenes, see Lamotte 1988: 242. For a depiction, from the latter site, of the stūpa covered with nāgas, see Burgess [1886] 1996: pl.40.2.

stūpa, built for him by King Ajātaśatru. It is to this single stūpa that Aśoka eventually comes to get the relics (*DA.*, 2:611–13; *Thūp.*, 181–83 = Eng. trans., Jayawickrama 1971: 44–46. See also *HmanNanY.* , 137–42 = Eng. trans., U Ko Ko 1983, 2:67–81; Bigandet [1858] 1979, 2:96–100; Chimpa and Chattopadhyaya 1980: 61).

This story would appear to be a more developed counterpart to the previously mentioned Sanskrit tradition of Mahākāśyapa's end-of-life visit to the different droṇa stūpas. It may also be intended to complement the elder's earlier actions at the First Buddhist Council; on that occasion, Mahākāśyapa called on members of the saṃgha to gather together the Buddha's teachings—his dharmakāya—here he gathers together the remains of his physical body—his rūpakāya.

Mahākāśyapa's collection of the relics from the droṇa stūpas (like Aśoka's) is an incomplete one. He too does not get the relics from the nāgas of Rāmagrāma, but this is not just because he knows the Buddha has reserved them for Sri Lanka, it is also because he thinks that they will be safe there. For Mahākāśyapa's motives, in his collection of the relics, are to safeguard and preserve them from unspecified "dangers." He is very worried—paranoid almost—that something will happen to the relics if they are left in the first seven droṇa stūpas; the Rāmagrāma relics he leaves untouched because they are well guarded by the nāgas, and so he is not anxious about them (*Thūp.*, 181 = Eng. trans., Jayawickrama 1971: 44).

This concern of Mahākāśyapa for the safety of the relics is said to lie behind the secrecy that envelops the whole of his undertaking. In fact, the very nature and purpose of the new relic-shrine itself are supposed to be kept undisclosed, so much so that King Ajātaśatru, when he commences the massive project of enshrining the relics, announces that he is making caityas for the Buddha's eighty leading disciples and not a stūpa for the Buddha. As the *Glass Palace Chronicle* put it, "everyone was told that shrines for the eighty disciples were being built at the place" (U Ko Ko 1983, 2:70; text in *Hman-Nan-Y.*, 137–38).[10]

The construction itself, however, is elaborate and opulent. Ajātaśatru has the site excavated to a depth of eighty cubits (c. 120 feet). The relics are placed inside (1) a yellow sandalwood urn or box (*karaṇḍa*) which, in turn, is placed inside seven others so that there are eight nesting yellow sandalwood boxes. These boxes are then put successively inside eight nesting yellow sandalwood miniature stūpas, which are then put inside (2) eight nesting red sandalwood boxes, and eight nesting red sandalwood stūpas, which are put inside (3) eight nesting ivory boxes and stūpas, which are put inside (4) eight nesting boxes and stūpas made of the

[10] For a Burmese list of the eighty disciples, see Mingun 1990–98, 6: part 1, xiv. See also Lagirarde 2000.

seven precious things, and so on and so forth through boxes and stūpas of (5) gold, (6) silver, (7) diamond, (8) ruby, (9) cat's-eye, and (10) crystal (*DA.*, 2:611–12; Thūp., 181–82 = Eng. trans., Jayawickrama 1971: 44–45; Bigandet [1858] 1979, 2:96–97). The alternating layers of boxes and stūpas curiously recall the alternating shrouds that envelopped the body of the Buddha, but what is significant here must be the numbers. There are exactly 8 × 10 = 80 boxes-cum-stūpas, a figure that seems to reflect the pretense that all this is for the eighty disciples of the Buddha. The outermost stūpa of crystal is said to be the size of the Thūpārāma in Sri Lanka. As large as this is, around it are built a series of still greater structures of different precious materials. These buildings are adorned with figures depicting all the past lives of the Buddha, as well as images of his father, King Suddhodana and his mother, Queen Mahāmāya (*DA.*, 2:612. See also Thūp., *182* = Eng. trans., Jayawickrama 1971: 45–46).

Alternatively, in later sources, the relics are said to be placed in a magnificent statue of Kanthaka, the horse on which the bodhisattva rode when he left the palace on the night of his great departure. The horse "was cast in solid gold . . . and lowered down into the huge pit, and around it were constructed seven walls of brick, mortar, precious stones, sandalwood, iron, [silver and gold], and inside the enclosure housing the golden horse was a pavilion of eleven tiers" (U Ko Ko 1983, 2:18–19; text in U Kala 1960: 76–77. See also *Hman-Nan-Y.*, 143 = Eng. trans., U Ko Ko 1983, 2:83).

Put together, these two traditions concerning the decorations and reliquary in the underground chamber suggest that what is being commemorated here is not so much the relics of the Buddha, but the relics of the bodhisattva-about-to-become the Buddha. Granted, depictions of the jātakas on and in stūpas are common enough, but generally they are a prelude to a longer narrative of the whole of the Buddha's life—a full biorama.[11] Here the representations stop with the figures of his father and mother—symbolizing the Buddha's birth and residence in the palace. The featuring of the horse Kanthaka as a reliquary suggests even more precisely the moment of the great departure; just as the real Kanthaka carried the bodhisattva out of his father's home, here the gold statue of Kanthaka carries his relics. But the "departure" has not yet occurred: around the gold image of the horse are built seven walls of various materials, recalling the seven ramparts of a traditional royal city, and more specifically, as we shall see, of Kapilavastu itself.[12] One understands better now

[11] See, for example, the chapter on the "figures in the relic chamber" of the Mahāthūpa in *Thūp.*, 227–38 = Eng. trans., Jayawickrama 1971: 107–23.

[12] For a description of the seven walls of the city of a cakravartin, see *D.*, 2:170 = Eng. trans., Davids 1899–1924, 2:200; and *MPS.*, 306. More generally, see Przyluski 1927.

some of the reasons for the enclosed nature of this underground chamber: this is a buddha who has not yet "come forth" and who will only do so later, when Aśoka arrives, gets into the chamber, pries open the trapdoor in the side of the golden horse, and removes the relic casket from within (U Kala 1960: 79 = Eng. trans., U Ko Ko 1983: 22–23; U Kin 1981: 793 = Eng. trans., U Ko Ko 1983, 2:7–8). We have, here, a first hint, that the "discovery" of the relics by Aśoka biographically repeats the bodhisattva's great departure, just as his later re-enshrinement of them corresponds to his enlightenment and reasserts his buddhahood.

In the meantime, the relics are kept waiting. Ajātaśatru has garlands of flowers placed in the enclosure as offerings, along with perfumes, banners, and five hundred gold oil-lamps. A resolution is made that the blossoms shall not wither, the perfumes not lose their scent, and the oil lamps not go out, until the relics are "dis-covered," and a gold plaque is inscribed with the message that, in the future, a righteous king named Aśoka will come and have these relics dispersed. It is clear, then, that all this is destined to keep the relics, provisionally, for the use of the future great monarch. A heap of gems is even left there, in the tomb, for him to offer to the relics (with a somewhat more demeaning message attached indicating that, comparatively speaking, Aśoka will be an indigent king) (*DA.*, 2:612–13; *Thūp.*, 182–83 = Eng. trans., Jayawickrama 1971: 46. See also Bigandet [1858] 1979, 2:97–98; U Kala 1960: 77 = Eng. trans., U Ko Ko 1983, 2:19).

Two things stand out about this structure, apart from its magnificence. The one, of course, is that it is to be kept secret. As one source puts it, "Complete secrecy was observed, not a single person knew that all this major undertaking was meant for the storage of the Buddha-relics" (U Ko Ko 1983, 2:70; text in *Hman-Nan-Y.*, 38). Great emphasis is placed on the fact that no one is to be told about the shrine for the Buddha's relics. A pretense is made that something else—a monument to the Buddha's disciples—is being built. Moreover, the whole structure is put underground, and the earth is then leveled over it, with only a small stone stūpa on top to mark the spot. Soon, this stūpa is overgrown by weeds and bushes, and it is as though the very existence of the place and its nature have been forgotten. So esoteric is this tradition, in fact, that, a few generations later, when King Aśoka searches for the relics, he apparently still believes them to be in the original eight droṇa stūpas. Thus, he first goes to the droṇa stūpa at Kuśinagarī and then to all the others, and it is only after he breaks them open and finds them all empty—devoid of any relics at all—that he starts making inquiries.[13] When a one-hundred-and-

[13] In this scenario, when Aśoka goes to the stūpa at Rāmagrāma (which presumably still did contain relics since Mahākāśyapa had left them there), he is unable to pierce the shell of the stūpa; the shovels of his men simply break. This is said to be due to the power of the nāgas.

twenty-year-old monk remembers that, when he was a seven-year-old novice, his master showed him an overgrown stone stūpa and told him to do homage there (without, however, explaining why), Aśoka figures out where to dig, and the site of the underground chamber is found (*Thūp.*, 189 = Eng. trans., Jayawickrama 1971: 53); *DA.*, 2:613–14. See also Bigandet, [1858] 1979, 132).

The question of why all this secrecy is necessary is one that has been addressed from a number of perspectives. Paul Bigandet ([1858] 1979, 2:96n), writing over a century ago, speculated that it, and the related security measures that I shall examine shortly, were due to the existence, either within or outside the saṃgha, "of a strong party . . . which was inimical to the worship paid to the remains of Buddha, and aimed at procuring their total destruction." Bigandet's own prejudices, however, may be showing through here. It is just as likely that the secrecy and security were intended to combat the danger of thievery, and the theft of relics, as is well known, is not usually motivated by antagonist feelings or a desire for destruction, but by the intense wish to possess sacred powerful objects (see Trainor 1992; Strong and Strong 1995; and, more generally, Geary 1978; Silvestre 1952).

The location of the secret relic chamber—underground—is surely not insignificant. On the one hand it, and also the story of the inscriptions that Ajātaśatru leaves there announcing the future arrival of Aśoka, have all the earmarks of a tradition intended to give legitimacy and antiquity to relics that were—as the story itself admits—lost and forgotten. We would have here, then, a story of the "invention" of the Buddha's relics, with all the delightful ambiguity that surrounds that word's meaning: (anciently) "discovery" and (presently) "making up."[14] Such a strategy of pseudo-esoterism is, of course, not unique in the history of Buddhism. As is well known, it was applied to texts and other "treasures" said to be buried until the time was ripe for their "[re]emergence."[15] And in China as well, "Aśokan" reliquaries were sometimes "found" buried underground, their presence revealed by lights or by the sounds of subterranean bells, a phenomenon that Bernard Faure (2002: 32–33) says "amounts to a discovery of China's Buddhist unconscious."[16]

[14] As in the "Invention of the True Cross"—a Christian relic that was also buried underground and lost until "discovered" by Constantine's mother Helena, in a secret location known only to a few. See Voragine 1993, 1:277–83.

[15] One thinks here of the Tibetan tradition of the buried and "rediscovered" treasures (*gTer ma*) which are mostly, although not exclusively, texts. See Gyatso 1996 and Mayer 1997.

[16] On the "archaeologia sacra" such phenomena inspired, see also Huang 1998: 490–91; Durt 1987: 6–7; Vetch 1981.

Relic Security and the Roman Robots

This theme of secrecy is reinforced by a second item of note in Ajātaśatru's underground chamber: the security measures that are set up in order to protect the place. Not only are the relics ensconced in a near-infinite regress of nesting reliquaries, not only are the doors to the various overarching buildings padlocked, but, in the underground chamber itself, images of ferocious animals are set up, along with special mechanical guards fashioned by none other than Viśvakarman, the divine engineer. These wooden figures move about with the speed of the wind, twirling swords in hand, ready to strike down anyone who would steal the relics (*Thūp.*, 182 = Eng. trans., Jayawickrama 1971: 46; see also *DA.*, 2:613; and Bigandet [1858] 1979: 32). They represent, thus, a further legitimating test for Aśoka: the relics will belong to the one who is clever enough or powerful enough or meritorious enough to be able to get around them.

Such mechanical security devices form a curiously persistent theme in the literature about relics in general and these relics in particular. When the hair relics brought by Trapuṣa and Bhallika are enshrined at the Shwe Dagon Pagoda in Rangoon, for instance, Indra fixes around the site wooden images brandishing swords who are kept constantly spinning by means of a clever mechanism (Pe Maung Tin 1934: 52–53; Strong 1998: 91).[17] Less spectacular, perhaps, was the alarm mechanism at the Temple of the Tooth in seventh-century Sri Lanka, which was set off automatically in the town if the doors to the lofty tower that served as a reliquary were so much as touched (*T.* 2066, 51:3c = Eng. trans., Lahiri 1986: 34).

In several versions of the story of Ajātaśatru's underground chamber, the mechanical armed guards are reduced to swords attached to a water wheel whose rotation prevents access to the relics. Aśoka manages to stop the wheel from spinning, although the way in which he does this differs from text to text. In Tāranātha's account, he simply diverts the water of the stream and can easily get through when the wheel stops turning (Chimpa and Chattopadhyaya 1980: 61). In another story, preserved in the last chapter of the *Ayuwang zhuan,* Aśoka throws plums into the water until they gum up the wheel's works. He thus manages to get through, only to find that the relics are also guarded by a nāga king. Aśoka is told that he will be able to obtain the relics only when his merit outweighs that of the nāga. Accordingly, two identical gold statues—one of Aśoka and the other of the nāga king—are fashioned and used to

[17] For a Chinese example of Buddhist buildings said to be protected by automatons that come out to keep enemies at bay, and mechanical animals that watch over the hours, see Forte 1988: 47.

weigh their relative merit. At first, the nāga king's image is twice as heavy as Aśoka's. Aśoka therefore undertakes some merit-making activities and soon the two images weigh exactly the same. Aśoka then makes still more merit, and eventually his statue becomes heavier than that of the nāga, and he is able to pass through (*T.* 2042, 50:131a = Fr. trans., Przyluski 1923: 425–27).[18]

In the *Thūpavaṃsa* and the *Commentary on the Dīgha Nikāya,* the revolving water wheel is replaced by moving mechanical men all held together and operated by a single mechanism. Aśoka's task, however, is simpler. The god Indra, perceiving the king's need to disarm these wooden figures and their whirling swords, summons Viśvakarman, the divine engineer who made the mechanical guards in the first place, and asks him for help. Viśvakarman comes down to earth disguised as a young archer, and, at Aśoka's request, he shoots an arrow exactly into the peg of the mechanism that holds the whole robot construction together. Aśoka is then able to pass and get the relics (*Thūp.,* 189 = Eng. trans., Jayawickrama 1971: 54. See also *DA.,* 2:614).[19]

The most elaborate story about these mechanical guardian figures, however, is the tale of the Roman robots, found in the *Lokapaññatti* (an eleventh-to-twelfth-century Pali cosmological text) and in related subsequent Burmese traditions (*LP.*, 157–61, 174–77 = Fr. trans., Denis 1977, 2:141–44, 153–54; U Kin 1957: 108–9 = Eng. trans., U Ko Ko 1983, 1:11–13; U Kala 1960: 76–77 = Eng. trans., U Ko Ko 1983, 2:15–20; see also Denis 1976). According to this tale, the mechanical robot guardians protecting King Ajātaśatru's underground relic chamber were made by an engineer who came from Rome (Roma-visaya).[20] Rome, the *Lokapaññatti* informs us, was famous for its experts in "spirit movement machines" (*bhūta-vāhana-yanta*), but the secret of their manufacture was well guarded, and was never to leave Rome. Any expert attempting to leave the city would be hunted down and killed by one of his own robots. The rest of the story is of epic proportions, but it may be summarized as follows: A young entrepreneur in Pāṭaliputra, after hearing about these wonderful Roman machine-beings, wants to learn the secret of their manufacture and to import them to India, so much so that, on his deathbed, he vows to be reborn in Rome. This occurs, and, in his next life, he marries the daughter of one of the Roman engineers and inherits

[18] In a similar story, in the *Aśokamukha-nāgavinaya-pariccheda* (see Handurukande 1967), Aśoka makes merit by worshiping the Buddha relics, and finds that gradually the nāga image prostrates itself more and more at the feet of his own image.

[19] In the Burmese sources used by Bigandet [1858] (1979, 2:132), the guardian nat is bribed into disarming the figures.

[20] Cambodian and Thai versions of the story have tended to resituate "Roma-visaya" ("Rome") either in Northwest India or Bengal. See Denis 1976: 114.

from him the secret of the robots. He wishes thereupon to return to India but knows that he will be killed when he tries to do so. He inserts, therefore, the blueprint for the manufacture of the robots into a cut he makes into the flesh of his thigh, and, setting out, he journeys as far as he can before being cut down by his robot pursuers. All seems lost but it turns out that, ahead of time, he instructed his own son to withdraw the secret plans from his thigh before cremating his body and to travel on with them to India. This, the young man is able to do, and, arriving in Magadha, he is just in time to be of service to Ajātaśatru, who was then seeking someone to build mechanical figures to protect the underground relic chamber. The guardians of the Buddha's relics are thus actually Roman robots, and they remain on duty underground for a whole century, until King Aśoka, seeking to obtain the relics, needs to disarm them. Not knowing how to do so, Aśoka seeks out the very same Roman engineer who made them, and who, we are led to believe, is still alive. With his help, the guardian figures are quickly disabled and Aśoka is able to collect the relics (*LP.*, 157–61 = Fr. trans., Denis 1977, 2:141–44).

What are we to make of this emphasis on mechanical protection devices for these relics? Jean Boisselier has pointed out that nothing even approaching such mechanisms has been found in any ancient stūpas. We seem, therefore, to be dealing with a fictional invention (see Denis 1976: 114–15). In Burma, however, miniaturizations of such schemes have been found. For example, as late as 1751, when a pagoda was dedicated at Shwebo, there were enclosed within it replicas of brass cannon (obtained from the British) and, more traditionally, "figures in silver and brass of elephants, horses, and soldiers armed with swords, spears, guns, bows and arrows, and facing outwards for the purpose of safeguarding the dedicated treasures in the relic chamber." It was believed, we are told, that these "would become endowed with life and motion, and that the soldiers would make use of the cannon, muskets, swords, spears, bow and arrows against any intruders" (Taw Sein Ko 1903–4: 152, 154).

Eugène Denis (1976: 113) tries to account for the story of the robots by reference to what he sees as a Southeast Asian fascination with "Roman," that is, Byzantine technology, and he cites a number of Byzantine works on "automatica" and "pneumatica"—spring-and-compression-propelled machinery designed to reproduce human movements.[21] Be this as it may, it is likely that we should also look elsewhere for an explanation for the popularity of these robots and other security devices.

Two possibilities suggest themselves. The first pursues the suggestion made above that the relics in the underground chamber, set in the horse Kanthaka, represent the Buddha not-yet-departed from his magnificent

[21] More generally, on Western influences on Buddhist notions of living icons, see Strickmann 1996: 170–74.

palace in his hometown of Kapilavastu. The protective devices would thus recall the security measures taken by the Buddha's father to thwart his son's departure. In one Buddha biography, for instance, we are told,

> Then King Śuddhodana met with his brothers . . . and said: "The brahmin soothsayers and fortune-tellers have predicted that my son . . . will become a cakravartin king if he does not wander forth. Therefore, we should watch him carefully and keep the city well-guarded." So they encircled the city of Kapilavastu with seven walls and seven moats, and iron doors were put in each city gate. Very loud bells were attached to the doors, so that whenever the doors were opened, they could be heard up to a distance of a league around. . . . Royal ministers, commanding armed men and riders, were posted outside on the walls, and they patrolled everywhere, keeping watch all around (*Sanghbh.*, 78–79; see also Rockhill 1907: 24).

In this light, it may be that the Roman robots and other armed guards described above were intended not only to keep thieves out but also to keep the relics in. In any case, in both instances, the process of emergence—of the bodhisattva from Kapilavastu and of the relics from the underground chamber—involves disarming or circumventing these opposition forces, by the gods in one case, by Aśoka in the other.

Unlike Śuddhodana and his men, however, the guardian "robots" of the relics are artificial mechanical devices. In a world where images of buddhas and bodhisattvas and deities frequently "come alive," this is an important point.[22] Unlike those images, and unlike actual sentient beings, the robots are never thought to be living, and this fact leads to a second possible line of interpretation. One of the problems that arises in the story of the relics at Rāmagrama (as well as in other tales) is that the guardian spirits of the relics (nāgas, nats, etc.) sometimes become so enamored of the objects in their care that they do not wish to give them up. Because of this understandable enthusiasm, the person who eventually comes to collect the relics—though he may be recognized as having a legitimate claim to them—inevitably ends up appearing as somewhat of a thief who is taking away the object of devotion of sincere Buddhist devotees. The flipside of this issue may be seen in the Sanskrit story of Aśoka at Rāmagrāma, where, unable to deny the appropriateness and seriousness of the nāgas' devotion, he refrains from "theft" and leaves the relics where they are.

When it comes to Ajātaśatru's underground chamber, however, Aśoka has no choice. He *must* acquire the relics; they have, after all, been predestined for him. So, the story must find a solution to the problem of the

[22] For East Asian Buddhist stories about such images, see Soymié 1984; Frank 1986: 151–57; Faure 1996: 43–46; McCallum 1994: 39–54. For non-Buddhist Indian examples, see Davis 1997: 15–50. For a broader comparative perspective, see Freedberg 1989: 283–316.

potential awkwardness of having him violate the devotion of their traditional guardians: it therefore replaces the nāgas by artificial, nonsentient robots. Being purely mechanical, they do not run the risk of becoming attached or otherwise devoted to the relics they protect. They may, of course, present would-be Aśokas with certain technical problems, that is, they have to, in one fashion or another, be put out of commission, but at least they do not present them any moral dilemmas, and make them neither commit murder nor leave Buddhist devotees without their object of devotion.

The Construction of the 84,000 Stūpas

After gathering together all the relics that he can, Aśoka sets out to accomplish his most famous legendary act: the redistribution and reenshrinement of the Buddha's śarīra into 84,000 stūpas throughout his realm of Jambudvīpa. There are a number of different accounts of this episode. I would like to present, first, a summary of the story as found in the Sanskrit *Aśokāvadāna* and then compare and contrast it to that found in the Pali tradition, before making some interpretative comments.

In the *Aśokāvadāna,* after collecting the relics from the seven droṇa stūpas (all but that of Rāmagrāma), Aśoka prepares for them 84,000 reliquaries of different precious materials. Each of these is said to consist of a box (*karaṇḍa)*, an urn (*kumbha*) and a cloth band (*paṭṭa*) presumably for tying down the lid of the urn (Burnouf 1876: 332n.2). These are to be enshrined in 84,000 stūpas that Aśoka has built throughout the earth as far as the surrounding ocean, in towns and countries wherever there is a population of at least 100,000 persons. The term used for *stūpa* here is *dharmarājikā,* a word that may be taken to mean "[a monument] of the king of dharma" (Strong 1983: 109n). The king of dharma may be either the Buddha or Aśoka himself. The distribution of the relics to the stūpas is undertaken not by ministers or the king's men, but by supernatural beings—*yakṣas*—who here are seen to be under Aśoka's command.

Two factors about the distribution and enshrinement stand out. First, the stūpas must be spread evenly throughout the realm. Thus, when the people of Takṣaśilā (in what is today Pakistan) claim thirty-six boxes of relics arguing that they have a population of thirty-six hundred thousand people, Aśoka turns them down, realizing that if he were to accede to their demand (and presumably the demands of others like them), there would not be enough relics to go around to all areas, and a lopsidedness in their distribution would occur. His method of turning down their request is said to exhibit "expedient means" (*upāya*): he announces to the Takṣaśilans that if they insist on having a number of relics commensurate to their population, he will simply have to have thirty-five hundred thousand of their people executed! They quickly withdraw their request.[23]

The second factor that stands out in this account is that Aśoka wants all 84,000 stūpas to be completed on the same day, at the same time. To accomplish this, he calls on the help of the elder Yaśas at the Kukkuṭārāma Monastery in the capital of Pāṭaliputra. Yaśas volunteers to hide the orb of the sun with his hand; this eclipse is seen throughout the world and acts as a signal to the yakṣas everywhere to complete the stūpas.[24] Finally, with the completion of all 84,000 stūpas, we are told that Aśoka, who has been known as "Aśoka the Fierce" (Caṇḍāśoka) comes to be known as "Aśoka the Righteous" (Dharmāśoka) (*Aśokāv.*, 53–55 = Eng. trans., Strong 1983: 219–21. See also *T.* 2042, 50:102a–b = Fr. trans., Przyluski 1923: 242–43; *T.* 2043, 50:135a–b = Eng. trans., Li 1993: 19–20).

This account, which is representative of the Sanskrit tradition, may be contrasted and compared to the version of the story found in the *Mahāvaṃsa* and a number of other Pali texts. Unlike the *Aśokāvadāna,* the *Mahāvaṃsa* does not directly link Aśoka's construction project to his collection of the relics from the droṇa stūpas. In fact, it speaks not of 84,000 stūpas (or *dharmarājikās*) but of 84,000 monasteries (*vihāras*). These, however, also presumably have stūpas associated with them, and in time, the Pali tradition was to make this connection explicit (see *Thūp.,* 188 = Eng. trans., Jayawickrama 1971: 53).

In the *Mahāvaṃsa,* the 84,000 vihāras are said to be in honor of the 84,000 sections of the Buddha's teaching[25]—his dharma—and Aśoka has them built in 84,000 towns all over his realm. The spread of the vihāras thus is symbolic of the spread of the dharma, and even more specifically, of the spread of the Buddha's "body of dharma," his *dharmakāya.* In accomplishing this, Aśoka calls not on the help of divine beings, such as yakṣas, but on the obedience and cooperation of local kings, who are ordered to build the 84,000 monasteries, while he himself, Aśoka, undertakes the construction in the capital of a great central monastery, the Aśokārāma. Here too there is an emphasis on simultaneity, although it is featured in a different way in the *Mahāvaṃsa* than in the *Aśokāvadāna.* Rather than an eclipse occurring, letters arrive from all 84,000 cities, at

[23] In *T.* 2043, 50:135a = Eng. trans., Li 1993: 19, Aśoka announces that he will send relics to every country that pays one hundred thousand taels of gold. The Takṣaśilans offer thirty-six hundred thousand taels and request thirty-six shares of relics, but Aśoka turns them down.

[24] The *Aśokāv.* does not specify that it is a signal for the yakṣas, but that is made clear in Xuanzang's account of the tale, where the arhat hiding the orb of the sun is not Yaśas but Upagupta. See *T.* 2087, 51:911b–c = Eng. trans., Li 1996: 225–26. In Burmese tradition (e.g., *Hman-Nan-Y.,* 142 = Eng. trans., U Ko Ko 1983: 81), a lunar eclipse marks the start of construction and another one, three years later, marks the end.

[25] On the division of the teaching into 84,000 sections, see Lamotte 1988: 148–49.

the same time on the very same day, announcing the completion of all of the vihāras. This happy coincidence is made possible by the supernatural powers of the arhat Indagutta, who more generally acts as "superintendent of work" for the whole project (see Witanachchi 1976). Aśoka then orders a great festival to be celebrated in all 84,000 monasteries at once. Lavish gifts are made to members of the saṃgha, and the vihāras are decorated with garlands of flowers, strings of lamps, and other appropriate adornments. The climax of this festival, however, comes with a miracle called "the unveiling of the world" (*lokavivaraṇa*), which enables Aśoka, standing in his central monastery in Pāṭaliputra, to see the whole of Jambudvīpa, bounded by the ocean, and all 84,000 vihāras in it. This experience, which I shall examine in greater detail below, is given to Aśoka so that he will cease being "Aśoka the Fierce" (Caṇḍāsoka) and come to be known as "Aśoka the Righteous" (Dharmāsoka) (*Mhv.*, 36, 45–47 = Eng. trans., Geiger 1912: 32–33, 41–42. See also *Dpv.*, 49 = Eng. trans., Oldenberg [1879] 1982: 154; *VinA.*, 48–49 = Eng. trans., Jayawickrama 1962: 43; and *Thūp.*, 188 = Eng. trans., Jayawickrama 1971: 52).

The Rūpakāya and the Dharmakāya

In the three-hundred page "preface" to his book, *Barabuḍur*, Paul Mus (1998: 280–81) argues that one of the things that Aśoka accomplishes, in his construction of the 84,000 stūpas, is the reunification of the two bodies of the Buddha that had become separate at the time of his parinirvāṇa: his physical form, or rūpakāya, and his doctrinal corpus, or dharmakāya.[26] We have seen how, in the *Mahāvaṃsa*, the 84,000 monasteries are specifically said to commemorate the 84,000 sections of the Buddha's teachings, his dharma. This is the dharmalogical side. The 84,000 stūpas are, as Mus (1998: 280) graphically put it, "the dharma in stone," and together they reconstitute the dharma body of the Blessed One. The number 84,000, however, has also been related to the traditional number of atoms in a *physical* body, although this association is not pointed to in our texts.[27] Be this as it may, it is clear that the relics themselves, as physical remnants of the Buddha's body, may also be associated with his rūpakāya.

It is possible to trace, in Buddhist literature, a certain bifurcation between acts of seeing the actual physical body of the Buddha, and "see-

[26] On early twofold notions of the buddha body, see Demiéville 1934: 176–77 and Lancaster 1974: 287–91. For complications, see Makransky 1997: 4–5 and Lamotte 1949–80: 711–12n.

[27] All references to this seem, ultimately, to be traceable to Legge [1886] 1965: 69n.1, who, however, fails to cite any source. I have been unable to track down this notion.

ing," or understanding, his doctrinal body, the corpus of his teachings. During the Buddha's lifetime, the conjunction of these two visions presented few difficulties. If one met the Buddha, one could see his rūpakāya with one's ordinary eye of flesh (*maṃsacakṣu*), and, by listening to and understanding his teaching, one could "see" his dharmakāya with one's eye of wisdom (*prajñācakṣu*).[28] With the death and parinirvāṇa of the Buddha, however, certain problems arose, for both bodies were dissolved and had to be recaptured, remembered, rehearsed. The rūpakāya was, as the second-century C.E. poet Mātṛceṭa laments, "scattered like sesame seed" (see Lévi 1910: 455); its remnants—the relics—were dispersed into the eight droṇa stūpas, and their unity was lost (see Demiéville 1934a: 176). On the other hand, the Buddha's teaching—his dharmakāya—was also in danger of dissipation, so that its remnants had to be preserved at the first Buddhist council, where the canon was rehearsed. Overall, however, there was a feeling that the two somatic dimensions of the Buddha—his dharma and his rūpa—had been separated at death (see Strong 1979: 223–25). Aśoka's great accomplishment—to bring them together again in the relics—made possible, once more, a complete experience of the Buddha.

The "Unveiling of the World" and the Descent from Trāyastriṃśa Heaven

Aśoka's joining (or rejoining) of these two bodies of the Buddha, however, is achieved only by their correlation with a third dimension of the experience of the buddha relics: the cosmological one. Mention has been made above of the visionary experience of the "unveiling of the world" (*lokavivaraṇa*) that Aśoka is granted in the *Mahāvaṃsa*. In this experience, occasioned by the monks, the king in his capital is given a vision of the whole of his kingdom, defined now by the 84,000 vihāras he has built. As one version of the story put it, "[T]he king, standing before the Aśokārāma Monastery, was able to see the entire continent of Jambudvīpa right to its shores touching the Great Ocean, the whole landscape studded with 84,000 shrines of his own construction. He saw all the details as though all the shrines were placed on the palm of his hand" (U Ko Ko 1983, 2:53; text in U Kala 1960: 90).

This visionary experience, however, is a phenomenon that is not limited to the occasion of Aśoka's construction of the stūpas. In one Pali commentary, the unveiling of the world (lokavivaraṇa) is said to be the same as the miracle called "making the world bright" (*lokappasādaka*),

[28] Both of these eyes are given a number of alternate names. On the correspondence between the different eyes and the different bodies, see, inter alia, Falk 1943: 114–15.

an illumination that enables all beings to see one another from the highest heaven to the deepest hell (*BuvA.*, 46 = Eng. trans., Horner 1978: 70). In the *Buddhavaṃsa,* Śāriputra performs this illuminatory miracle for the benefit of five hundred monks (*Buv.*, 4 = Eng. trans., Horner 1975: 5). Generally speaking, however, it is connected to the event of the Buddha's descent at Saṃkāśya from the Trāyastriṃśa Heaven, where he spent a rains-retreat preaching to the gods, his mother among them.[29] According to Buddhaghosa, as the Buddha and the gods come down from the Trāyastriṃśa Heaven on the triple ladder made for them and are met in Saṃkāśya by the assembled crowds of devotees, not only is there a revelation of the whole world, but also a breakdown of the barriers between gods and men. For this is an occasion on which humans can see gods (*deva*) and gods can see humans, face to face, without the one having to look down or the other having to look up (*Vsm.*, 392 = Eng. trans., Ñyāṇamoli 1976: 429).

The importance of *seeing* (*darśana*)—one's god, one's guru, one's fellow humans—in Indian religious traditions is well known. It is a moment of coming together that is both devotional and soteriological (see Eck 1981; Swearer, forthcoming). In the case of the descent from Trāyastriṃśa, however, not only can humans and gods see each other; they are also able to see the Buddha. This is is an important point since, mythologically speaking, the absence of the Buddha during his rains-retreat in the Trāyastriṃśa Heaven may be seen as a sort of dry-run for his parinirvāṇa. Indeed, his unannounced departure for that heaven leads the assembled faithful to lament his disappearance as though he were gone forever (*DhA.*, 3:218 = Eng. trans., Burlingame 1921, 3:48). The Buddha's descent from heaven at Saṃkāśya, then, is symbolic of an overcoming of his absence in the eyes of the faithful, an occasion that is marked by an "unveiling of the world," in which gods, humans, and buddha can all see one another.

There also appears in this story the theme of the two bodies of the Buddha. In the *Questions of King Milinda,* for instance, the lokavivaraṇa at the time of the Buddha's descent from heaven is presented as an occasion for laypersons to realize the four noble truths. This would seem to amount to a vision of the dharmakāya. As Rhys Davids (1890–94, 2:249n.) points out in a footnote, however, the Sinhalese text also interprets the lokavivaraṇa as an occasion on which the Budha's rūpakāya—his physical body— is made manifest in all of its glory. The same duality of vision is made even

[29] On the Buddha's descent from Trāyastriṃśa heaven, see Strong 2001: 115–17 and Huntington 1986. For a bibliography, see Lamotte 1988: 339–40. For sources that relate it to the miracle of the "unveiling of the world," see below and *Mil.*, 350 = Eng. trans., Davids 1890–94, 2:248–49; *Dāṭh.*, 123 = Eng. trans., Law 1925:22; and *JA.*, 4:266 = Eng. trans., Cowell 1895–1907, 4:168.

more explicit in the version of the story that is retold in the Mahāyānist *Mahāprajñāpāramitā-śāstra.* There, two of the individuals who are said to welcome the Buddha at Saṃkāśya—the arhat Subhūti and the nun Utpalavarṇā—each greet him in their own way. Subhūti, the champion of the perfection of wisdom, is meditating on emptiness in a cave. He realizes that the Buddha is about to descend from Trāyastriṃśa Heaven and wonders whether or not he should go to Saṃkāśya to welcome him, since, after all, it is a time when "gods will see humans and humans will see gods." But then he reflects that the Buddha always said that the best way to see the Buddha is to see him in his dharmakāya with one's eye of wisdom (prajñācakṣu). He therefore goes to "meet" the Buddha while remaining in meditation in his cave. Quite different is the case of the nun Utpalavarṇā, who is eager to see the physical body of the Buddha, so much so that, in her eagerness, she transforms herself into a great cakravartin king and is thus able to take her place at the front of the crowd at Saṃkāśya. In this way, she becomes the very first person to salute the Buddha's rūpakāya. The text of the śāstra, true to its prajñāpāramitā heritage, praises Subhūti as the one who has truly seen the Buddha, and denigrates Utpalavarṇā; nonetheless, we have here a situation, recognized as a time of "unveiling of the world," in which both bodies of the Buddha can be and are seen, albeit by different individuals (*T.* 1509, 25:137a = Fr. trans., Lamotte 1949–80: 634–36). Much the same thing is true of the lokavivaraṇa at the time of Aśoka's building the 84,000 stūpas, except that the Buddha (in his relics) is returning not from the Trāyastriṃśa Heaven but from parinirvāṇa.

The Divine Eye and the Buddha's Smile

Paul Mus (1998: 280–81) has argued that Aśoka's "lokavivaraṇa" is tantamount to the cosmic circumambulation (pradakṣina) of the cakravartin. According to the *Cakkavatti Sīhanāda sutta,* at the beginning of each cakravartin's reign, a great wheel—the wheel of dharma—appears in mid-air in front of the king, as a sign of his righteousness. It then leads him in a great cosmic conquest of the world. It takes him to the East, South, West, and North, as far as the great ocean in every direction, and wherever it rolls, he meets with no resistance. Finally, the wheel takes Aśoka back to his capital at the center of the world, and there it remains, miraculously suspended in mid-air over the royal palace, an illuminating emblem of his sovereignty, visible to all (*D.,* 3:61–63 = Eng. trans., Davids 1899–1924, 3:62–64). The lokavivaraṇa, according to Mus (1964) is a sort of freezing in time in a single moment, a solid cinema of what is here expressed as a process. In both instances, there is a visitation or vision of the realm, as a result of which the king becomes established in his capital as a dharmarāja.

The vision that Aśoka has of the world, however, is also not without recalling the similar vision had by the Buddha in the second watch of the night of his enlightenment. Aśoka sees, with his royal (deva) eye, the entirety of his realm and all the beings in it. The Buddha sees, with his divine (deva) eye, beings throughout the cosmos moving through the pathways of rebirth (*Sanghbhv.,* 1:118 = Eng. trans., Strong 2002: 17). Coming on top of the remembrance of his own previous existences in the first watch of the night, such a vision adds to that a cosmological dimension. It provides a realization of the common situation of all creatures throughout the cosmos, of the final alikeness and interrelationship of all beings. It is a vision of the universe as an open book in which nothing is hidden and where, consequently, there is no place to hide. This, as we shall see, constitutes an important part of the Buddhist experience of enlightenment.

A more proactive expression of this vision, perhaps, may be seen in stories about the Buddha's smile, which likewise involves a salvific illumination of the universe. In Sanskrit *avadāna* literature, descriptions of the Buddha's smile abound. A stock passage repeated over twenty times in the *Avadānaśataka* asserts that "it is the norm that whenever blessed buddhas manifest their smile, blue, yellow, red, and dazzlingly white rays issue forth from their mouth, and some go down and some go up. Those that go down enter the [various hells] and . . . those that go up [the various heavens]" (Strong 2002: 27; text in *Avś.,* 297). In both places, the rays alleviate the sufferings of beings, in several ways. In the hells, for instance, they do this physically (by heating the cold hells and cooling the hot ones); they also do it psychologically (by illuminating the hells so as to enable the beings there to see one another and so to realize that they are not alone); and finally they do this salvifically, by projecting a magical image of the Buddha into the hells, an image that lets the beings there see his body and that engenders their devotion, enabling them to cast off their remaining bad karma and be reborn among the gods or humans, as "vessels of the truth" (Strong 2002: 27; text in *Avś.,* 297). What we have here, once again, is a revelation of the cosmos as a whole that makes it possible, first, for beings to see each other; second, for beings to see the physical form (rūpakāya) of the normally absent Buddha; and third, for beings to realize the truth of the Buddha's teaching—to see his dharmalogical form (dharmakāya).

From Centrifugality to Centripetality: The Power of Compassion

The Buddha's smile, as well as his second watch experience may be taken as expressions of his compassion for others. The same may be said of the spread of his relics. In building the 84,000 stūpas, Aśoka is causing the

Buddha's relics to be dispersed "far and wide" (*Aśokāv.*, 50 = Eng. trans., Strong 1983: 217). It will be recalled that, in chapter one, we saw that the motivation for such a dispersal was that it was done "out of compassion for living beings" by buddhas who had not been able to complete their mission in their lifetime (*Buv.*, 102 = Eng. trans., Horner 1975: 99). Now, however, we can see that there are different possible modes for the expression of this spread of compassion.

With Aśoka, it appears that the relics have truly "gone galactic."[30] By building the 84,000 stūpas, and placing himself at the center, the Mauryan monarch manages to assert and reinforce the maṇḍalaic unity of the whole empire. But it is important to realize that there is a certain progression in this achievement, and that it involves certain roads not taken. In considering together as a whole the various legends of the distribution of the Buddha's relics, we can see that Aśoka (or in some texts, Mahākāśyapa) first corrects the *centrifugal* forces that originally caused the relics to be taken off to the eight droṇa stūpas where they reinforced the local loyalties and rivalries of petty kingdoms—their tribal republicanism. The "war of the relics" even though it never actually broke out, left the Buddha's body fragmented and unorganized, with the relics in danger of flying off centrifugally forever. Aśoka puts an end to this.

In doing so, however, he rejects also the *centralizing* monopolizing forces exhibited by Mahākāśyapa and Ajātaśatru who, in bringing all the relics together in the capital, chose to hide them underground and jealously guard them from the view and even the knowledge of others. If the first centrifugal phase can be thought of as the split up and dispersal of the Buddha and his teaching among his many devotees, that is, his disciples (śrāvakas, arhats), the metaphor here, for this centralization, would be the pratyekabuddha—the "buddha for oneself" whose realization is "all there," but who fails to make that realization available to others. Politically and sociologically, this would amount to a totalitarian system in which all power and authority rested in one single somewhat paranoid ruler.

Over and against this, Aśoka opts instead to "*centripetalize*" the relics, to distribute them outward in a way that allows them to exist locally, while at the same time emphasizing their ongoing ties to the center, their ultimate unity and interconnection. Like the rays of the Buddha's smile, which do not diffuse out endlessly but cycle back to the person of the Blessed One, the relics that Aśoka sends out remain connected to him at the hub. This makes for a conceptual structure that precludes potential "centers out there" in the distribution of the relics. There can be no lopsidedness in this maṇḍalaic scheme, something that is graphically illustrated in the story of the Takṣaśilans, who are refused more than a single share of relics. At the

[30] The expression is inspired by the work of Tambiah (1976: 102ff)

same time, what keeps capital and provinces—center and periphery—together is the vision that the relics make possible, a vision of the whole, a vision that we saw epitomized in the event of the unveiling of the world, a vision that is everyone's but also, of course, Aśoka's. Aśoka at the center "looks down upon the world" in ways that recall the bodhisattva, at the moment of his birth in Lumbinī, when he views all four directions, or a bodhisattva such as Avalokiteśvara, whose very name ("the lord who looks down [with compassion]") expresses such a vision.[31] All of this can perhaps best be summarized in the form of a table (see table 3).

TABLE 3
Modes of distribution of the Buddha's relics following his parinirvāṇa

Movement of relics	*Locale of relics*	*Major actors*	*Homologous political ideology*	*Homologous soteriological ideal*	*Experience engendered by the relics*
centrifugal	8 droṇa stūpas	Droṇa and the eight rulers	Tribal republicanism	Arhat	Fragmentation (War of Relics)
centralizing	single underground chamber	Ajātaśatru and Mahākāśyapa	Totalitarianism	Pratyeka-buddha	Esoterism
centripetal	84,000 stūpas	Aśoka	Maṇḍalaic kingship of cakravartin	Bodhisattva/ buddha	Compassion for the world as a whole

The Festival of the Relics

The "unveiling of the world" (lokavivaraṇa) is only one aspect of a greater festival of relics that Aśoka is said to celebrate as the culmination of his construction of the 84,000 stūpas. Merely hinted at in the *Aśokāvadāna,* it is announced by royal messengers in the *Mahāvaṃsa:* "On the seventh day from this day shall a festival of all the ārāmas be kept, in every way, in all the provinces" (*Mhv.*, 46 = Eng. trans., Geiger 1912: 41). This is then described as a time when lavish gifts are given to the saṃgha, when the monasteries and streets are adorned with strings of lamps and garlands of flowers, when music is played, sermons are preached, and the eight precepts are observed. Aśoka participates in the festivities, wearing all his adornments, accompanied by his wives, minis-

[31] On these connections, see Mus 1964a. The name "Avalokiteśvara" is commonly interpreted as meaning "the lord who looks down [upon the world with compassion]." More generally on its etymology, see Holt 1991: 31; and Yü 2001: 13–14.

ters, and troops. The monks and nuns too are there in their numbers (*Mhv.*, 47 = Eng. trans., Geiger 1912: 41–42).

Later texts were to develop this scene even further. The *Ārya-mañjuśrīmūlakalpa,* for instance, specifies that Aśoka himself visited all of the stūpas and made offerings to them, in a chariot loaded with gold, silver, copper, and various ornaments (*AMMK.*, 27 = Eng. trans., Lamotte 1988: 241). But it was the legend of the elder Upagupta, recounted in the *Lokapaññatti* and other texts, that was to make this celebration the center of a whole new saga and cause it to become a paradigm of sorts for stūpa festivals throughout Southeast Asia (*LP.*, 162–74 = Fr. trans., Denis 1977, 2:144–52; see also Strong 1992: 186–208). Upagupta is recruited by Aśoka and the saṃgha to help protect the festival from disruption by Māra. The details of this story need not concern us here, except to mention that Upagupta is successful in taming Māra, and that, in the process, he gets Māra to take on, for him, the physical form (rūpakāya) of the Buddha so that he (Upagupta), as well as all others present (including monks, laypersons, and Aśoka) can see what the Blessed One looked like (*LP.*, 173 = Fr. trans., Denis 1977, 2:152; *Hman-Nan-Y.*, 162 = Eng. trans., U Ko Ko 1983, 2:108; see also Strong 1992: 98–117 and 188ff.; Duroiselle 1904). In some versions of the tale, in fact, we are told that this vision of the Buddha's rūpakāya is what inspires the monks who are present to go on and stage the "unveiling of the world" so that Aśoka can see all 84,000 shrines that symbolize the Buddha's dharmakāya (U Kala 1960: 89–90 = Eng. trans., U Ko Ko 1983, 2:50–53; U Kin 1957:120 = Eng. trans., U Ko Ko 1983, 1:41–42). Here again we can see the pairing of rūpakāya and dharmakāya expressed in a different way.

The celebration of the actual festival of the stūpas, however, involves several other factors. I have dealt with the *Lokapaññatti*'s description of this event elsewhere (see Strong 1992: 154–57), and so here I would like to focus on versions of the story that were incorporated into a number of later Burmese chronicles, and that have not yet been given the attention they deserve. These, as they themselves admit, are derivatively based on the *Lokapaññatti,* but they present some interesting additional pieces of information.[32] The *Glass Palace Chronicle.* for instance, begins its account as follows:

[32] I am only able to do this thanks to the generosity and the translations made for me by the late U Ko Ko, formerly of the University of Mandalay. His translations, some of which have already been used in this chapter, cover sections of one eighteenth-century Burmese work, the *Mahayazawingyi* (= U Kala 1960), and three nineteenth-century ones, the *Mahawin Wutthu* (= U Kin 1957), the *Jinathapakāsani* (= U Kin 1981), and the *Glass Palace Chronicle* (= *Hman-Nan-Y.*), and remain, unfortunately, unpublished. They are contained in two notebooks in my possession and so are cited as U Ko Ko 1983, volumes 1 and 2. For the most part, I shall quote U Ko Ko's words directly, with only a few slight alterations.

> The relics that King Asoka brought from Rājagaha were divided into several portions, one being meant for the royal city of Pāṭaliputta and the rest to be spread over several parts of his kingdom—numbering 84,000 in all. There at the riverbank at Pāṭaliputta, a plot of land one-and-a-half kosas [about 1,000 meters] in extent was levelled flat and thereon was built the Mahazedi [Mahā-cetiya = Aśoka's Mahāstūpa] on a lavish scale. Then the king said to the assembly of monks: "Reverend Sirs, there are now 84,000 shrines and monasteries all over my kingdom, built by me, and I wish to hold a veneration ceremony lasting seven years, seven months, and seven days" (U Ko Ko 1983, 2:91–92; text in *Hman-Nan-Y.*, 159).

The *Mahayazawingyi* adds to this a few details of its own. Aśoka specifies that all people taking part in the celebration shall take refuge in the Triple Gem and observe the eight precepts, and he is said to decorate the royal city with jewels "so that it dazzled like Tāvatiṃsa [Skt.: Trāyastriṃśa], the home of the gods" (U Ko Ko 1983, 2:41; text in U Kala 1960: 86).

Most of our sources then emphasize the size of the crowd participating in the festival. They do this by focusing on the fact that Aśoka brings with him to worship the relics a fourfold army that is called *akkhobhaṇī*—a term that would appear to be related both to the Pali words for "unshakeable" (*akkhobhana*) and for one of the greatest numbers imaginable (*akkhobhiṇī* = 10^{41}). Like all four-fold armies, the akkhobhaṇī consists of elephants, chariots, cavalry, and infantry, but, in fact, this amounts to quite a diverse crowd, for, as one text puts it, in an akkhobhaṇī army,

> Each elephant has three riders—front, middle, and back—two spear-holders on the right and another two on the left, and behind them four attendants, and at the back of them all, in charge of the elephant's tail, one more attendant. Together with one [person] in charge of feeding, each elephant has thirteen people that accompany it. Each chariot has one driver, one assistant driver on either side, and one spear-holder on either side, so that it has five persons that go along with it. Each horse has one rider, one spear-holder on either side and one orderly so that it has four persons along with it. One elephant is surrounded by a hundred chariots. One chariot is surrounded by a hundred horses, and one horse is surrounded by a hundred [foot]-soldiers. Again each soldier is attended by a hundred women, each of whom has a hundred female-servants to look after her needs.
>
> An [akkhobhaṇī] "army" consists of nine thousand elephants [+ attendants], nine hundred thousand chariots [+ attendants], ninety million horses [+ attendants], nine billion soldiers, nine hundred billion women, and ninety trillion female-servants (U Ko Ko 1983, 2:42–44; text in U Kala 1960: 86–87).

None of this, of course, includes the monks present for the occasion, who are said to number eight billion, or the nuns who are put at ninety-nine million (U Kala 1960: 87 = Eng. trans., U Ko Ko 1983, 2:44). It is noteworthy that most of the laypersons in attendance at the relics festival are women, even though they are clearly placed in a subordinate position. Most of the monastics, however, are monks.

Apart from the vast numbers of people at the festival, the illumination that takes place is also emphasized. The *Glass Palace Chronicle* specifies that oil lamps are brilliantly lit everywhere in a circle around the Mahāstūpa, whose radius measures one-and-a-half *yojanas* (an area about thirty-six miles in diameter) (U Ko Ko 1983, 2:102; text in *Hman-Nan-Y.*, 161). Other texts are more modest and reduce the figure down to half of a yojana (U Kala 1960:86 = Eng. trans., U Ko Ko 1983, 2:41; and U Kin 1957: 116 = Eng. trans., U Ko Ko 1983, 1:32). In either case, we have here a ritual equivalent of the illumination / unveiling of the world discussed earlier.

Aśoka's Autocremation

This theme of ritual illumination and offering is furthered by an event that, in the *Lokapaññattti* and subsequent texts, is presented as the climax of the whole celebration of Aśoka's lokavivaraṇa: his decision to set himself on fire, thereby transforming his own body into a human lamp. The one experience (the unveiling of the world) is said to inspire the other (Aśoka's fiery offering of himself). As the *Mahawin wutthu* puts it,

> Seeing before him, spread all over the continent of Jambudīpa, all the 84,000 shrines and monasteries in a clear vision . . . , his [Aśoka's] faith and liberality were multiplied several times over. In this way he was led to prepare for the highest form of charity—that of offering himself in an oblation of fire. With that end in view, the king had himself wrapped in oil-soaked cotton, which was then set ablaze. This resulted in flames that leaped to a height of seven yojanas. All this while the king kept his meditation on . . . the Buddha and this concentration gave him so much protection that the raging fire did no harm whatsoever. On the contrary, the king felt a cooling sensation as though besmeared with sandalwood. This fire oblation went on for seven days, at the end of which the king bathed himself, circumambulated the Mahazedi with his retinue three times, fed the monks, listened to the doctrine, and proceeded to his palace (U Ko Ko 1983, 1:42–44; text in U Kin 1957: 20–21. See also U Kala 1960: 90–91 = Eng. trans., U Ko Ko 1983, 2:53–56; *Hman-Nan-Y.*, 163 = Eng. trans., U Ko Ko 1983, 2:110–11; *LP.*, 174 = Eng. trans., Strong 1992: 207–208).

The importance of this event in defining Aśoka is clear not only from its being featured as the climax of his great festival, but also from the fact that these sources make this same deed into something that the Buddha himself is said to have prophesied about Aśoka (*Hman-Nan-Y.*, 160 = Eng. trans., U Ko Ko 1983, 2:96–97; see also U Kala 1960: 83 = Eng. trans., U Ko Ko 1983, 2:33–34; and U Kin 1957: 112 = Eng. trans., U Ko Ko 1983, 1:23). Clearly then, this fiery self-offering became an important part of Aśoka's self-definition. In chapter 4, I already connected this act, and others like it, to the event of the Buddha's [auto]-cremation at the time of his parinirvāṇa, in which he too became a sort of human torch, wrapped in a thousand oil-soaked cloths. Here, however, we may see a difference betwen the two scenarios. The Buddha's burning resulted in a particular transformation: his physical presence, formerly embodied in his rūpakāya, became embodied in his relics. Aśoka, however, is transformed in a different way: when the fire engulfing him finishes burning, nothing has happened to his physical body—he is still present here on earth—and no relics have been produced. And yet, it may be that the experience deifies him, for, shortly thereafter, we are told, he dies and is reborn in heaven, the "world of the gods"(*devaloka*) (*LP.*, 177 = Fr. trans., Denis 1977, 2:154).

Conclusion

In her study of state sponsorship of relic veneration in contemporary Myanmar, Juliane Schober (1997: 220) points out that such things as the construction of stūpas by kings and royal patronage of the Buddha's rūpakāya "create a field of merit and source of political legitimation separate and distinct from . . . the saṃgha," one that "diminish[es] the saṃgha's [traditional] position as a religious institution and source of merit and charisma" (Schober 1997: 242). Though meant to depict modern Myanmar, this conclusion is perhaps not without a certain applicability to some of the legends we have looked at in this chapter.

In Aśoka's "centripetalizing" of the Buddha's relics and his celebration of the relics festival, Buddhist monks tend to become adornments to the king and / or facilitators of the royal vision, rather than independent focal points of devotion. Thus the arhat Yaśas (or Upagupta in Xuanzang's account) serves Aśoka by signaling the moment for the enshrinement of the relics; and Indagutta plays a similar role in the *Mahāvaṃsa*. And when Aśoka stands on the Aśokārāma in the midst of the assembled saṃgha, it is the monks who make possible for him the unveiling of the world, for him and everyone to view his kingdom, Jambudvīpa, as far as the cosmic ocean. Such a vision, as we have seen, puts an end to alternative worldviews—to a realm governed by centrifugal forces, in which the relics are controlled by autonomous local rulers and saṃghas, and to a scenario of centralization in which they are all hoarded in a single place, and esotericized as the secret source of power of a single ruler such as Ajātaśatru, or of a single saṃgha patriarch such as Mahākāśyapa. Aśoka's dealings with the relics thus emphasize a middle course between two poles, but it is a middle course that insures that he and the rulers throughout Asia who followed his example played a key role in the ongoing preservation, distribution, veneration, and definition of the relics of the Buddha's body.

At the same time, there can be seen in Aśoka's actions toward the relics a series of acts that recall and replicate some of the major stages of the Buddha's biography. First, he liberates the relics from Mahākāśyapa's underground stūpa, where they were enshrined in a reliquary in the form of the bodhisattva's horse Kaṇṭhaka surrounded by seven bejewelled walls recalling the seven ramparts of a royal city. This, we have seen, is tantamount to a reenactment of the bodhisattva's great departure from Kapilavastu. Secondly, Aśoka's distribution of the relics into 84,000 stūpas and his vision of those stūpas that mark the 84,000 sections of the dharma, in the miracle of the unveiled world (lokavivaraṇa), brings to mind the Buddha's use of his divine eye in the second watch of the night of his awakening, as well as his reappearance in this world after his descent from the Trāyastriṃśa Heaven. Finally, Aśoka's autocremation, in which his body burns as a torch in honor of the Buddha's relics for seven days and nights, recalls, as we have seen, the event of the Buddha's own parinirvāṇa.

Chapter Six

PREDESTINED RELICS: THE EXTENSION OF THE BUDDHA'S LIFE STORY IN SOME SRI LANKAN TRADITIONS

ON ONE of his tours of what is now Northeastern Thailand and Laos, the Buddha stopped on the banks of the Mekong River, at a place that had been visited by the three previous buddhas of this aeon. He received alms from the local king, and then predicted that, after his parinirvāṇa, his "breast bone relic" (*urangadhātu*) would be enshrined at that spot. Upon returning to India, he entrusted his disciple, Mahākāśyapa, with the task of making sure that this enshrinement took place, and then again, just before passing away, he reminded Ānanda, "Do not allow the fire to consume my body until [Mahākāśyapa] has obtained the Breast-bone Relic to take to Dōi Kapaṇagīrī" (Pruess 1976: 27). Those were, in fact, the Buddha's last words, according to a local chronicle. And when Mahākāśyapa finally did arrive in Kuśināgarī, just after he venerated the Buddha's feet but prior to the lighting of the pyre, "the Breast-bone Relic, wrapped in a woolen cloth, miraculously emerged from the golden casket and hovered above the right palm of the disciple" (Pruess 1976: 27). Mahākāśyapa took the relic and subsequently flew across the sea with it and had it enshrined in what is now Wat Phra That Phanom in Northeastern Thailand (Pruess 1976: 30, 1976a: 177).

Similar stories may be found elsewhere: A Mon tradition features a tooth relic promised by the Buddha to the people of Thaton, in Lower Burma, which was taken there from his funeral pyre by the arhat Gavāṃpati (see Shorto 1970; *Sās.*, 35–37 = Eng. trans., Law 1952: 40–42; and Strong 2002a). A Northern Thai tradition features a relic predicted for Wat Haripuñjaya in Lamphun, which was taken there after the Buddha's parinirvāṇa to await the moment when, thanks to a guardian crow, it would be rediscovered under the latrine of King Ādittarāja (eleventh century) (see Swearer and Sommai 1998: 125–33; *Jin.*, 77–80 = Eng. trans., Jayawickrama 1968: 106–9; Swearer 1976: 8–9; Notton 1926–32, 2:44ff.). And a Laotian tradition features a journey made by the Buddha to the future site of Wat Muang Sing, where he foretells the enshrinement of his neckbone, his whetstone, and his razor, on a hill called Doi Chiangteum (see Lafont 1957: 47; Cohen 2000). In these and other tales, we have examples of what may be called predicted or predestined relics, that is, relics whose enshrinement in a particular place occurs after the time of the Buddha but is said to have been foretold by him while he was still alive.

The connection of such predictions or "resolutions" (adhiṣṭhāna; Pali: *adhiṭṭhāna*) to relics is spelled out in the *Questions of King Milinda*. There, it is asked how it is that miraculous manifestations (such as displays of bright lights, etc.) can take place at the relic shrines of saints who have already passed away. Given that these arhats are now "absent" from the world in parinirvāṇa, how can their ongoing "powers" be manifest? The Venerable Nāgasena explains that there are three ways in which such post-parinirvāṇa "miracles" can occur: by virtue of the resolve and faith of devotees, by virtue of the actions of gods, and by virtue of a resolution (adhiṭṭhāna) made by the parinirvāṇized saint in question *prior* to his death (*Mil.*, 309 = Eng. trans., Davids 1890–84, 2:174–75). Buddhas as well as arhats are thus thought to have the ability to determine the fate of their own relics after passing away. This is important for it is one of the modes in which the paradox of presence and absence of the Buddha in his relics is resolved: the Buddha is absent, but his ongoing will is present and manifests itself in particular ways.[1] As one (late-twelfth-century?) text put it, "Even after his extinction, the long-standing compassion of [the Blessed One] who had done what had to be done, did not itself become extinct" (*Jināl.*, 49 = Eng. trans., Gray 1894: 110).

In this chapter, I shall limit myself to a consideration of three relics whose post-mortem manifestations are said, in the Sri Lankan chronicles, to be the subject of five great adhiṣṭhānas (resolutions) made by the Buddha on his deathbed. The first three of these adhiṣṭhanas are closely related to one another and concern miracles that will be manifested by the bodhi tree, whose southern branch will be sent for transplanting in Sri Lanka by King Aśoka. More specifically, the Buddha declares that the bodhi branch will detach itself from the tree and, of its own accord, plant itself in a vase; illuminate the whole world with multicolored rays of light; and enter a bank of high cold mist and clouds (see Childers 1909: 155, s.v. "himo") and remain concealed there for seven days.[2] The Buddha's next adhiṣṭhāna—his fourth—concerns the fate of his right collarbone relic,

[1] Trainor (1997: 163) has called attention to this important aspect of Buddhist relics. Berkwitz (2001: 161 and forthcoming) argues that the Buddha's adhiṣṭhānas instill moral / emotional feelings of gratitude in later devotees.

[2] The order and time of resolution of these three individual adhiṣṭhānas, however, vary from text to text. The *Mhv.* seems to repeat the second and third of them twice—once in Bodhgaya and once in Anurādhapura. The *VinA.* reverses the order of the second and third.

which he determines will be enshrined in the Thūpārāma in Sri Lanka, where it will manifest the miracle of double-appearances such as the Buddha himself performed at Śrāvastī.[3] Finally, the Buddha makes a fifth adhiṣṭhāna: he resolves that the droṇa measure of his relics that will have gone to Rāmagrāma (see chapter 5) will in due course be enshrined in the Mahāthūpa in Sri Lanka, and will, at that time, also take on the appearance of the Buddha and perform the Twin Miracle (*Mbv.*, 147; *Mhv.*, 138 = Eng. trans., Geiger 1912: 120; and *VinA.*, 92 = Eng. trans., Jayawickrama 1962: 82). All three of these relics are promised to Sri Lanka, but each of them presents a slightly different perspective on the ways in which relics can be seen acting as self-determined extensions of the Buddha's life story.[4]

The Transplanting of the Bodhi Tree and the Multiplication of Relics

Buddhist traditions about the bodhi tree are multifarious, and it is not possible to consider all of them here.[5] According to the *Aśokāvadāna*, after Aśoka had built the 84,000 stūpas, his faith "was particularly aroused by the tree of awakening" at Bodhgaya, and he began making great offerings to it. This provoked the jealousy of his wife, Tiṣyarakṣitā, who craved some of that devotion and attention for herself. Malignantly, she hired a sorceress to destroy the bodhi tree, and might have succeeded had the plot not been uncovered in time (*Aśokāv.*, 93–94 = Eng. trans., Strong 1983: 257–58). Before the tree recovered, however, when it looked as though it might wither away, Aśoka himself felt faint and exclaimed, "When I look at the king of trees, I know that, even now, I am looking at the Master. If the tree of the Lord should come to perish, I too shall surely expire!" (*Aśokāv.*, 93 = Eng. trans., Strong 1983: 257).[6]

[3] For studies of the great miracle at Śrāvastī, see Foucher 1917 and Mus 1934: 198–213. For a Pali version of the story, see *DhA.*, 3:198–216 = Eng. trans., Burlingame 1921, 3:35–47; for a Sanskrit version, see *Div.*, 143–66 = Fr. trans., Burnouf 1876: 144–68.
[4] In addition, mention might be made of the forehead bone relic (*nalāṭadhātu*) which will not be studied here but which is featured in the fourteenth-century *Dhātuvaṃsa* (see Trainor 1997: 146–47) as predestined for Sēruvila, and which was touched upon in chapter 3.
[5] On the bodhi tree in general, see Higashimoto and Nanayakkara 1972. On the bodhi tree in Sri Lanka, see Nissanka 1994; on its central position in Anurādhapura, see Wickrematne 1987: 54–55. For the chronicle of its coming to Sri Lanka, see *Mbv.* On its cult in Sri Lanka, see De Silva 1980: 67–69. On the recent transformation of the worship of the bodhi tree, see Gombrich 1981 and Gombrich and Obeyesekere 1988: 384–410.
[6] For a discussion of this episode and a comparison with the variant story found in the *Mhv.*, see Strong 1983: 125–27.

This sense that the bodhi tree can replace the Buddha in his absence is true not only of the original tree at Bodhgaya but also of other bodhi trees as well, which are thought to stem from it. This is made clear in a number of texts. The *Kalingabodhi jātaka,* for instance, recounts the frustration of the people of Śrāvastī who, one day, find they have nobody to venerate when they go to the Jetavana and find the Buddha "out," gone off on a trip somewhere. To remedy this situation, upon his return, the Buddha allows Ānanda to plant a bodhi tree in front of the Jetavana. It grows miraculously quickly from a fruit from the original tree gathered by Mahāmaudgalyāyana at Bodhgaya, and it then serves as a substitute focus for people's devotions whenever the Buddha is not in residence (*JA.,* 4:228–29 = Eng. trans., Cowell 1895–1907, 4:142–43).[7] Much the same point is made in a verse of the *Jinālaṅkāra,* where the Buddha is quoted as saying, "When I am gone, the dharma and vinaya which I taught you will be your Master, as well as my bodily relics, the seat of awakening, and the most excellent bodhi tree. They too will also be your Master, after I am gone. I allow you to establish the bodhi tree and the relics in my place, and to venerate them in order to obtain the way to bliss" (*Jināl.,* 49 = Eng. trans., Gray [1894] 1981: 110).

At the same time, the paradigmatic worshiper of the bodhi tree is said to be the Buddha himself, who spent the second week after his enlightenment contemplating the tree "with unblinking eyes" (*JA.,* 77 = Eng. trans., Jayawickrama 1990: 104). Indeed, even today, a verse commonly recited by worshipers of the bodhi tree starts with this reminder: "I bow my head to the very pure king of bodhi trees that was venerated for seven days by the Master himself [who gazed at it] with tears flowing from his . . . wide-open eyes" (Barua 1994: 122; see also De Silva 1980: 67). This is noteworthy for it helps us understand the double importance of this relic. On the one hand, it represents the Buddha himself; on the other hand, by worshiping it, the devotee imitates an act of the Buddha, and so further identifies him or herself with him. In this way both the relic and the relic-worshiper recall the departed Master.

According to the Pali chronicles, it is not a seed of the original bodhi tree at Bodhgaya but its whole southern branch that is cut and taken to the Sri Lankan capital, Anurādhapura. The story is as follows: One day, Princess Anulā, the sister-in-law of the Sri Lankan king Devānampiya Tissa, forms the wish to be ordained. However, this is not possible for there are, as yet, no nuns in Sri Lanka, and it takes a quorum of ten nuns legitimately to carry out new ordinations. The elder Mahinda (King Aśoka's son) therefore recommends that his sister, Sanghamittā, who is a fully ordained *bhikṣuṇī,* be invited to come from India to the island,

[7] This is very similar to certain stories about the origins of buddha images. See Swearer forthcoming: ch. 1; Strong 2002: 39–41; Carter 1990.

along with a quorum of nuns. At the same time, he specifies that she should bring with her a branch of the bodhi tree, since the bodhi trees of the three previous buddhas of this aeon were also transplanted to Sri Lanka (*VinA.*, 90 = Eng. trans., Jayawickrama 1962: 80; and *Mbv.*, 144–45).[8]

When the Sri Lankan delegation sent by Devānampiya Tissa and Mahinda arrives in Pāṭaliputra to ask that Sanghamittā be sent back with them, Aśoka is first aggrieved at the thought of losing his daughter. She, however, explains to him that it is her mission to join her brother and ordain women on the island, and so he agrees to let her go. He is also not quite sure how he feels when she asks him to let her take with her a branch of the bodhi tree, but his advisers recount for him the story mentioned above about the Buddha's deathbed resolutions, and he quickly realizes it is his duty to make the transplantation of the tree possible.

He therefore prepares a golden vase, and, approaching the bodhi tree, he makes offerings to it and then draws, with red arsenic, a line around the southern branch of the tree, and makes an "act of truth," declaring, "If the great bodhi [tree] should be established in the island of Lankā, . . . let it plant itself in this golden vase of its own accord" (*Mbv.*, 149–50). The limb breaks off and then hovers in mid-air over the pot prepared for it. Miracle then gives way to horticulture: Aśoka, makes other marks on the bottom of the branch and from them grow first ten large roots and then ninety smaller roots, and only then does the actual planting of the branch in the pot take place (*VinA.*, 91–95 = Eng. trans., Jayawickrama 1962: 80–84; see also *Mbv.*, 147–50; *Mhv.*, 140–47 = Eng. trans., Geiger 1912: 122–27).

The transplanted branch is then taken on a barge down the Ganges to the sea, where it is put on a ship that will transport it to Sri Lanka. It is accompanied by representatives of different castes, clans, and guilds,[9] as well as by Sanghamittā and eleven other nuns. The subsequent high seas journey of the bodhi tree is not without its own adventures. In mid-ocean it has to be defended from the nāgas. They want to have the tree to worship it and threaten to sink the boat, until Sanghamittā chases them off using her magical powers. But then, recognizing the genuineness of their devotion, she allows them to take the bodhi tree down to their underwater nāga abode and lets them venerate it for a limited period of time—seven days. It then proceeds on to the port of Jambukoḷa in Northern Sri Lanka, where it is welcomed with great ceremony and devotion by Devānampiya Tissa, who wades out neck-deep in the water to receive it. It

[8] On the bodhi trees of all twenty-eight of the past buddhas, see Liyanaratne 1983.

[9] On these groups and their relationship to the later specialists involved in the care of the bodhi tree at Anurādhapura, see Hettiaratchi 1994 and Seneviratne 1994: 199ff. The groups are sometimes said to be at the origin of caste distinctions in Sri Lanka. See Pragnasara 1994: 174–75.

is transported by cart to the capital and planted on the grounds of Mahāmeghavana Park, at the very spot where the bodhi trees of the three previous buddhas of this aeon had been (*Mhv.,* 118–24 = Eng. trans., Geiger 1912: 104; *Dpv.,* 89–90 = Eng. trans., Oldenberg 1982: 196–97). This festival is attended not only by the king and by the elder Mahinda and the eldress Sanghamittā, but also by nobles from all over the island and by all the people of the capital. In the midst of the festivities, the bodhi tree remains hidden in a cloud bank for seven days, this miracle (one of those that had been predicted by the Buddha) being connected to the relic's power to make it rain.[10] The festivities over, Sanghamittā is able to ordain Queen Anulā and many of her followers as the first Sri Lankan nuns (*VinA.,* 96–99 = Eng. trans., Jayawickrama 1962: 85–88; see also *Mhv.,* 148–54 = Eng. trans., Geiger 1912: 128–32; and *Mbv.,* 153–60).

The story of the bodhi tree does not stop here, however, for soon after it takes root in Anurādhapura, it produces five fruit. These are given to the king, who is told to plant them. From them grow bodhi tree saplings—eight from the first fruit, and then a total of thirty-two more from the other four. The first eight saplings are planted at eight different places all over Sri Lanka, all of them connected to the saga of the tree's coming to the island or to the cycle of legends surrounding Sanghamittā and Mahinda (*Mhv.,* 154 = Eng. trans., Geiger 1912: 133; *VinA.,* 100 = Eng. trans., Jayawickrama 1962: 88–89; *Mbv.,* 161–62).[11] The thirty-two bodhi tree saplings grown from the other four fruit taken from the Anurādhapura tree are likewise planted all over the island, but with a slightly different scheme in mind. They are evenly spread out at locations said to be correlated with the so-called "yojana stūpas"—the reliquaries built "at every league" [yojana] by King Devānampiya Tissa.[12]

The story of those yojana stūpas, in brief, recalls that after coming to Sri Lanka and converting King Devānampiya Tissa, Mahinda bemoans the fact that there is nothing for him to venerate on the island, adding that it has been a long time since he has seen the Buddha. This statement confuses the king, who knows that the Buddha parinirvāṇized long before Mahinda was born. Mahinda explains that he was talking not about the living Buddha but about his relics, for "when you see the relics, you

[10] To this day, especially at the end of the dry season, the veneration of the bodhi tree (often by women) with pots of water is thought to be able to make the rain clouds appear. See De-Silva 1980: 67–68, 233–34.

[11] The eight sites, from north to south, are listed as Jambukoḷa, Tivakka, the Thūpārāma, the Issarasamaṇārāma, Paṭhamacetiya, Cetiyagiri, Kāṭaragāma, and Candanagāma.

[12] The names of these sites, as preserved in the Sinhala *Bodhivaṃsa,* may be found in Pragnasara 1994: 180–81. According to the *Dpv.,* 88 = Eng. trans., Oldenberg [1879] 1982: 196, the island of Sri Lanka is thirty-two yojanas long; the stūpas would thus span the whole island.

see the Victorious One" (*Mhv.*, 133 = Eng. trans., Geiger 1912: 116). At this, Devānampiya Tissa offers to build a stūpa—the first in Sri Lanka—if Mahinda will only provide some relics. Mahinda does this by sending his nephew, the novice Sumana, back to India to request some relics of his grandfather Aśoka. Sumana manages to get from Aśoka the Buddha's begging bowl filled with bodily relics (sarīradhātu), and he takes these to Sri Lanka, where they are temporarily enshrined at Cetiyagiri (Mount Missaka) (*Mhv.*, 134 = Eng. trans., Geiger 1912: 117; *Dpv.*, 79–80 = Eng. trans., Oldenberg 1982:186; *Thūp.*, 197 = Eng. trans., Jayawickrama 1971: 65; *VinA.*, 74 = Eng. trans., Jayawickrama 1962: 74). In due time, Devānampiya Tissa arranges for these relics to be distributed throughout the island and enshrined in the same places as the thirty-two bodhi-tree saplings.[13]

The *Thūpavaṃsa* tells the same story in a short chapter entitled "The Account of the [building] of stūpas at every league" [*Yojanathūpakathā*], which immediately follows the account of the arrival of the bodhi tree. Here, we are informed that

> King Devānampiya Tissa had the relics which filled the bowl that the Buddha had used for his meals and which were deposited at Cetiyagiri brought, and he had them enshrined in stūpas he had built throughout the island of Sri Lanka, at distances of one league from each other. But the Buddha's bowl he kept in the royal palace where he paid homage to it. (*Thūp.*, 204–5 = Eng. trans., Jayawickrama 1971: 74)[14]

As the source (i.e., the container) of the other relics, the bowl remains in the capital while its contents (the relics) are spread out to the provinces, just as the main bodhi tree takes root also in the capital, while its offshoots are transplanted in the provinces. In this way, the Aśokan maṇḍalaic pattern of relic distribution on Jambudvīpa is replicated locally in Sri Lanka.

There is a difference, however, between the bodhi tree saplings and the relics. Thus far, the various distributions of relics that we have encountered (by Droṇa to the eight kings at the time of the parinirvāṇa, by Aśoka in the construction of the 84,000 stūpas, and here by Devānampiya Tissa in the establishment of stūpas at every league) have all been brought about by a process of *division,* an apportionment of relics, carried out by men. In the case of the spread of the bodhi tree, the process is one of growth and *multiplication,* made possible, perhaps not insignificantly, by a woman, Sanghamittā. To be sure, the southern branch of the

[13] As we shall see, on his way back to the island, Sumana also stops off in Indra's heaven, where he also acquires the collarbone relic of the Buddha.

[14] On the almsbowl of the Buddha, see chapters 7 and 8. As we shall see, the bowl, along with the tooth, becomes an important symbol of royal sovereignty.

original bodhi tree at Bodhgaya is cut (or rather, it cuts itself) off from its parent root, but thereafter it does nothing but grow, give off new shoots, and produce new fruit. And it is these offshoots that are planted throughout the island. A number of other traditions take up this theme of multiplication and proliferation. Thus, according to a text known as the *Cullabodhivaṃsa,* not only were there 8 + 32 bodhi tree seedlings grown from the first five fruits of the Anurādhapura bodhi tree, but, in addition, at least thirty-two other bodhi plants, sprung from the roots of the original tree at Bodhgaya, were brought to Sri Lanka at various times by various kings and arhats and were planted in different locations throughout the island. Morever, over a dozen others were planted from seedlings taken from the bodhi tree planted by Ānanda at the Jetavana monastery (discussed earlier). In this way, virtually every important bodhi tree on the island was given a pedigree and traced back to the original (see Pragnasara 1994: 181–82).[15]

I would suggest that we have here an important new metaphor for the spread of relics in Buddha lands: one which emphasizes reproduction and spread and descent (i.e., lineage) over division and controlled distribution. This metaphor makes perfect sense in the case of the bodhi tree, which, though a relic, reproduces itself like a plant. But it was applied also to bodily relics of the Buddha, which, in parts of Southeast and East Asia, were seen as able miraculously to reproduce themselves, to multiply prolifically.[16]

The Collarbone Relic and Its Enshrinement in the Thūpārāma

The second relic that is the subject of one of the Buddha's deathbed resolutions is his right collarbone (Pali: *dakkhiṇa-akkhaka*), which, like the southern branch (*dakkhiṇa-sākhā*) of the bodhi tree, was predestined for Sri Lanka.[17] The saga of this relic is connected to the story of the arhat Sumana touched on earlier. It will be remembered that Sumana, sent by his uncle Mahinda to India to get relics, brings back from Aśoka the Buddha's bowl filled with relics of the Blessed One. On his way back to Sri Lanka, however, still acting under Mahinda's instructions, Sumana also

[15] This proliferation was not limited to Sri Lanka. For instance, in 1817, a delegation of Thai monks took six cuttings from the Anurādhapura bodhi tree back with them to Ayutthya. See Lingat 1930: 12.

[16] For example, the tooth relic brought to Myanmar by Gavāṃpati, which, like the bodhi tree, was "predestined" by the Buddha (for enshrinement in the Mon city of Thaton), proceeds to clone itself into thirty-two separate teeth, the original to be kept in the capital and the others in the thirty-two provinces of the kingdom. See Shorto 1970: 16–17 and 1963.

[17] This relic should not be confused with the Buddha's neckbone (Pali: *gīvaṭṭhi*), which the elder Sarabhū took from the Buddha's funeral pyre directly to Sri Lanka, where it was

stops off in the Trāyastriṃśa Heaven, and there he makes another request for the sake of his adopted homeland. Addressing the god Indra, he asks him why he has remained so indifferent to the fate of Sri Lanka, which he has vowed to protect. Indra, a little taken aback perhaps, replies that he cares greatly for Sri Lanka and asks in what way can he help. Sumana tells him, "You have in your possession two relics, the right eye-tooth and the right collar-bone [of the Buddha]. Of these, continue to honor the right eye-tooth, but give me the collar-bone" (Jayawickrama 1971: 65; text in *Thūp.*, 197–98).[18] Indra, like Aśoka before him, readily complies with this request and gives up the relic, which Sumana then takes back to Sri Lanka and hands over to the elder Mahinda.

We are not told how Indra acquired this collarbone relic in the first place, but we already know how he got the right eyetooth which, along with it, was kept in the Cūḷāmaṇi stūpa in his heaven.[19] He stole it from the brahmin Droṇa, who had concealed it at the time of his distribution of the relics, intending to keep it for himself. According to Buddhaghosa's *Commentary on the Dīgha Nikāya,* when Droṇa showed the relics to the assembled kings, they became distracted, lamenting the passing of the Blessed One and the destruction of his body. Knowing them to be thus preoccupied, Droṇa seized the opportunity to take the right tooth relic of the Buddha and hide it in his turban. Indra, however, peering down from on high, could see what he had done, and "thinking 'this brahmin is not able to honor this tooth in a suitable way, I should therefore take it,' he removed it from inside [Droṇa's] turban, put it in a golden urn, took it to heaven, and enshrined it in the Cūḷāmani-cetiya" (*DA.*, 2:609).[20]

There is no suggestion that the collarbone of the Buddha was likewise stolen by Indra, but there is some doubt, in the story, as to its authenticity. When it is first taken to the capital by Mahinda, King Devānampiya Tissa, in fact, decides to test it, something he does with no other relic. "If," he declares, "this is truly the relic of the Sage, let my royal umbrella bow down of its own accord, let my elephant get down on its knees, and let this reliquary, together with its relics, descend upon my head" (*Mhv.*,

enshrined in the Mahiyangana stūpa. See *Thūp.*, 210 = Eng. trans., Jayawickrama 1971: 80; and *Mhv.*, 6, where Geiger (1912: 5) wrongly translates *gīvaṭṭhi* as "collar-bone." According to a Thai inscription, this neckbone as well as a hair relic (or magically produced duplicates) were taken from Mahiyangana to Sukhothai in the early fourteenth century. See Griswold and Prasert 1972: 72 and 127n. A Laotian tradition asserts its presence at Wat Muang Sing in Northern Laos. See Lafont 1957: 47.

[18] See also *Mhv.*, 134–35 = Eng. trans., Geiger 1912: 117); *VinA.*, 84 = Eng. trans., Jayawickrama 1962: 75). On the right eyetooth in Indra's possession, see chapter 7.

[19] The same stūpa also enshrined the hair that the bodhisattva cut at the time of his great departure. See chapter 2.

[20] For a study of this passage and its elaboration in the *Dhātuvaṃsa,* in which Droṇa is accused of further thefts, see Trainor 1997: 123, 132.

135 = Eng. trans., Geiger 1912: 118; see also *Thūp.*, 198 = Eng. trans., Jayawickrama 1971: 66). All this immediately comes to pass, and the king is thus assured of the genuineness of the relic. There then follows the account of its enshrinement in the Thūpārāma. At Mahinda's recommendation, Devānampiya Tissa places the reliquary urn on top of the elephant, and it sets off with it until the animal finally stops at the place of the future stūpa.[21] This, we are told, happens also to be the forgotten site (overgrown with bushes and thorns) wherein were deposited the water pot, the monastic belt, and the bathing cloth of the previous buddhas Kakusandha, Konāgamana, and Kassapa, respectively.[22] The king's men have the site cleared and then attempt to take the collarbone relic down from the elephant, but the elephant will not allow it to be removed and put down at a place lower than himself.[23] The people therefore gather lumps of clay from the dry bed of a nearby tank (the country was suffering from a drought), and use the clay to make bricks, which they pile up to the height of the elephant. This allows them to take the relic from the elephant without lowering it. At the same time, it marks the start of the construction of the great stūpa. When the time comes for the enshrinement of the collarbone in the stūpa, the relic rises up into the air and manifests the miracle of double appearances that the Buddha had predicted it would. This involves the relic not only emitting flames but also showering down sprays of water that fall as rain all over the island, thereby solving the drought. Finally, the king and all his retinue pay great homage to the relic and deposit it in the stūpa, and the story ends with a verse: "Thus the Lord of the world, even though he has gone to parinirvāṇa, works in various ways for the benefit and happiness of humankind. How much more would he do so when alive?" (*Thūp.*, 198–200 = Eng. trans., Jayawickrama 1971: 66–68. See also *Mhv.*, 135–38 = Eng. trans., Geiger 1912: 118–20; and *VinA.*, 85–90 = Eng. trans., Jayawickrama 1962: 75–80).

It is interesting to contrast this tale with the account of the transplanting of the bodhi tree given above. As we have seen in the case of the tree of awakening, what is emphasized is pedigree and descent. The bodhi trees throughout Sri Lanka stem from the bodhi tree at Anurādhapura, which stems from the bodhi tree at Bodhgaya, which represents the

[21] For a discussion of the route taken by the elephant, complete with maps, see Masefield 1994–95, 2:677–79.

[22] This detail, found in the *Thūp.*, appears also in *Ext.Mhv.*, 147, and in *Mbv.*, 142. See also *Mhv.*, 118, 121, 124 = Eng. trans., Geiger 1912: 104, 106, 108. *Dpv.*, 89 = Eng. trans., Oldenberg [1879] 1982: 196 pairs these relics with the droṇa of bodily relics enshrined in the Mahāthūpa, which is discussed later.

[23] A relief in the Mathurā museum showing an elephant with, over its back, the inscription "the collarbone relic of the Lord" may be a depiction of this scene. See Konow [1929] 1991: 45.

Buddha. The transmission of embodiment is by virtue of lineage, and the transportation of the relics is generally by ordinary means. Although the severing of the southern branch of the bodhi tree is not unaccompanied by miracles, the account of its transplantation is horticultural in tone and is accomplished by humans. So too is its transport to Sri Lanka: the bodhi branch, in its pot, does not fly through the air, but must be shipped down the Ganges, carried aboard a vessel, disembarked in Northern Sri Lanka, and taken by cart to the capital.

In sharp contrast to this is the story of the collarbone relic, which, we are not told how, has made its way to a divine abode, Indra's heaven. Its transmission to Sri Lanka is accomplished in an instant, by an arhat who demands it of Indra, and who then flies with it through the air. Its enshrinement in the Thūpārāma is likewise accompanied by miraculous displays, this time occasioned by the relic itself. Here the emphasis is not on lineage but on the supernatural. This is a distinction to which I will return more fully in chapter 7.

Duṭṭhagāmaṇī, the Rāmagrāma Relics, and the Mahāthūpa

Mention has already been made of the share of buddha relics that ended up in the hands of the nāgas at Rāmagrāma. As we have seen in chapter 5, in the *Mahāvaṃsa,* when Aśoka considers getting these relics from the nāgas, he refrains from doing so because some arhats tell him that they are, in fact, destined for later enshrinement in Sri Lanka by the future king Duṭṭhagāmaṇī. The text also indicates that this was asserted by the Buddha himself, who, on his deathbed, is quoted as declaring, "Of the eight droṇas of my bodily relics, one will be venerated first by the Koḷiyas of Rāmagrāma . . . and then in the kingdom of the nāgas, until at last it shall come to be enshrined in the Great Stūpa on the island of Sri Lanka" (*Mhv.,* 246 = Eng. trans., Geiger 1912: 210). It comes as no surprise then, that an event involving these same relics (that they would take on the form of the Buddha and manifest the Twin Miracle) should have been the subject of the last of the Buddha's deathbed resolutions (adhiṣṭhāna).

The whole first part of the rather chauvinist saga of Duṭṭhagāmaṇī-Abhaya (who ruled Sri Lanka in the first century B.C.E.) cannot be examined here. The story of his father, Kākavaṇṇatissa, who enshrined the forehead bone and a hair relic of the Buddha at Sēruwila (see chapter 3), and who married Vihāramahādevī; the birth of their two sons, Gāmaṇī and Saddhatissa, in Rohaṇa in the southern part of the island; Gāmaṇī's conflict with his father and his exile to the central highlands for twelve years; his conflict with his brother and acquisition of the throne; his rallying of "Sinhalese" forces and recapture of the "Tamil" dominated North for the glory of the Buddhist Order; his going into battle with a buddha relic in the lance that served as his standard; his defeat of the "foreign" King Eḷāra; and his reunification of the island—all have become the subject of myth and oral tradition, and are treated extensively in the *Mahāvaṃsa* and other sources (see *Mhv.,* chs. 22–25).[24]

My main concern here will be Duṭṭhagāmaṇī's building of the Mahāthūpa (Great Stūpa) in Anurādhapura, and his enshrining of the Rāmagrāma relics therein.[25] These events form the chief focus of the *Thūpavaṃsa,* which devotes its last chapters to an account of the construction of the stūpa, the decoration of its relic chamber, the obtaining and enshrining of the relics, and the closing up of the stūpa and death of Duṭṭhagāmaṇī (*Thūp.,* chs. 12–16 = Eng. trans., Jayawickrama 1971: 95–144. See also *Mhv.,* chs. 28–32 = Eng. trans., Geiger 1912: 187–227). Taken together, these form a remarkable account of the ritual building of a stūpa and enshrining of relics, which is worth examining in some detail.

The Building of the Stūpa

The story begins with a reminder of the predestined nature of the enterprise. Duṭṭhagāmaṇī passes by a stone pillar that had been set up by his ancestor, Devānampiya Tissa, with an inscription to the effect that his descendent would in the future build a great stūpa in this place (*Thūp.,* 219, 201 = Eng. trans., Jayawickrama 1971: 95, 73; see also *Mhv.,* 219 = Eng. trans., Geiger 1912: 187; Berkwitz 2001: 162). Inspired by this, Duṭṭhagāmaṇī decides to undertake the project. He reflects, however, that during his war with the Tamils, he already levied high taxes on the people, and worries about further impositions on them. The solution that presents itself is one of divine intervention. Indra, realizing the king's need for bricks, asks the divine architect, Viśvakarman, to go and create bricks on the bank of a river about a league from the city, in a northerly direction. The next day, the bricks are discovered by a hunter, who bestows them upon the king. Simultaneously, other building materials miraculously appear and are made available. They each come from villages or areas located at varying distances in the cardinal and intermediate directions: gold nuggets from the northeast, copper from the east, various kinds of precious stones from the southeast, silver from the

[24] For a structuralist study of twenty-eight different oral and written versions of the myth, see Robinson 1968; see also Greenwald 1978. On the stūpa of the lance relic at the Maricavaṭṭi Vihāra, see *Thūp.,* 211–16 = Eng. trans., Jayawickrama 1971: 82–90. Interestingly, *Dpv.,* 99–100 = Eng. trans., Oldenberg [1879] 1982: 207–8 limits its account of Duṭṭhagāmaṇī to a few verses.

[25] The Mahāthūpa is currently known as the Ruvanvälisäya. For discussions of its architectural importance, see Paranavitana 1946: 6–7, 14–15, et passim.

south, pearls from the west, and four large gems from the northwest.[26] In this way, the gathering of materials for the construction of the great stūpa involves an initial circumambulation of the site, not to mention the establishment of a tributary relationship between the periphery and the center (*Thūp.*, 219–21 = Eng. trans., Jayawickrama 1971: 95–99; see also *Mhv.*, 219–24 = Eng. trans., Geiger 1912: 187–90).

With the materials amassed, the building of the stūpa can begin. First, the king's men lay a foundation of crushed stone, pounded down by elephants. Then various layers of clay, rocks, and metal are put down to establish a base. Then, on an auspicious day, comes the time for the placing of the first ceremonial brick. This is an occasion for a great festival to which the entire order of monks and the whole population of the city are invited. Barbers and bath attendants are stationed at the entrances to the site so that the people coming can freshly shave and wash. Food, colorful garments, flowers, and perfumes are also provided, free of charge. The king himself, wearing all of his regalia, arrives at the site surrounded by forty thousand men and hosts of beautiful dancing women playing diverse instruments.

With its ceremonial laying out of bricks, the occasion, as we shall see, is marked not only by the construction and consecration of a brahmanical sacrificial altar, but also by Buddhist references. Great offerings of cloth for monastic robes and foodstuffs for the saṃgha are prepared and set forth, and soon thousands of monks begin to arrive, not only from the capital and from Sri Lanka, but from famous Buddhist sites in India and beyond. In the *Thūpavaṃsa* (see Jayawickrama 1971: 102), no fewer than fourteen great elders with a total entourage of 1,456,000 monks gather for the occasion, arriving from such foreign places as Rājagṛha, the Jetavana, Pāṭaliputra, Bodhgaya, Gandhāra, Pallava (Persia?), Allasandā in the Yonaka kingdom (i.e., one of several possible "Alexandrias" located in what is today Afghanistan), and Mount Kailāśa. This, then, is to be a "world assembly" of Buddhists from all over, intended in part to establish Sri Lanka as a new international center of the faith.

In the very middle of this great assembly, Duṭṭhagāmaṇī takes his place, surrounded by four great arhats who bear significant symbolic names: Buddharakkhita to the east, Dhammarakkhita to the south, Sangharakkhita to the west, and Ānanda to the north. The first three names, of course, recall the Triple Gem of Buddhism, the Buddha, Dharma, and Saṃgha, while the last is the name of the Buddha's chief attendant and favorite disciple. Ānanda's positioning on the northern side, moreover, re-

[26] Curiously, no mention is made of the southwest. This is either an oversight in the text, or because that direction (from the Mahāthūpa) is barred by a major body of water, the Tissa Tank.

calls his place at the Buddha's deathbed in Kuśināgarī. This is significant for, as we shall see, the Buddha's relics in the Mahāthūpa will be layed out in "parinirvāṇa mode," that is, in the shape of the Buddha lying on his right side with his head to the north, just as he lay at the time of his death.

The main part of the initial ritual consists in tracing the circumference of the stūpa that is to be built on the prepared site and then laying the first eight ceremonial golden bricks. Perfumed clay and mortar are prepared by two senior monks and eight young officials, all named Suppatiṭṭhita ("Well-Established"), set the eight bricks in the eight directions. These are followed by eight silver bricks. Once these rituals are over, an elder named Piyadassī preaches a sermon, as a result of which forty thousand laypersons, eighteen thousand monks, and fourteen thousand nuns attain arhatship (*Thūp.*, 222–26 = Eng. trans., Jayawickrama 1971: 100–106; *Mhv.*, 225–32 = Eng. trans., Geiger 1912: 191–97).

The time for the real, actual construction has come, and Duṭṭhagāmaṇī now finds himself trying to hire a good contractor. He interviews several builders but rejects them all on the grounds that they propose using too much dirt and this will result in weeds and trees growing on the stūpa. Finally, he finds a person who states he will pound, sift, and grind the little earth he plans to use in such a way that no weeds will ever grow. Duṭṭhagāmaṇī then asks him what shape he will give to the stūpa, and he replies by splashing some water in a bowl so as to make a perfect bubble: that will be the shape of the monument. Duṭṭhagāmaṇī agrees to this and arranges payment for the builder. He also sets up great reserves of cash, garments, ornaments, foodstuffs, etc., to pay the manual labor who will do the actual building. Both householders and monastics will participate in the work, but all, Duṭṭhagāmaṇī insists, must be duly compensated for their participation. This is not a just a matter of generosity and unwillingness to oppress the people; it is also that he, the king, wants to reap all of the merit from the enterprise.[27] Thus, when a couple of monks try to sneak in donations of their own (the one a handful of clay that he specially prepared to make it look like the clay at the worksite, the other a brick made to resemble the bricks brought to the site by the gods), their subterfuges are unmasked by the ever-vigilant master builder, who countertricks them into accepting lavish gifts, which he then reveals as being payment for their attempted donations (*Thūp.*, 227–30 = Eng. trans., Jayawickrama 1971: 107–12).

[27] Lest this seem a little selfish, the text also points out that the rewards even for working for wages on the stūpa are rebirth in one of the heavens, due to the fervent joy aroused by such work. See *Thūp.*, 230 = Eng. trans., Jayawickrama 1971: 112.

The Making of the Relic Chamber

Eventually, with the advance of construction, it is time to make the relic chamber. For this, two novices who are arhats are asked to bring, from the northern continent of Uttarakuru, six golden-colored stone slabs, each one measuring forty-by-forty meters.[28] The chamber is to be a perfect cube in the midst of the stūpa. One slab will serve as the floor, one as the lid, and the other four as the walls. There then follows an elaborate description of the decoration of the relic chamber, which, like the stūpa in general, has both narrative and spatial aspects to it. In the very center is set up a silver replica of the great bodhi tree at Bodhgaya, perfect in every detail, about twenty meters in height, with leaves and fruits made of various kinds of gems and precious materials. It is overhung by a canopy of priceless cloth festooned with pearls and adorned with golden bells, and it is surrounded by an enclosure-railing made of seven precious things. Under the tree is set a solid gold image of the Buddha, with nails of crystal, lips, palms and soles of coral, and hair of blue sapphire. All around are set up representations of various biographical events that took place in Bodhgaya: the attack of Māra and his hordes, and various incidents during the seven weeks following his enlightenment, including the contemplation of the bodhi tree with unblinking eyes, the walking back and forth in meditation, the sitting under the hood of the nāga Mucilinda, the receipt of food from the merchants Trapuṣa and Bhallika, and the decision to preach the Dharma.[29]

The decorations of the great stūpa, however, are not limited to the time of the Buddha's awakening. They go on to depict subsequent life story scenes, including the Buddha's first sermon, the ordination of Yaśa and his friends, the conversion of the three Kāśyapa brothers, the visit of King Bimbisāra, the acceptance of the Veṇuvana monastery, the return home to Kapilavastu, the ordination of Rāhula, of Nanda, and of the rest of the Śākyas, the acceptance of the Jetavana monastery, the Twin Miracle at Śrāvastī, the Buddha's preaching of the Abhidharma to his mother in the Trāyastriṃśa heaven, the descent from that heaven at Sāṃkāsya, the preaching of a whole series of sermons, the decision to give up his life, the last meal at Cuṇḍa's house, the passing away into parinirvāṇa, the lamentations of the deities, the worship of his feet by Mahākāśyapa, the

[28] Though these dimensions are extraordinary, reliquary chambers could, in fact, be quite large. In 1797, Hiram Cox, the British Resident at Rangoon, visited the site of the Mingun pagoda, then in the process of being built, and measured the relic chamber to be a quadrangle sixty-one feet and six inches per side, eleven feet deep, and with walls almost thirteen feet thick. See Cox 1821: 106.

[29] On different accounts of the seven post-enlightenment weeks, see Strong 2001: 77–81.

cremation of his body, and the division of the relics by Droṇa (*Thūp.*, 233–34 = Eng. trans., Jayawickrama 1971: 115–16; see also *Mhv.*, 239–42 = Eng. trans., Geiger 1912: 203–6).

But this visual biographical narrative does not stop here. Interestingly, it now circles back to the beginning, for, we are told, Duṭṭhagāmaṇī then has put into the relic chamber depictions of all of the jātaka stories, including detailed representations of scenes from the Viśvantara story. Then there are scenes showing his life in Tuṣita heaven, his descent into his mother's womb, his birth in Lumbinī, the seven steps he took after birth, the prediction of the soothsayer, the first meditation under the rose apple tree, his marriage to Yaśodharā, the birth of Rāhula, his seeing the three signs of the old, diseased, and dead persons, his revulsive experience in the harem, his great departure from Kapilavastu, his cutting his hair, his encounter with King Bimbisāra, his partaking of the milkrice offered him by Sujātā, and his arrival at the seat of enlightenment under the bodhi tree in Bodhgaya (*Thūp.*, 234–35 = Eng. trans., Jayawickrama 1971: 116–18).[30]

Donald Swearer (forthcoming: ch. 8), in his study of the consecration of buddha images in Northern Thailand, has shown how the ritual, though it involves a recalling of the whole life story of the Buddha, ends up centering on his awakening, that is, on the event that makes the bodhisattva into the Buddha. Much the same thing seems to be going on in the decoration of this relic chamber, which centers on the event of the Buddha's enlightenment, but presents it in a biographical context, as the starting and ending point for a life-story narration that moves forward to the parinirvāṇa and then circles back to the past lives and the birth. I shall return to the importance of this later, in the conclusion to this chapter. For now, suffice it to say that, using both statues and paintings, Duṭṭhagāmaṇī makes what I have called a "biorama" of the Buddha, depicting inside the stūpa his entire life story.

The depictions in the relic chamber, however, are not purely biographical. They are also devotional, for, in addition to representations recalling the life of Śākyamuni, there are included in the stūpa statues of differents deities who, as we shall see, attend the festival of the final enshrinement of the relics in the stūpa, and are depicted as permanently protecting and paying homage to the relics: the four guardian lords of the four directions bearing swords, the thirty-two deities bearing flower offerings, the thirty-two divine maidens bearing lighted torches, the twenty-eight yakṣa-generals, and hosts of other gods, goddesses, and godlings, shown with clasped hands, dancing, playing musical instruments, waving garments, and proffering such things as golden water-pots, mirrors, flowering

[30] *Mhv.*, 242 = Eng. trans., Geiger 1912: 206–7 greatly abbreviates this section.

branches, representations of the sun and the moon, lotus blossoms, parasols, etc. (*Thūp.*, 235 = Eng. trans., Jayawickrama 1971: 118–19). So many things and figures, in fact, are placed in the relic chamber that later on doubts are said to arise as to whether there was room enough inside for all of them, and it has to be explained that their placement, without crowding, is made possible only through the combination of the wondrous powers of the king, the gods, and the arhats (*Thūp.*, 237–38 = Eng. trans., Jayawickrama 1971: 122–23).

The Acquisition and Enshrining of the Relics

One thing, however, is missing in all these preparations: the relics! Indeed, rather strikingly, the whole construction of the Mahāthūpa and the elaborate decoration of the relic chamber take place without Duṭṭhagāmaṇī having yet obtained the relics he wishes to enshrine therein. Paul Mus (1935, 2: 210–11) has remarked that this is a general feature of such stories, going so far as to say, "Stūpas were not built for relics; relics were only added (and sometimes not added at all) to stūpas after they were built."[31] This, of course, is a bit of an exaggeration. We have already seen that the Thūpārāma was built by Devānampiya Tissa for the Buddha's collarbone when it had already been brought to the island. But the "stūpa first, relics later" pattern was not unusual. An extreme example may be found in the story Xuanzang tells of a stūpa built by a minister named Rāhula in Kāpiśi, in present day Afghanistan. After finishing the monument, Rāhula had a dream in which he was told that his stūpa had no relic, but that on the morrow, a man would offer one to the king, and he should obtain it and enshrine it. Accordingly, Rāhula received from the king a promise that he could have the first thing brought the next day to the palace as tribute. This turned out to be a buddha relic. Fearing, however, that the king would renege on his promise and not let him keep it, Rāhula hurried with the relic to the stūpa, intending to enshrine it as soon as possible. The king's men, realizing his intention, moved to stop him. As they were about to intercede, however, a great crevice all of a sudden opened miraculously in the cupola of the stūpa. Rushing in, Rāhula quickly deposited the relic inside. In his haste to get out, however, he caught the hem of his garment on the stones inside the chamber and was immured within as the crevice closed up again just before the arrival of the king's men. Ever since, Xuanzang adds, a black aromatic oil has oozed out from a crack in the stūpa's cupola.[32]

[31] Mus, of course, wants to argue here for the symbolic value of the stūpa as more than just a funerary tumulus. See also Foucher 1905–18, 1:52.

[32] *T.* 2087, 51:874a–b = Eng. trans., Li 1996: 42. See also Beal 1884, 1:60–61.

In the story of Duṭṭhagāmaṇī's Mahāthūpa, the arrival of the relics is more anticipated. Though the relic chamber is completed in their absence, there is every expectation that they will be delivered, and they are thought of as crucial to the completion of the monument. In this light, their arrival and enshrinement in the prepared chamber may be seen as what will consecrate the stūpa, what will make this biorama "come alive" in much the same way as the opening of the eyes of a buddha image changes it, in the words of Robert Knox (1958: 155), from "a lump of ordinary metal" into "a god."[33]

Duṭṭhagāmaṇī is very clear that the responsibility for obtaining relics for his stūpa lies not with him but with the saṃgha, so, when construction of the relic chamber is complete, he goes to the monks and tells them that it is time for them to fetch the relics, since he intends to enshrine them the very next day. Fortunately, the elders know that the Rāmagrāma relics in question are now in the kingdom of the nāgas, and need only be fetched by someone with supernatural powers. Accordingly, they deputize a sixteen-year-old novice named Soṇuttara, who is endowed with such powers, to go and get them (*Mhv.,* 245–46 = Eng. trans., Geiger 1912: 209–10).

Soṇuttara, in fact, is so quick that he can afford to take his time. He waits until he hears the sound of the music indicating that the enshrinement festivities are about to begin, before entering into the fourth level of trance and diving down to the palace of the nāga king Mahākāḷa. In no uncertain terms, he announces that he has come for the relics that have been predestined for enshrinement in the Mahāthūpa. Mahākāḷa, however, is loath to give up the relics, for he hopes that by honoring them he will be able to be reborn in heaven. Accordingly, he tells his nephew, the nāga Vāsuladatta, to hide them. Vāsuladatta does this by swallowing the whole reliquary urn and going off to the foot of Mount Meru. Mahākāḷa then tells Soṇuttara that he can have the relics if he can find them, thinking that the novice's powers will not be up to the task. He is sadly mistaken, however. Granted this permission, Soṇuttara wastes no time; he stretches out his arm, making it very long and slender, and reaches down into Vāsuladatta's stomach and removes the relics. He then absconds with them back to Sri Lanka before the nāgas completely catch on to the fact that they have been bested (*Thūp.,* 241–44 = Eng. trans., Jayawickrama 1971: 127–31; *Mhv.,* 249–52 = Eng. trans., Geiger 1912: 212–15).

This, of course, is much the same story as the *Dhātuvaṃsa* tale, considered in chapter three, about the elder Siva who retrieves the hair relics

[33] On the opening of the eyes of the images, see Swearer, forthcoming: ch. 8. For Sri Lanka, see Gombrich 1966 and Ruelius 1978.

of the Buddha from the belly of the nāga Jayasena. Kevin Trainor (1997: 117ff., and 1992) has studied both of these stories in the context of a discussion of the "theft of presence" that accompanies the "stealing" of relics. But clearly there are other things going on as well. As Trainor (1997: 133–34) himself affirms, the cases of Soṇuttara and Siva are rather different from the more selfish case of Droṇa's theft of a relic, discussed previously, or, for that matter, from the case of Indra, who takes the tooth from Droṇa. Moreover, the fact that, in the text, Mahākāḷa—three times—gives Soṇuttara permission to take the relics if he can find them would seem to be an important mitigating factor, pointing to the realization that what we have here is not really theft so much as legitimate appropriation of a relic that needed to pass through an intermediary.

We shall encounter again, in the next chapter, a similar case of a tooth relic being recaptured from some nāgas who want to worship it, but it may be good to pause here to consider some of the implications of this legendary motif. Historians of religions might, when interpreting such stories, see them as initiatory scenarios, rites of passage involving a journey into the deep, or into the belly of the monster, a "return" to watery, dark, chaos, followed by a reemergence into light, structure, and order (see Eliade 1958: 35ff.). In the particular Buddhist context at hand, this notion of passage and rebirth may still be there, but the nāgas themselves are more specifically symbolic of a number of other things.

First of all, as has already been mentioned, candidates for ordination, in the Theravāda Buddhist tradition at least, are called *nāgas,* an appellation that is meant to denote their liminal status. No potential monk can become ordained without becoming a nāga first, but anyone becoming a monk ceases to be a nāga, since nāgas are not allowed in the saṃgha. Indeed the reason candidates for ordination are called *nāgas* is in memory of an actual serpent (nāga) who changed himself into human form and became a monk under false pretenses, but then was excommunicated by the Buddha when his true identity was discovered.[34] The nāga state is thus something that needs to be abandoned, but it is also something that needs to be passed through on the way to its abandonment. The same may perhaps be said of relics, for which enshrinement in a stūpa may be a kind of ordination.[35] No relic can become enshrined without undergoing a "rite of passage," symbolized here by "passing through" or at least being in the possession of nāgas.

In this light, it should also be pointed out that though nāgas are great merit-makers (and so accumulators and hoarders of wealth), they cannot

[34] For a discussion of this story and its relation to ordination, see Strong 1992: 191–93. According to the Vinaya, animals and spirits cannot become ordained.

[35] The same is true of the consecration of images, which has been seen as a type of ordination. See Bentor 1996: 41.

attain enlightenment. Soṇuttara points this out in his encounter with Mahākāḷa. The latter tries to argue that the relics would be better off left in the nāga world, where far greater offerings can be made to them than any that could be given in Sri Lanka. Soṇuttara, however, replies that buddhas esteem the dharma far more than they do material wealth and the relics should be enshrined in a place where beings can achieve enlightenment (*Thūp.*, 243 = Eng. trans., Eng. trans., Jayawickrama 1971: 129). The implication here seems to be that relics—like buddhas—are not only recipients of donations, and so facilitators of merit, but also active propagators of the dharma. What this means, of course, is that the passage of relics through nāgas to the world of humans is also a symbolic passage from religious action solely oriented toward merit-making and improving one's karma to religious action also aimed at dharmic realization.

Thirdly, however, nāgas also represent indigenous forces, chthonic and aquatic spirits who are specifically connected with fertility of the land and rainfall.[36] Buddhism's ambiguous relationship to such indigenous serpent spirits is well known (see Bloss 1973; Rawlinson 1986). Nāgas (as well as yakṣas, nats, phīs, devatās, etc.) must be tamed, must be converted to Buddhism and so must leave behind their baser nature; yet their cults must also be absorbed into the Buddhist context, and their power needs to be harnessed and used. In fact, relics can become a focal point for this process. Thus, as we shall see in chapter 7, the tooth relic, having passed through and bested nāgas on the way to Sri Lanka, becomes important in part for its nāga-like powers, its rain-making function and its ability to act as a guarantor of prosperity and fertility of the land.[37] More immediately, it is significant here that the nāgas, having been bested by Soṇuttara, do not definitively lose all of the relics taken from them. When they realize what has happened they first of all mourn their loss, but then, grief-stricken, they go to the saṃgha and complain that, bereft of relics, they no longer have any means of making merit. Taking compassion on them, the monks agree to let them have a token portion of the relics back and, happy, they go back to their abode. Indeed, the nāga king, Mahākāḷa, apparently bearing no grudge, later returns to Anurādhapura for the enshrinement celebration (*Thūp.*, 243 = Eng. trans., Jayawickrama 1971: 130–31).[38]

That enshrinement is attended by hosts of deities, along with monks and laypersons. The relics are placed in an urn and set on a golden throne

[36] For descriptions of rain-making rituals involving nāgas in different parts of the Buddhist world, see Archaimbault 1968; Porée-Maspero 1962–69, 1:233–82; DeGroot 1893: 148–59; Ruppert 2003.

[37] For another manifestation of this kind of syncretism, which relates the tooth of the Buddha not to a nāga but to the fang of a yakṣa, see Hocart 1931: 4.

[38] This is not unlike Aśoka's decision to leave some token amount of relics in each of droṇa stūpas when he opens them up. See chapter 5.

crafted by the divine artificer, Viśvakarman, and brought by Indra. Brahmā, invisible, holds an umbrella of divine sovereignty over them, and Duṭṭhagāmaṇī likewise offers his own umbrella of state to the relics, thus conferring his kingship on them. The arhat Indagutta creates a metal canopy over the whole universe to ward off any interferences by Māra,[39] and the assembly of monks chants the whole of the sūtra piṭaka. When it comes time for the actual enshrinement of the relics, Duṭṭhagāmaṇī, carrying the reliquary urn on his head, circumambulates the stūpa and then descends into the relic chamber, together with the company of monks. As he is about to remove the urn from his head and place it on the magnificent throne prepared for it, the urn itself rises up into the air, opens, and the relics come out of their own accord. Ascending further into the air, they take on the shape of the Buddha's body, complete with its thirty-two major and eighty minor marks of the great man, and, in this form, they display once again the Twin Miracle that the Buddha put on at Śrāvastī, thereby fulfilling the fifth of the Buddha's deathbed resolutions.

Seeing this, no fewer than one hundred and twenty million gods and humans attain arhatship and countless others the first three fruits of the path. Then, after displaying other miracles, the relics once again enter the urn and descend upon the king's head. The king holds the urn in his hands, and, opening it, takes out the relics, and determines that if they are to remain undisturbed and a refuge to humans forever, they will assume the shape of the Buddha in parinirvāṇa and come to rest on the jeweled couch prepared for them. It is, finally, in this shape—that of the Blessed One lying on his right side, stretched out with his head to the north—that the relics are permanently enshrined. The relic chamber is then closed up by two novices, Uttara and Sumana, who put the forty-by-forty-meter cover-slab in place and seal it, while the arhats in the assembly make a final resolution that the perfumes inside the relic chamber shall never dissipate, that the garlands therein shall never wither, that the lamps shall never go out, and that the relic chamber itself shall never be broken into by thieves (*Thūp.*, 247 = Eng. trans., Jayawickrama 1971: 135).

It is instructive to compare this scene with that of the enshrinement of the relics by Mahākāśyapa in the underground stūpa built by King Ajātaśatru. There the relics, in a private, secret ceremony, were placed inside the golden image of the horse Kanthaka, and the flowers and lamps and other devotional offerings were timed to last only until the moment when Aśoka should break into the stūpa, and bring forth the relics, an act

[39] Indagutta thus plays here a role similar to that of Upagupta at Aśoka's great stūpa festival. See Witanachchi 1976.

which, it will be recalled, repeated the Buddha's great departure. Here, in the case of the Mahāthūpa, a different biographical episode is remembered: In a public ceremony attended by millions, the relics are layed out in the shape of the Buddha in parinirvāṇa, after his whole life, and especially his awakening, has been recalled by the biorama built all around. And from this stūpa, there will be no emergence or new departure; the relic chamber is sealed permanently, and the flowers, lamps, and devotional offerings, meant to last forever, are frozen in timelessness. This is a stūpa that apparently recalls the presence not of the living but of the dying Buddha.

The Death of Duṭṭhagāmaṇī and Burial Ad Sanctos

With the closing of the relic chamber, work promptly resumes on finishing the construction of the Mahāthūpa's dome and spire. Just as promptly, however, Duṭṭhagāmanī falls deathly ill, and royal authority is turned over to his younger brother and heir, Tissa. Knowing that the king will die before the stūpa can be completed, Tissa arranges for a visual subterfuge: He has a mantle of great sheets of white cloth made and painted to resemble the top of the dome of the stūpa, mounting thereupon a spire of wicker and bamboo, the whole decorated to look like the real thing. He then declares to the king that work on the stūpa is finished. Duṭṭhagāmaṇī asks to see it and circumambulates it, carried on his litter. Then, lying in front of the stūpa, contemplating it, he summons an old companion, the elder Theraputtābhaya, who had been by his side through twenty-eight major battles and who now comforts him with the words of the Buddha that all things are subject to dissolution. The king then has the record of his good deeds that are inscribed in his "book of merit" (*puññapothaka*) read out to him,[40] and, rejoicing in his heart at all he has managed to accomplish, he tells his friend that for twenty-four years he has served the order of monks and would now have his body serve it one more time: his wish is to be cremated within sight of the Mahāthūpa on the consecrated terrace (*mālaka*) reserved for ritual acts (*Thūp.*, 248–52 = Eng. trans., Jayawickrama 1971: 136–42; *Mhv.*, 257–63 = Eng. trans., Geiger 1912: 220–25). The implication seems to be that his body is to become a lamp offering to the relics, an act reminiscent of Aśoka's autocremation at his own great stūpa in Pāṭaliputra.

At this point, the end is near. The assembled monks begin to chant the dharma, and gods from various heavenly abodes swing down in chariots from the sky, invisible to all but the king, each imploring him to choose

[40] On the use of such merit books, commonly read at deathbeds, see Rahula 1956: 254.

their heaven. Duṭṭhagāmaṇī, uncertain what to tell them, asks the monks which heaven is the most beautiful, and the elder Theraputtābhaya tells him "Tuṣita heaven," which is what he chooses.[41] Then, lying there, gazing at the Mahāthūpa, he finally passes away, and his wish comes true: he is instantly reborn in one of the heavenly chariots, which takes him straight to Tuṣita after circumambulating the stūpa three times. His body is then taken and cremated as he wished, in the very shadow of the stūpa, at a place that comes to be known as the "King's terrace" (*Thūp.*, 253 = Eng. trans., Jayawickrama 1971: 143).

No mention is made of any relics of Duṭṭhagāmaṇī, and indeed, given his status as king, his rebirth in heaven, and his lack of enlightenment, one would not necessarily expect him to have any. Nor are we told what happens to the remains of his cremated body (bits of charred bone and ashes), but it is logical to assume they were kept in or near the Mahāthūpa, which meant so much to him. Indeed, there existed in Buddhism a custom of collecting what remained of the dead after cremation, placing that in a small urn or stūpa and disposing of it at a stūpa site made holy by the relics of the Buddha or some other saint.

This pattern has been likened by Gregory Schopen (1987, 1994a, and 1996) to the "burial ad sanctos" tradition commonly found in Western medieval cathedrals (see Ariès 1981: 32–40; Duval 1988). Like their Western counterparts (and like their Indian megalithic predecessors—see Schopen 1995), Buddhists developed cemeteries in which the ashes and bones of the more-or-less ordinary dead were placed in small stūpas clustered around or in the vicinity of more major ones containing the relics of the special dead.[42] The pattern at one representative Indian site (Bodhgaya) was described long ago by Monier-Williams ([1889] 1964: 396–97):

> Another remarkable characteristic of this spot [Bodhgaya] is that it was converted into a kind of Buddhist Necropolis, teeming with the remains of generations of the Buddha's adherents contained in relic-receptacles called Stūpas, some of which have been brought to light, while countless others still remain to be unearthed.
>
> The fact was that immense numbers of pilgrims from all parts of India and the outlying countries once thronged in crowds to Buddha-gayā, and nearly every pilgrim brought with him a Stūpa or relic-shrine of some kind, according to his means, and deposited it as a votive offering in this hallowed region, either with the object of acquiring religious merit for himself, or of

[41] Tuṣita is the abode of Maitreya and, as *Thūp.*, 254 = Eng. trans., Jayawickrama 1971: 144 later makes clear, Duṭṭhagāmaṇī is destined to be reborn as Maitreya's chief disciple and to rejoin his parents there who will also be reborn within the future buddha's family.

[42] More recently, Richard Salomon (1999: 81) has suggested that not only bones of bodies but also Buddhist texts were ritually buried in this way.

promoting the welfare of the deceased in other states of being. . . . Generally the votive Stūpa contained the relics of deceased relatives—perhaps the ashes of a father or mother, or pieces of bone, or a small fragment of a single bone placed in an earthen vessel or casket of some other material, and buried in the interior of the Stūpa.[43]

Much the same thing seems to be going on at the Mahāthūpa in Anurādhapura, and not only with regard to the possible remains of Duṭṭhagāmaṇī. Indeed, just prior to Duṭṭhagāmaṇī's death, right after the relic chamber is sealed up, he has the drum of proclamation beaten throughout the city to announce the following: "Let those who wish to deposit relics (dhātu) at the Great Stūpa bring their relics and enshrine them." Then, we are told, "[T]he multitude, each one according to his means, had urns made of gold, silver and so forth and placing relics therein deposited them on the surface of the gold coloured stone slab above the enshrined relics. And all the relics thus deposited were about a thousand" (Jayawickrama 1971: 135; text in *Thūp.*, 247; see also *Mhv.*, 256 = Eng. trans., Geiger 1912: 218). The Mahāthūpa, then, did not only enshrine the remains of the Buddha, but also, in close proximity to him, the remains of a thousand Sri Lankan Buddhists. In this context, it makes perfect sense that the remains of Duṭṭhagāmaṇī might have been added to them.

Such a supposition is, in fact, reinforced by archaeological finds. One of the architectural features of the Mahāthūpa in Anurādhapura, as well as some of the other large stūpas of Sri Lanka, is the existence, at the four cardinal points, of projecting structures known as "vāhalkaḍas" (Paranavitana 1946: 52–53). The purposes of these gateway projections long perplexed archaeologists, but excavations of the remains of one of them at the Mahāthūpa in 1946 revealed "a large number of [stūpa-shaped] limestone caskets and earthenware urns" imbedded in the structure itself, along with beads, ornaments, and other trinkets that had been "thrown into the mortar, probably by devotees while the work of building was in progress" (Paranavitana 1940–47: xliii). In these caskets and urns there were smaller reliquaries of crystal or gold sheet containing ash or small fragments of bone, some of which bore inscriptions. These were unfortunately undecipherable, but two similar caskets at the Abhayagiri Stūpa were inscribed as containing the relics (dhātu) of the wife and the mother of an early Sri Lankan king. Paranavitana concludes that although "the vāhalkaḍas may not have been constructed for the express purpose of

[43] For examples at other sites see Schopen 1987 and 1994a. Richard Salomon (1999: 81n.16) has suggested that the same pattern developed around the Buddha's skull bone, which was enshrined at Haḍḍa, where "a particularly large number of human bones seem to have been enterred."

enshrining these cinerary urns . . . the people [perhaps primarily people of consequence] probably preserved the ashes of their loved ones and, when vāhalkaḍas were being built, took that opportunity to have these cinerary urns deposited in the fabric of the sacred edifice" (Paranavitana 1940–47: xlv).[44]

Schopen (1994a: 287–89) has compared this Buddhist method of disposing of what is left of the cremated dead at stūpa sites to the Hindu practice of carefully collecting the charred bones and ashes of the deceased and disposing of them in the Ganges or at some other sacred river ford (*tīrtha*). There is much to be said for this parallelism. In Hinduism, such a disposal of the remains of the dead is aimed at insuring rebirth in heaven, or, alternatively, liberation (*mokṣa*) at the end of one's next incarnation (Parry 1994: 24). The same would certainly seem to be true in the case of Buddhism. Duṭṭhagāmaṇī's ascent to Tuṣita heaven (after dying in the shadow of the Mahāthūpa) is witnessed by all those present, and his enlightenment in his next incarnation is guaranteed by virtue of his relationship to Maitreya, whose chief disciple he becomes. In both these cases, then, the sacrality of the site, occasioned by the goddess Gangā or by the Buddha, acts as a kind of soteriological conduit for the deceased.

There is another dimension, however, to the case of Duṭṭhagāmaṇī and, more generally, to the Buddhist tradition of burial ad sanctos. Duṭṭhagāmaṇī's desire to see the completed stūpa (and the pretense at completing it), his eagerness to be in its presence in his final hours, suggests that the same devotional relationship may be continued in death. Proximity to the Buddha's relics thus makes possible not only rebirth in heaven, but a kind of ongoing devotional contemplation (*darśana)* within the sacred realm created by the stūpa.[45] In the Buddhist context, it might be stated that burial ad sanctos provides a kind of "darśan for the dead."

This does not mean, however, that the presence of the relics and the life story of the Buddha inside the stūpa remain completely inaccessible to the living. In a passage that the *Thūpavaṃsa* includes in its account of the building of the stūpa and that the *Mahāvaṃsa* fits in elsewhere, we are told the story of Bhātiya, a king who ruled Sri Lanka a century after Duṭṭhagāmaṇī. He was very devoted to the Mahāthūpa, having once had the entire monument smeared with sandalwood paste. One day, as he ascended onto the stūpa's terrace, through the eastern gate, he heard the sound of arhats reciting the dharma. Thinking it was coming from the

[44] The vāhalkaḍas have been linked with the platforms often found on stūpas in South India known as *āyakas,* a term that Prematilleke (1966: 70) relates to *āyāga-paṭa,* meaning "a tablet in homage of a departed ancestor." Such āyākapaṭas have been found at the sites of one of the earliest stūpas in Vaiśālī (see Sinha 1991: 2).

[45] On the importance of the theme of "seeing" the Buddha and its connection to relics, see Trainor 1997: 173–88. On darśan in India, generally, see Eck 1981.

southern gate, he went there, but found no one. Still hearing it, he went on to the western and then the northern gate, but still without discovering the reciters. It was then that he realized the chanting was coming from *inside* the relic chamber, and the desire to see inside the stūpa arose in him.[46] Making a firm resolve, he prostrated himself on the terrace and determined not to eat or move until the arhats took him inside and showed him the relics. The arhats, in the midst of their chanting, were apparently oblivious to what was going on, so the god Indra, realizing Bhātiya's determination, decided to intervene. Penetrating inside the stūpa, he explained to the arhats that the king had heard them reciting the dharma and would not move until he was let in. Out of compassion for him, they then instructed an elder to bring the king inside, show him around, and then see him out. When the king reemerged, he had the figures he had seen in the chamber etched in gold and arranged in a pavilion that was a sort of replica of the relic chamber. These figures were known as "pilot" (*niyāmaka*) figures because they could lead devotees to a realization of what was inside the stūpa. And every year, they were taken out and shown to the people who, on one occasion at least, were so filled with joy that each family gave one son to enter the saṃgha (*Thūp.*, 236–37 = Eng. trans., Jayawickrama 1971: 120–21; *Ext.Mhv.*, 278–80).

Conclusion

We have in this chapter seen several examples of the extension of the Buddha's life story in relics in the context of Sri Lanka. The bodhi tree, the collarbone, and the Rāmagrāma droṇa of relics are all predestined for the island, and are transmitted there in various ways. The bodhi tree is requested from King Aśoka, taken to Sri Lanka on a ship by Sanghamittā, planted by King Devānampiya Tissa in Anurādhapura, from where it proliferates and spreads all over the island. The collarbone relic is gotten from the god Indra by the novice Sumana, honored by an elephant, and enshrined in the very first stūpa in Sri Lanka, the Thūpārama. At the same time, Sumana brings back, from Aśoka, the Buddha's begging bowl filled with relics, which, like the bodhi tree, are spread throughout the island. Finally, the Rāmagrāma relics are taken, rather forcefully, from the realm of the nāgas by Soṇuttara, who returns to have King Duṭṭhagāmaṇī enshrine them in the Mahāthūpa already built for them.

Considered together, these traditions reinforce the notion that Sri Lanka has become the land of the Buddha, outshining even India in its possession of relics. We shall see, in chapter 7, similar claims being made

[46] On the theme of sounds coming from buried reliquaries, see also Faure 2002: 40 and Huang 1998: 495. For another example, see *T.* 2087, 50:874a = Eng. trans., Li 1996: 42.

about China and Japan. Considered individually, however, these traditions exhibit different strategies of presence, different ways in which the Buddha is made manifest in his relics on the island. By way of conclusion, here, I would like to focus on one of these strategies, namely the phenomenon of miracles exhibited by the relics.

To various degrees, all of the predestined relics examined in this chapter manifest displays of supernatural powers. Indeed, the exhibition of such powers is one of the chief features of the adhiṣṭhānas that the Buddha makes about them. Some of these miracles seem simply designed to underline the point that the relic has a will and inviolability of its own, which, of course, is the same as the will and inviolability of the Buddha. Thus the bodhi tree branch will, of its own accord, miraculously sever itself from the tree at Bodhgaya, thereby demonstrating the will of the Blessed One. At the same time, however, this reinforces the sense of its sacrality and identity with the Buddha: this is a relic that no man (i.e., Aśoka) dare cut with a knife or saw, lest he cut the Blessed One himself.

The bodhi tree branch is also said to emanate multicolored rays of light that illuminate the whole world. On a lesser scale, such displays are, in fact, rather routine for Buddhist relics. The Chinese pilgrims to India make note of countless instances in which relics or stūpas glow mysteriously or light up the night sky. One noteworthy example will have to suffice here: Once, when Xuanzang was living in Nālandā, he and an Indian disciple of his named Jayasena decided to go to Bodhgaya to see the annual exhibition of the Buddha's relics at the Bodhi temple. They observed that some of the bead-like relics were small, but some of the bigger ones were unusually large and glossy. Later that night, Jayasena expressed some doubts to his master, telling him that all the relics he had ever seen at other temples were quite small, no larger than a grain of rice. Why were these so big? And he wondered aloud whether or not these Bodhgaya relics were genuine. Xuanzang agreed with him that he too had some doubts about the matter. Just then, however, the lamp in the room went out, and the two monks could see a very bright light outside. They went out and saw that the whole sky was lit up by rays of multicolored light that were shooting out of the relic stūpa. The lights remained for quite a while and then gradually circled the stūpa and reentered into it. Then the sky became dark again and the stars came out. And "having witnessed [all this]," the text concludes, "[they] were freed from the net of doubt" (Li 1995: 128–29; text in *T.* 2053, 50: 244b).

The story shows graphically that one of the functions of a relic's miraculous display is to overcome people's doubts about the genuineness of the relic. And in this, the emanation of light is significantly effective, because, in fact, the emanation of light is something that the living Buddha also does. As is well known, the Buddha's golden body generally glows with a halo "a fathom wide," and, on special occasions, he can illuminate the whole cosmos (as we saw, for example, in the discussion of the "unveiling of the world" in chapter 5). Thus, when a relic gives off rays of light, it is, of course, manifesting "numinous powers" (Kieschnick 2003: 34), but it is more specifically affirming its identity with the Buddha.

The overcoming of doubts is also at work in the miracles that the collarbone relic and the Rāmagrāma/Mahāthūpa relics are predestined to perform. They will both, according to the Buddha's adhiṣṭhānas, put on a display of the Twin Miracle, just prior to their enshrinement. As we have seen, this supernatural display was first performed by the Buddha when defeating the heretics at Śrāvastī, and in some ways it remains the Buddhist miracle par excellence. The repetition of it by these relics is thus a repetition of a major act in the Buddha's lifetime—something that further identifies them with him.

One suspects, however, that there is something more going on here, that there is a reason why this particular miracle was featured. It is sometimes argued that this miracle is called the "Twin Miracle" because of the double appearance in it of both fire and water, and, indeed, certain texts indicate that this is the reason. However, it seems more likely, as Alfred Foucher (1917: 156–57) has argued, that the name originally designated the Buddha's ability, equally manifest at Śrāvastī, to reproduce himself, either by creating (as he does in some versions of the story) a "twin" buddha with whom he converses, or by filling the sky with a multitude of buddhas, as he does in other texts and in the iconography (see Strong 2001: 110–11). The miracle at Śrāvastī, then, is an event in which the Buddha shows his ability to create a replica—a double—of himself. In this way, it helps reinforce, at least in principle, the notion that the Buddha can coexist with another buddha—a twin—and it thereby serves to legitimate the concept of a relic as a substitute for the Buddha.

At the same time, the context in which it does this is important. The miracle at Śrāvastī takes place just prior to the rains retreat, which the Buddha spends preaching to his mother in the Trāyastriṃśa Heaven. I have argued elsewhere that the Buddha's absence during this rains retreat represents in some ways a dry-run for his more permanent absence in nirvāṇa. The people in Śrāvastī have no idea where he has gone and mourn his departure as though he has passed away (see Strong 2001: 112–13). Significantly, then, the creation of doubles comes at a time when worries about the absence of the Buddha are particularly strong and need to be assuaged. So important is the manifestation of this cloning power that, in fact, the creation of doubles continues right through the time of the Buddha's absence. First, whenever he needs to interrupt his preaching to the

Trāyastriṃśa gods so as to go on his almsround (which he does in the Northern continent of Uttarakuru), he creates a double of himself in heaven so that his sermon will go on without stopping (*DhA.*, 3:222 = Burlingame 1921, 3:51). Secondly, back on earth, another kind of "double" is made of him at this time. This is not a relic, but something akin to it: the sandalwood image that King Prasenajit has made and installed in the Buddha's place, in an effort to help human beings who are longing for the Buddha to overcome his absence.[47]

[47] See *T.* 2085, 51:860b = Eng. trans., Li 2002: 181. Xuanzang (*T.* 2087, 51:898a = Eng. trans., Li 1996: 160) claims the king involved here was Udayana, but see Gombrich 1978; Bizot 1994: 103ff; *Paññāsa-j.* 2:414, 424–35 = Eng. trans., Jaini 1986, 2:103–04, 114–16. For other sources, see Demiéville 1937a: 211.

Chapter Seven

FURTHER EXTENSIONS OF THE BUDDHA'S LIFE STORY: SOME TOOTH RELIC TRADITIONS

PETER BROWN, in his study of the development of the cult of Christian saints (1981: 88), has emphasized the importance of the mobility of relics in the spread and decentralization of Christianity. Unlike sacred sites such as Jerusalem and Rome, which were fixed in particular places, relics could be translated to new areas to establish new centers, sometimes on the very periphery of Christendom. In this, relics were an effective complement to the practice of pilgrimage; they brought the saints to the people instead of taking the people to the saints.[1]

We have seen so far a number of Buddhist examples of the same phenomenon, from the hair relics taken by Trapuṣa and Bhallika to Burma, to the instances examined in the last chapter of relics predestined for Sri Lanka. All of these relics were translated, in one fashion or another, to new locales, where they came to define new foci of devotion, anchored new cosmic centers, and legitimated temporal reigns so that, once translated, they tended to stop their movement. They were enshrined—buried—in magnificent stūpas such as the Shwe Dagon, the Thūpārama, or the Mahāthūpa, or planted firmly in the ground like the Bodhi tree at Anurādhapura. And there, tradition asserts, they have remained to this day, at spots often already made holy by the relics of previous buddhas.

In this chapter, I want to look at traditions concerning buddha relics that stay "on the move" a bit longer, whose identity is not caught up in the site—the place—to which they are predestined, but in other things. What these things are varies from one context to another so that, in this chapter, the emphasis will keep changing as we explore not only different relic traditions but the evolution of particular ones. To give all of this detail some focus, I will concentrate on various tooth relics (especially the one that ended up in Sri Lanka), although I will examine a few other types of relic as well, such as the Buddha's almsbowl, which was closely associated with that tooth relic.

[1] On the movement of relics, see also Geary 1978 and Frolow 1961.

Tooth relics tend to be the subjects of long sagas recounting their many movements. They are relics that go from country to country, to heaven or the realm of the nāgas, that get stolen or go into exile, that undergo epic adventures, again and again. Perhaps for this reason, they are inclined not to be the subject of specific resolutions—adhiṣṭhānas—by the Buddha, and they tend to be enshrined not in stūpas but in "temples," or monastic buildings, or palaces. From these places, they can be removed and carried in processions or put on display on special occasions. Thus, as we shall see, the Sri Lankan tooth as well as the tooth relics in the Chinese capital of Chang'an were annually the focus of great festivals during which they were paraded through the streets.[2] An extension of this can be seen in the phenomenon of such relics being taken on tours of foreign countries—a practice that continues to this day.

It is probable that teeth, like hair and many other body parts, have multiple psychological and symbolic resonances in most cultures (see MacCulloch 1921). In Buddhist literature, one of their meanings centers around the fact that teeth are the only bones of the living body that are commonly visible while a person is still alive. They thus provide a glimpse of what the body is and will become, and so serve as reminders of impermanence that help to bridge the divide between life and death (see *Vsm.*, 1:20–21 = Eng. trans., Ñyāṇamoli 1976, 1:21–22). In this sense (as well as for a variety of other reasons), they may be ideal candidates for relics.

At the same time, of course, it should be remembered that the Buddha's teeth (*danta*) are special. As a mahāpuruṣa, he is said to have forty of them, and these are described as being white, set close together, and even (see Burnouf 1852: 565). In some texts, all forty of these escape from the cremation fire, and are distributed far and wide (see *Jin.*, 37 = Eng. trans., Jayawickrama 1968: 53). Unlike the metamorphosed droṇa relics that appear as jasmine buds, pearls, or nuggets of gold, these tooth relics are still recognizable as teeth.[3] As such, they became popular objects of veneration throughout the Buddhist world (see Wylie [1897] 1966: 61–73; Faure, forthcoming). For instance, according to Xuanzang, "hundreds and thousands" of people came "every day from far and near" to venerate a tooth relic of the Buddha in Kanyākubja. So numerous, in fact, were the pilgrims there that the caretakers of the shrine started charging a large entrance fee in an effort, they said, to cut down on the size of the

[2] The same was true of the Buddha's fingerbone, whose celebration, however, took place only once every thirty years, at least in theory.

[3] This does not mean that they necessarily resemble ordinary human teeth in size. For descriptions and drawings of the Sri Lanka tooth presently in Kandy, see Cumming 1892: 292 and Da Cunha 1875: 141.

crowds—something that occasioned considerable disgruntlement among those who had traveled great distances to see it.[4] The relic itself was about one-and-a-half inches long, it was kept in a precious casket, and it had a special luster that caused it to change colors. On *poṣadha* days, it was set on a high cushion, and great multitudes of people offered incense and flowers, though, miraculously, no matter how high the blossoms were piled up, the relic itself was never covered (Li 1996: 150; text in *T.* 2087, 51:895c).

Other such tooth relics, featured at a variety of pilgrimage sites, are mentioned by Xuanzang as being located in Baktra, in Nagarahāra, and in Kashmir.[5] East of Bamiyan, he visited a monastery where there were enshrined a tooth of the Buddha, a tooth of a pratyekabuddha (over five inches long), and a tooth of a cakravartin king.[6] And at the so-called Tamasāvana monastery in Cīnabhukti were enshrined the tooth relics of numerous arhats.[7] Many of these same sites had been visited by Faxian, who, in addition, mentions a tooth relic in Hilo (Haḍḍa in present day Afghanistan).[8] He says little about it except that its cult was the same as the cult, in the same locale, of the Buddha's uṣṇīṣa bone, which he describes in some detail. It was taken out of its chamber each morning and set on a pedestal outside the temple, where it was worshipped first by the king and then by prominent men of the community and then by the populace as a whole. Outside the gate, vendors sold flowers and incense to worshipers who wished to make offerings (*T.* 2085, 51:858c = Eng. trans., Li 2002: 172–73).

Tooth relics, thus, are many, and all of them became the object of multifarious legends and cults. In this chapter, I would like to examine only a few of these, using them to make more general comments about the nature of buddha relics and the many dimensions of their associations. I will start with the story of a tooth visited by Xuanzang in Kashmir. I will then turn to examine traditions about the four eyeteeth of the Buddha. Consistent with this book's focus on South Asia, I will examine primarily legends and cults surrounding the tooth that ended up being enshrined in Sri Lanka, but I will also give some brief attention to the others for comparative purposes.

[4] Admission was also charged for much the same reason for viewing the Buddha's *uṣṇīṣa* relic near Nagarahāra: one coin for viewing it and five for making plaster impressions of it from which one's fortune could be told. See *T.* 2087, 51:879b = Eng. trans., Li 1996: 69.

[5] *T.* 2087, 51: 872c, 878c, 887b = Eng. trans., Li 1996: 35, 66, 107–108.

[6] *T.* 2087, 51: 873b = Eng. trans., Li 1996: 38.

[7] *T.* 2087, 51: 889c = Eng. trans., Li 1996: 119.

[8] On archaeological finds in Haḍḍa, see references in the index to Salomon 1999.

The Kashmiri Tooth: Relics and Elephants

When Xuanzang visited Northwest India, in the first half of the seventh century, scarcely a hundred years had passed since the great persecution of Buddhism by the Ephthalite Huns, and the extensive destruction by them of monasteries and actual relics in Kashmir and Gandhāra (see chapter 8). In those days, we are told, Kashmiri Buddhist monks scattered and went into exile. One bhikṣu, who is not named, fled to India where he spent his time visiting various sacred sites. When he heard that the persecution had ended, he set out to return to Kashmir. On the way he met a herd of wild elephants who were running amok. Seeking to avoid them, he climbed a tree, but the elephants, seeing him, pushed the tree over and grabbed him with their trunks. They did not kill him, however, but carried him into the forest and took him to a sick elephant who was suffering from a bamboo splinter in his foot. The monk removed the splinter, disinfected the wound, and bandaged it with a piece of his robe. In gratitude, all the elephants brought the monk fruits to eat, and the sick elephant then presented him with a golden casket. The next day, they carried him out of the forest on their backs. They left him where they had originally found him, and then, after bowing down to him, went away. The monk opened the casket and found inside a tooth relic of the Buddha, which he took with him to enshrine in his home monastery.[9]

On his way back to Kashmir, the unnamed monk came to a rapid river, which he had to cross by ferry. In mid-stream, the boat threatened to capsize. The other passengers, worried that they would drown, surmised that the monk must have had with him some buddha relic, and that the nāgas of the river, known to desire such relics, were seeking to overturn the boat to get it. Accordingly, they searched the monk's possessions and found the tooth. At their insistence, the monk agreed to throw it into the river to assuage the nāgas and calm the waters.[10] As he did so, however, he promised to return and retrieve the relic from the nāgas. And indeed, we are told, the monk then spent the next three years learning the proper rituals for taming nāgas. When he was ready, he returned to the spot, built an altar on the riverbank, subdued the nāga king, and got him to re-

[9] See *T.* 2053, 50: 248a–b = Eng. trans., Li 1995: 149–50. The story is also recounted in Hsüan-tsang's own memoirs; see *T.* 2087, 51:887b = Eng. trans., Li 1996: 107–8.

[10] The magical use of relics as an offering to appease spirits of nature become violent is a well-known theme. Much the same thing almost happened to the tooth relic being carried home by the Chinese pilgrim Wu-kong (see Liu 1996: 47). The same practice is found in Christianity. Thus, Saint Helena throws one of the nails from the true cross overboard to calm a storm on the Adriatic, which ever since has been a benign body of water.

turn the tooth. He then finally was able to continue on his way to Kashmir, where he enshrined the tooth in his home monastery.[11]

We have already looked at the significance of nāgas (snake divinities) in the sagas of relics' journeys to their places of enshrinement (see chapter 6). Here I want to focus on their association with elephants, who are also commonly called nāgas. In fact, in legend and cult, buddha relics in general, and tooth relics in particular, are often connected to elephants. Three themes in particular may be highlighted: the legendary devotion of elephants toward relics, the connection between tooth relics and elephants' tusks, and the role of elephants as symbols of sovereignty.

It may perhaps be suggested that the elephants, in the story of the Kashmiri tooth, do not really know what it is that they have in their possession—that they are innocent of the contents of the casket they hand over, in gratitude, to the monk who helps them. This, however, would be to belie a well-established Buddhist tradition featuring elephant devotees of relics. The Chinese pilgrim Faxian describes the overgrown stūpa of the Buddha's relics at Rāmagrāma as being tended to by a herd of wild elephants, who make offerings of flowers to it and sweep and water the ground with their trunks.[12] Elephants are likewise shown venerating reliquaries on early bas-reliefs.[13] Part of this is due to the association of elephants (nāgas) with snake-divinities (nāgas), who are also enthusiastic guardians of relics, but more generally, elephants are thought to know naturally how to honor relics. We have seen one example of this already (in chapter 6) in the story of the elephant who refused to allow the collarbone relic to be taken down from his back as this would leave him higher than it.

One of the possible reasons for this affinity of elephants and tooth relics, of course, is that elephants have tusks (danta), which, in Sanskrit, are eponymous with teeth and tooth relics. Clearly, tusks are important. For instance, the Buddha himself, in the impregnation dream of his mother, Queen Māyā, appears as a six-tusked white elephant, as he does also in a famous jātaka tale.[14] It may be that some of the enormous tooth

[11] *T.* 2087, 51: 887b = Eng. trans., Li 1996: 107–8. Actually, the tooth relic was not to remain at that particular temple for long. Some years later, King Śīlāditya (Harṣa) went to Kashmir to venerate it, but the monks there refused to show it to him and hid it. When it was finally located, Śīlāditya, irked, simply appropriated the relic and took it home with him. See *T.* 2053, 50: 248b = Eng. trans., Li 1995: 150.

[12] *T.* 2085, 51: 861b = Eng. trans., Li 2002: 187. See also Legge [1886] 1965: 69). It has been suggested that such stories may be based on the behavior of real elephants (at least African elephants) toward the bones of their own dead. There is no indication of this in the texts.

[13] See the bas-relief from Amarāvatī, in Snellgrove 1978: 32.

[14] For a bibliography on the "Ṣaḍdantajātaka," see Lamotte 1949–80: 716–17n.

relics, said to be of the Buddha and exhibited in various Chinese temples, were, in fact, actually elephant's teeth (see DeGroot [1886] 1977: 179n.1; Hart [1888] 1972: 204). More generally, elephant tusks often figure in connection with relic worship. In some instances, they may be set up before tooth relic shrines as permanent votive offerings (see Cumming 1888: 186). The elephants that are shown venerating reliquaries in early bas-reliefs are always tuskers (see Snellgrove 1978: 32), as are those that are depicted at the entrance way to the Temple of the Tooth (Daḷadā Māligāwa) in Kandy, Sri Lanka (see Hocart 1931: plate 7). Full tusks are not very common on South Asian elephants, but, in Kandy, to this day, the elephant who carries the tooth relic in the annual Esala perahera, must be a tusker. He must also be male. This is connected not only to issues of perceived female impurity and pollution, but also may have phallic overtones.[15]

Be this as it may, the elephant, like the tooth relic, became in Sri Lanka an emblem of sovereignty. It comes as no surprise, perhaps, that the name of the great tusker who, until his death a few years ago, always carried the tooth relic of the Buddha in Kandy, was "Rāja" [king]. Rāja, moreover, was exactly the same age as the then-president of Sri Lanka, J. R. Jayawardene. When Rāja's mahout was killed (and he himself slightly injured) by a jeep driven by a drunken army officer on New Year's eve of 1987, this was taken as a very inauspicious sign, and there were immediate rumors of an impending military coup. More traditionally, a great white elephant is, after the Wheel, the second of the seven "treasures" of a cakravartin king (see *D.*, 2:174 = Eng. trans., Davids 1899–1924, 2:204), and kings themselves, riding their elephants, are often compared to Indra, the king of the gods, atop his great divine mount, Airāvaṇa (*JA.*, 3: 392 = Eng. trans., Cowell 1895–1907, 3:237). Possession of a state elephant, like possession of a tooth relic, as we shall see, not only legitimizes rule but also acts as an auspicious guarantee of order, prosperity, and fertility.

But possession of an elephant, whether by a cakravartin or another king, also assumes the taming of that elephant, and in the Kashmiri tooth story that we are considering here, the elephants encountered by the monk are, at least initially, wild, and are inhabiting their own natural realm. There are several Buddhist legends featuring the taming of an elephant gone amok, most notably by the Buddha (*Vin.* 2:194ff = Eng. trans., Horner 1938–52, 5:273ff.). Stanley Tambiah (1970: 71), com-

[15] Michel Strickmann (1996: 243–90) has explored the sexual and erotic significance of elephants (and elephant tusks) in Buddhist and more broadly in Asian tantric traditions. It has also been suggested that, in Sri Lanka, the tooth and the almsbowl relic, which, as we shall see, "form an inseparable pair" (Geiger 1960: 213) until the fourteenth century, recall the Śaivite lingam and yoni.

menting on one such tale, interprets the wild elephant as a symbol of unfettered royal power, of the spirit of nature that must be controlled by religious forces, represented by a monk or novice. In the relic tale we are considering here, the taming of the elephant is done by compassion—by the monk's tending to the wound of the injured elephant and removing the cause of his suffering. The elephants as a result become devotees of the monk and give him the tooth relic of the Buddha.

But elephants, once tamed by a monk or novice must be abandoned by them. An elephant (nāga) may be an appropriate mount for a candidate for ordination (nāga), but that is because it is a symbol of royalty that is to be given up.[16] Fully ordained monks, as a rule, do not ride on elephant back. Taking leave of an elephant can thus be a powerful symbol of giving up one's royal sovereignty, one's princely status. In the "Vessantara jātaka," we have a good example of this. It is the prince's giving away of the state elephant that signals his own forced abandonment of his kingdom and occasions his own wandering forth into a homeless state (*JA.*, 6: 487–90 = Eng. trans., Cowell 1895–1907, 6:252–54). In the present story of the Kashmiri tooth, the scenario is rather different, but the effect is the same: Having "tamed" the wild elephants, the monk (and the relic) must now depart from them. Indeed, the procession out of the forest on elephant back, and the dismounting and departure from this animal-symbol of sovereignty recalls some sense of a wandering forth.

The Eyeteeth of the Buddha

Unlike the Kashmiri tooth whose story, recounted by Xuanzang, seems to have been a local or regional legend, the four eyeteeth (canines) of the Buddha have a pan-Buddhist pedigree. It will be remembered that they are first mentioned at the very end of the *Mahāparinirvāṇa sūtra.* In a verse addendum to that text, we are told that of these tooth relics, "the first is venerated in [Indra's] Heaven of the Thirty-Three [gods]; the second in the beautiful city of Gandhāra; the third is in the realm of the king of Kalinga; and the fourth is worshiped in Rāmagrāma by the king of the nāgas" (*MPS.*, 450. See also *D.* 2:167 = Eng. trans., Davids 1899–1924, 2:191).[17] In what follows, I shall be paying most attention to the third of these teeth, the Kalinga tooth, which eventually was transmitted to Sri

[16] Here and in what follows, the same could be said, of course, of horses, who are more commonly used in ordination ceremonies. Both beasts are symbols of royalty although, as Eugene Wang (2003) has pointed out, they may have different connotations.

[17] These four canine teeth (*daṃṣṭra*) are sometimes given special mention in lists of the thirty-two marks of the mahāpuruṣa (see Demiéville 1937: 204), but generally they are singled out only in the catalogs of the eighty secondary marks (see Burnouf 1852: 599–600).

Lanka. Some initial consideration, however, may first be given to the other three.

Curiously, little further mention is made of the fourth tooth—the Rāmagrāma relic—unless we are to understand that it was brought to Sri Lanka along with the droṇa portion of relics that was taken from the nāgas by the novice Soṇuttara.[18] Traditions about the second tooth—that which was taken to Gandhāra—are somewhat more plentiful, although they remain multiple and rather confused. It is often claimed that this was the tooth that was seen in Nāgarahāra, in Northwest India, by Faxian (c. 400 C.E.) and Daorong (in the mid fifth century) (*T.* 2085, 51:858c = Eng. trans., Li 2002: 173; *T.* 2092, 51:1021c = Eng. trans., Wang 1984: 244; Demiéville 1937: 204).[19] Faxian, however, also mentions another important tooth in the Northwest (*T.* 2085, 51:857c = Eng. trans., Li 2002: 167), and other sources speak of a tooth that was said to have been in Udyāna, not far from Gandhāra. It somehow got to Khotan, in Central Asia, and then to Nanjing, the capital of the Southern Chi dynasty (*T.* 2059, 50:411c; see Pelliot 1936: 281–82n.).[20] In 522 C.E., it was reportedly stolen, but it reappeared mysteriously and opportunely in 557 during a celebration of the enthronement of the Emperor Wudi, just in time to help legitimate his accession.[21]

Huang Chi-chiang (1998: 501) has pointed out that this tooth relic's main political significance seems to have been in the South during the Southern dynasties (up until the mid sixth century), whereas in the North, its functions were more or less filled by the fingerbone relic, which then dominated in importance throughout the Tang Dynasty (starting in the early seventh century).[22] Nonetheless, during the Tang Dynasty, a

[18] See chapter 6. There is occasional mention of a second tooth in Sri Lanka, that may or may not have been the Rāmagrāma tooth. See *Jin.*, 54 = Eng. trans., Jayawickrama 1968: 74; Trainor 1997: 149; and Pridham 1849: 327–28.

[19] When Xuanzang came to the place in the seventh century, however, it was no longer there. See *T.* 2087, 51:878c = Eng. trans., Li 1996: 66.

[20] See also Huang 1998: 499. It was said to have been brought there by a monk named Faxian (424–498—not to be confused with the more famous pilgrim Faxian, whose name is written with different characters).

[21] Huang 1998: 500–501 and De Groot 1919: 27. See also Faure, forthcoming, who calls this a real "coup de théâtre."

[22] Traditions about the fingerbone relic cannot be gone into here. Suffice it to say that it was one of the most important relics in the whole of Chinese Buddhism. On its history and its worship by a succession of emperors, in theory every thirty years, see Gernet 1956: 228ff; Ch'en 1973: 267–71; Huang 1998: 503–29; Chen 2002a: 37–48, 98–103; Sen 2003: 64–76. For the Confucian Han Yu's vehement objections to it, see Dubs 1946 and Hartman 1986: 95, 139–40, 158. On the spectacular archaeological finds at the Famen si (one hundred kilometers from Xian) where the relic was enshrined throughout the Tang Dynasty and rediscovered in 1987, see Whitfield 1989, 1990; Zhang 1990; Han Jinke 1994; Zhu 1990; and Michaelson 1999: 148–62.

Udyāna / Khotan tooth was enshrined in the capital of Chang'an, in one of the four temples said to possess tooth relics (see later discussion). And today, scholars of the Chinese Buddhist Association claim that it is this same tooth that is housed in the Tooth Relic pagoda that the Chinese government built in the 1960s in the Western Hills just outside of Beijing (despite the fact that, physically, it appears to be a molar rather than a canine) (Buddhist Association of China 1966: 6–7, 25; Chao 1959: 36–37). This is the tooth that the Chinese Communist government, in the second half of the twentieth century, sent on a number of tours of South and Southeast Asia, which we shall return to at the end of this chapter.

Daoxuan's Tooth

The tooth relic that achieved greatest fame in East Asia, however, was not the Gandhāra / Udyāna relic but the first tooth on the *Mahāparinirvāṇa sūtra* list—the relic that went to Indra's heaven. It became the subject of numerous legendary traditions, only some of which can be touched upon here. The advent of this relic to China is consistently connected to the figure of Daoxuan (596–667), the patriarch of the Vinaya School, who reportedly received the tooth during a nocturnal visitation from a divinity connected to Indra. How this tooth got to Indra's heaven in the first place is a topic that is addressed by several rival traditions. We have already seen in the Pali tradition that it was stolen by Indra from Droṇa's turban. According to a more elaborate legend that became well known in China, Korea, and Japan, it was first stolen by a speedy demon who, in Japanese sources, is usually called Sokushikki ("Demon Fleet-Foot"). This demon, however, was immediately chased by an even faster divinity who quickly caught him and recovered the tooth, which he then delivered to Indra.[23] The divinity who catches the demon is generally identified as the god Skanda (Ch.: Weito-tian; Jpn.: Idaten), here also presented as one of the deities who appears regularly in a series of nocturnal visions had by Daoxuan (Péri 1916: 45–53; Strickmann 1996: 273 and 2002: 218–19). Indeed, it is on one of these occasions that Skanda (or, alternatively, a deity named Naḍa) delivers the tooth to Daoxuan, out of gratitude for his having imparted to him the three refuges and eight precepts (see Strong and Strong 1995: 8).[24]

Daoxuan's receipt of this celestial tooth is a key moment in its mythical history, for it marks the relic's return to earth. It also helps explain its

[23] The chase of the demons eventually came to be featured as a dance in a Nō drama by Zeami (see Strong and Strong 1995: 27–28). For a variant on this story, see Demiéville 1937: 204.

[24] On the connection, more generally, of Daoxuan's visions to relics, see also Shinohara 1988: 212–14.

move from India to China, while imbuing it with the prestige of a new miraculous origin and the legitimacy of being associated with a great Vinaya master. Indeed, along with his contemporary Xuanzang (559–664), Daoxuan was one of the great figures of Chinese Buddhism in the mid-seventh century. In this regard, it is interesting to contrast the tale of Daoxuan's acquisition of the tooth "from heaven" with the tradition that credits Xuanzang with bringing a tooth relic with him back from India, the long hard way, overland. According to Xuanzang's biography, upon his return to China in 645 C.E., he brought with him "over six hundred Mahāyāna and Hīnayāna texts . . . seven statues of the Buddha and more than a hundred grains of śarīra relics" (Li 1995: 343; text in *T.* 2053, 50:279a).[25] No mention is made specifically of a tooth being among these relics, but a later Japanese tradition claims that there was one and that it was eventually taken to Japan by the monk Gishin, and kept in Tendai and Fujiwara circles (Faure 1996: 165).

In these two modes of transmission—from heaven and overland, sudden and gradual—it is possible to detect two modes of movement, and more generally two ways of viewing relics in medieval China, which, to be sure, were often mixed together but may be differentiated for the sake of analysis. Simply put, there are relics as miracles and relics as mementos of lineage. On the one hand, relics with established pedigrees were passed on from generation to generation, from master to disciple. On the other hand, relics also appeared miraculously, either by the intervention of deities as in the case of Daoxuan, or simply as the result of the faith of monks or rulers, as in the case of the very first relic in China, which manifested itself in a vase (in 248 C.E.) so that the Sogdian monk Kang Senghui would have something to show to the local ruler (see Kieschnick 2003: 32).

Some years ago, Koichi Shinohara (1988: 145), in an important study of Chinese monks' biographies, helpfully distinguished between two types of sources: stūpa inscriptions that tended to be narrative chronicles or life histories of monks and were emphatic of status and genealogy, and that were modeled perhaps on the more general Chinese tradition of funeral stelae inscriptions; and miracle stories that emphasized the supernatural and marvelous. Somewhat the same thing may perhaps be found in the case of relics. Both as miracles and as mementos of lineage, relics obviously serve to legitimate rulers, monks, and monasteries, but they do so in different ways. Miracle relics that are given to or produced for rulers are signs of their charisma or that of the monks who receive them; memento relics that are offered to them are signs of lineage or inheritance, or of tribute.

At the same time, these different genres of relic reflect different attitudes toward Buddhism, and specifically toward India. Relics as memen-

[25] On the over-land trade in relics more generally, see Liu 1996: 45–48 and Sen 2003: 74–75.

tos see an India that may be far away but that is real, that can be reached and returned from by pilgrims, through persistence and hard work. This India calls to mind a former time and a distant place, and emphasizes the theme of transmission or transport to the East rather than of transference. On the other hand, miraculously appearing relics, whether brought by a divinity or spontaneously coming into being in a place, call to mind the transport or transferral to East Asia of an India that has become abstract and of a Buddha who has become eternalized. Indeed, once a temple or monk or ruler "has" the Buddha in the form of a relic, India itself need no longer be visited; in fact, India as the homeland of the Buddha and the Dharma need no longer exist—something that was stated explicitly in later Japanese traditions that likewise emphasize the "transfer to the East" of the tradition (see Strong and Strong 1995: 24). The gradual disappearance of Buddhism in India and the difficulties of making a journey there probably also contributed to this sentiment.

Daoxuan's's tooth, as the tooth from Indra's heaven came to be called (see Huang 1998: 501), was actually just one of four tooth-relics enshrined in the capital of Chang'an during the Tang Dynasty, though it is the only one said to have come there miraculously (Reischauer 1955: 300–303; text and discussion in Ono 1964–69, 3:351–64; see also Weinstein 1987: 125, 143). There, it was the focus of an annual festival that took place every March. The Japanese pilgrim Ennin's account of it has been summarized by Kenneth Ch'en:

> The various monasteries arranged and offered all kinds of medicines, foods, fruits, flowers, and incense to the Buddha's tooth. The tooth itself [kept in a storied hall] was the object of adoration of all the famous monks in the city. As for the common inhabitants, they rushed to make donations to the relic. One man donated a hundred *shih* [bushels] of rice and twenty *shih* of millet, another donated copious quantities of biscuits, while a third donated enough cash to provide the meals for the monks in the various monasteries in the city. In addition, people tossed coins like rain toward the hall where the tooth was kept. (Ch'en 1973: 266–67; text in Ono 1964–69, 3:351; see also Reischauer 1955: 300–301)

Such worship, however, was proscribed (along with veneration of the Buddha's fingerbone relic), during the great government crackdown on Buddhism that occurred in 845 C.E. during the reign of Emperor Wu (see Reischauer 1955: 340), and, though there are signs that it regained some of its former position soon thereafter,[26] the Tang Dynasty was not to last much longer. In the centuries that followed, however, a number of new

[26]Just eight years after the crackdown, in 853, the emperor himself personally visited the tooth, which was back at the Zhuangyan si. See Strong and Strong 1995: 5 and Huang 1998: 527.

traditions developed asserting that Daoxuan's tooth was now housed in a variety of places. These cannot be examined here. Suffice it to say that at least five rival overlapping claims located it, more or less during the same periods, in five different sanctuaries: the Xiangguo si, in what is now Kaifeng in Honan Province;[27] the Jōjū-ji temple in Kyoto;[28] the Engaku-ji and other temples in Kamakura;[29] the palace of the King of Koryo in Korea;[30] and the Sennyū-ji temple in Kyoto, which still claims to possess the tooth today.[31]

The Kalingan / Sri Lankan Tooth

According to a relatively late Pali tradition, the three eyeteeth that we have looked at so far and that were most famous in East Asia, got to their initial places of enshrinement as the result of a double theft. As mentioned in chapter 4, they were all originally stolen by Droṇa, at the time of his distribution of the bodily relics to the eight kings. The one that he hid in his turban was later filched by Indra and became "Daoxuan's tooth." The second that he hid on his person was then stolen by a man who took it to Gandhāra. And the last one that he hid between his toes was stolen by some nāgas who absconded with it to Rāmagrāma (Trainor

[27] The relic was enshrined there in 983 C.E. by the Song Emperor Taizu. His successor, Taizong, had it tested by fire. When it escaped from the flames, he composed an encomium in its honor. Similar expressions of praise were promulgated by subsequent emperors and all three eulogies were eventually inscribed on an imperially ordered stele at the temple. In 1072, the Japanese Tendai monk Jōjin visited and worshiped the relic there. See Soper 1948: 24–25.

[28] The fourteenth-century Japanese chronicle the *Taiheki* claims that Daoxuan's tooth relic had been there since the early ninth century. See McCullough 1979: 236.

[29] A fourteenth-century tradition claims that the tooth was brought to Kamakura from a temple in China as a result of an order by the shōgun Sanetomo (r. 1193–1219), who dreamt that he was a reincarnation of Daoxuan and thus entitled to the relic. In time, it was enshrined in the Engaku-ji, where it became the focus of various state-sponsored *shari-e* (relic ceremonies). Toward the end of the fourteenth century, the tooth is said to have been moved to the Shōkoku-ji in Kyoto (the Japanese namesake of the Xiangguo si), where it may have disappeared during the chaos of the Ōnin wars (1467–77). See Faure 1996: 164; and Ruppert 2000: 249–51. There is no trace of an old reliquary at the Shōkoku-ji today, but the neighborhood on the East side of the temple is still called "Tō-no-dan" ("Stūpa-steps"). The original shari-den in Kamakura, however, still stands today at the Engaku-ji. See Mutsu 1918: 138–42.

[30] For the saga of this relic, supposedly obtained from Daoxuan himself by the Korean monk Uisang (635–702), who then saved it from the Chinese emperor's attempts to destroy it, and brought it to Korea, where it later underwent numerous adventures at the time of the Mongol invasion, see Ha and Mintz 1972: 227–30.

[31] Brought to the Sennyū-ji in 1255 by Tankai, a disciple of the temple founder Shunjō, the relic became the subject of a nō play attributed to the famous dramatist Zeami. A shari-e (relic worship ritual) is still held annually at the temple. See Strong and Strong 1995.

1997: 132). This little tale not only shows the distribution of relics to the three realms of heaven (the gods), earth (the humans), and the underworld (the nāgas), but it also makes the rather chauvinist point that the only given (i.e., not stolen) tooth relic was the Kalinga relic that eventually went to Sri Lanka.

Despite the Kalinga tooth's relatively recent association with the so-called Temple of the Tooth in Kandy, historically speaking, this relic provides another example of a "relic on the move" in more senses than one. The traditions about it are worth examining in some detail as they will allow us to see several new dimensions to the South Asian cult of the Buddha's remains.

The saga of this relic's various overland and overseas peregrinations is recounted in a number of sources. According to the Pali *Dāṭhāvaṃsa* (Tooth Chronicle),[32] a disciple of the Buddha, named Khema, acquired this tooth from the remains of the Blessed One's funeral pyre and gave it to Brahmadatta, the king of Kalinga (roughly present day Orissa). Brahmadatta enshrined it in his capital city, which was appropriately known as Dantapura (Toothville), and there it was duly worshiped by the people and several generations of kings (*Dāṭh.*, 120 = Eng. trans., Law 1925: 15–16). The identity and location of Dantapura have been much debated (see Herath 1994: 35–36). A number of scholars have claimed it to be none other than Puri, in Orissa, site of the famous temple to Jagannātha (lit., "Lord of the World"—a form of Viṣṇu / Kṛṣṇa), and they have gone on to note parallels between the festival of Jagannātha and the current festival of the tooth in Kandy (see Eliot 1921, 3:26n; Forbes [1840] 1994, 2:217–19; Goloubew 1932: 467). More recently, other scholars have argued that the identification with Puri is wrong and have concluded that Dantapura should be identified with the town of Dantavuram, on the Vaṃśadhārā River, some hundred miles Southwest of Puri (Herath 1994: 38–39; Krishnarao 1929: 112).

In any case, according to the *Dāṭhavaṃsa,* it is in Dantapura that the tooth, after a while, becomes the target of persecution by non-Buddhist Nigaṇṭhas.[33] Despite the inclination of the city's inhabitants toward

[32] The text as we have it, according to Law (1925: ii), may be dated to the thirteenth century. The edition I shall use (*Dāṭh.*) is that of Rhys Davids. An edition in devanāgarī and an English translation may be found in Law (1925). In 1874, Sir Muttu Coomārā Swāmy published an English translation that was then popularized in French (see De Milloué 1884: 309ff). A Thai version of the text was translated into English by James Low (1848). A briefer version of the story is found in *Jin.*, 66–71 = Eng. trans., Jayawickrama 1968: 88–94. Another, sometimes with interesting variants, is in the *Rājāvaliya* (see Gunasekara 1900: 45–46).

[33] The name "Nigaṇṭha" often refers to the Jains, but, as Phyllis Granoff (1996: 82) has pointed out with specific reference to this story, it can also mean "any non-Buddhist who is hostile to the Buddhist faith."

Buddhism, the Niganṭhas (Skt.: Nirgrantha) seek to turn first the local king, Guhasīva, and then the Indian emperor, Paṇḍu, against the relic. Paṇḍu, a Hindu devotee of the gods, is not pleased to find that his subjects are worshiping "the bone of a dead man," and he eventually has the tooth brought to the capital of Pāṭaliputra. There he orders its destruction by fire. A big heap of charcoal is lit for this auto-da-fé, but, when the relic is thrown into it, a great lotus blossom emerges from the flames and receives the tooth relic, which is thus miraculously preserved, unscathed. King Paṇḍu, however, is not about to give up. He quickly orders that the relic be placed on an anvil and smashed with a hammer. This is done, but the tooth, instead of breaking into pieces, merely sinks into the anvil and remains stuck there, half visible, emitting rays of light in all directions (*Dāṭh.*, 125–26 = Eng. trans., Law 1925: 22–24). He then puts the relic into a tank of water, but it begins to swim about like a royal swan.[34] He puts it into a pit in the ground and has the place trampled by elephants, but the relic emerges on a lotus blossom. Finally, one last attempt is made to get rid of the tooth, by tossing it into an open moat that is filled with foul, rotting dead bodies. Instantly, the moat is transformed into a delightful pool in the midst of a beautiful park. Witnessing all this, Paṇḍu at last becomes convinced of the superior merit of the Buddha and his religion, and, taking refuge in the Triple Gem, he converts and becomes a doer of good deeds. Fixing the relic on the top of his crown, he then places it on his own throne, worships it with great offerings, and builds a temple for it, encrusting it with brilliant jewels. In time, however, he allows the tooth to go back to Dantapura in Kalinga where it is re-enshrined (*Dāṭh.*, 131–35 = Eng. trans., Law 1925: 30–34).

The theme of the attempted destruction of a relic—specifically a tooth relic—by a nonbelieving monarch is one that became fairly common in the Buddhist world.[35] In China, for instance, a relic miraculously produced by the Sogdian monk Kang Senghui in the mid-third century C.E. was subjected to repeated tests by the third-century king of Wu, Sun Quan (*T.* 2059, 50:325b = Eng. trans., Kieschnick 2003: 32; see also Sen 2003: 60). Much later, the emperor Taizong tried unsuccessfully to destroy a Buddha's tooth relic by fire (Soper 1948: 25). A Korean tradition records the failure of the emperor Huizong to sink a tooth relic at sea (Ha and Mintz 1972: 233). In Japan, in 552 C.E., unsuccessful attempts were made to smash one of the very first relics introduced into that country. It was first placed on an anvil and hit with a hammer; the anvil and the hammer were smashed but the relic remained intact (see Deal 1995: 220).

[34] This is a common relic miracle. For another example, see Griswold and Prasert 1972: 63.

[35] In Roman Catholic tradition, too, the testing of relics, most commonly by fire, was one of the ways of asserting their authenticity. For the ritual, see Dooley 1931: 26–27; for examples, see Snoek 1995: 329–32; for a discussion, see Head 1993.

Finally, as we have seen in the introduction to this book, the Portuguese, in the sixteenth century, captured a Buddha's tooth in Sri Lanka and took it to Gõa, where they publically pulverized it in a mortar, burned the pieces in a brazier, and tossed the ashes in the river, only to find the relic reappear on the island shortly thereafter.

The conclusion in all these cases is the same: Buddhist relics cannot be destroyed, at least not by heretical non-Buddhists. But the methods of attempted destruction are significant. In the case of the Dantapura relic (and in the examples just given) four ways are tried: destruction by fire, by smashing, by water, and by burial. These four correspond to the four methods of disposing of the dead in India: cremation, dismemberment, immersion, and interment. In other words, what is literally being attempted here is to hold a funeral for the relic, something that is, of course, doomed to failure since the relic, by its very nature, has already emerged from a funeral. From a Buddhist perspective, this is in line with the adamantine nature of buddhahood, but it may also be that this experience of the relic—this almost ritualistic miraculous reminder of its indestructability—amounts to a sort of reconsecration, a reaffirmation of the relic's being beyond life and death. And yet the ritual threat to the relic is important because, although it is not realized, it simultaneously serves as a reminder of the impermanence that relics are subject to, and to which, as we shall see in chapter 8, they eventually succumb at the end of the aeon. Thus, the paradoxical dialectic of life and death, presence and absence, permanence and impermanence, is maintained.

If, in these scenarios, the Buddha's tooth cannot be destroyed, it can, however, be stolen, and, as the *Dāṭhavaṃsa* story goes on, there is still concern for its safety. Thus, a few years later, when Dantapura is threatened by an invading army that seeks to capture the relic, the king tells his daughter, Hemamālā, and his son-in-law—a handsome young man appropriately named Danta (Tooth)—to flee the city with the relic, and to take it to Sri Lanka, where the king is known to be a friend and ally (*Dāṭh.*, 136–38 = Eng. trans., Law 1925: 35–37. See also Gunasekara 1900: 45). Going south, Danta and Hemamālā first stop by the side of a river. There they bury the tooth relic in a pile of sand, and, dwelling nearby, they go daily to venerate it.[36] Soon, however, a great nāga king, coming up the river, sees the rays of light emanating from the sand stūpa, and, realizing that a buddha relic is buried at the spot, he makes himself invisible and quickly swallows the casket with the tooth relic inside. He then goes and lies down on the slopes of Mount Meru. When Danta and Hemamālā arrive for their regular worship, they find the relic is gone. Distraught, they call on a passing arhat for help. He comes to their aid by

[36] On the practice of making sand stūpas on the banks of rivers, see Gabaude 1979. On the making of sand buddha-images in the same locale, see Hou 1984.

taking on the form of the divine king of birds, Garuḍa, archfoe of all nāgas and greatly feared by them. As Garuḍa, he confronts the nāga king and bullies him into delivering up the casket and the relic, and Danta and Hemamālā then proceed on their way. (*Dāṭh.*, 138–40 = Eng. trans., Law 1925: 37–39).[37] Once again, we have here an example of the "passage through nāgas" theme that we examined in chapter 6.

When Danta and Hemamālā finally arrive in the Sri Lanka, they are received by King Sirimeghavaṇṇa (362–409 C.E.) who has an old building in the palace compound refurbished for the tooth and renamed the Dāṭhādhātu-ghara ("House of the Tooth Relic"). An annual festival for the relic is instituted (*Cūḷ.*, 6–7 = Eng. trans., Geiger 1929, 1:7–8).[38] Moreover, as mentioned, from this time until at least the fourteenth century, the tooth relic comes to form "an inseparable pair" (Geiger 1960: 213) with the bowl relic brought over originally at the time of Mahinda (see chapter 6).

For the next six hundred years and more, the tooth and the bowl apparently remain in the capital of Anurādhapura, although they are only occasionally mentioned in the accounts of this period (see *Cūḷ.*, 27, 51, 154 = Eng. trans., Geiger 1929, 1:37, 69, 182; and Herath 1994: 49). There are at least two possible reasons for this dearth of references. First, it may be that, in this period, the tooth was closely associated with the Abhayagiri sect, while the island's chronicles were written, for the most part, by members of the rival mainline Mahānikāya sect. Second, as we have seen in chapter 6, there were other more important (i.e., predestined) and more established (i.e., immovable) foci of devotion already in the capital—the bodhi tree, the Mahāthūpa, and the Thūpārama—and it may be that the tooth could simply not compete with them (Herath 1994: 53).

When the capital is moved to Polonnaruva in the eleventh century, however, the tooth (and the bowl) move with it, and come into their own, while those other less movable relics stay behind, rooted in Anurādhapura. Indeed, from this time on, "the Tooth Relic seems to have been the most prominent object of worship in Sri Lankan Buddhism" (Herath 1994: 84; see also Wickremeratne 1987: 57). The subsequent history of the tooth on the island has been dealt with in detail by others and need

[37] Julia Shaw (2000: 35) has argued that this portion of the *Dāṭh.* is modeled on a *Mahābhārata* passage in which snakes guard the elixir of immortality and have to be defeated by Garuḍa and the gods. See also Van Buitenen 1973–75, 1:89.

[38] At this point, the *Dāṭh.* comes to an end but the *Cūḷ.* and certain chronicles in Sinhalese take over the narrative. These include the *Daḷadā Sirita* (written in 1325), the *Daḷadā Pūjāvaliya* (also from the fourteenth century), and the eighteenth century *Siṃhala Daḷadā Vaṃsaya* (see Herath 1994: 10–22).

not occupy us here. Suffice it to say that, over the next five hundred years or so, the tooth and bowl stay on the move, following the centers of power as they shift back and forth from Pollonaruva to Rohaṇa, Kotmale, Dambadeniya, Beligala, Yapahuwa, Southern India, Kurunegala, Gampola, and Koṭṭe (see Herath 1994: 27–75; Sirisoma 1988).

At some point during this time, the bowl relic drops out of the picture. According to Marco Polo, Genghis Khan sent an expedition to Sri Lanka in 1284, where it acquired not only the bowl of the Buddha, but some of his hair and two of his teeth (molars) as well. With these prizes, it then returned to China. "And when they drew near to the great city of Cambaluc, where the Great Kaan was staying . . . the whole population went forth to meet those reliques, and . . . received them with great joy and reverence" (Yule and Cordier 1993, 2:320).[39] This event, however, is not recorded in the Sri Lankan chronicles. In fact, the last reference to the bowl in the *Cūḷavaṃsa* appears to be the mention of its joint worship with the tooth by King Parakkamabāhu IV in 1325 C.E. (*Cūḷ.*, 515 = Eng. trans., Geiger 1929, 2:207). There are some cryptic references to a bowl relic in some early sixteenth-century inscriptions at Gadaladeniya monastery, near Kandy. There is also some speculation that in the mid-sixteenth century Don Juan Dharmapala (see next paragraph) may have sent the bowl relic to the Burmese (together with a tooth relic). The bowl and the tooth are said by some to be together, even today, in a pagoda in Sagaing in Burma (see Weerasinghe 1969: 63–64). On the other hand, a popular tradition has it that the bowl relic is actually still today enshrined in the base on which the tooth relic casket rests in the Daḷadā Māligāwa in Kandy (see Weerasinghe 1969: 64).[40]

Be this as it may, by 1561, according to the Portuguese, the tooth (sans bowl) was in far Northern Sri Lanka, since that is where they claim to have captured it during their invasion of Jaffna.[41] They took it (or whatever it was they actually seized) back with them to Gōa, in India, where,

[39] The bowl is further described as being "of a very beautiful green porphyry" and as potentially having the properties of a "vase of plenty," since, we are told, the Mongols "find it written in their Scriptures that the virtue of that dish is such that if food for one man be put therein it shall become enough for five men" (see Yule and Cordier 1993, 2:320).

[40] An alternative claim holds that it is (or was until the late nineteenth century, when it was stolen) enshrined in a small dagoba at the northwest corner of the Nātha dēvālaya across the street. See Holt 1991: 183.

[41] This was not the first time the relic was thought to have been captured. In the thirteenth century, it was taken briefly to South India by Pāṇḍyan rulers (see Herath 1994: 74–75), and, according to a Chinese source (*T.* 2087, 51:938c–39a = Eng. trans., Li 1996: 353–55), it was seized in 1411 by the Ming Dynasty admiral, Zheng He, who returned with it to China. On the aborted earlier attempt by the Tang Dynasty monk Ming Yuan to steal it and take it home with him, see Liu 1996: 32, 47 and Lahiri 1986: 33–34.

as we have seen, they destroyed it in a public ceremony.[42] It was not long, however, before the tooth reappeared on the island. Don Juan Dharmapala, the Christianized king of Koṭṭe, soon claimed that he had had the relic all along, and promptly offered it to the king of Pegu (along with his own "daughter" in marriage) to seal an alliance with them (De Couto 1783, 18:77 = Eng. trans., Tennent 1859, 2:218–19).[43] Not long thereafter, Konnappu Bandāra, who had attacked Kandy for the Portuguese but then turned against them, claimed he too was in possession of the tooth relic. He then used it, as well as his marriage to a Kandyan princess, as part of his attempt to legitimize his usurpation of the Kandyan throne (*Cūḷ.*, 529 = Eng. trans., Geiger 1929, 2:228; see also Sirisoma 1988: 46; Da Cunha 1875: 138–39; K. M. DeSilva 1981: 118). This is the first mention in the *Cūḷavaṃsa* of the tooth's being enshrined in Kandy, where it remains today.

Relics and Rule

It is clear from all this that possession of the tooth (and the bowl prior to its eclipse) came to be viewed in Sri Lanka as an important symbol of sovereignty over the nation. Kings could not be consecrated if they did not possess the tooth and could not retain power if they lost it (Herath 1994: 95–99). But possession of a relic was not simply a matter of ownership or inheritance. It was also, as David Wyatt (2001: 35) has argued in a different context, a sign of a ruler's ability to handle an "extremely powerful object," and thus a sign of his own merit and "enormous sacral power." As centers of power shifted, the tooth (along with the bowl) became a movable palladium of kingship; at the same time, it was also a "symbol of nationalism which unified the Sinhalese against foreign rulers" (Herath 1994: 163). For example, Parakkamabāhu I (1153–86) used the recapture of the relics as a rallying cry for his troops. "I have heard," he told his men, "that the routed enemy, in their flight, have taken the most excellent venerable relic of the almsbowl and the tooth, and may flee across the sea with them. If that happens, this land of Lanka

[42] See De Couto 1783, 17:316–17, 428–33 = Eng. trans., Tennent 1859, 2:213–16. See also Da Cunha 1875: 127–31, and, for a full study of this episode, Strong 1997. Some have claimed that what the Portuguese destroyed was just a replica of the tooth (see Forbes [1840] 1994, 2:220; Karunaratne 1984: 285; and Hocart 1932: 3). Such facsimiles certainly existed (see Goloubew 1932: 454n.), and we know, from epigraphical evidence (Herath 1994: 82), that a mid-fifteenth-century monarch used to wear a replica of the tooth as an amulet on his person.

[43] Supposedly, this tooth was eventually enshrined in Ava. In the mid-nineteenth century, two Sri Lankan monks at the court of Ava caused some degree of controversy when they expressed doubts about its genuineness. On the subsequent attempt to resolve the matter, see Jacobs 1860: 129.

will become empty. . . . Therefore, work together, . . . capture the enemy army, and quickly send me the most excellent tooth relic, and the venerable almsbowl" (*Cūḷ.*, 347–48 = Eng. trans., Geiger 1929, 2:31).

Already in Anurādhapura, the temple of the tooth tended to be located in or near the palace compound, where it was the locale for a daily cult. Xuanzang, for example, basing himself on hearsay since he never visited Sri Lanka, states that it was right next to the royal palace, and he describes it as being "several hundred feet high and decorated with pearls and rare gems. A signal post is installed on the temple, with a huge ruby fixed on it that issues a refulgent light that shines brightly as a star when viewed at a distance day or night. The king bathes the tooth relic three times a day with scented water and burns powdered incense as an offering, in an extremely opulent manner" (Li 1996: 331; text in *T.* 2087, 51:934a). In the Polonnaruva period, this proximity and relationship of king and relic continued, and, as we have seen, possession of the tooth became almost a sine qua non for legitimate rule.

Much the same thing was still true in the early nineteenth century when the British captured the relic in Kandy. As John Davy ([1821] 1969: 275), the British governor's physician who toured Kandy in 1817, put it, "The effect of its capture was astonishing, and almost beyond the comprehension of the enlightened. . . . Now (the people said) the English are indeed masters of the country; for they who possess the relic have a right to govern" (see also Malalgoda 1976: 118). But the British quickly realized that possession of the tooth alone was not enough; of necessity it entailed ritual. Thus, when they first secured Kandy, they not only allowed for an elaborate *perahera* (procession) to reinstall the tooth, but they organized it and participated in it, having the "Drums of His Majesty's 3rd Ceylon Regiment" replace some of the Kandyan "tom-tom" beaters, and having Mr. D'Oyly, the British leader in Kandy walking directly behind the tusker bearing the relic, and then going barefoot up to the altar and making offerings to the tooth in his official capacity (DeSilva 1972: 2; Malalgoda 1976: 119n.). For the next thirty years, the British were not only the guardians of the Buddha's tooth but also the sponsors of its cult, and it was only in 1847 that, succumbing to increasing pressure from missionaries on the island and Christian societies in England, they finally gave up their ritual role and entrusted custody of the tooth to a committee, consisting of the chief lay official of the temple, the Diyawaḍana Nilame, and the elders of the Malwatte and Asgiriya monasteries, the same committee of three that remains in charge of the temple to this day (Malalgoda 1976: 120).

State sponsorship of ceremonies and the maintenance of the Temple of the Tooth take money, and so it comes as no surprise to find that throughout much of Sri Lankan history, kings, their ministers, and members of the royal family were among the chief donors to the tooth relic. Their offerings included not only such things as villages, forest lands, fields, precious articles, money, slaves, cattle, and elephants, but also, at times, government-imposed taxes, such as the quarter-percent customs duty one king levied—for the sake of the tooth—on all goods imported through any of Sri Lanka's nine seaports, or the sales tax on liquor (*toddy*) imposed by another, or the fines collected from shops that stayed open on *poya* (*poṣādha*) days (Herath 1994: 65–66, 114, 132–34).[44]

There were several reasons for the king to manifest such support of the tooth. On the one hand, as we have seen, it bolstered his sovereignty by allowing him to exhibit traditional models of dharmic rule and piety, originally set by Aśoka and by the cakravartin ideal. At the same time, however, the tooth (and the bowl) were thought to have special powers of insuring the prosperity of the nation and fertility of the land. Probably from the time of its first arrival on the island, the tooth was thought to protect the kingdom from "famine, calamity and revolution" (Gunawardana 1979: 229). According to a seventh-century Chinese account, Sri Lankans believed that if the tooth relic were ever lost, the country would be devoured by demons (*T.* 2066, 51:3c = Eng. trans., Lahiri 1986: 34). In other words, it would return to the condition that it was in prior to the first apocryphal "civilizing" visit by the Buddha.

More specifically, the tooth (and especially the bowl relic during the Anurādhapura period) was thought to produce rainfall.[45] The fourth-century king, Upatissa, for example, put an end to a drought by filling the Buddha's bowl relic with water, and sprinkling it as he followed a cart on which a newly fashioned gold image of the Buddha was taken through the streets of the city (*Cūḷ.*, 15 = Eng. trans., Geiger 1929, 1:19). This, it was said, was what the Buddha's disciple Ānanda had done long ago with the Buddha's bowl, when Vaiśālī was suffering from a famine and pestilence due to a drought (Herath 1994: 43; see also *KhpA.*, 164 = Eng. trans., Ñāṇamoli 1997: 178). In the twelfth century, at Parakkamabāhu's great festival of the tooth relic, the procession was preceded by a rain cloud that kept just ahead of the parade and "filled all the ponds and rivers" but without ever raining down on the festivities themselves (*Cūḷ.*, 359 = Eng. trans., Geiger 1929, 2:43). The lengthy description of the translation of the tooth and bowl relics to the town of Sirivaḍḍhana, in the thirteenth century, specifies that the sound of the drums mimicked the

[44] For a somewhat similar list of wealth, lands, and persons given over to a buddha relic in twelfth-century Thailand, see Wyatt 2001: 11. Gregory Schopen (1997: 258ff) has spoken of the Buddha as the "owner" of property in medieval Indian monasteries, and it is clear here that we have a similar instance of such ownership.

[45] Herath (1994: 163) proposes this as one of the four reasons for the tooth's prominence during and after the Polonnaruva period.

thunderclaps of Pajjunna, the god of rain (*Cūḷ.*, 475 = Eng. trans., Geiger 1929, 2:163). A few years later, in the midst of a terrible dry spell, the monks were asked to circumambulate the capital with the tooth relic while making a firm resolve: "the heavens shall rain." The very next day, it poured (*Cūḷ.*, 487–88 = Eng. trans., Geiger 1929, 2:177–78). The *Daḷadā-sirita,* a fourteenth-century Sinhala ritual manual still in use at the Temple of the Tooth, prescribes that "when rain does not fall the Tooth-relic should be worshipped" (Hocart 1931: 37), and one of the verses that closes the daily veneration of the relic requests that "the god send down rain in due time and promote the welfare of crops" (Hocart 1931: 27; see also Gunawardana 1979: 229). Even today, this verse is recited, and, as is well known, the annual Esala perahera has as one of its purposes rain-making, a fact that may be connected to the title of the chief lay official of the Temple of the Tooth, the Diyawaḍana Nilame, which originally meant "water-bearer" (see Holt 1991: 186).

Pūjā and Perahera: God, King, and Monk

The royal connections of the tooth relic were also reflected in some of the features of the regular cultic rituals that were carried out for it, some of which can still be seen today. Juliane Schober has distinguished between two forms of relic veneration, which she calls the "Ānanda modality," emphasizing personal service and devotion, and a more public "royal modality" involving social relations of power and hegemonic pursuits, diplays and processions (Schober 1996: 203–8, and 1997). Similarly, Victor Goloubew has distinguished between two "ritual programs" focused on the relic at the Temple of the Tooth in Kandy. On the one hand, there is what he calls the "daḷadā-king," the tooth relic-as-ruler; on the other, there is "the very holy daḷadā," in which the relic-as-personal savior comes to the fore.

The "daḷadā-king," Goloubew explains, "necessitates the constant presence, in the temple and its dependencies, of numerous servants and lay officials, administrators, secretaries, musicians, cooks, night watchmen, shoulder-pole carriers, torch bearers— a whole personnel . . . that is approximately the same as the entourage of a sovereign" (1932: 460–61). In this way, the relic's daily "royal needs" are taken care of. Every day, at dawn, in a set of rituals that was first established in the fourteenth century and that continues up to the present, the tooth is awakened and offered water with which to wash its hands, a toothstick, water for a bath, a towel to dry the face, another towel for the body, fresh clothes, a seat, a fan, a fly-whisk, the sound of a bell, sweet-smelling camphor, lights, perfumes, flowers, and then a full meal, consisting of water to drink, gruel, rice, curry, and sweetmeats. Then, after a pause, during which the relic is left alone to eat, the meal is cleared away and a chew of betel is offered. Finally, the sanctum is fumigated with incense, swept, and then closed. Similar rituals, with some variations, occur at midmorning and then again in the evening (see Seneviratne 1978: 38–60; Hocart 1931: 18–33; Devendra 1984).

It is sometimes argued that all these rituals—the bathing, feeding, etc.—assume belief in a literal presence of the Buddha in his relic. Such an argument, however, ignores the complex nature of ritual action. More fruitfully, anthropologists such as H. L. Seneviratne (1978: 38ff) have shown how these maintenance rituals emphasize the "deva" status of the tooth relic, its treatment as king, but also as god. Indeed, generally speaking, these rituals closely resemble the daily *pūjā* performed for Hindu deities, and they assume a recognition of divinity and royalty in the relic.

At the same time, however, the identity of the relic (and of the Buddha) as a monk is appreciated. For example, the fresh clothes that are offered are specified as being the triple monastic robe. The sound of the bell that is rung is said to recall the sound of the preaching of the dharma (Hocart 1931: 21–23). Also, in recognition of the Buddha's monastic status, the evening meal contains no solid foods but only juices and other sweets (Seneviratne 1978: 54). Moreover, the daily ritual is prefaced by the recitation of Pali verses that are unambiguously Buddhist and serve to frame the ritual as a whole (Hocart 1931: 20; Seneviratne 1978: 42; Goloubew 1932: 464n). In this official cult, then, the tooth relic is really three things: god, king, and monk.

This, of course, is also true of the Buddha, biographically speaking. The various identities taken on by the tooth, I would argue, replicate the movement of Śākyamuni's own life story, in that he proceeds from existence as a deity in Tuṣita Heaven, to birth in this world as a royal prince, to wandering forth as a monk to achieve enlightenment as a buddha. In the broader scope of his biography, which includes his previous lives, it is possible to see that he has, in fact, often been a king, a god, or an ascetic (i.e., a *śramaṇa,* the prototype of a monk). According to a count made by T. W. Rhys Davids, in the Pali jātaka collection, the bodhisattva is an ascetic eighty-three times, a king eighty-five times, and a deity sixty-three times (Davids 1880: ci). He also appears as other things, of course (merchants, ministers, various kinds of animals, etc.), but, if we view his biography synchronically (as relics encourage us to do), one is tempted to conclude that the Buddha primarily "is" these three things. Thus the fact that the tooth relic can be treated as though it were a god and a king and a monk makes sense not only because the Buddha himself has been all three of those things in his lifetimes, but also because he "is" them.

More concretely, this tripartide distinction is also helpful in understanding another aspect of the cult of the Sri Lankan tooth relic: the fact that it participates in periodic processions called *peraheras*. Unlike relics that were ensconced in stūpas, the tooth (and the bowl), as we have seen, were enshrined in halls, sometimes in monasteries, sometimes on the grounds of the palace. From these places, they could be taken out on festive occasions and paraded through the streets or exposed for the veneration of the faithful. The best-known of these tooth relic processions is the one that is carried out in modern times, the so-called Esala perahera, which is held every year in July / August in Kandy, and has become one of Sri Lanka's most famous tourist attractions.[46] As a celebration, however, this festival was originally a ritual in honor of Viṣṇu.[47] Robert Knox (1958: 149–50), who witnessed the Kandy perahera in 1681, makes no mention of the tooth, but speaks of the chief deity in the procession as "Allout neur Dio," whom he calls the "God and Maker of Heaven and Earth." This refers to "Alutnuvara Deva"—one of the names of Viṣṇu at the time in Sri Lanka (see Holt 1991: 186; Goloubew 1932: 467). The other two deities at the perahera mentioned by Knox are "Cotteragom Dio" and "Potting Dio." These are the god Kataragama and the goddess Pattini who still participate in the perahera. In the eighteenth century, during the reign of Kīrti Śrī, the tooth relic and the "god" Nātha (= Avalokiteśvara) were added to the procession in an attempt to "buddhaize" the festival, and that is the way the festival has been celebrated ever since (see Holt 1991: 186, and 1996: 31–32; Swearer 1982: 304–8).

According to a tradition current in the early nineteenth century, this was done so as to please a delegation of visiting Thai monks who wondered why the Buddha had no place in this major festivity (Pieris 1956: 136). Kīrti Śrī's actions made sense, however, in light of a long history of processional festivals celebrating the tooth relic. The first account we have of such an occasion is that of Faxian, who visited Sri Lanka at the start of the fifth century, not many years after the arrival of the relic on the island. As we saw in chapter 2, according to Faxian, ten days before the start of the festival, a man dressed in royal robes and sitting on a large caparisoned elephant, beat a drum and reminded everyone that the Buddha, during three uncountable aeons, had performed great bodhisattva deeds. He then recalled a number of jātakas, which segued into an account of the Buddha's last life up until his attainment of parinirvāṇa. The herald ended by proclaiming that, since that event of the parinirvāṇa "1,497 years ago,"[48] the Blessed One can no longer be seen and the world has lived in sadness. But, ten days hence, the Buddha's tooth would

[46] For a modern description of the Esala festival, see DeSilva 1980: 210–15.
[47] For an early description of the Kandy Esala festival, see Pieris 1956: 135–38, where the account by the Disave of Vellassa, first published in 1817, is reprinted.
[48] This would put the date of the parinirvāṇa c. 1,087 B.C.E. For a summary of what chronologists have made of this bit of information, see Bechert 1995: 279–80.

be brought out and taken to the Abhayagiri-vihāra (*T.* 2085, 51:865a–b = Eng. trans., Li 2002: 206). The implication, of course, is that this will be a chance to *see* the Buddha once again, and indeed, monks and laypeople are encouraged by this herald to make the roads smooth and well adorned and to prepare a great supply of flowers and incense in anticipation of making merit. Ten days later, at the festival itself, the narrative of the jātakas is repeated, but in a different, more figurative way; as we have seen, the tooth relic, in procession, "skins the cat" of its former lives by passing through two lines of banners depicting all five hundred jātaka tales (*T.* 2085, 51:865b = Eng. trans., Li 2002: 206–7; see also Legge [1886] 1965: 106).

Once again, we can see how biographical narrative, or at least biographical recall—including lives as king, god, and monk—can function in the context of relics. But what is most emphasized here, in the final analysis, is the monastic connection, since the perahera, as Faxian describes it, is a procession that is heading for the Abhayagiri monastery. The relic itself, as we have seen, is normally kept in royal circles, in a temple by the palace, but every year, after this procession, it spends the three months of the rains retreat as a "monk" at the Abhayagiri. Ninety days later, it is returned to its place in the city (*T.* 2085, 51:865b = Eng. trans., Li 2002: 207; see also Legge [1886] 1965: 106–7).

A somewhat different emphasis may be found in another example of a tooth relic procession sponsored by Parakkamabāhu I in the twelfth century. This monarch had built, for the occasion, in the middle of the city of Polonnaruva, a splendid house (*ghara*) for the relic, which is likened to the assembly hall of the king of the gods. Here, then, the procession will not be to a monastery but to a centrally located shrine with divine and royal associations. From the royal gate onward, the king has the road made perfectly level for a distance of one league and decorated with triumphal arches, palm trees, banana trees, and vases filled with flowers and banners and pennons, so that the whole looked like Indra's heaven. All of this culminates, once the tooth and the bowl arrive in their temple in the center of the city, in a great festival of lights, lasting seven days and nights (*Cūḷ.*, 356–60 = Eng. trans., Geiger 1929: 39–43; see also Gunawardana 1979: 228–29).

Here, clearly, the deva/king side of the relic is brought to the fore. More specifically, I would suggest that this Polonnaruva procession, which includes the relics' re-establishment in the center of the city and the celebration of the festival of lights, recalls not only the example of Aśoka, but the myth of the cakravartin who follows with all his entourage the great wheel of the dharma, which arises for him and then establishes itself back in the center of his kingdom, an event that confirms his status as a righteous monarch (see *D.*, 3:58–79 = Eng. trans., Davids 1899–1924, 3:53–76). This would seem to be the mythic model for relic peraheras in which the sovereignty and dharmic nature of the king is asserted or reasserted. Indeed, in the *Cūlavaṃsa,* the tooth and bowl are sometimes specifically compared to the jewel-wheel of a cakravartin, and their veneration is said to make at least one king feel like the great righteous ruler Mandhātar (*Cūl.*, 453 = Eng. trans., Geiger 1929, 2:138).[49] The same association may be found in China. When the Japanese pilgrim Jōjin visited the Buddha's tooth in Kaifeng in 1072, for example, an imperial emissary had to open the building for him, and the relic itself was housed in the "Hall of Seven Treasures," a reference to the regalia of cakravartins (see Soper 1948: 24–25).

Personal Piety

The second of Goloubew's "ritual programs" at the Temple of the Tooth—that which focuses on the "very holy relic"—emphasizes personal dedication and acts of sacrifice toward the relic, whether inspired by communal concerns or not. In China, we know that such manifestations of devotion toward relics could be quite frenzied, recalling ancient New Year's celebrations in which men and women "wasted their goods, destroyed their inheritance, . . . and exhausted their family fortunes" (Gernet 1956: 232, quoting Granet 1926, 1:321–22). In Sri Lanka, things appear to be somewhat more subdued, yet not fundamentally different. For instance, at a special exhibition of the tooth outside of its reliquary—the first in fifty-three years—held in May 1828, the relic was brought in procession, on the back of a great tusker through two lines of elephants kneeling in homage. People thronged the route, their cries of "Sadhu" swelling "into a grand and solemn sound of adoration" (Forbes [1840] 1994, 1:292). Then, for three days and nights, they vied with one another in making donations—jewelry, coins of all denominations, cloth, monastic robes, flowers, areca nuts, betel leaves, etc.—to the relic, which was displayed on a lotus blossom made of gold on top of a silver table (Forbes [1840] 1994, 1:293–94; see also Colebrooke 1836).

A second example of such personal piety is more down to earth and contemporary, and needs little elucidation. It is taken from an anonymous letter that appeared in the Colombo *Daily News* in the summer of 1991, and it testifies not only to the emotions but also the motivations of individual devotees:

[49] In this regard, it is noteworthy that the very first shrine built for the tooth in Sri Lanka, the Dāṭhādhātughara in Anurādhapura, was originally called the "House of the Dharma-Wheel" (Dhammacakkageha). See Herath 1994: 92.

[I]n Kandy, about thirty years ago, there was a special exposition of the sacred Tooth Relic.[50] I was an ordinary housewife, managing the house and four young children. My husband had gone to work and would come back only in the evening. My mother was visiting us and, on reading the newspaper, she came to know about the special exposition. She expressed a keen desire to worship the Relic again. The maligawa [temple of the tooth] had a special significance for her and her mother before her. Countless were the times we children accompanied them to worship there. . . .

When my mother expressed her wish to worship the Tooth Relic, I was in a quandary because she could not travel by bus and there were no hiring cars in the vicinity. I had to wait till my husband came home after work, in the evening. When I told him about my mother's wish, he agreed to drop us at the maligawa and came back to be with the children. . . . We joined the tail-end of the queue. The exposition was nearly over when we got a chance to worship the Sacred Relic [but] fortunately for us the officiating priest knew my mother well, as she was a regular worshipper. He told her that she could remain there to see the Relic casket being put back for safety in the inner shrine room. My mother was overjoyed as the longer she worshipped, the happier she was.

I gazed in wonder and amazement at the richness of the offerings. Beautiful jewellery was being put back, to adorn the casket. As the inventory was being read out, I marvelled at the people and places they came from. I was struck by the piety and devotion that prompted them to make such offerings. Many were the offerings made by Siamese and Burmese [pilgrims] and I loved looking at these foreign people who were seated on a low platform right through the exposition. Foreigners were rare then. . . .

[I then looked down at] the most valuable piece of jewellery I had, my own engagement ring, a sovereign gold one with a blue sapphire in the middle and eight tiny diamonds round it. . . . I looked at it long and lovingly, as that was my husband's first valuable gift to me. I thought to myself "Why don't I offer this to the Lord Buddha? So many people, for so many centuries, have made such valuable offerings. If I keep this, I may lose it, or if I give it to my children they may not value it. But, if I offer it here, it will be here, long after I am no more." (Anonymous 1991: 17)

The letter goes on to tell how she finally decides to make her offering, and to relate how a problem the family was having with getting some work done on their driveway and a culvert was resolved the very next day. And it concludes, "I am certain that it was the merit I had acquired by offering my ring that solved the problem. Every action has a reaction

[50] This was not an actual viewing of the tooth itself, but an exposition of the tooth in its casket, outside of its usual shrine.

they say and that good kamma (Pali for "Karma") of mine had an immediate result. I did not have to wait till after death to reap the benefit of a generous action" (Anonymous 1991: 17).

The Tours of the Chinese Tooth

We have, so far, encountered a number of different ways in which tooth relics may be thought to extend further the life story and presence of the Buddha. There is one final context in which I would like to look at this theme. That is the more-or-less modern phenomenon of Buddha's teeth and other relics being taken on tours of other countries. In doing this, I want to focus primarily on the tour—to Sri Lanka in 1961—of the "Chinese tooth relic" that was then and is still today kept in a pagoda near Beijing. I think this tour is worth chronicling for its own sake. More generally, however, it should help us push our inquiry beyond traditional boundaries and, as we enter a realm of internationalism, look at problems such as the question of how Buddhists view relics that are in the possession of others (non-Buddhists).

The Beijing tooth may or may not be the Udyāna / Khotan tooth that was in Chang'an in the Tang Dynasty (which, in turn, may or may not be the tooth mentioned in the *Mahāparinirvāṇa sūtra* as being taken to Gandhāra). Its modern history begins in 1900. In that year, during the Boxer Rebellion, the Zhaoxian pagoda in the Western Hills outside of Beijing was destroyed by cannon fire, by Western Imperialist troops who wanted to punish the monks of the nearby Lingguang monastery for having harbored Boxers (Arlington and Lewisohn 1987: 301). In the rubble of the foundations, the monks from that monastery found a box inscribed with the words "The Holy Tooth Relic of Śākyamuni Buddha. Written by Shan-hui on the 23rd day of the 4th month in the 7th year of Tien-hui [963 C.E.]" Inside the box was a molar wrapped up in a piece of silk (Chao 1959: 36–37, and Buddhist Association of China 1966: 6–7, 25).

The newly discovered tooth was initially kept by the monks at the monastery near the ruined pagoda, until 1955 when it was handed over to the recently founded Chinese Buddhist Association, which put it in a display case at its headquarters in Beijing. There it was noticed by the Burmese ambassador, who reported its existence to Premier U Nu, who mentioned it to Premier Zhou Enlai, who is supposed to have then generously offered it to the Burmese people saying, "Take it—we have no use for it" (Welch 1972: 181, but see also 553n.35). Delighted, U Nu promptly sent a delegation to China to receive the tooth. When they got there, they found that the relic was no longer simply displayed in an ordinary glass case but was now housed in a jewel-encrusted golden reliquary, and that it was no longer to be given to the Burmese people but simply loaned to them, to be sent on a tour of their country for a period of eight months (Welch 1972: 181).[51]

The tour was a great success. The tooth was welcomed at the Rangoon airport by President Ba U, Premier U Nu, members of the Supreme Court and the legislature, secretaries of the Army, Navy, and Air Force, ministers of various governmental departments, foreign diplomats, monks, nuns, and a huge crowd. U Ba U proclaimed, "Many thanks to Chairman Mao, Premier Chou, the Chinese government and the Chinese People. Through their profound friendship the historic wish of the Burmese people is now fulfilled. . . . The tooth of the Buddha is now visiting our land. . . . Long live the friendship between the peoples of China and Burma!" (see Welch 1972: 183).

The Chinese, it should be said, were not the first modern state to use Buddhist relics on such propaganda tours. In the early 1950s, the British had already returned, with great fanfare, to India, the relic of the Buddha's chief disciples, Śāriputra and Mahāmaudgalyāyana, which Alexander Cunningham had uncovered at Sāñcī in 1851 and ferreted away to the Victoria and Albert Museum in London (Daulton 1994).[52] Soon thereafter, the Indian government, through the Maha Bodhi Society, sent these relics on a tour of Sri Lanka, and the French then sponsored their visit, along with a Buddha relic, to Cambodia, where they were received with great ceremony by King Sihanouk (Barthes 1952). The Sri Lankans, in turn, got into the act. In the same year, they arranged for one of their Buddha relics to stop off in Vietnam on its way to being presented to the people of Japan on the occasion of the Second World Congress of Buddhists in Tokyo, in 1952 (see De Berval 1952: 703).[53]

It is possible that the Chinese were inspired by the success of these tours. Not long thereafter, they, in fact, joined the World Fellowship of Buddhists, and began sending delegates to its conferences (Welch 1972: 210–11). It was soon after that that they undertook their negotiations with U Nu and the Burmese. Moreover, the tooth's tour of Burma was so successful that the government decided to take its relic diplomacy more seriously. In 1957, it undertook the construction of a new Buddha's

[51] Chao (1956: 14) presents this scenario in a somewhat different light. For photographs of the reliquary in the Guangji si (Chinese Buddhist Association headquarters), see Buddhist Association of China 1956: 10–11.

[52] For some of the mysteries involved in this translation, see Prasad 1981.

[53] On subsequent Sri Lankan gifts of relics to Cambodia and Vietnam, see Narada 1953 and Nouth Oun 1953.

Tooth Relic Pagoda, near the site of the old one outside of Beijing, at a cost of over half a million dollars. It was fifty meters high, in "traditional" Chinese architectural style, its finial resplendent with gold leaf (Buddhist Association of China 1966: 9–10). In 1964, the building was dedicated in the presence of Buddhist delegations from ten different countries, including North and South Vietnam. A great procession was held to translate the tooth to its new sanctuary, and a joint statement was issued condemning United States bombing in Southeast Asia (Welch 1972: 219–20).

Prior to that time, however, in 1961, the tooth relic itself was sent on a second tour, to Sri Lanka. The New China News Agency, as Holmes Welch (1972: 183) put it, "released a torrent of despatches" about this trip. The articles are official, more or less predictable, emphasizing the size of the crowds, the receptions given by high government officials, and the reunion of the two teeth (the Beijing and Kandy relics) as symbolizing the new friendship between the people of the two nations.[54] In many ways, the coverage in the *Ceylon Daily News* is more interesting for our purposes. It starts with some front-page reports from Beijing on the activities of the Sri Lankan delegation sent to China to accompany the relic back to the island (31 May 1961, p. 1; and 2 June 1961, p. 1). A few days later, it details some of the preparations being made in Sri Lanka for welcoming the relic upon its arrival: the Governor General, the Prime Minister (Mrs. Bandaranaike), and the Chinese Ambassador are all said to be planning to go to the airport, and arrangements are being made for exhibiting the relic in Colombo, in a special pavilion at the Daḷadā Māligāwa in Kandy, and at other important sites throughout the island (7 June 1961, p. 1).

Yet, at the same time, we get the first indication that not all Sri Lankan Buddhists were necessarily happy with this planned tour. In a separate article, on the very same day, a potential rift on this issue is made public between the two chief monks (*mahānāyakas*) of the Asgiriya and Malwatte vihāras, the two leading monasteries of the principal sect, the Siyam Nikāya. The Malwatte mahānāyaka announced that he would decline the invitation to go to the airport to welcome the relic, since he "was not feeling well and was busy with preparations for ordination ceremonies." The Asgiriya mahānāyaka, on the other hand, declared that he *would* go to the airport and chant sūtras there *despite* the fact that he had developed a rash on his face (*Ceylon Daily News*, 7 June 1961, p. 1). This snub by the Malwatte elder is important not only because of his leadership role in the Sri Lankan saṃgha, but also since he is one of the three

[54] See the mimeographed *Survey of China Mainland Press* (Hong Kong), Nos. 2508–14, 2516–18, 2521–25, 2528–33, and 2556–66.

members of the committee that is in charge of the temple of the tooth in Kandy, the other two being the Asgiriya mahānāyaka, and the lay custodian of the tooth, the Diyawaḍana Nilame.

Three days later, the tooth arrived. A few headlines will allow us to trace quickly the first part of its tour. In Colombo, "75,000 Venerate Relic Daily," and "Chinese Bring Greetings to Ceylon Buddhists" (12 June 1961). In Anurādhapura, the visit was especially successful; it was timed to coincide with the traditional celebration of Poson Poya, a day that marks the advent of Buddhism to the island, and that is especially celebrated in Anurādhapura. The relic was exhibited directly opposite the bodhi tree. "Big Crowds in Anurādhapura!" announced the *Ceylon Daily News* (27 June 1961), and "One Mile Queue at Anurādhapura Braves Rain to Venerate Relic" (28 June 1961).

I do want to say a few more words, however, about the visit of the relic to Kandy, which, in many ways, was intended to be the highpoint of the whole tour since there, after all, the two teeth of the Buddha would come together. The visit to Kandy, although generally successful, was marked by two events. The Asgiriya mahānāyaka and the lay custodian of the tooth, the Diyawaḍana Nilame, Mr. C. B. Nugawela, had both agreed to participate fully in the reception of the tooth in Kandy, but the head of the Malwatte sect still refused. For him, the relic was not genuine and the Chinese Communists were not to be trusted. Despite considerable pressure from different sources,[55] he declared in no uncertain terms, "I have decided not to associate myself with this event, and under no circumstances will I alter my decision" (*Ceylon Daily News*, 28 June 1961, 1).

The ceremonies in Kandy thus were conducted without him. The reception of the tooth went off smoothly. Even though the Chinese tooth did not get to be carried by Rāja, the big tusker reserved for the Sri Lankan tooth, a great perahera was organized and the tooth was installed in a grand pavillion right in front of the Daḷadā Māligāwa. Thousands of people came. The next day, however, in what could only be interpreted as a very inauspicious event, Mr. Nugawela, the Diyawaḍana Nilame who played a major role in the occasion, died rather suddenly of a heart attack. "He was 74," the obituary reported, "he had had a busy day the day before receiving the Chinese relic" (*Ceylon Daily News*, 3 July 1961, p. 3). The tooth relic went on and finished its tour, but the overwhelming propaganda success the Chinese had hoped for did not really materialize, and, on August 10, the relic returned to China.

The "Great Cultural Revolution" of 1966–76 was not a good time for the practice of Buddhism in China. Many temples were damaged or destroyed and open devotions disappeared altogether. Even the officials of

[55] See, for example, the "special article" by G. P. Malalasekera on the front page of the *Ceylon Daily News* (27 June 1961).

the state-supported Chinese Buddhist Association laid low. Little is known about what happened to the Buddha's tooth relic and its brand new pagoda during this chaotic period, except that they escaped damage and were shown, at least once, to foreign visitors, during a lull in the revolutionary fervor, in 1972.[56] In the 1990's, however, the Chinese tooth relic resurfaced and resumed its tours. Notably, in 1994, it went on a forty-five day tour of Myanmar at the invitation of the military-dominated State Law and Order Restoration Council, which, as Juliane Schober has pointed out, "relied increasingly on its patronage of Buddhist relics and symbols . . . in the absence of a secular, constitutional legitimation of state powers" (Schober 2000: 47).[57]

Since then, the other great Chinese relic—the fingerbone, recovered by archaeologists at the Famen si in 1987—has followed the tooth on other tours. In 1996, it was sent to Thailand, and then again, in 2002 to Taiwan where it was paraded through the streets and venerated by hundreds of thousands of devotees for over a month.[58] Two quotes, both of which should be taken seriously, may suffice to sum up the two sides—devotional and political—of the occasion. Soon after the arrival of the relic, a Taiwanese monk was quoted by the Associated Press as saying, "Looking at the bone is like seeing the Buddha himself,"[59] while a Mainland Chinese official declared, "We hope Buddha's finger [can] inspire friendly love and peace across the Taiwan Strait."[60] The latter sentiment, however, should probably be read in the context of the earlier journey, in 1998, of yet another relic—a tooth—said to have been smuggled out of Tibet to India during the Cultural Revolution, and then sent in a pronationalist move to Taipei "for safe-keeping."[61]

Such "relic diplomacy," or "relic warfare," especially when practiced by secular governments, has sometimes been criticized as hypocritical. And yet the use of relics in this way has a long history, starting perhaps with King Aśoka who, in an attempt to better his relations with foreign peoples (e.g., Sri Lanka and Devānampiya Tissa), also agreed to send relics overseas. Moreover, as we have seen in the case of the Kandyan kings, and the British colonialists, this is not the first time that "nonbelievers" have used relics to help show their support for Buddhism and/or legitimate their rule.

[56] On this visit made by myself and my wife, and the circumstances that led to it, see Strong 1973, and Strong and Strong 1973.

[57] See also Schober 1997, which contains a detailed account of the events of this visit.

[58] See contributions to buddha-l@ulkyvm.louisville.edu, by Wong Weng Fai (posted 16 April 1998, 9:13 a.m.) and by James Benn (posted 16 April 1998, 9:14 a.m.).

[59] http://www.cnn.com/2002/WORLD/asiapcf/east/02/23/taiwan.buddha/.

[60] See http://www.cnn.com/2002/WORLD/asiapcf/east/02/23/taiwan.buddha/.

[61] See the contributions to buddha-l@ulkyvm.louisville.edu by Wong Weng Fai (posted 16 April 1998, 9:13 a.m.) and by James Benn (posted 16 April 1998, 9:14 a.m.); and see Kieschnick 2003: 47.

Conclusion

In an interesting work not without relevance to the study of relics, Melissa Schrift (2001) shows how Mao Zedong badges in modern day China not only commemorate events in the life of the chairman, but develop life stories and cults of their own that go far beyond the original intentions of their creators. In this chapter, I have examined tooth relic traditions to illustrate an assortment of "moves" that some relics make after the death of the Buddha, extensions of his biography that enable "the Buddha" to do things he never did and go places he never went during his lifetime in human form. These relics travel, in a variety of modes, from one country to another. Tied to kingship rather than pilgrimage sites, they keep on moving from capital to capital, where they serve to legitimate rule. They also are taken on peraheras at festival times, processing through cities the way the wheel of a cakravartin king might circumambulate the cosmos. They are implored to inspire troops and win wars. They are asked to insure fertility and make it rain as though they were deities. They are given respect as though they were monks. And, as we have just seen, they go on diplomatic / devotional tours of foreign nations, even in modern times.

None of these movements was predicted by the Buddha. None is part of the biographical blueprint for all tathāgatas. These relics tend not to be enshrined in places that have been hallowed by buddhas of the past. They represent, therefore, new life-story departures in Śākyamuni's career, while, at the same time, remaining connected to him, in the mind of devotees. We can see here one of the ironies of relics that extend the Buddha's biography: ceasing to be mere expressions of the Buddha's life (or of episodes therein) they are freed from "re-presenting" him, and so are able to "present" him afresh in ways not seen before. "Being" the Buddha, they are paradoxically able to do new things that "the Buddha" never did.

Chapter Eight

RELICS AND ESCHATOLOGY

As IS WELL KNOWN, one of the basic messages of Buddhism is the lesson of impermanence. All things that arise from a cause are subject to dissolution; nothing, not even the Buddha, not even the Buddha's teaching, lasts forever. The same may be said of the Buddha's relics, which, insofar as they embody the departed master and his dharma and replicate and extend his biography, are subject to the same law of impermanence.

This does not, however, mean the end of the world. In Buddhism, eschatology (like cosmogony) is never quite as absolute as it is in traditions such as Christianity, which have a more linear notion of time. The end of this world is followed by the creation of a new one that is very much like this one, and the disappearance of one buddha (and his dharma) is followed by the advent of another buddha, whose life and teachings differ little from those of his predecessors. Buddhist eschatology thus tends to be a dialectic between themes of continuity and termination, and it is perhaps not surprising that relics, which similarly hold in tension themes of the disappearance of a buddha and of his ongoing presence, should be featured in some of these scenarios. In what follows, I want to examine three traditions in which relics make eschatological transitions from "our" buddha, Śākyamuni, to the next buddha, Maitreya. The first concerns the Buddha's begging bowl, his pātra, which became an important relic of use in certain circles; the second features the robe of the Buddha, which he passed on to his disciple Mahākāśyapa, and which the latter then delivered to Maitreya; and the third is the story of the parinirvāṇa of the relics—the coming together and extinction of all the Buddha's remains, just prior to the advent of Maitreya. Each puts a slightly different emphasis on the balance of continuity and discontinuity.

The Buddha's Bowl: A Recycled Relic

We have already encountered a number of traditions about the Buddha's bowl, most notably those that associate it with the tooth relic in Sri Lanka. In addition, however, there developed a variety of other legends that seem to have had a separate existence of their own. When the

Chinese pilgrim Faxian passed through what is now Peshawar in Western Pakistan, at the very end of the fourth century C.E., he had the opportunity to venerate the Buddha's begging bowl, which was enshrined in a monastery there. The bowl itself, he reports, had a capacity of about four litres, and had four concentric rings around the top marking the rims of the original bowls of which it was made (*T.* 2085, 51:858c = Eng. trans., Li 2002: 171).[1] Unlike the bowls of ordinary monks, this bowl of the Buddha was made of stone, and actually consisted of four bowls that were found by the four guardian gods of the four quarters on Mount Vinataka (the sixth of the seven concentric mountain chains that surround Mount Sumeru—see Sadakata 1997: 26, 190–91). As we saw in chapter 3, they brought the bowls to the Buddha at the time of the food offering made to him by Trapuṣa and Bhallika; and the Blessed One, unwilling to slight any of the deities, accepted them all and pressed them together to make a single bowl.

Twice a day, in Peshawar, just before noon and in the evening, the bowl relic was brought out to receive the offerings of devotees, and, miraculously, when poor people put a few blossoms into it as an offering, it would fill up instantly, but when rich people gave thousands of flowers, it would never get full (*T.* 2085, 51:858b–c = Eng. trans., Li 2002: 171). Faxian also recounts the story of a Yuezhi king, a fervent Buddhist, who invaded the country and tried to carry off the bowl, but was unable to move it, even when eight elephants were yoked to it.[2] He concluded that the time for him to own the almsbowl had not yet come, and so he built a monastery and a stūpa in its honor on the spot (*T.* 2085, 51:858b = Eng. trans., Li 2002: 171).

By the time Xuanzang passed through the region in the seventh century, however, the time for the bowl to move had apparently come, for it was gone, and only the foundation of the pavilion in which it had been placed remained. Several explanations for this have been given. Some scholars have argued that there was a significant shift to the West of the trade routes to Central Asia, about a century before Xuanzang's time, and that this contributed to a general decline of parts of Gandhāra (Kuwayama 1982, 1990: 945–46; Sen 2003: 169). Others have pointed to the invasions of the Ephthalite Huns under Mihirakula, whose persecution of Buddhism in the sixth century saw the extensive destruction of

[1] Faxian's observations are largely corroborated by the testimony of other pilgrims. See *T.* 2059, 50:343b–c, 338b–339a, 337a–b = Eng. trans., Kuwayama 1990: 947.

[2] On the parallels between this story and an Uigur legend about the immovability of a piece of the stone crib of Christ, see Olschki 1950: 163. Similarly, a thousand elephants were not able to move a golden bowl given to the infant Śākyamuni (see *Sanghbhv.*, 1:57 = Eng. trans., Rockhill 1907: 18).

monasteries in Gandhāra and Kashmir.[3] Xuanzang himself, however, reports that the bowl "is now in Persia," and further hints that it had spent time in several different countries (*T.* 2087, 51:879c = Eng. trans., Li 1996: 70). In this he is reflecting, perhaps, a legendary tradition about the peregrinations of the Buddha's bowl, movements that were said to have taken place already or that were projected into the future and so connected to the eschatological theme of the coming of Maitreya.

The fullest version of this story is perhaps that which Faxian heard from an Indian monk, in Sri Lanka. There, he was told that the Buddha's almsbowl, which originally had been kept in Vaiśālī, was now in Gandhāra (where, in fact, Faxian had just seen it). After several hundred years, it would go to the land of the Western Yuezhi.[4] Then, in succession, after intervals each of a few hundred years, it would reside in Khotan, Kucha, Sri Lanka, and China. After that, it would return to India from where it would go up to the Tuṣita Heaven. There, Maitreya would welcome it, and honor it for seven days.[5] From the Tuṣita Heaven, it would then return to Jambudvīpa, where, after a while, it would be acquired by a nāga king who would carry it to his underwater palace in the sea. Sometime prior to Maitreya's birth, it would reemerge from the realm of the nāgas and return to its place of origin on Mount Vinataka, where it would redivide into its original four component bowls. In due time, these would be taken by the four guardian kings of the four quarters, who would offer them to Maitreya right after he attained buddhahood. And, like his predecessor Śākyamuni, he would accept them all and press them together to form a single bowl. Eventually, the same cycle would repeat itself with Maitreya's successor. In this way, Faxian concludes, all one thousand buddhas of this auspicious aeon (bhadrakalpa) would actually use the same bowl (*T.* 2085, 51:865c = Eng. trans., Li 2002: 208–9; see also Zürcher 1982: 3; Kuwayama 1990: 959–60).

Faxian claims that this story was based on Indian oral tradition, but, in fact, variants of it have been found in a number of Chinese Buddhist literary sources.[6] The bowl's initial move to Gandhāra, for instance, seems to echo a legend according to which it (along with the scholar Aśvaghoṣa)

[3] On Mihirakula, see Pandit 1968: 40n.; Naudou 1968: 9–10; Wang-Toutain 1994: 72; and Chavannes 1903: 417.

[4] It was this move, perhaps, that the king of the Yuezhi was unsuccessful at jump-starting in the story recounted earlier.

[5] This episode is depicted on a stone relief from Amarāvatī (see Monius 2001: 97).

[6] Anne Monius (2001: 98–100) has also drawn attention to parallels between Faxian's account of the bowl relic and the bowl called Amutacurapi (lit., "that which generates the nectar of immortality"), which is featured in the great Tamil Buddhist epic, *Maṇimēkalai*. Like the Buddha's bowl, Amutacurapi is connected with the future Buddha, and moves from place to place (within the more limited confines of South India), bringing prosperity, fertility, and morality wherever it goes.

was part of a ransom paid by a city in "middle India" to a great conquering king of the Yuezhi (see *T.* 2046, 50:183c = Eng. trans., Li 2002a: 12; Kuwayama 1990: 961; Wang-Toutain 1994: 64). More significant is the tradition that emphasizes the bowl's going to China. This has been studied by Erik Zürcher and Françoise Wang-Toutain, who have shown that the bowl is an important symbol of the propagation and prosperity of Buddhism. Indeed, more generally, wherever the bowl lands (it moves by flying through the air), disasters and epidemics will be avoided and the virtues of the Buddha will be manifest. The dharma will flourish and the people will be happy. As one text puts it, "In all the countries it passes through, sovereigns and subjects will be healthy and happy; crops and silk will be in abundance, and people will rejoice and have no worries" (*T.* 392, 12:114b = Fr. trans., Wang-Toutain 1994: 67; see also Strickmann 1996: 105).[7]

The flipside of this, of course, may be found in those traditions that correlate the absence of the bowl, or its disappearance from a region or from this earth, with the decline of the dharma and the advent of bad times. Most radically, when, prior to the advent of Maitreya, the bowl leaves this world for the land of the nāgas, the whole of Jambudvīpa will be shaken by earthquakes and plunged into darkness (*T.* 386, 12:1076a = Fr. trans., Wang-Toutain 1994: 69). Worse, the dharma will then gradually be extinguished, and human life will shorten until it reaches a span of only five years; "rice, butter, and oil will all vanish away, and men will become exceedingly wicked. The grass and trees which they lay hold of will change into swords and clubs, with which they will hurt, cut, and kill one another" (Legge [1886] 1965: 110; text in *T.* 2085, 51:865c; see also Li 2002: 209).

An alternative scenario predicts that a heretical king (Mihirakula in one source) will break the bowl into pieces. As a result, monks will gradually cease to follow the Vinaya rules, and, bit by bit, become laicized. They will turn to tilling and planting the soil, to hoarding money and robbing others, and they will cease reciting the dharma (*T.* 386, 12:1075–76 = Eng. trans., Kuwayama 1990: 965–66; see also Wang-Toutain 1994: 71–72; Shinohara 2003).

According to the Chinese Vinaya Master Daoxuan, this breaking of the bowl relic by a heretical king was, in fact, foretold by an event during the Buddha's own lifetime. Once, in Rājagṛha, Rāhula, acting as the Buddha's monastic attendant, was washing the Blessed One's bowl in a nāga pond when it accidentally broke into five pieces. The Buddha did not blame Rāhula. Instead he repaired the bowl with some molten lead, and

[7] In China, the bowl came also to be associated with the millenarian Maitreyan hero Candraprabha ("Prince Moonlight"), on whom see Zürcher 1982.

used the occasion to predict that, in the future, after his demise, bad monks and nuns would fail to respect the integrity of the dharma and would divide the Vinaya into five different versions and the Tripiṭaka into five parts. The breaking of the bowl thus foretells the breaking of the dharma and the discipline (*T.* 2122, 53:1008a–b = Fr. trans., Wang-Toutain 1994: 78–79; see also Shinohara 2003).

Still, according to Daoxuan, who, as a visionary, tends to elaborate his own versions of legends, this bowl that was broken and repaired was not the stone bowl brought by the four guardian kings but a clay bowl that had been presented to the Buddha at the time of the offering of milkrice. It was given to him then by a mountain deity who had received it from the previous buddha Kāśyapa, with instructions to pass it along at the appropriate moment. After it was repaired by the Buddha, Indra and the guardians of the four quarters fashioned thousands of stone replicas of it which were placed in thousands of stūpas all over the Buddhist world, so that straying Buddhists everywhere would be able to correct their behavior. In time, Daoxuan predicts, the original broken and repaired bowl will be made faultlessly whole again and passed on to Maitreya (*T.* 2122, 53:1008c = Fr. trans., Wang-Toutain 1994: 80; and *T.* 386, 12:1077b = Eng. trans., Shinohara 2003).

In all of these scenarios, it is clear that the bowl is not only a relic of use but also a relic of re-use. It participates in a cosmic biographical scheme that is greater than just the life of Śākyamuni. It is a token that is passed on from buddha to buddha. This makes it a somewhat different kind of relic, one that marks both the going of one tathāgata and the coming of another. At the same time, it signals the fluctuations of the dharma. In this capacity, it not only is periodically broken down into its component parts (its component bowls) and then reassembled, but it also moves about to different countries. It participates in and signals the spread of Buddhism. As Anne Monius (2001: 100) has put it, its peregrinations serve to "map out the central locations of the Buddhist world envisioned by [the] narrative." It effectuates a great circumambulation of the world—both the world of humans and of the gods and nāgas—bringing the dharma everywhere before returning to its point of origin. In this, once again, it is not unlike the dharma wheel of a great cakravartin king that appears at the beginning of his reign and leads him on a great tour of the world before disappearing at the time of his withdrawal from kingship, and then reappearing for the next cakravartin. As with the bowl, when the wheel does not appear, disorder, disaster, and decline ensue, but when it does, all is right with the world (*D.*, 3:58–79 = Eng. trans., Walshe 1987: 395–406).

The Buddha's Robe

Another object that is transmitted from buddha to buddha, although in a slightly different manner, is the relic of the robe. This tradition is complicated by the fact that the Buddha, during his career, is said to have worn at least two different kinds of robes: a set of "dust-heap robes" (*pāṃśukūla*) characteristic of the ascetically inclined "forest tradition" of monks, and a set of magnificent, costly robes made of expensive cloth, more typical, perhaps, of the "town-monk" tradition.[8] Each type of robe is the subject of several different, sometimes overlapping, and not always consistent legends.

We have already seen, in chapter 2, one tale of the origin of the robe the bodhisattva acquired right after his great departure; it was made of the discarded garments of ten pratyekabuddhas who passed into parinirvāṇa. Another tradition claims that, six years later, after the bodhisattva had practiced austerities for a while, that robe became worn out, and he was in need of something to cover his nudity. Accordingly, he looked around and found, in a cremation ground, the discarded cloth (pāmśukūla) that had enveloped the body of a servant girl who had died in the household of the nearby village chief. The bodhisattva took the cloth, washed it, and sewed it together under a tree at a spot that became known as Pāṃśukūlasīvana ("[The Place of] Sewing-the-Dustheap-Robe"). Thereafter, that was the robe that he wore (*Lal.*, 194–95 = Eng. trans., Bays 1983: 405–6).

Three other stories highlight a rather different kind of robe. One is the account of the sumptuous cloth given to the Buddha by the doctor Jīvaka. According to one version of this legend, Jīvaka had received, as payment for his medical services, a waterproof piece of cloth worth one hundred thousand coins. This he then offered to the Buddha, who had Ānanda cut it up and sew it into a cloak. There was so much cloth, however, that Ānanda was also able to make a triple robe (*tricīvara*) for the Buddha as well as an underrobe for himself and a cloak for Rāhula, and there was still enough left over to clothe other members of the community (*GilgMss.* 3, 2:48).

A second story features the garment that the Buddha's disciple Mahākāśyapa gave to the Buddha in exchange for his dustheap robe. According to this tale, which is found both in the Pali and the Sanskrit traditions, when Mahākāśyapa became a monk, inclined toward asceticism, he wished to make himself a paṃśukūla robe of discarded rags, but he could not find any. He therefore cut up his householder's clothes,

[8] On these two traditions in Buddhism, see Tambiah 1984: 53–77.

which were worth a hundred thousand pieces of gold, and sewed them back together again. The result was a monastic robe, but one made of expensive, high-quality cloth. One day, the Buddha happened to notice that Mahākāśyapa's robe was "soft," and mentioned this. Mahākāśyapa promptly offered his "soft" robe to the Blessed One, in exchange for the latter's "rough" robe of hemp, and he then wore this rag-robe of the Buddha for the rest of his life—until, as we shall next see, the coming of the future buddha Maitreya (*T.* 1509, 25:225a = Fr. trans., Lamotte 1949–80: 1399; and *S.* 2:219–22 = Eng. trans., Davids and Woodward 1917–30, 2:146–50).

In this eschatological context, a third story of a very expensive robe offered to the Buddha should be mentioned. According to the *Za bao zang jing* and a number of other Chinese anthologies of Buddhist tales, the Buddha's aunt and foster mother, Mahāprajāpatī, once made a robe for the Blessed One out of a fabric with golden threads, but he refused it, telling her to give it to the saṃgha. Mahāprajāpatī protested, pointing out that she had suckled and raised the Buddha, and made this garment especially for him, but he adamantly declined. So Mahāprajāpatī went to the saṃgha, but not one of the monks, starting with the abbot, would accept her robe, until it was finally taken by the bodhisattva Maitreya, who was then apparently a monk under Śākyamuni (*T.* 203, 4:470a = Eng. trans., Willemen 1994: 112–13; see also Chavannes 1934, 3:46–47 and 4:210). Here again, then, we have the theme that a robe used by or made for Śākyamuni is also destined for the next buddha.

Given all these stories, it is not altogether clear what became *the* Buddha's robe, nor even what he was wearing at the time of his death. Apart from what it says about his unburnt shrouds (see chapter 4), the *Mahāparinirvāṇa sūtra* is silent on the subject.[9] Xuanzang, however, reports that when the Buddha's mother came down from heaven to view her deceased son's body, still in its coffin between the two sal trees, she saw not only him but also, nearby, his "*saṃghāṭi* (double robe), alms bowl and pewter staff" (Li 1996: 189; text in *T.* 2087, 51:904b). Moreover, Xuanzang himself claims to have seen, in shrines in Northwest India, that same pewter staff, as well as "the Tathāgata's upper robe, made of fine cotton of a yellowish red color . . . in a precious casket" (Li 1996: 69; text in *T.* 2087, 51:879b). The Pali tradition also records the post-parinirvāṇa preservation of various robe relics. For example, the last chapter of the *Buddhavaṃsa,* which provides a kind of verse summary of the fate of all the relics of the Buddha after his cremation, specifies not only that his bowl and staff are in Vajirā, but that his "lower robe" (*nivāsana*) is in

[9] The *MPS.* does mention, however, two expensive pieces of golden fabric, given by the Malla Putkasa, in which Ānanda dresses the Buddha prior to his arrival at Kuśinagarī. See Przyluski 1920:152ff. and Bareau 1970–71, 1:282–99.

Kusaghara, his monastic belt or girdle in Pāṭaliputra, his bathing cloth in Campā, and his "yellow robe" (*kāsāya*) in Brahmā's heaven (*Buv.*, 102 = Eng. trans., Horner 1975:98–99; see also *Jin.*, 37–38 = Eng. trans., Jayawickrama 1968: 53–54).

It is not specified how these robe-relics were transmitted to these places or who preserved them, but, in fact, monks' robes (along with their bowls) were important pieces of property that took on additional significance by being passed on to others after their death. Thus, in the story of the cremation of the Buddha's disciple, Śāriputra, the novice, Cunda, not only gathers up Śāriputra's bodily relics (which he places in his water strainer), but he also takes his robe and his bowl.[10] These were obviously not only "relics of use" but relics "to be used," and the right to possess them was a bone of some contention among monks and laity alike (see Schopen 1994).

In fact, in East Asia, especially in the Chan / Zen tradition, the "transmission of the robe" (and to a lesser extent of the bowl)—whether literal or symbolic—became one of the primary means of asserting the passing on of one's teaching lineage, something that was traced all the way back to the Buddha (or at least to the founder of Chinese Chan, Bodhidharma).[11] Moreover, in China, as Anna Seidel has pointed out, the "Dharma robe" came to be thought of as a kind of Daoist talisman (*fu*) or dynastic treasure (*bao*), half of a single bipartide reality, the other half of which is the dharma. According to the magical principles of efficacy governing such objects, possession of the one half (the robe) necessarily entails and guarantees possession of the other (the dharma), and possession of the dharma makes one into a buddha—an awakened master.[12] As Bernard Faure (1995: 342) has put it: "[T]hose who wear the . . . Dharma robe, become *ipso facto* Buddhas."

Mahākāśyapa and the Buddha's Robe

The robe relic that most interests us here, however, is the robe that is preserved by Mahākāśyapa for transmission on to Maitreya. In Sanskrit sources, this is usually identified as the hempen rag-robe or dustheap

[10] For Pali sources, see Nyanaponika and Hecker 1997: 54 and Migot 1954: 474. On Sanskrit sources, see Schopen 1994: 44–60.

[11] See on this Faure 1995; Adamek 2000; Kieschnick 2003: 103–7. Unfortunately, I was unable to consult Anna Seidel's article, "Den'e" [the transmission of the robe] forthcoming in *Hōbōgirin*, fasc. 8.

[12] See Faure 1995: 341–42. On treasures and talismans in the Daoist context, see also Seidel 1983: 310ff and Kaltenmark 1960. The identification of the robe with the dharma did not, however, go uncontested in Chan circles; for instance, the sixth patriarch, Huineng, is sometimes said to have put an end to its transmission. See Kieschnick 2003: 106 and Yampolsky 1967: 176.

robe (paṃśukūla), which, as we have seen, the Buddha gave to Mahākāśyapa in exchange for the latter's softer garment.[13] Mahākāśyapa does not pass it on to his own dharma-heir (Ānanda), but instead resolves that his body and the robe the Buddha gave him shall not decay but remain on him, perfectly preserved, until the end of this buddha-age and the advent of the next.[14] Accordingly, when Mahākāśyapa either passes away in parinirvāṇa or goes into a long-term trance,[15] his body is not cremated but is immured inside Mount Kukkuṭapāda, which opens to receive it. The site, variously located in Northern India, became famous as a pilgrimage center and was visited by both Faxian (*T.* 2085, 51:863c–864a = Eng. trans., Li 2002: 199), and Xuanzang (*T.* 2087, 51:919c = Eng. trans., Li 1996: 264–65).

There are many versions of this story but one of the most developed is that found in a text called the *Mi le da cheng fo jing* (The Discourse on Maitreya's Great Attainment of Buddhahood). It tells how Maitreya will knock on the summit of Mahākāśyapa's mountain and then open it the way a cakravartin opens a city gate. The god Brahmā will then anoint Mahākāśyapa's head with oil, strike a gong, and blow the conch shell of the dharma. All this will be enough to awaken the saint from his samādhi trance; he will get up, prostrate himself in front of Maitreya, and offer him the robe of the Buddha, saying, "The great teacher Śākyamuni, . . . shortly before his parinirvāṇa, confided this monastic robe to me so that I could give it to you, O Venerable One" (*T.* 456, 14:433b = Ger. trans., Deeg, forthcoming; Leumann 1919: 276–78).[16] Elsewhere, Mahākāśyapa, coming out of his trance, expresses his good fortune at having been able to meet *two* buddhas in his lifetime. He then launches into a long sermon explaining how the "leftover disciples," initiated but not brought to final nirvāṇa by one buddha, are usually saved by the next. He then displays his magical powers and enters parinirvāṇa (Emmerick 1968: 332–33).[17]

[13] See *Aśokāv.*, 90 = Eng. trans., Strong 1983: 254; *T.* 2042, 50:114c = Eng. trans., Fr. trans., Przyluski 1923: 331; and*T.* 2043, 50:154a = Eng. trans., Li 1993: 114. See also *T.* 1545, 27:698b = Fr. trans., Lamotte 1949–80: 191–92. In other texts, however, the identity of the robe is not altogether clear. Xuanzang, for instance, claims it was the sumptuous robe referred to earlier that Mahāprajāpatī had offered the Buddha and that he had kept and given to Mahākāśyapa (*T.* 2087, 51:919c = Eng. trans., Li 1996: 264; see also Kieschnick 2003: 104).

[14] In the *Abhidharmakośa* (La Vallée Poussin [1923–31] 1980, 5:120), this is said to be the result of an adhiṣṭhāna.

[15] There is some disagreement among the texts as to whether or not Mahākāśyapa is actually dead at this point or has entered the trance of cessation. See Strong 1992: 63.

[16] The moment of transmission was captured in the cliff-face sculpture at the Japanese Maitreyan center at Mount Kasagi. See Brock 1988: 222.

[17] For other versions of this story, see Jaini 1988: 74–76, and Deeg forthcoming.

Like the Buddha's bowl, then, the robe relic becomes another bridge between buddhas, a marker of the transmission of the dharma, over time, rather than through space. Unlike the bowl, however, and unlike the robes monks receive from their masters, it does not become an object of re-use. As far as I know, there are no traditions that tell of Maitreya actually putting on Śākyamuni's robe. One of the reasons for this is the point made, in virtually every version of this story, that since beings in Maitreya's time will be much bigger than they were at the time of Śākyamuni, Mahākāśyapa will seem tiny by comparison. In fact, in one text, Maitreya's disciples are very contemptuous of Mahākāśyapa since his head seems to them to be no larger than that of an insect (*T.* 456, 14:433b = Ger. trans., Leumann 1919: 276; see also Lamotte 1949–80: 191n), and, in a Pali version of the legend, he is actually said to be cremated in the palm of Maitreya's hand (see Saddhatissa 1975: 44). It is clear that any robe worn by such a being would be an impossible fit for Maitreya; indeed, in one text, when Maitreya receives it, it is said barely to cover two fingers of his right hand and two fingers of his left, and his disciples marvel at how small Śākyamuni must have been (Jaini 1988: 75; see also Leumann 1919: 277).[18] In other words, while the legend of the bowl relic serves to emphasize recycling and continuity from one buddha to the next, the legend of the robe stresses change and discontinuity. All buddhas of the bhadrakalpa will use the same bowl, but they will not wear the same robe.

Finally, one other difference between the bowl relic and the Buddha's dustheap robe should be mentioned here. Symbolically, as we have seen, the bowl represents the health of the dharma. The same is true of the Buddha's "Dharma robe" which became an object of transmission in Chan / Zen lineages. The symbolism of the pāṃśukūla that Mahākāśyapa passes on to Maitreya is a bit different, however. The dustheap robe's association with shrouds and death is well known. As we have seen above, the Buddha is said to make his from the burial cloth of a young woman. There could hardly be a more graphic reminder of the truth of impermanence—that, enveloped in such a garment, one is symbolically, a living corpse. Buddhist monks, however, need not only come to a realization that death is suffering, but also that life, that is, birth—is suffering. In this regard, a variant of the story of the "origin" of the Buddha's robe, found in a late Pali text called the *Paṃsukūlānisaṃsaṃ* (The Account of the Advantages of the Dustheap Robe) may be of some interest. There we are told that the robe that the Buddha acquired at the end of his practice of austerities

[18] Maitreya is said, in a number of sources, to be eighty-eight cubits (c. forty-four meters) in height. See Saddhatissa 1975: 55 and Meddegama and Holt 1993: 49. It is curious and noteworthy in this regard that the same point is never made, to my knowledge, about the Buddha's bowl, which, presumably would have been too small for Maitreya as well.

was made from a piece of cloth that had enveloped the body of the unborn fetus of a young woman who had died in the advanced stages of pregnancy. Indeed, when the Buddha picks up the cloth, the decaying fetus and placenta fall to the ground (*Brapaṃsukūla.,* 67–68 = Fr. trans., Martini 1973: 71–72). Here the paṃsukūla seems to recall an amniotic sac or caul as well as a shroud. In fact, in the Southeast Asian traditions that the *Paṃsukūlānisaṃsaṃ* may reflect, this double correlation was worked out in detail, so that not only were the three kinds of monk's robes said to equal the three layers of the dead body's shroud, but they were also given detailed intra-uterine significance: the outer robe (*saṃghāṭī*) symbolized the amniotic sac; the upper robe (*uttarāsanga*), the placenta; the inner robe (*antarvāsa*), the meconium pocket; and the monastic belt, the umbilical cord (Bizot 1981: 69–70 and 1980: 246).[19] Bizot interprets this double symbolism in terms of an inititiatory rebirth-scenario in which the wearer of the pāṃśukūla is likened to both a corpse and a foetus. However, in a broader context, it is also possible to see Buddha's pāṃśukūla as a symbol of liminality, a transitional object that concretizes the rite of passage from the death of one buddha to the birth of the next.

The Decline of the Dharma and the Parinirvāṇa of the Relics

Both the bowl and the robe are technically relics of use. Another eschatological scenario features the bodily relics of the Buddha, and here the theme of *discontinuity* between buddhas is emphasized. Mention has already been made, several times, of the "final extinction" of the Buddha's relics. I would like, at this point, to present that tradition in greater detail, relating it first to the more general notion of the decline of the dharma.

There are many scenarios outlining the gradual disappearance of the Buddha's teaching. In East Asia, a threefold scheme—featuring the succession of ages of the "True Dharma," the "Counterfeit Dharma," and the "End of the Dharma"—came to prevail (see Nattier 1991: 65ff). A somewhat different threefold scenario was featured in South Asia in texts such as the *Questions of King Milinda.* There, three successive periods are posited during which various features of Buddhism decay and disappear. There is, first, a period of the disappearance of the possibility of attaining enlightenment (*adhigama*), which is said to be followed, secondly, by a period of the disappearance of the observance of the precepts (*paṭipatti*), and then, thirdly, by the disappearance of external symbols or signs (*linga*) of the religion (*Mil.,* 133–34 = Eng. trans., Davids [1890–94]

[19] Similarly, in East Asia, the Buddha's robe is likened to an amniotic sac (as well as a shroud). See Faure 1995: 362. For a good depiction of the three monastic robes, see Kieschnick 2003: 91.

1963, 1:190). Variants on this scheme may be found in several Pali commentaries. For instance, in the *Commentary on the Samyutta Nikāya,* we find that the disappearance of the attainment of enlightenment (adhigama) and the disappearance of precept-observance (paṭipatti) are followed by a third period that sees the disappearance of the knowledge of the scriptures (*pariyatti*) (*SA.,* 2:202).[20]

The fullest development of this scenario in the Theravāda world, however, seems to have been a fivefold scheme that combined elements from these two lists and added to them a period of the disappearance of the relics (dhātu). This perhaps is most systematically spelled out in Buddhaghosa's *Commentary on the Anguttara Nikāya.*

First, we are told, the death of the Buddha ushers in a thousand-year period of the disappearance of the attainments (adhigama). During this time, there is a gradual decline in the ability of people to reach the four fruits of the path. Initially, they lose the capacity to attain arhatship, and then, over time, the ability to reach the lesser stages of of nonreturning, of once-returning, and of entering the stream (*AA.,* 1:87).

Secondly, when the last stream-enterer passes away, there will be a second thousand-year period marked by the disappearance of the observances (paṭipatti). During it, even though they can no longer become enlightened, beings will, at first, still observe all the moral precepts, including the most minor ones. But then, gradually, they will violate more and more of the precepts until they maintain only the four *pārājikas* (against sexual relations, theft, taking life, and laying false claims to supernatural powers). This period will come to an end when the last monk who has not violated these precepts dies (*AA.,* 1:87–88).

Thirdly, it will be followed by a millenium that will see the disappearance of knowledge of the scriptures (pariyatti). Evil kings will rule and famine will result in people failing to support the community of monks. Without their support, learning will suffer, and, gradually, knowledge of the texts will disappear. The first text to be forgotten will be the last of the seven texts of the Abhidharma piṭaka, the *Paṭṭhāna.* This will be followed by Abhidharma texts 6, 5, 4, 3, 2, and 1, that is, the *Yamaka, Kathāvatthu, Puggalapaññatti, Dhātukathā, Vibhanga,* and *Dhammasangaṇi.* When the whole of the Abhidharma disappears, the sūtras will start to be forgotten, one nikāya at a time. The first to go will be the *Anguttara Nikāya,* starting with the "Book of the Elevens" and counting down all the way to the "Book of the Ones."[21] That will be followed by the

[20] For variants on this scheme, see *VibhA.,* 431 = Eng. trans., Ñāṇamoli 1996, 2:179; *DA* 3:898. In these two texts, the knowledge of the scriptures (the *tripiṭaka*) is said to disappear first. See also Griswold and Prasert 1973: 98–99.

[21] *A.* is divided into sections, according to the number of things categorized together in the sūtras in each section.

Samyutta Nikāya, the *Majjhima Nikāya,* and the *Dīgha Nikāya,* section by section, chapter by chapter, sūtra by sūtra, in reverse order. No mention is made here of the *Khuddaka Nikāya,* the "Collection of Little Texts," but there is reference to the jātakas that are part of the *Khuddaka Nikāya.*[22] The first jātaka to be forgotten will be the last one, the story of Prince Viśvantara (Pali: Vessantara), and the last to go will be the first one, the "Apaṇṇakajātaka." In this way, not only will the scriptures gradually be erased, but so too will knowledge of the life of the Buddha.[23] The disappearance of the sūtras, however, will still leave the Vinaya, but it too will gradually be forgotten, first, the *Parivāra* or "Appendix," then the *Khandhaka*, then the explanations of the rules for nuns, and of the rules for monks, until finally all that will be left is the Pāṭimokkha code. When it too is forgotten, the period of the disappearance of knowledge of the teaching will come to an end (*AA.*, 1:88–89).

Fourthly, over the next period of a thousand years, physical symbolic signs (linga) of Buddhism such as the yellow monastic robe and the monks' bowl will slowly disappear. Monks will begin to use gourds and calabashes on their begging rounds, and carry them on poles. Gradually, in their manner of begging and in their dress, they will come more and more to resemble Jains and other non-Buddhists. Eventually they will give up their robes altogether and wear only yellow rags around their wrist or neck. What this represents is not only an end of the characteristic mark of a monk but a return of the robes to their component parts, since monastic robes are supposed to be made up of rags sewn together. But even this last symbolic connection will be abandoned when, along with their wives (sic), "monks" will wonder "of what good is this yellow strip of cloth?" and throw it away (*AA.*, 90–91; see also Griswold and Prasert 1973: 100).

Finally, that will usher in the fifth and last period of decline that will see the disappearance of the relics (dhātu) of the Buddha. It should be pointed out, in this context that the Buddha is said actually to undergo three parinirvāṇas: the complete extinction of the defilements (*kleśa*), which occurs at the time of his enlightenment; the complete extinction of the aggregates (*skandha*), which occurs at the time of his death; and the complete extinction of his relics (dhātu), which eschatologically marks the final end of his *sāsana,* and occurs prior to the advent of the next

[22] On the special status of the *Khuddaka Nikāya* , see Lamotte 1988: 156–61.

[23] In *DA.* 3:899, and *VibhA.*, 432 = Eng. trans., Ñāṇamoli 1996, 2:180, no mention is made of the jātakas. Instead, the last sūtra texts to go are two-stanza passages such as the questions of Āḷavaka and the questions of Sabhiya, both from the *Sutta Nipāta* (which is also part of the *Khuddaka Nikāya*). See *Sn.,* 31–32 and 91–102 = Eng. trans., Norman 1996: 30–31 and 86–93. Significantly, these two sūtras are said to date from the time of the previous buddha Kassapa (Skt.: Kāśyapa).

buddha Maitreya (*AA*., 1:90).[24] This final event is spelled out in some detail by Buddhaghosa who, here, is worth quoting directly:

> Then, the relics, not receiving honor and veneration in various places, will, by the power of the resolve of the buddhas, go to those places where they will receive honor and veneration. Over time, however, the honor and veneration in such places will cease. [At the time of the withdrawal of the dispensation, the relics in this island of Sri Lanka will assemble and go to the Great Stūpa (in Anurādhapura). From the Great Stūpa, they will go to the Rājāyatana Shrine in Nāgadīpa, and thence to the great bodhi tree throne (in Bodhgaya). Also, the relics from the nāga, deva, and Brahmā worlds will likewise gather at the throne of the great bodhi tree. Not a single relic, even so small as a mustard seed, will be lost en route. All the relics at the great bodhi tree throne will come together in a heap like a single mass of gold, emitting six-colored rays of light. They will illuminate ten thousand world systems.][25] Taking on the form of the Buddha, they will display the glory of the Buddha's body seated crosslegged on the throne of awakening. They will fully manifest all of the thirty-two major and eighty minor marks of the great man as well as a fathom-wide aura around the Buddha, and they will perform a miracle as on the day of the twin-miracle (at Śrāvastī). Among the beings who will go to that place, there will be not a single human, but all the gods in ten thousand universes will assemble and lament: "Today the Dasabala (i.e., the Buddha) has parinirvanized; from now on there will be darkness."[26] Then, from the relic-body, a fire will leap up. [It will reach up as high as Brahmā's heaven, and burn as long as there are relics, even the size of mustard seeds. When the relics are consumed, the fire will go out],[27] and that body will become non-existent. Then the assembly of gods, as on the day of the parinirvāṇa of buddhas, will pay their respects with divine perfumes, garlands, and musical instruments, and circumambulate (the place) three times, and declaring "May we in the future see and receive a buddha being born," they will each return to their own place. This is what is called the disappearance of the relics (*AA*. 1:91).[28]

[24] See also *DA*., 3:899; *Anāg*., 36 = Eng. trans., Warren 1896: 484–85; Coedès 1956: 5ff.; Gombrich 1971: 291–93, who quotes a contemporary Sri Lankan monk and also the *VibhA*., 432–33 = Eng. trans., Ñāṇamoli 1996, 2:181.

[25] The text in brackets is added from *DA*, 3:899–900. See also *AA*., 91n.9, and *VibhA*., 433 = Eng. trans., Ñāṇamoli 1996, 2:181.

[26] In *VibhA*., 433 = Eng. trans., Ñāṇamoli 1996, 2:181; and *DA*. 3:900, the gods lament, "Today, the Master has parinirvanized, today the dispensation is withdrawn, this now is the last time we will see him," and, we are told, "they will feel more emotion than they did even on the day of the Buddha's parinirvāṇa. Except for non-returners and arhats, they will not be able to stand firm by their own power."

[27] Added from *DA*. 3:900. See also *VibhA*., 433 = Eng. trans., Ñāṇamoli 1996, 2:181.

[28] See also *DA*., 3:899–900; *Anāg*., 36 = Eng. trans., Warren 1896: 484–85; Reynolds and Reynolds 1982: 330.

A number of comments can be made about this event, which marks the ultimate end of Śākyamuni's biography. First, it is clear that the disappearance of the Buddha's relics, here, is put in the context of the systematic dismantling of the other two refuges of Buddhism. To begin with, the community is gradually whittled away: with the disappearance of the attainments, the ārya saṃgha, consisting of arhats, nonreturners, oncereturners and stream-winners, vanishes. Then ordinary monks cease to observe the precepts and the customs of the community, until, gradually, they can no longer be distinguished from other groups. In other words, there is a remerging of Buddhists into commonality, a loss of distinctiveness and separate identity. At the same, the dharma that marked this distinctiveness, vanishes, piṭaka by piṭaka, as the scriptures are lost, text by text, in reverse canonical order. What had been built up is now built down. Finally, the Buddha himself goes in the same way, as knowledge of the Buddha's life, and of his jātakas is lost, and then the relics.

The assembly of all the relics in Bodhgaya reverses the dispersions effectuated by the Buddha himself and by disciples such as Trapuṣa and Bhallika (chapter 3), by Droṇa at the time of the parinirvāṇa (chapter 4), by Aśoka a century later (chapter 5), and by the predictions (adhiṣṭhāna) of the Buddha (chapter 6). It even puts an end to the unpredicted movements of relics such as the Buddha's teeth (chapter 7). We saw (in chapter 1) that relics of some previous buddhas are "dispersed" and spread far and wide out of compassion, out of a sense that particular buddhas believe that their mission on earth is not yet complete and needs to be carried on by their relics. Previous buddhas who have finished dispensing the dharma in their lifetime do not have their relics spread far and wide; instead, their remains stay "in one single compact mass, like an image made of gold" (*BuvA.*, 141 = Eng. trans., Horner 1978: 202). Thus the gathering of Śākyamuni's relics here, into a heap "like a single mass of gold," signals the end of his mission. At the same time, the Pali texts that recount the parinirvāṇa of the relics make it clear that their disappearance is a necessity precisely so that the advent of another buddha—Maitreya—can take place (*VibhA.*, 431 = Eng. trans., Ñāṇamoli 1996, 2:179–81).[29] With the relics gone, there will be no overlap between buddhas and their dispensation.

And yet, certain traditions, not so committed, perhaps, to the nonsimultaneity of buddhas, shied away from the total destruction of the

[29] In this regard, it is noteworthy that, in Cambodia, the gathering of relics is also something that is recalled in a non-eschatological context, at the time of the consecration of new buddha images, when all the relics of Lankā and of the whole of Jambudvīpa—as well as those in heaven and the nāga world, as well as the four canine teeth, the right and left collar bone, and all the hairs—are invoked to come and enter the statue. See Bizot 1994: 113 and Swearer, forthcoming: ch. 8.

relics. Thus, in the *Nandimitrāvadāna,* translated by Xuanzang, we find a somewhat different eschatological vision. In this non-Theravādin text, it is asserted that, when the time comes for the parinirvāṇa of the relics, they will all be brought together from the different directions by the sixteen great arhats (*luohan*) and enshrined in a magnificent stūpa. Then that stūpa, after being duly worshiped, will slowly disappear by *sinking down into the earth* until it comes to rest at the cosmic level of the golden wheel underlying our universe (*T.* 2030, 49:14 = Eng. trans., Li 1961: 12; see also DeVisser 1922–23: 63–64; Lévi and Chavannes 1916: 13).[30] Here, then, the relics are not destroyed by fire but put into a final reliquary, which itself disappears. This seems to be a less absolute "extinction" than in the Theravādin scenario. The relics are no longer to be found on the face of the earth, and so the way is cleared for Maitreya to come, but the possibility is also left for a future buddha to pull those relics back up from the depths, just as Śākyamuni did with the remains of the previous Buddha Kāśyapa at Toyikā (see chapter 1).

It will be remembered that the Chinese pilgrim Daorong, with whom we began the preface to this book, saw a sinking stūpa in Afghanistan in the fifth century and was told that when it completely disappeared under the surface of the earth, that would mark the end of the Buddha's teaching (*T.* 2092, 51:1022 = Eng. trans., Wang 1984: 245). Now we can see that the gods who witness that actual end, who are there at the parinirvāṇa of the relics, mourn this final passing of Śākyamuni, but, at the same time, they look forward to being present at the birth of the next buddha, Maitreya. It is clear, then, that, though the disappearance of the relics marks the end of Śākyamuni's biography and of his dispensation, it does not spell the end of Buddhism.

Conclusion

We have seen in this chapter that, when they are considered in an eschatological context, relics that are extensions of the Buddha's biography make one think about the transitions between one buddha and the next. The Buddha's bowl, his robe, and the scenario of the parinirvāṇa of his bodily relics all express this process of passage, but they do so to various extents and in a variety of ways.

Faxian declares that all one thousand buddhas of the bhadrakalpa will use the same bowl, brought to them each time at the start of their preach-

[30] The level of the golden circle supports the cakravāla world system. It itself rests on a circle of water, which rests on a circle of wind, which in turn rests on empty space. See Sadakata 1997: 25.

ing career by the guardian kings of the four quarters. And yet, each time it passes on, the bowl undergoes a crucial transformation: it separates into its component parts and then is made whole again. It is, in other words, both a new bowl and an old bowl. In this way, the dialectic of continuity and discontinuity, of permanence and impermanence, is maintained (even though, in the end, as always in Buddhism, impermanence wins out, since this pattern is discontinued with the end of the bhadrakalpa).

Buddhist monastic rag-robes (like begging bowls) are made up of component parts—strips of cloth (the number varies depending on the type of robe) that are sewn together to make the whole garment. Just as the "rims" of the four bowls that the Buddha squeezes together are still visible on his (and any monk's) begging bowl, so too are the "seams" between the different pieces of cloth in the robe (see Faure 1995: 338, 369; Kieschnick 2003: 92). If the Buddha's pāṃśukūla were totally like the buddhas' bowl, one would expect an eschatological scenario in which it disintegrated or was cut up into its separate pieces sometime after Śākyamuni's parinirvāṇa, only to be resewn together and redyed by Maitreya. That, however, is not the case. Instead, the robe makes possible the linkage between, at most, two buddhas (Śākyamuni and Maitreya), but it itself does not make that transition. Each buddha will have his own robe.[31]

In a previous chapter, the point was made that "relics of use" have a double potency in that they both symbolize the Buddha and can be used by devotees in the same way that the Buddha used them. This was true of the bodhi tree, which could be viewed as the Buddha and also be "viewed as the Buddha viewed it" (see chapter 6). It is true also of the "Dharma robe" that was passed on and worn by successive masters in Chan / Zen lineages. And it is also true of the pāṃśukūla robe—but only for Mahākāśyapa, who wears it. It is not true for Maitreya, for whom the paṃśukūla loses half of its double potency when he receives it, since he does not and cannot wear it. Unlike the bowl that becomes a relic of use for all buddhas, the robe remains always a relic of one buddha—Śākyamuni. As such, it can be honored but never appropriated by Maitreya.

[31] This view was not accepted universally. On the one hand, the tradition is divided as to whether the Buddha's robe also linked him to the previous buddha Kāśyapa. In most sources it does not. For instance, in the *Paṃsukūlānisaṃsa* (*Brapaṃsukūla,* 67 = Fr. trans., Martini 1973: 71), when Śākyamuni acquires his paṃsukūla, he declares not that he is inheriting the robe of previous buddhas but that he is imitating them in acquiring one: "This is the first paṃsukūla. . . . The Buddhas of the past wore paṃsukūla; I therefore, will wear one too." But, in Daoxuan's reworking of the robe legend, he is said to get the robe from a tree spirit whom Kāśyapa had requested to pass it on to him (see Kieschnick 2003: 104). On the other hand, Daoxuan, who seems to model his account of the robe on the legend of the bowl, also says that the Buddha stated that "his saṃghāti robe was worn by all the Buddhas, past and future, in order to achieve liberation" (see Shinohara 2000: 313).

This hints at another scenario of transition with a slightly different take on the question of continuity and discontinuity. More generally, it can be said that a different buddhology may be at work here: soteriologically speaking, the bowl is a relic that will take a devotee to the time and place of every buddha—any buddha. The robe is a relic that will take a devotee to the time and place of Maitreya, but there and then, Maitreya will take over.

Finally, buddhology is also clearly at work in the case of the parinirvāṇa of the relics. The Pali scenario, as we have seen, is characteristic chiefly of the Theravāda tradition, which resists allowing the overlap of buddhas, and hence the relics are completely destroyed before the advent of Maitreya. The *Nandimitrāvadāna* is less absolute, however, in its declaration of noncontinuity. In the one case the dialectic of continuity and discontinuity has been resolved; in the other, it is left potentially open.

CONCLUSIONS

I have assumed, throughout this book, that there is no relic without a story and there is no story without a context. I have tried to tell some of the stories and explore some of the contexts of some of the relics of the Buddha, and it now remains to sum things up. To a certain extent, this has already been done in the individual "conclusions" at the end of each chapter. But those "conclusions" were made within contexts of their own. What I would like to do now, with the benefit of hindsight, is to revisit those chapters, in order, and to review their findings. But I want to do this not simply by recapitulating them but by discussing a set of ten topics that I think emerge from them and that are important in any consideration of the various dimensions of Buddha relics. The ten topics are relics and the biographical process, relics and buddhology, relics and the spread of Buddhism, the episodic nature of relics, relics and the demands of *darśan,* relics and the post-liminal state, relics and polity, strategies of legitimation, relics as performative objects, and the dialectic of continuity and discontinuity.

Relics and the Biographical Process

In my introduction, I set out some of the limitations of this study, namely its focus on relics of the Buddha (especially bodily relics), and then enunciated the theory that relics of the Buddha can best be understood as *expressions and extensions of his biography.* There is a sense in which the whole rest of the book may be seen as an unpacking and illustration of this thesis. Several things are implicit in it, however. The first is a rejection of views of the presence and absence of the Buddha in his relics that are grounded in theistic notions of immanence or transcendence. Relics of the Buddha, as we have seen, are more spreaders and continuators of the Buddha's presence than incarnations of him. Connected to this is a second implicit understanding that the Buddha's life story does not stop with his death, just as it does not begin with his birth. Buddhologists have come to accept accounts of the previous lives (jātakas) of the Buddha as part of his overall biography; it is also important to consider his "posterior lives" (his relics) as part of the same continuum. Finally, also implicit in this is an understanding of the Buddha's life story as a process that reflects a Buddhist view of the nature of reality. As we have seen, buddhas come and buddhas go, something that may be hinted at in the very word that buddhas use to refer to themselves: tathāgata. As is well known, in Sanskrit and Pali, depending on how one reads the saṃdhi, this can mean either "Thus-Come-One" (tathā-āgata) or "Thus-Gone-One" (tathā-gata). Given the ambiguity, I have always been tempted to translate the term as "Thus-Come-and-Gone-One." In any case, the implication is that the Buddha comes and goes in the same way that previous buddhas have and that future buddhas will. At the doctrinal level, of course, the same process of coming and going is happening ontologically, and is expressed in the view that is said to epitomize the teaching of all tathāgatas, namely that they explain the *origin* and *cessation* of all elements of existence (dharmas). Relics, too, as we have seen, share in the expression of this process.

In biographical terms, moreover, within the life story of a single buddha, it may be possible to detect a series of "comings and goings." For instance, the Buddha's descent from Tuṣita Heaven into his mother's womb and his birth in Lumbinī are a coming into this world, while his great departure from Kapilavastu is a going away from it. His awakening at Bodhgaya and decision to preach is another coming into this world, while his parinirvāṇa is a going away. Finally, the collection of his relics represents a third coming into this world, while the parinirvāṇa of those relics is a last departure. The various phases of the Buddha's overall life story—his previous life phase, living buddha phase, and relic phase—thus are strung out linearly, but they also repeat themselves cyclically. In other words, the relics, as extensions of the Buddha's biography, recount the tale of his last coming and going, but, as we have seen in this book, the thrust of their narrative is the same as that of the Buddha's earlier life periods, and the same as his overall biography. The Buddha's relics not only extend the Buddha's biography, they also repeat his life and death.

Relics and Buddhology

It is clear in all this that one's understanding of the relics will depend on one's understanding of the nature of the Buddha. Obviously, there is no one Buddhist view of relics, even though relics are a pan-Buddhist phenomenon. We saw one example of this variety in the introduction, in my brief discussion of dharma relics, which reflect the views of those for whom the presence of the Buddha is to be found more in his teachings than in his physical body, more in "books" than in "bones." I chose not to consider dharma relics in this study, but obviously they reflect a different understanding of the Buddha.

In chapter 1, dealing with the relics of previous buddhas, another buddhological context came to the fore. This was the doctrine—stated or unstated—of the non-overlap of buddhas through time, which posits that one tathāgata must be completely gone before the next one can come. According to this view, the relics of the previous buddha Kāśyapa or those of Prabhūtaratna, as extensions of their life stories, should not coexist with the life of the Buddha Śākyamuni. In examining various versions of the story of Kāśyapa's relics at Toyikā, however, we saw a spectrum of ways that various texts, depending on their buddhology, handled this problem. Some (such as the Theravāda sources) recognized the doctrine and eliminated or never developed the overlap. For them, there were no bodily relics in Kāśyapa's shrine. Others (such as the *Lotus Sūtra*) ignored (or deliberately undermined) the doctrine and affirmed the overlap, while still others adopted a middle position that allowed Kāśyapa's relics to be present but portrayed them as remaining inert. In a somewhat similar vein, there was an analogous spectrum of positions on the question of the soteriological effectiveness of relics (i.e., stūpas) of previous buddhas in bringing devotees to enlightenment. In both cases, we can see how doctrinal stances about the nature of the Buddha can affect a traditions's understanding of relics. But, of course, this is a symbiotic relationship and the reverse is equally true: relics can influence a tradition's understanding of the nature of the Buddha.

Relics and the Spread of Buddhism

Another contextual issue that emerged in chapter 1 (but also in many later chapters) was the use of relics—in this case relics of previous buddhas—to incorporate non-Buddhist—in this case brahmanical—traditions into Buddhism. Simply put, relics were seen as an effective means for spreading Buddhism into areas where it had previously not existed, for extending the presence of the Buddha there. That this was one of the intended purposes of relics is further reflected in the tradition, also studied in chapter 1, that whether or not previous buddhas have their relics "dispersed" throughout the world after their parinirvāṇas depends on whether or not they have finished their careers of conversion and compassion.

Kāśyapa's stūpa at Toyikā, as we have seen, was previously a local shrine, venerated by local brahmins, until it was "redefined" as belonging to the previous buddha. Such redefinitions are not unusual in the history of religions. The Buddha's actions at Toyikā are somewhat akin to those of Saint Paul in Athens when he proclaimed that the "altar to the unknown god" was actually one to the Christian god (see Acts 17:22ff). But there is a difference in the case of Toyikā. As we have seen, the identification of the local shrine as being that of a *previous* buddha (and not one of Śākyamuni's) incorporates it into the Buddhist fold while still managing to keep it in the background. The understanding that relics of previous buddhas are not to be worshiped independently but always in conjunction with the cult of Śākyamuni (Toyikā is advertised as a place where *two* buddhas can be honored simultaneously) helps reinforce this status.

The identification with previous buddhas also serves to give antiquity to the redefinition of sites. As Buddhism moved into new areas, the claim could be made that, in fact, it had already once been there. The same was true in Burma and in Sri Lanka, where sites such as the Shwe Dagon were given a pedigree of antiquity and déjà-vu sanctity by the relics of all three previous buddhas of this aeon. Much has been said about the "movability" or "transportability" of relics in both Buddhism and Christianity, something that makes them ideal tools for the spread of the tradition. But, in Buddhism at least, we need also to think about the "discoverability" of relics, their role in inspiring what Hubert Durt (1987: 17) has called a Buddhist *archaeologia sacra*. The bones of the previous buddha Kāśyapa were not brought to Toyikā; they were found there. The same is true of the many sites in Southeast and East Asia associated not only with relics of previous buddhas but, less anciently, with the "rediscovered" relics of Śākyamuni said to have been brought there at the time of King Aśoka, or even by the Buddha himself.

Whether discovered or transported, however, relics were usually among the first objects featured by Buddhist missionaries in new lands. They were often presented as impressive and effective sources of magical power, but part of their lure, as John Kieschnick (2003: 52) has pointed out, was that they were "a distinguishing characteristic of Buddhist devotion that no other religious tradition could match." In other words, relics came to be seen not just as spreaders of the presence of the Buddha, but also as exotic emblems of the uniqueness of this new religion of Buddhism—some thing that brahmanism, Confucianism, or Shintō did not have.

The Episodic Nature of Buddha-relics

In chapter 2, I examined the somewhat anomalous tradition of relics of the bodhisattva, and saw how stories about relics of the Buddha in his past lives, and in his youth prior to his enlightenment, underscored an understanding of the bodhisattva as being defined, prospectively, by his future buddhahood. Here, the relics were seen to "pre-present" rather than "re-present" the Buddha, thus challenging the assumption that relics are always "remnants" (Latin: reliquiae) of someone who has already attained sainthood (awakening). Indeed, as "essences" (Sanskrit: dhātu) or "bodies" (śarīra), relics do not necessarily have a temporally posterior relationship to buddhahood, something that was graphically illustrated by the infant Gautama's embryonic relic / reliquary palace, as well as by the case of the bodhisattva's bones in the jātaka of the tigress (where again, different buddhological contexts resulted in a spectrum of different renditions of the story).

One of the features of relics of the Buddha that emerged in this chapter, however, is that they tend to be episodic in nature. This was true, as well, of virtually all of the rest of the relics looked at in the rest of this book. At first hand, at least, relics tend not to embody "the Buddha" in the abstract but to recall and give expression to particular events in his lifetime. This, in part, accounts for the many differences among them. Clearly, a relic that recalls the moment of the Buddha's embarkation on the path (Sumedha's hair) is rather different from one that recalls his intra-uterine life (the amniotic palace), or one that recalls the gift of milkrice (the bowl), or one that recalls his great departure (the relics in Ajātaśatru's underground chamber), or one that marks his concern for the ongoing faith of two laymen right after his enlightenment (the hairs given to Trapuṣa and Bhallika), or one that recalls his visit to Sri Lanka (the footprint on Adam's Peak), or those that recall his parinirvāṇa and cremation (the relics distributed by Droṇa). It is, of course, possible to argue that these are all different types of objects: that a hair is not a bowl and is not an amniotic palace, or a footprint, or a collection of remains from the cremation fire. But no mention of these physical differences is highlighted in the texts. Rather, what primarily differentiates them are the stories told about them, stories that connect them to different episodes in the Buddha's life.

Be this as it may, these stories are always embedded in a greater story. The bodhisattva relics discussed in chapter 2, for instance, all looked forward to the bodhisattva's awakening at Bodhgaya. They thus were seen to refer not so much to the same event as to the greater process of the achievement of buddhahood. More generally, the biographical episodes that are recalled by relics can be said to be part of the greater narrative comprising the whole life of the Buddha, which, as Steven Collins (1992: 241) has pointed out, is "implicitly present [whenever] an enshrined relic is venerated." Relics may thus be biographically episodic, but, at another level, they recall in the minds of devotees the *whole* of that biography; they are expressions of the overall narrative of the Buddha's life and death. This, as we have seen, is sometimes reinforced by their setting in reliquaries or stūpas that are, in effect, "buddha bioramas."

Relics and the Demands of Darśan

In chapter 3, I dealt with hair relics and footprints, and there a new contextual issue arose: what to do when the Buddha cannot be seen, when it is not possible to be in his presence and have a devotional relationship with him that, in India, is called *darśan* (literally, "seeing")? Obviously, the answer given in the stories examined in this chapter was that darśan could be had with and through the Buddha's relics.

It is important that, biographically speaking, this question and solution were first posited not with regard to the absence of the Buddha after his parinirvāṇa, but with regard to his absence during his lifetime. In this context, three types of situations seem to be important in stimulating the creation of relics. First, there are rather straightforward cases in which the Buddha has gone off somewhere, or is "in retreat," or is otherwise in a place where devotees or visitors cannot get to him. Such, for example, was the situation of the wives of King Bimbisāra, who requested that some hair relics be enshrined in their harem, as a convenient solution to the problem of their isolation. Secondly, there are cases such as that of Trapuṣa and Bhallika, who were permanently going to a place, a foreign country (their homeland) where there was no buddha, and who requested a relic so as to be able to continue to see him, as well as to be able to introduce him to their fellow countrymen and women. Finally, it is important to realize that humans were not the only parties interested in the worship of relics. Autochthonous deities (such Mahāsumana on Adam's Peak), gods (such as Indra), and nāgas (such as Jayasena) all desired darśan as well, but lived in places that the Buddha rarely visited. As we have seen, however, relics could be enshrined in their heavens, or in their underwater palaces, or in certain places like riverbeds, where they could be worshiped by both people and nāgas depending on the height of the water, or on mountain tops, where they were accessible to gods descending and humans ascending. One of the purposes of relics in this context seems to have been to enlarge the number and nature of devotees.

In all these cases, we have examples of relics making darśan possible to beings when the Buddha was absent during his lifetime. The situation was not radically different after the Buddha's death. Paul Mus (1935, 1:74, 190) has spoken of the Buddha's parinirvāṇa as "a new kind of absence," but, in fact, relic-wise, it meant only a switch from a "lateral extension" of the possibilities of darśan to a "longitudinal one." Thus, after the parinirvāṇa, it remains still possible to "see" the Buddha, as Aśoka's son Mahinda made clear in Sri Lanka when he arranged for relics to be brought from India because, "when one sees the relics, one sees the Buddha" (*Mhv.*, 133 = Eng. trans., Geiger 1912: 116). In this regard, it might also be pointed out that, in the tradition of "burial ad sanctos" looked at in chapter 6, we have simply another longitudinal extension of the possibility of darśan, not just after the death not of the Buddha, but after the death of the devotee as well.

Relics and the Post-liminal State

In chapter 4, I examined the event of the Buddha's parinirvāṇa, and theorized that various aspects of his obsequies, the prescribed "duties to the corpse" (śarīrapūjā) marking his final departure, were at the same time involved in the production and preservation of his ongoing relics. In this respect, the Buddha's funeral is not so much an account of his death as one of his transformation, the division of his remains marking the start of a new phase of his career. The parinirvāṇa is thus a pivotal biographical moment, between two phases of the Buddha's life story—his living human phase and his relic phase. It is a rite of passage that ensures the transition from the one to the other.

In his classic study of rites of passage, Arnold Van Gennep (1960: 146) showed that funerals too should be considered as rites of passage, in which all three ritual phases—separation, transition (liminality), and incorporation into the new state—are present. This makes sense in terms of the dead who are heading for some sort of afterlife (heaven, or hell, or rebirth). But the question arises of what happens in the funeral of someone who has put an end to passage, who, like the Buddha and other saints, has escaped from saṃsāra. My conclusion, of course, is that this problem is somewhat artificial; in the Blessed One's parinirvāṇa and cremation, the new steady state that is passed into is that of the relics.

For this reason, perhaps, the Buddha's funeral, which buddhologists have tended to treat as though it were solely a rite of separation, is actually both a rite of separation and of incorporation. The bodily relics that are collected after his cremation similarly can be looked at in two ways. They are markers of his passage, witnesses to the truth of his impermanence, but, at the same time, they are liberated by the death of the Buddha to become the subject of new narratives that will recall not only the Buddha's life gone by but extend it in significant ways.

Relics and Polity

In chapter 5, I focused on the key role played by King Aśoka in the post-parinirvāṇa period of the Buddha's biography. Three events involving relics were examined: first, the collection of the relics from the eight droṇa stūpas either by Aśoka or by Ajātaśatru and Mahākāśyapa, who had them enshrined in a single secret underground chamber; secondly, the redistribution of those relics by Aśoka into 84,000 reliquaries, culminating in a vision of the world marked by those reliquaries; and, thirdly, Aśoka's final celebration of a great festival of relics.

Biographically, I drew parallels between Aśoka's actions and three episodes of the Buddha's life. The collection of the relics from Mahākāśyapa's underground chamber was related to the event of the Buddha's great departure; Aśoka's visionary experience of the world was compared to the Buddha's enlightenment experience at Bodhgaya and his performance of the Twin Miracle at Śrāvastī; and Aśoka's autocremation in honor of the relics was connected to the Buddha's own parinirvāṇa and cremation productive of the relics. This suggests a new dimension for the biographical paradigm, one in which a relic saga gives expression to a succession of episodes in the life story of the Buddha.

But the thrust of this chapter was to relate these relic traditions to various understandings of Buddhist polity. And here it is possible to distinguish three notions of how to govern the state. As we saw, in his final dedication of the 84,000 stūpas, Aśoka *centripetalizes* the relics and the state, thereby resolving a tension between *centrifugal* forces (as seen in the "war of the relics" between the eight kings resulting in the disorganized set of the droṇa stūpas), and *centralizing* forces (as seen in Mahākāśyapa and Ajātaśatru's underground chamber). The Buddha's body goes from being fragmented, to being whole but hidden away, to being seen and correlated to the cosmos, thanks to Aśoka.

Aśoka's "galactic polity," as Stanley Tambiah (1976: 102) called it, became, of course, a model for rulers throughout the Buddhist world. But we should not lose sight of the other paradigms implicit in this tale, since they may help us understand certain aspects of certain rulers. Duṭṭhagāmaṇī's construction of the Mahāthūpa, for example, appears to have at least as much in common with Mahākāśyapa and Ajātaśatru's building of the underground chamber as it does with the Aśokan paradigm. At least the hoarding of relics and control of all materials are telltale parallels. This is important because it means that the later use of relics by Buddhist sovereigns in East Asia and elsewhere is not necessarily based solely on the "galactic polity," even when the example of Aśoka is evoked.

Strategies of Legitimation

In chapter 6, I examined the spread of "predestined relics" to countries beyond India (in this case, Sri Lanka) in moves that were still determined by resolutions (adhiṣṭhānas) that had been made by the Buddha during his lifetime. One of the contextual issues that emanates from this consideration is the question of the charismatic legitimation of these relics. Obviously, the Buddha's adhiṣṭhānas provide one important source of legitimacy to these traditions, but the stories themselves reveal several others.

Stanley Tambiah (1984: 335) has spoken of the "objectification of charisma" in such things as "talismans, amulets, charms, regalia [and] palladia," and he goes on to describe some of the ways in which this is achieved. Similarly, Kevin Trainor (1997: 145) has spoken of "strategies of authoritative presence" evident in various relic traditions. In what follows, I would like to do much the same thing in terms of the relics examined in chapter 6. In addition to the affirmation of their predestined status, there seem to have been three ways in which the objectification of charisma in these relics could take place.

First, there was the affirmation of the importance of lineage, evident in the case of the bodhi tree, which, by virtue of its organic nature and reproductive capacity, made possible the passing on of the relic from generation to generation and its spread all over the island. Thus, virtually every important bodhi tree in Sri Lanka was an ultimate offshoot or an offspring of the tree in Anurādhapura (and so of the tree in Bodhgaya). This I see as a metaphor for the common transmission of relics and other things from master to disciple according to their lineages (*paraṃparā*). This method of legitimation characterizes most ordinary, generic buddha relics held in Sri Lankan temples (see Gombrich (1971: 106). We saw a similar example, in chapter 8, in the case of the robe and bowl that were passed on within Chan circles. Another textual South Asian example may be seen in the case of the Buddha's forehead relic, which was mentioned briefly in chapter 3, and that is the subject of a chronicle, the *Dhātuvaṃsa*. It was originally part of the share of relics in the possession of the Mallas, but was appropriated by Mahākāśyapa soon after the Buddha's parinirvāṇa. The chronicle then traces its transmission through a succession of teachers both Indian and Sri Lankan. As Kevin Trainor (1997: 148, slightly modified) describes it: "The text records the names of seven elders who carry the relic across north India, temporarily enshrining it in the actual structures in which the Buddha resided—in Vaiśālī, Śrāvastī, Sārnāth, the Veṇuvana, and Kauśāmbī. Each of these elders hands the relic over to his successor, announcing the prediction of the relic's ultimate destiny. . . . The final Indian elder, Mahādeva, brings the relic to the Rohaṇa region [in Sri Lanka] where it is venerated by a lay-disciple named Mahākāḷa [and eventually passed on to King Kākavaṇṇatissa, who has it enshrined in Sēruvila]."

A second sign of charisma was the performance of miracles. This, we have seen, was a feature exhibited by all the predestined relics examined in chapter 6, and, in fact, the manifestation of such miracles was often a specification of the Buddha's adhiṣṭhāna about them. Such miracles not only assert a relic's extraordinary power and sacrality, but also can connect it directly to the Buddha's biography in the case of miracles that recall those paradigmatically performed by the Buddha, such as the Twin Miracle at Śrāvastī.

Finally, there was, in the case of the relics sealed into the Mahāthūpa by Duṭṭhagāmaṇī, what might be called an esoteric strategy of charisma building, one in which the glories of the relics are kept hidden, known directly only to a few, and only secondarily to others. In these traditions, the reliquary (i.e., the stūpa) takes over the charismatic focus. Thus, devotees are more inspired by the sight of the dome of the Mahāthūpa than by relics inside, or by the magnificent spire of the Shwe Dagon than by the knowledge that it encases some hair relics.

Relics as Performative Objects

In chapter 7, I dealt with the "further further" spread of relics by focusing on the unpredicted movements of tooth relics. Although there are many themes that emerged in the course of this consideration, one of the most prominent is perhaps what could be called the tradition of relics as "performative objects." Like performative utterances, performative objects "do" things by virtue of their very nature, in the right ritual / cultural / emotional / religious environment. In the case of the Kalingan / Sri Lankan tooth, we saw how it variously legitimated kingship, following the ruler wherever he went; it guaranteed law and order; it inspired troops; it justified war; it promoted peace; it furthered fertility by making it rain; it unified the nation; it satisfied the desires and needs of individuals and collectivities; it reasserted social structures and hierarchies; it attracted pilgrims from at home and abroad; it made merit for individual devotees; it received visits from other tooth relics. In these and other various actions, as we have seen, it continued to be treated as a monk, but also could be identified with kingship and divinity. Similar lists of things done by relics could be drawn up for other traditions throughout Asia. In some of these actions, relics are merely doing the things that the Buddha has done. They are thereby repeating actions that marked the life of the Buddha, but in some cases, they are taking off on their own, so to speak, extending the biography of the Blessed One by doing new things.

The Dialectic of Continuity and Discontinuity

Finally, in chapter 8, which dealt with eschatology, we came to the end of the Buddha's biography and the end of his relics. We saw the different ways in which the bowl and the robe marked (or rather will mark) the transition from one buddha to another, in particular from Śākyamuni to Maitreya. This is an important issue because, as I have stated elsewhere, "Buddhists today can . . . best be thought of as living devotionally in between two buddhas, trying to recollect, on the one hand, the glories of Śākyamuni, and looking forward, on the other hand, to the coming of Maitreya" (Strong 2002: 41). These eschatological relics help them do both of these things.

At the same time, taken together, the traditions about these relics help engender reflection on the dialectic of continuity and discontinuity. As we have seen, the Theravādin myth of the future parinirvāṇa and disappearance of the relics unambiguously asserts the final ending of Śākyamuni's biography. And yet, another version of the story, in the *Nandimitrāvadāna,* though perhaps also shutting the door, nonetheless leaves it unlocked. In the final analysis, then, stories about relics of the Buddha help us to think not only about the life but also about the death of the Blessed One, and about the processual reality that he described and which his life and death reflected. Almost by nature, relics toy with the opposition between "gone" and "not gone." On the one hand, they are, themselves, living entities: they can grow, they can emit rays of light, they can fly up into the air and perform miracles, they can take on the shape of the Blessed One, they can respond to the faith of devotees, they can do all the things the Buddha could do, and then some. They not only express his life story but extend it and the scope of his activities. On the other hand, they are also reminders of impermanence, of the death of the Buddha, of the end and destruction of his body, of the fact that it was split up into grains the size of mustard seeds and spread throughout the world, or buried beneath huge stūpas, sealed into chambers, never to be opened again . . . until, of course, the end of the Buddha age, when Śākyamuni's relics will reemerge and all come alive once more. Only to "die" and disappear again. Only to make way for the next buddha and his relics. Put all together, then, the sides of this dialectical paradox make relics the powerful embodiment of the process of arising and cessation that characterizes all buddhas and all things.

BIBLIOGRAPHY

Adamek, Wendi L. 2000. "Robes Purple and Gold: Transmission of the Robe in the *Lidai fabao ji* [Record of the Dharma-Jewel through the Ages]." *History of Religions* 40:58–81.

Adikaram, E. W. 1946. *Early History of Buddhism in Ceylon.* Colombo: M.D. Gunasena.

Akanuma Chizen. 1994. *A Dictionary of Buddhist Proper Names.* Delhi: Sri Satguru.

Aksland, Markus. 2001. *The Sacred Footprint: A Cultural History of Adam's Peak.* Bangkok: Orchid.

Alabaster, Henry. 1871. *The Wheel of the Law.* London: Trübner.

Allchin, Frank Raymond. 1957. "Sanskrit *Eḍūka*—Pāli Eluka." *Bulletin of the School of Oriental and African Studies* 20:1–4.

———. 1980. "A Note on the 'Asokan' Stūpas of Pātan." In *The Stūpa: Its Religious, Historical and Architectural Significance.* Edited by Anna Libera Dallapicolla. Wiesbaden: Franz Steiner. Pp. 147–56.

Allione, Tsultrim. 1984. *Women of Wisdom.* London: Routledge and Kegan Paul.

Almond, Philip C. 1988. *The British Discovery of Buddhism.* Cambridge: Cambridge University Press.

Altekar, A. S. 1956. "The Corporeal Relics of the Buddha." *Journal of the Bihar Research Society.* Buddha Jayanti Special Issue. 2:501–11.

Anguttara Nikāya. 1885–1900. 5 vols. Edited by R. Morris and E. Hardy. London: Pali Text Society.

Anonymous. 1953. "Nouvelles bouddhiques—Les grandioses cérémonies de Sanchi." *France-Asie* 84:472–74.

Anonymous. 1991 "An Offering to the Tooth Relic (A True Story)." *Daily News* (Colombo). June 1, p. 17.

Anuman Rajadhon. n.d. *Essays on Thai Folklore.* Bangkok: Duang Kamol.

Apadāna of the Khuddaka Nikāya. 1925–27. 2 vols. Edited by Mary E. Lilley. London: Pali Text Society.

Archaimbault, Charles. 1966. "La fête du T'at à Ḷuong P'răbang." In *Essays Offered to G. H. Luce.* 2 vols. Edited by Ba Shin, Jean Boisselier, and A. B. Griswold. Ascona: Artibus Asiae. 1:5–47.

———. 1968. "Les rites pour l'obtention de la pluie à Luong P'răbang." *Bulletin de la Société des Etudes Indochinoises,* n.s. 43:199–217.

———. 1972. *La course de pirogues au Laos: Un complexe culturel.* Ascona: Artibus Asiae.

Ariès, Philippe. 1982. *The Hour of Our Death.* Translated by Helen Weaver. New York: Oxford University Press.

Arlington, L. C. and William Lewisohn. [1935] 1987. *In Search of Old Peking.* Hong Kong: Oxford University Press.

Aśokāvadāna. 1963. Edited by Sujitkumar Mukhopadhyaya. New Delhi: Sahitya Akademi.

Aṣṭasāhasrikāprajñāpāramitā sūtra. 1960. Edited by P. L. Vaidya. Darbhanga: Mithila Institute.

Auboyer, Jeannine. 1987. "A Note on 'the Feet' and Their Symbolism in Ancient India." In *Kusumañjali: New Interpretations of Indian Art and Culture*. Delhi: Agam Kal Prakashan. 1:125–27.

Aung-Thwin, Michael. 1981. "Jambudīpa: Classical Burma's Camelot." *Contributions to Asian Studies* 16:38–61.

Avadānakalpalatā of Kṣemendra. 1959. 2 vols. Edited by P. L. Vaidya. Darbhanga: Mithila Institute.

Avadāna-śataka. 1958. Edited by P. L. Vaidya. Darbhanga: Mithila Institute.

Bakker, H. 1991. "The Footprints of the Lord." In *Devotion Divine: Bhakti Traditions from the Regions of India: Studies in Honour of Charlotte Vaudeville*. Edited by Diana L. Eck and Françoise Mallison. Groningen: Egbert Forsten. Pp. 19–37.

Bapat, P. V. and A. Hirakawa, 1970. *Shan-Chien-P'i-P'o-Sha: A Chinese Version by Sanghabhadra of Samantapāsādika*. Poona: Bhandarkar Oriental Research Institute.

Bareau, André. 1962. "La construction et le culte des stūpa d'après les vinayapiṭaka." *Bulletin de l'Ecole Française d'Extrême-Orient* 50:229–74.

———. 1963. *Recherches sur la biographie du Buddha dans les sūtrapiṭaka et les vinayapiṭaka anciens I: De la quête de l'éveil à la conversion de Śāriputra et de Maudgalyāyana*. Paris: Ecole Française d'Extrême-Orient.

———. 1966–74. "Le *Dīpaṃkarajātaka* des Dharmaguptaka." *Mélanges de sinologie offerts à Monsieur Paul Demiéville*. 2 vols. Paris: Institut des Hautes Etudes Chinoises. 1:1–16.

———. 1970–71. *Recherches sur la biographie du Buddha dans les sūtrapiṭaka et les vinayapiṭaka anciens: II. Les derniers mois, le parinirvāṇa et les funérailles*. 2 vols. Paris: Ecole Française d'Extrême-Orient.

———. 1974. "La jeunesse du Buddha dans les sūtrapiṭaka et les vinayapiṭaka anciens." *Bulletin de l'Ecole Française d'Extrême-Orient* 61:199–274.

———. 1974a. "Sur l'origine des piliers dits d'Aśoka, des stūpa et des arbres sacrés du bouddhisme primitif." *Indologica Taurinensia* 2:9–36.

———. 1974b. "Le parinirvāṇa du Buddha et la naissance de la religion bouddhique." *Bulletin de l'Ecole Française d'Extrême-Orient* 61:275–99.

———. 1975. "Les récits canoniques des funérailles du Buddha et leurs anomalies: Nouvel essai d'interprétation." *Bulletin de l'Ecole Française d'Extrême-Orient* 62:151–89.

———. 1979. "La composition et les étapes de la formation progressive du *Mahāparinirvāṇasūtra* ancien." *Bulletin de l'Ecole Française d'Extrême-Orient* 66:45–103.

———. 1982. "Légende bouddhique." *Corps écrit*. 3:19–24.

———. 1987. "Lumbinī et la naissance du futur Buddha." *Bulletin de l'Ecole Française d'Extrême-Orient* 76:69–81.

———. 1987a. "La fin de la vie du Buddha selon l'*Ekottara-āgama*." *Hinduismus und Buddhismus. Festschrift für Ulrich Schneider.* Freiburg: Hedwig Falk. Pp. 13–37.

———. 1988–89. "Etude du bouddhisme." *Annuaire du Collège de France: Résumé des cours et travaux.* Paris: Collège de France. Pp. 533–47.

———. 1989–90. "Devadatta et le premier schisme bouddhique." *Oriente e Occidente (Pūrvāparam) 1989–1990.* Pp. 1–14.

———. 1991. "Les agissements de Devadatta selon les chapitres relatifs au schisme dans les divers vinayapiṭaka." *Bulletin de l'Ecole Française d'Extrême-Orient* 78:87–132.

Barrett, T. H. 2001. "Stūpa, Sūtra, and Śarīra in China, c. 656–706 C.E." *Buddhist Studies Review* 18: 1–64.

Barthes, Jean. 1952. "Les reliques sacrées à Phnom-Penh." *France-Asie* 8, no. 78:951–56.

Bartholomeusz, Tessa J. 1994. *Women under the Bō Tree: Buddhist Nuns in Sri Lanka.* Cambridge: Cambridge University Press.

Barua, D. K. 1994. "Buddhist Literary Masterpieces on the Bodhi Tree." In *Maha Bodhi Tree in Anuradhapura, Sri Lanka.* Edited by H.S.S. Nissanka. New Delhi: Vikas. Pp. 119–68

Basham, A. L. [1951] 1981. *History and Doctrines of the Ājīvikas.* Delhi: Motilal Banarsidass.

Bays, Gwendolyn. 1983. *The Voice of the Buddha: The Beauty of Compassion.* 2 vols. Berkeley: Dharma.

Beal, Samuel. [1875] 1985. *The Romantic Legend of Śākya Buddha.* Delhi: Motilal Banarsidass.

———. [1883] 1975. *The Fo-Sho-Hing-Tsan-King.* New Delhi: Motilal Banarsidass.

———. 1884. *Si-Yu-Ki: Buddhist Records of the Western World.* 2 vols. London: Kegan Paul, Trench and Trübner.

Bechert, Heinz. 1995. "The Dates of the Buddha and the Origin and Spread of the Theravāda Chronology." In *When Did the Buddha Live? The Controversy on the Dating of the Historical Buddha.* Edited by Heinz Bechert. Delhi: Sri Satguru Publications. Pp. 253–86.

Benard, Elisabeth. 1988. "The Living Among the Dead: A Comparison of Buddhist and Christian Relics." *The Tibet Journal* 13:33–48.

Bendall, Cecil, and W.H.D. Rouse. [1902] 1971. *Śikshā-samuccaya: A Compendium of Buddhist Doctrine Compiled by Śāntideva.* Delhi: Motilal Banarsidass.

Benn, James A. 1998. "Where Text Meets Flesh: Burning the Body as an Apocryphal Practice in Chinese Buddhism." *History of Religions* 37:295–322.

———. 2002. "Fire and the Sword: Some Connections between Self-Immolation and Religious Persecution in the History of Chinese Buddhism." Paper presented to the Conference on Death and Dying in Buddhist Cultures, Princeton University, May.

Bentley, James. 1985. *Restless Bones.* London: Constable.

Bentor, Yael. 1994. "Tibetan Relic Classification." *Tibetan Studies (Proceedings of the Sixth Seminar of the International Association for Tibetan Studies).* Edited by Per Kvaerne. Oslo. Pp. 16–30.

———. 1995. "On the Indian Origins of the Tibetan Practice of Depositing Relics and Dhāraṇīs in Stūpas and Images." *Journal of the American Oriental Society* 115:248–61.
———. 1996. *Consecration of Images and Stūpas in Indo-Tibetan Tantric Buddhism.* Leiden: E. J. Brill.
Berg, Charles. 1951. *The Unconscious Significance of Hair.* London: George Allen and Unwin.
Berkwitz, Stephen C. 2001. "Emotions and Ethics in Buddhist History: The *Sinhala Thūpavaṃsa* and the Work of Virtue." *Religion* 31:155–73.
———. Forthcoming. "History and Gratitude in Theravāda Buddhism." *Journal of the American Academy of Religion.*
Beyer, Stephan. 1974. *The Buddhist Experience: Sources and Interpretations.* Encino, Calif.: Dickenson.
Bhattacharya, Sachchidananda. 1960. *Select Asokan Epigraphs.* Calcutta: Firma K. L. Mukhopadhyay.
Bidyalankarana, H. H. Prince. 1935. "The Buddha's Footprints." *Journal of the Siam Society* 28:1–12.
Bigandet, Paul. [1858] 1979. *The Life or Legend of Gaudama.* 2 vols. Delhi: Bharatiya.
Bizot, François. 1971. "La figuration des pieds du Bouddha au Cambodge." *Asiatische Studien / Etudes asiatiques* 25:407–39.
———. 1980. "La grotte de la naissance." *Bulletin de l'Ecole Française d'Extrême-Orient* 67:221–73.
———. 1981. *Le don de soi-même.* Paris: Ecole Française d'Extrême-Orient.
———. 1988. "Les traditions de pabbajā en Asie du Sud-Est." *Abhandlungen der Akademie der Wissenschaften, Göttingen, Philologisch-Historische Klasse,* ser. 3, 169:24–48.
———. 1994. "La consécration des statues et le culte des morts." In *Recherches nouvelles sur le Cambodge.* Paris: Ecole Française d'Extrême-Orient. Pp. 101–39.
Bloch, Jules. 1950. *Les inscriptions d'Asoka.* Paris: Les Belles Lettres.
Bloch, Maurice, and Jonathan Parry. 1982. *Death and the Regeneration of Life.* Cambridge: Cambridge University Press.
Bloss, Lowell W. 1973. "The Buddha and the Nāga: A Study in Buddhist Folk Religiosity." *History of Religions* 13:36–53.
Boisvert, Matthieu. 1996. "Death as Meditation Subject in the Theravāda Tradition." *Buddhist Studies Review* 13:37–54.
Boucher, Daniel. 1993. "The *Prātityasamutpādagāthā* and Its Role in the Medieval Cult of the Relics." *Journal of the International Association of Buddhist Studies* 14:1–27.
Brock, Karen L. 1988. "Awaiting Maitreya at Kasagi." In *Maitreya , the Future Buddha.* Edited by Alan Sponberg and Helen Hardacre. Cambridge: Cambridge University Press. Pp. 214–47.
Brown, Peter. 1981. *The Cult of the Saints.* Chicago: University of Chicago Press.
Brown, Robert L. 1990. "God on Earth: The Walking Buddha in the Art of South and Southeast Asia." *Artibus Asiae* 50:73–107.

———. 1997. "Narrative as Icon: The *Jātaka* Stories in Ancient Indian and Southeast Asian Art." *Sacred Biography in the Buddhist Traditions of South and Southeast Asia.* Edited by Juliane Schober. Honolulu: University of Hawai'i Press. Pp. 64–112.

———. 1998. "Expected Miracles: The Unsurprisingly Miraculous Nature of Buddhist Images and Relics." *Images, Miracles, and Authority in Asian Religious Traditions.* Edited by Richard H. Davis. Boulder: Westview. Pp. 23–35.

Brown, W. Norman. 1968. "The Metaphysics of the Truth Act (Satyakriyā)." In *Mélanges d'indianisme à la mémoire de Louis Renou.* Paris: E. de Boccard. Pp. 171–77.

Bryner, Edna. 1956. *Thirteen Tibetan Tankas.* Indian Hills: Falcon Wing's Press.

Buddhacarita. 1972. Edited by E. H. Johnston. Delhi: Motilal Banarsidass.

Buddhavaṃsa and Cariyāpiṭaka. 1974. Edited by N. A. Jayawickrama. London: Pali Text Society.

Buddhist Association of China. 1956. *Buddhists in New China.* Peking: Nationalities Publishing House.

———. 1966. *The Buddha's Tooth-Relic Pagoda.* Peking: Buddhist Association.

Burgess, James. [1886] 1996. *The Buddhist Stupas of Amaravati and Jaggayyapeta.* New Delhi: Archaeological Survey of India.

Burlingame, E. W. 1921. *Buddhist Legends.* 3 vols. Cambridge: Harvard University Press.

Burnouf, Eugène. 1852. *Le Lotus de la bonne loi.* Paris: Imprimerie Nationale.

———. 1876. *Introduction à l'histoire du buddhisme indien.* 2nd. ed. Paris: Maisonneuve.

Bynum, Caroline Walker. 1995. *The Resurrection of the Body in Western Christianity, 200–1336.* New York: Columbia University Press.

Caldwell, Ian, and Ann Appleby Hazlewood. 1994. "'The Holy Footprints of the Venerable Gautama': A New Translation of the Pasir Panjang Inscription." *Bijdragen tot de Taal-, Land- en Volkenkunde* 150:457–80.

Calvin, John. 1970. *Three French Treatises.* Edited by Francis M. Higman. London: Athlone.

Campany, Robert. 1995. "A la recherche de la religion perdue: 'Aśokan Stūpas,' Images, and the Cult of Relics in Early Medieval China." Paper presented to the American Academy of Religion Buddhist Relics Seminar, Philadelphia.

Carter, Martha L. 1990. *The Mystery of the Udayana Buddha.* Naples: Istituto Universitario Orientale.

Carus, Paul. 1897. "A Buddhist Priest's View of Relics." *The Open Court* 11:122–25.

Chakesadhātuvaṃsa. 1885. Edited by Ivan Minayeff in *Journal of the Pali Text Society* 4:5–16.

Chao Pu-chu. 1956. "New Ties among Buddhists." *China Reconstructs* 5, no. 4:12–15.

———. 1959. "The Story of the Buddha's Tooth-Relic." *China Reconstructs* 8, no. 9:36–37.

Chapin, Helen B., and Alexander Soper. 1971. *A Long Roll of Buddhist Images.* Ascona: Artibus Asiae.

Charpentier, Jarl. 1918. "Heilige Fussabdrücke in Indien." *Ostasiatische Zeitschrift* 7:1–30.

Chavannes, Edouard. 1894. *Mémoire composé à l'époque de la grande dynastie T'ang sur les religieux éminents qui allèrent chercher la loi dans les pays d'occident.* Paris: E. Leroux.

———. 1903. "Voyage de Song Yun dans l'Udyāna et le Gandhāra." *Bulletin de l'Ecole Française d'Extrême-Orient* 3:379–441.

———. 1934. *Cinq cent contes et apologues extraits du Tripiṭaka chinois.* 4 vols. Paris: Adrien Maisonneuve.

Chen Jinhua. 2002. *Monks and Monarchs, Kinship and Kingship: Tanqian in Sui Buddhism and Politics.* Kyoto: Scuola Italiana di Studi sull'Asia Orientale.

———. 2002a. "*Sarīra* and Scepter: Empress Wu's Political Use of Buddhist Relics." *Journal of the International Association of Buddhist Studies* 25:33–140.

Ch'en, Kenneth K. S. 1956. "Economic Background of the Hui-ch'ang Persecution." *Harvard Journal of Asiatic Studies* 19:67–105.

———. 1964. *Buddhism in China.* Princeton: Princeton University Press.

———. 1973. *The Chinese Transformation of Buddhism.* Princeton: Princeton University Press.

Childers, Robert Caesar. 1909. *A Dictionary of the Pāli Language.* London: Kegan Paul, Trench, Trübner.

Chimpa (Lama) and Alaka Chattopadhyaya. 1980. *Tāranātha's History of Buddhism in India.* Calcutta: K. P. Bagchi.

Chiovaro, F. 1967. "Relics." *New Catholic Encyclopedia.* New York: McGraw Hill. 12:234–40.

Ch'ŏn Hye-Bong. 1972. "Dhāranī-Sutra of the Early Koryŏ." *Korea Journal* 12:4–12

Coedès, Georges. 1956. "Le 2.500e anniversaire du Bouddha." *Diogène* 15:1–16.

Cohen, Paul T. 2000. "Lue across Borders: Pilgrimage and the Muang Sing Reliquary in Northern Laos." In *Where China Meets Southeast Asia.* Edited by Grant Evans. Bangkok: White Lotus. Pp. 145–61.

Colebrooke, William M. G. 1836. "Account of a Ceremonial Exhibition of the Relic Termed 'the Tooth of Buddha,' at Kandy, in Ceylon, in May 1828. Translated and abridged from the original Singhalese, drawn up by a Native Eye-Witness." *Journal of the Royal Asiatic Society* 3:161–64.

Collins, Steven. 1992. "*Nirvāṇa,* Time and Narrative." *History of Religions* 31:215–46.

———. 1997. "The Body in Theravāda Buddhist Monasticism." In *Religion and the Body.* Edited by Sarah Coakley. Cambridge: Cambridge University Press. Pp. 185–204

———. 1998. *Nirvana and Other Buddhist Felicities.* Cambridge: Cambridge University Press.

Commentary on the Dhammapada. 1906–15. 5 vols. Edited by H. Smith and H. C. Norman. London: Pali Text Society.

Cone, Margaret, and Richard Gombrich. 1977. *The Perfect Generosity of Prince Vessantara.* Oxford: Clarendon.

Conze, Edward. 1951. *Buddhism: Its Essence and Development*. New York: Harper Torchbooks.
———. 1959. *Buddhist Scriptures*. Harmondsworth: Penguin.
———. 1973. *The Perfection of Wisdom in Eight Thousand Lines and Its Verse Summary*. Bolinas: Four Seasons Foundation.
———. 1975. *The Large Sutra on Perfect Wisdom*. Berkeley: University of California Press.
Couvreur, Walter. 1967. "Nieuwe Fragmenten van het Catuṣpariṣat-, Mahāparinirvāṇa-, Mahāsudarśana-, en Mahāvadānasūtra." *Orientalia Gandensia* 4:167–73.
Cowell, E. B. 1895–1907. *The Jātaka or Stories of the Buddha's Former Births*. 6 vols. London: Pali Text Society.
Cox, Hiram. 1821. *Journal of a Residence in the Burman Empire, and More Particularly at the Court of Amarapoorah*. London: J. Warren.
Cūḷavaṃsa. 1925–27. 2 vols. Edited by Wilhelm Geiger. London: Pali Text Society.
Cumming, C. F. Gordon. 1888. *Wanderings in China*. Edinburgh: William Blackwood.
———. 1892. *Two Happy Years in Ceylon*. New York: Charles Scribner's.
Cummings, Mary. 1982. *The Lives of the Buddha in the Art and Literature of Asia*. Ann Arbor: Center for South and Southeast Asian Studies, University of Michigan.
Cunningham, Alexander. 1854. *The Bhilsa Topes, or Buddhist Monuments of Central India*. London: Smith, Elder.
Da Cunha, J. Gerson. 1875. "Memoir on the History of the Tooth-relic of Ceylon." *Journal of the Bombay Branch of the Royal Asiatic Society* 11:115–46.
Dallapicolla, Anna Libera, ed. 1980. *The Stūpa: Its Religious, Historical, and Architectural Significance*. Wiesbaden: Franz Steiner.
Damrong Rājānubhāb. 1973. *Monuments of the Buddha in Siam*. Translated by Sulak Sivaraksa and A. B. Griswold. Bangkok: Siam Society.
Danforth, Loring M. 1982. *The Death Rituals of Rural Greece*. Princeton: Princeton University Press.
Dantinne, Jean. 1983. *La splendeur de l'inébranlable (Akṣobhyavyūha)*. Vol. 1. Louvain-la-neuve: Institut Orientaliste.
Darmesteter, James. 1880. *The Zend-Avesta, Part I: The Vendīdād*. Oxford: Clarendon.
Das, Asha. 1994. *The Chronicle of Burma. Cha-Kesadhātuvaṃsa*. Delhi: Pratibha Prakashan.
Das, Nobin Chandra. 1893. "Rukmāvatī." *Journal of the Buddhist Text Society of India* 1, pt. 4:1–6.
Das, Sarat Chandra. [1902] 1970. *A Tibetan-English Dictionary*. Delhi: Motilal Banarsidass.
Dāṭhāvaṃsa. 1884. Edited by T. W. Rhys Davids, in *Journal of the Pali Text Society*. Pp. 109–50.
Daulton, Jack. 1994. "The Relics of Sariputta and Moggallana: From Ancient India to Modern Burma." M.A. thesis, Northern Illinois University.
Davids, C.A.F. Rhys., and F. L. Woodward. 1917–30. *The Book of Kindred Sayings*. 5 vols. London: Pali Text Society.

Davids, T. W. Rhys. 1880. *Buddhist Birth Stories or Jātaka Tales*. London: Trübner.

———. [1890–94] 1963. *The Questions of King Milinda*. 2 vols. New York: Dover.

———. 1899–1924. *Dialogues of the Buddha*. 3 vols. London: Pali Text Society.

———. 1901. "Aśoka and the Buddha Relics." *Journal of the Royal Asiatic Society*. Pp. 397–410.

Davids, T. W. Rhys, and Hermann Oldenberg. [1882–85] 1975. *Vinaya Texts*. 3 vols. New Delhi: Motilal Banarsidass.

Davids, T. W. Rhys and William Stede. 1925. *Pali-English Dictionary*. London: Pali Text Society.

Davis, Richard H. 1997. *Lives of Indian Images*. Princeton: Princeton University Press.

Davy, John. [1821] 1969. *An Account of the Interior of Ceylon and of Its Inhabitants*. Dehiwala: Tisara Prakasakayo.

•Deal, William E. 1995. "Buddhism and the State in Early Japan." In *Buddhism in Practice*. Edited by Donald S. Lopez, Jr. Princeton: Princeton University Press. Pp. 216–27.

De Berval, René. 1952. "La réception de la relique du Bouddha." *France-Asie* 8, no. 76:702–11.

De Couto, Diogo. 1783. *Da Asia. Dos feitos, que os Portuguezes fizeram na conquista, e descubrimento das terras e mares do Oriente*. Vols. 17–18. Lisbon: Regia Officina Typographica.

Deeg, Max. Forthcoming. "Das Ende des Dharma und die Ankunft des Maitreya. Endzeit- und Neue-Zeit-Vorstellungen im Buddhismus (mit einem Exkurs zum Kāśyapa-Legende)." Manuscript.

DeGroot, J. J. M. [1886] 1977. *Les fêtes annuellement célébrées à Emoi (Amoy)*. Translated by C. G. Chavannes. San Francisco: Chinese Materials Center.

———. 1893. *Le code du Mahāyāna en Chine*. Amsterdam: Johannes Müller.

———. 1919. *Der Thūpa: Das heiligste Heiligtum des Buddhismus in China*. Berlin: Verlag der Akademie der Wissenschaften.

Dehejia, Vidya. 1991. "Aniconism and the Multivalence of Emblems." *Ars orientalis* 21:45–66.

———. 1996. "The Animated World of the Toranas." In *Unseen Presence: The Buddha and Sanchi*. Edited by Vidya Dehejia. Mumbai: Marg. Pp. 36–57.

De Marco, Giuseppe. 1987. "The Stūpa as a Funerary Monument: New Iconographical Evidence." *East and West* 37:191–246.

De Mély, F. 1890. "Les reliques du lait de la vierge." *Revue archéologique* 15:103–16.

Demiéville, Paul. 1924. "Les versions chinoises du Milindapañha." *Bulletin de l'Ecole Française d'Extrême-Orient* 24:1–258.

———. 1934. "Buppatsu . . . buddhakeśa . . . les cheveux du Buddha." In *Hōbōgirin*. Tokyo: Maison Franco-Japonaise. 2:169–71.

———. 1934a. "Busshin . . . buddhakāya . . . corps de Buddha." In *Hōbōgirin*. Tokyo: Maison Franco-Japonaise. 2:174–85.

———. 1937. "Butsuge . . . dent de Buddha." In *Hōbōgirin*. Tokyo: Maison Franco-Japonaise. 3:203–5.

———. 1937a. "Butsuzō . . . buddhapratimā . . . icone." In *Hōbōgirin*. Tokyo: Maison Franco-Japonaise. 3:210–15.

De Milloué, Léon. 1884. "Le Dāṭhāvança ou Histoire de la dent relique du Buddha Gotama." *Annales du Musée Guimet* 17:309ff.

Denis, Eugène. 1976. "La *Lokapaññatti* et la légende birmane d'Aśoka." *Journal asiatique* 264:97–116.

———. 1977. *La Lokapaññatti et les idées cosmologiques du bouddhisme ancien*. 3 vols. Lille: Université de Lille.

De Queyroz, Fernaõ de. 1930. *The Temporal and Spiritual Conquest of Ceylon*. 2 vols. Translated by S. G. Perera. Colombo: A. C. Richardson.

DeSilva, Haris. 1972. "The Tooth Relic—A Palladium of Sinhalese Royalty." *Times of Ceylon Annual*. Pp. 1–3.

DeSilva, K. M. 1981. *A History of Sri Lanka*. Berkeley: University of California Press.

DeSilva, Lily. 1981. *Paritta: The Buddhist Ceremony for Peace and Prosperity in Sri Lanka*. Colombo: Government Printing House.

DeSilva, Lynn. 1980. *Buddhism: Beliefs and Practices in Sri Lanka*. 2nd ed. Colombo: Ecumenical Institute.

DeSousa, Francisco. [1710] 1978. *Oriente conquistado a Jesus Cristo*. Vol. 1. Porto: Lello and Irmão.

Devendra, D. T. 1984. "Daḷadā Māligāva." In *Encyclopaedia of Buddhism*. Edited by Jotiya Dhirasekera. Colombo: Government of Sri Lanka Printing Press. 4:287–94.

DeVisser, Marinus Willem. 1922–23. "The Arhats in China and Japan." *Ostasiatische Zeitschrift*. 10:60–102.

Dīgha Nikāya. 1911. 3 vols. Edited by J. Estlin Carpenter. London: Pali Text Society.

Dissanayake, Wimal. 1993. "Body in Social Theory." In *Self as Body in Asian Theory and Practice*. Edited by Thomas P. Kasulis. Albany: State University of New York Press. Pp. 21–36.

Divyāvadāna. 1886. Edited by E. B. Cowell and R. A. Neil. Cambridge: Cambridge University Press.

Dooley, Eugene A. 1931. *Church Law on Sacred Relics*. Washington, D.C.: Catholic University of America Press.

Douglas, Mary. 1966. *Purity and Danger*. London: Routledge and Kegan Paul.

Dubs, Homer H. 1946. "Han Yü and the Buddha's Relic: An Episode in Medieval Chinese Religion." *The Review of Religion* 11:5–17.

Duncan, Jonathan. 1808. "An Account of the Discovery of Two Urns in the Vicinity of Benares." *Asiatic Researches* 5:131–32.

Duroiselle, Charles. 1904. "Upagutta et Māra." *Bulletin de l'Ecole Française d'Extrême-Orient* 4:414–28.

———. 1905. "Notes sur la géographie apocryphe de la Birmanie." *Bulletin de l'Ecole Française d'Extrême-Orient* 5:146–67.

———. 1911–12. "The Hlèdauk Pagoda and Its Relics." *Annual Report of the Archaeological Survey of India*. Pp. 149–51.

———. 1920–21. "The Talaing Plaques on the Ananda." *Epigraphia Birmanica* 2:parts 1–2.

Durt, Hubert. n.d. "Nouvelle approche de l'imaginaire bouddhique: Le culte des reliques, des reliquaires et des images." Unpublished manuscript.

———. 1979. "Chōrai, ch. ting li. Hommage du sommet de la tête." In *Hōbōgirin*. Paris: Adrien Maisonneuve. 5:371–80.

———. 1979a. "Chōsō, ch. ting siang. Protubérance-cranienne." In *Hōbōgirin*. Paris: Adrien Maisonneuve. 5:421–30.

———. 1987. "The Meaning of Archaeology in Ancient Buddhism—Notes on the Stūpas of Aśoka and the Worship of the 'Buddhas of the Past' According to Three Stories in the *Samguk Yusa*." *Bul gyo ue So Kwahak / Buddhism and Science*. Seoul: Tongguk University. Pp. 1223–41.

———. 1992. "Récit de l'apparition du Buddha, sortant du cercueil, à sa mère, Mahāmāyā." Paper delivered at the Scuola di Studi sull'Asia Orientale, Kyoto, Japan.

———. 1996. "L'apparition du Buddha à sa mère après son nirvāṇa dans le *Sūtra de Mahāmāyā* et le *Sūtra de la mère du Buddha*." In *De Dunhuang au Japon: Etudes chinoises et bouddhiques offertes à Michel Soymié*. Edited by Jean-Pierre Drège. Geneva: Droz.

———. 1998. "Two Interpretations of Human-Flesh Offering: Misdeed or Supreme Sacrifice." *Journal of the International College for Advanced Buddhist Studies / Kokusai bukkyōgaku daigakuin daigaku kenkyū kiyō* 1:57–83.

———. 1999. "The Offering of the Children of Prince Viśvantara / Sudāna in the Chinese Tradition." *Journal of the International College for Advanced Buddhist Studies / Kokusai bukkyōgaku daigakuin daigaku kenkyū kiyō* 2:147–82.

———. 2000. "Du lambeau de chair au démembrement. Le renoncement au corps dans le bouddhisme ancien." *Bulletin de l'Ecole Française d'Extrême-Orient* 87:7–22.

———. 2000a. "The Casting-off of Mādrī in the Northern Buddhist Literary Tradition." *Journal of the International College for Advanced Buddhist Studies / Kokusai bukkyōgaku daigakuin daigaku kenkyū kiyō* 3:133–58.

Durt, Hubert, Krishnā Riboud, and Lai Tung-hung. 1985. "A propos de 'stūpa miniatures' votifs du ve siècle découverts à Tourfan et au Gansu." *Arts asiatiques* 40:92–106.

Duval, Yvette. 1988. *Auprès des saints corps et âme: l'inhumation "ad sanctos" dans la chrétienté d'orient et d'occident du iiie au viie siècle*. Paris: Etudes Augustiniennes.

Eck, Diana L. 1981. *Darśan: Seeing the Divine Image in India*. Chambersburg: Anima.

Eckel, Malcolm David. 1992. *To See the Buddha*. San Francisco: Harper.

Edgerton, Franklin. 1953. *A Buddhist Hybrid Sanskrit Grammar and Dictionary*. 2 vols. New Haven: Yale University Press.

Eggeling, Julius. [1900] 1972. *The Śatapatha Brāhmaṇa*. 5 vols. Delhi: Motilal Banarsidass.

Eire, Carlos M. N. 1986. *War against the Idols: The Reformation of Worship from Erasmus to Calvin*. Cambridge: Cambridge University Press.

Eliade, Mircea. 1958. *Rites and Symbols of Initiation*. Translated by Willard R. Trask. New York: Harper and Row.

Eliot, Charles. 1921. *Hinduism and Buddhism*. 3 vols. London: Edwin Arnold.

Emmerick, R. E. 1967. *Tibetan Texts Concerning Khotan*. London: Oxford University Press.

———. 1968. *The Book of Zambasta*. London: Oxford University Press.

———. 1970. *The Sūtra of Golden Light*. London: Luzac.

Extended Mahāvaṃsa. [1937] 1988. Edited by G. P. Malalasekera. Oxford: Pali Text Society.

Falk, Maryla. 1943. *Nāma-Rūpa and Dharma-Rūpa*. Calcutta: University of Calcutta.

Faure, Bernard. 1991. *The Rhetoric of Immediacy: A Cultural Critique of Chan/Zen Buddhism*. Princeton: Princeton University Press.

———. 1992. "Relics and Flesh Bodies: The Creation of Ch'an Sites." In *Pilgrims and Sacred Sites in China*. Edited by Susan Naquin and Chün-fang Yü. Berkeley: University of California Press. Pp. 150–89.

———. 1995. "Quand l'habit fait le moine: The Symbolism of the *Kāsāya* in Sōtō Zen." *Cahiers d'Extrême-Asie* 8:335–69.

———. 1996. *Visions of Power: Imagining Medieval Japanese Buddhism*. Translated by Phyllis Brooks. Princeton: Princeton University Press.

———. 1999. "A Jewel of a Woman: Medieval Ideology and Wishful Thinking." Paper presented to the 1998–99 Evans-Wentz Conference on "Buddhist Priests, Kings, and Marginals: Medieval Japanese Buddhism." Stanford University, May.

———. 1999a. "Relics, Regalia, and the Dynamics of Secrecy in Japanese Buddhism." In *Rending the Veil*. Edited by Elliot R. Wolfson. New York: Seven Bridges. Pp. 271–87.

———. 2002. "Les cloches de la terre: Un aspect du culte des reliques dans le bouddhisme chinois." In *Bouddhisme et lettrés dans la Chine médiévale*. Edited by Catherine Despeux. Louvain: Editions Peeters. Pp. 25–44.

———. Forthcoming. "Datō: Le culte des reliques dans le bouddhisme." In *Hōbōgirin*, vol. 8. Paris: Adrien Maisonneuve.

Feer, Léon. 1891. *Avadāna-çataka: Cent légendes (bouddhiques)*. Paris: Ernest Leroux.

Fernando, Sujatha. 1970. "A Pilgrimage to Nithupathpane-Girihanduseya." *The Buddhist Vesak Annual* 41:91–93.

Fickle, Dorothy H. 1979. *The Life of the Buddha Murals in the Buddhaisawan Chapel*. Bangkok: National Museum Fine Arts Department.

Filliozat, Jean. 1963. "La mort volontaire par le feu et la tradition bouddhique indienne." *Journal asiatique* 251:21–51.

Fleet, J. F. 1906–1907. "The Tradition about the Corporeal Relics of the Buddha." *Journal of the Royal Asiatic Society*. Pp. 341–63, 665–71, 881–913.

Fontein, Jan. 1981. "Notes on the *Jātakas* and *Avadānas* of Barabuḍur." In *Barabuḍur: History and Significance of a Buddhist Monument*. Edited by Luis O. Gómez and Hiram W. Woodward, Jr. Berkeley: Asian Humanities.

Forbes, Jonathan. [1840] 1994. *Eleven Years in Ceylon*. 2 vols. New Delhi: Asian Educational Services.

Forchhammer, Emile. 1883. *Notes on the Early History and Geography of British Burma: 1. The Shwe Dagon Pagoda*. Rangoon: Government Press.

Forte, Antonino. 1988. *Mingtang and Buddhist Utopias in the History of the Astronomical Clock: The Tower, Statue and Armillary Sphere Constructed by Empress Wu*. Rome: Istituto Italiano per il Medio ed Estremo-Oriente.

Foucaux, Philippe Edouard. 1860. *Rgya tcher rol pa. Histoire du Bouddha Sakya Mouni traduite du tibétain*. Paris: Benjami Duprat.

———. 1884. *Le Lalita Vistara—Développement des jeux*. Paris: Ernest Leroux.

Foucher, Alfred. 1905–18. *L'art gréco-bouddhique du Gandhara*. 2 vols. Paris: Leroux.

———. 1917. "The Great Miracle at Śrāvastī." In *The Beginnings of Buddhist Art*. Paris: Paul Geuthner. Pp. 147–84.

———. 1943. "A propos de la conversion au bouddhisme du roi Indo-Grec Ménandre." *Mémoires de l'Académie des Inscriptions et Belles Lettres* 48, part 2:1–37.

———. 1987. *La vie du Bouddha d'après les textes et les monuments de l'Inde*. Paris: Adrien Maisonneuve.

Fournereau, Lucien. 1895. *Le Siam ancien*. Paris: Ernest Leroux.

Frank, Bernard. 1986. "Vacuité et corps actualisé: Le problème de la présence de 'Personnages Vénérés' dans leurs images selon la tradition du bouddhisme japonais." *Corps de dieux: Le temps de la réflexion* 7:141–70.

Freedberg, David. 1989. *The Power of Images: Studies in the History and Theory of Response*. Chicago: University of Chicago Press.

Frolow, Anatole. 1961. *La relique de la vraie croix: Recherches sur le développement d'un culte*. Paris: Institut d'Etudes Byzantines.

Frye, Stanley. 1981. *The Sūtra of the Wise and the Foolish (mdo bdsans blun) or the Ocean of Narratives (üliger-ün dalai)*. Dharmsala: Library of Tibetan Works and Archives.

Gabaude, Louis. 1979. *Les cetiya de sable au Laos et en Thaïlande*. Paris: Ecole Française d'Extrême-Orient.

Geary, Patrick J. 1978. *Furta Sacra: Thefts of Relics in the Central Middle Ages*. Princeton: Princeton University Press.

Geiger, Wilhelm. 1912. *The Mahāvaṃsa or the Great Chronicle of Ceylon*. London: Pali Text Society.

———. 1929. *Cūḷavaṃsa being the More Recent Part of the Mahāvaṃsa*. 2 vols. London: Pali Text Society.

———. 1960. *Culture of Ceylon in Medieval Times*. Edited by Heinz Bechert. Wiesbaden: Otto Harrassowitz.

Germano, David. 1994. "Embracing the Buddhas' Blazing Absence: The Philosophy of Relics in the Tibetan *sNying thig* Pure Land Cult." Paper presented to the American Academy of Religion Seminar on Buddhist Relics, Chicago.

Gernet, Jacques. 1956. *Les aspects économiques du bouddhisme dans la société chinoise du ve au xe siècle*. Saigon: Ecole Française d'Extrême-Orient.

———. 1960. "Les suicides par le feu chez les bouddhistes chinois du ve au xe siècle." In *Mélanges publiés par l'Institut des Hautes Etudes Chinoises*. 2 vols. Paris: Presses Universitaires de France. 2:527–58.

Gilgit Manuscripts. 1939–59. 9 vols. Edited by Nalinaksha Dutt. Srinagar and Calcutta: Research Department.

Gjertson, Donald E. 1989. *Miraculous Retribution: A Study and Translation of T'ang Lin's* Ming-pao chi. Berkeley: Berkeley Buddhist Series.

Gnoli, Raniero. 1978. *The Gilgit Manuscript of the Sanghabhedavastu*. 2 vols. Rome: Istituto Italiano per il Medio ed Estremo Oriente.

———. 1978a. *The Gilgit Manuscript of the Śayanāsanavastu and the Adhikaraṇavastu*. Rome: Istituto Italiano per il Medio ed Estremo Oriente.

Goloubew, Victor. 1932. "Le temple de la dent à Kandy." *Bulletin de l'Ecole Française d'Extrême-Orient* 32:441–74.

Gombrich, Richard. 1966. "The Consecration of a Buddha Image." *Journal of Asian Studies* 26: 23–36.

———. 1971. *Precept and Practice: Traditional Buddhism in the Rural Highlands of Ceylon*. Oxford: Clarendon Press.

———. 1972. "Feminine Elements in Sinhalese Buddhism." *Wiener Zeitschrift für die Kunde Südasiens* 16:67–93.

———. 1978. "Kosala-Bimba-Vaṇṇanā." In *Buddhism in Ceylon and Studies on the Religious Syncretism in Buddhist Countries*. Edited by Heinz Bechert. Göttingen: Vandenhoeck and Ruprecht. Pp. 281–303.

———. 1980. "The Significance of the Former Buddhas in the Theravādin Tradition." *Buddhist Studies in Honour of Walpola Rahula*. Edited by Somaratna Balasooriya et al. London: Gordon Fraser. Pp. 62–72.

———. 1981. "A New Theravādin Liturgy." *Journal of the Pali Text Society* 9:41–73.

Gombrich, Richard, and Gananath Obeyesekere. 1988. *Buddhism Transformed. Religious Change in Sri Lanka*. Princeton: Princeton University Press.

Goody, Jack. 1997. *Representations and Contradictions: Ambivalence Towards Images, Theatre, Fiction, Relics and Sexuality*. Oxford: Blackwell.

Goonasekere, Lakshmi R. 1966. "Bhallika." In *Encyclopaedia of Buddhism*. Edited by G. P. Malalasekera. Colombo: Government Press. 2:685–87.

Goswamy, Brijinder Nath. 1980. "Introductory Speech: The Stūpa—Some Uninformed Questions about Terminological Equivalents." In *The Stūpa: Its Religious, Historical, and Architectural Significance*. Edited by Anna Libera Dallapicolla. Wiesbaden: Franz Steiner. Pp. 1–11.

Grabar, André. 1946. *Martyrium: Recherches sur le culte des reliques et l'art chrétien antique*. 2 vols. Paris: Collège de France.

Granet, Marcel. 1926. *Danses et légendes de la Chine ancienne*. 2 vols. Paris: Presses Universitaires de France.

Granoff, Phyllis. 1996. "The Ambiguity of Miracles: Buddhist Understandings of Supernatural Power." *East and West* 46:79–96.

Gray, James. [1894] 1981. *Jinālaṅkāra or "Embellishments of Buddha by Buddharakkhita*. London: Pali Text Society.

Greenwald, Alice. 1978. "The Relic on the Spear: Historiography and the Saga of Duṭṭhagāmaṇī." In *Religion and Legitimation of Power in Sri Lanka*. Edited by Bardwell L. Smith. Chambersburg: Anima. Pp. 13–35.

Griswold, A. B. 1967. *Towards a History of Sukhodaya Art*. Bangkok: National Museum.

Griswold, A. B. and Prasert ṇa Nagara. 1972. "King Lödaiya of Sukhodaya and His Contemporaries." *Journal of the Siam Society* 60, no. 1:21–152.

———. 1973. "The Epigraphy of Mahādharmarājā I of Sukhodaya." *Journal of the Siam Society* 61:71–179.

Grosnick, William. Forthcoming. "Tathāgatagarbha." In *Encyclopedia of Buddhism.* Edited by Robert Buswell. New York: MacMillan.

Guillon, Emmanuel. 1983. "Notes sur le bouddhisme Mōn." *Nachrichten der Akademie der Wissenschaften Göttingen, Philologisch-Historische Klasse.* Pp. 43–76

Gunasekara, B. 1900. *The Rājāvaliya or a Historical Narrative of Sinhalese Kings.* Colombo: George J. A. Skeen.

Gunawardana, R.A.L.H. 1979. *Robe and Plough: Monasticism and Economic Interest in Early Medieval Sri Lanka.* Tucson: University of Arizona Press.

Gyatso, Janet. 1996. "Drawn from the Tibetan Treasury: The *gTer ma* Literature. In *Tibetan Literature: Studies in Genre.* Edited by José Ignacio Cabezón and Roger R. Jackson. Ithaca: Snow Lion. Pp. 147–69.

Ha Tae-hung and Grafton K. Mintz. 1972. *Samguk Yusa: Legends and History of the Three Kingdoms of Ancient Korea.* Seoul: Yonsei University Press.

Hall, H. Fielding. 1914. *The Soul of a People.* London: MacMillan.

Halliday, Robert. 1917. *The Talaings.* Rangoon: Superintendent of Government Printing.

———. 1923. "*Slapat Rājāwan Datow Smin Ron:* A History of Kings." *Journal of the Burma Research Society* 13:5–67.

Hallisey, Charles. 1996. "Relics as Memory Sites in the Buddhist Literature of Medieval Sri Lanka." Paper presented to the American Academy of Religion Seminar on Buddhist Relics, New Orleans.

Hallpike, Christopher. 1987. "Hair." In *Encyclopedia of Religion.* Edited by Mircea Eliade. New York: MacMillan. 6:154–57.

Hamilton, Sue. 1995. "From the Buddha to Buddhaghosa: Changing Attitudes toward the Human Body in Theravāda Buddhism." In *Religious Reflections on the Human Body.* Edited by Jane Marie Law. Bloomington: Indiana University Press. Pp. 46–63.

Han Jinke. 1994. *Fa Men Temple.* N.p.: Shaanxi Tourism.

Handurukande, Ratna. 1967. "Aśokamukha-nāgavinaya-pariccheda." In *Encyclopaedia of Buddhism.* Edited by G. P. Malalasekera. Colombo: Government of Ceylon Press. 2:196–97.

Hara, Minoru. 1980. "A Note on the Buddha's Birthstory." *Indianisme et bouddhisme.* Louvain: Institut Orientaliste. Pp. 142–57.

Hardy, R. Spence. [1850] 1989. *Eastern Monachism.* Delhi: Sri Satguru.

———. [1853] 1995. *A Manual of Buddhism.* New Delhi: Munshiram Manoharlal.

Harrison, Paul. 1992. "Is the Dharma-kāya the Real 'Phantom Body' of the Buddha?" *Journal of the International Association of Buddhist Studies* 15:44–94.

———. 1998. *The Pratyutpanna Samādhi Sutra.* Berkeley: Numata Center for Buddhist Translation and Research.

Hart, Virgil C. [1888] 1972. *Western China. A Journey to the Great Buddhist Centre of Mount Omei.* Taipei: Ch'eng Wen.

Härtel, Herbert. 1991. "Archaeological Research on Ancient Buddhist Sites." *The Dating of the Historical Buddha / Die Datierung des historischen Buddha.* Edited by Heinz Bechert. Göttingen: Vandenhoeck and Ruprecht. 1:61–84.

Hartman, Charles. 1986. *Han Yü and the T'ang Search for Unity.* Princeton: Princeton University Press.

Harvey, Peter. 1984. "The Symbolism of the Stūpa." *Journal of the International Association of Buddhist Studies* 7:67–93.

Hazlewood, Ann Appleby. 1986. *In Praise of Mount Samanta.* London: Pali Text Society.

Head, Thomas. 1993. "Bodies of Truth: The Genesis and Abandonment of the Ritual Proof of Relics by Fire." Paper delivered to the Davis Seminar, Princeton University.

Heiler, Friedrich. 1961. "Reliquien." In *Die Religion in Geschichte und Gegenwart.* 3rd. ed. Tübingen: J.C.B. Mohr. 5:1043–47.

Henderson, Gregory, and Leon Hurvitz. 1956. "The Buddha of Seiryōji." *Artibus Asiae* 19:5–55.

Herath, Dharmaratna. 1994. *The Tooth Relic and the Crown.* Colombo: n.p.

Hertz, Robert. 1960. "A Contribution to the Study of Collective Representations of Death." In *Death and the Right Hand.* Trans. Rodney and Claudia Needham. Glencoe: Free Press. Pp. 27–86.

Hettiaratchi, S. B. 1994. "Arrival of *Bodhaharakulas*—the Great Attempt to Indianize the Island." In *Maha Bodhi Tree in Anuradhapura, Sri Lanka.* Edited by H.S.S. Nissanka. New Delhi: Vikas. Pp. 66–89.

Hickman, Brian. 1975. "A Note on the Hyakumantō Dhāraṇī." *Monumenta Nipponica* 30:87–93.

Higashimoto, Keiki, and S. K. Nanayakkara. 1972. "Bodhi Tree." In *Encyclopaedia of Buddhism.* Edited by G. P. Malalasekera. Colombo: Government of Ceylon Press. 3:249–52.

Hiltebeitel, Alf. 1998. "Introduction: Hair Tropes." In *Hair: Its Power and Meaning in Asian Cultures.* Edited by Alf Hiltebeitel and Barbara D. Miller. Albany: State University of New York Press. Pp. 1–9.

Hirakawa Akira. 1963. "The Rise of Mahāyāna Buddhism and Its Relationship to the Worship of Stūpas." *Memoirs of the Research Department of the Toyo Bunko* 22:57–106.

Hman-Nan-Yazawindawgyi [Glass Palace Chronicle]. 1883. Mandalay: n.p.

Hocart, A. M. 1931. *The Temple of the Tooth in Kandy.* London: Luzac.

Hofinger, Marcel. 1954. *Le congrès du Lac Anavatapta (vies de saint bouddhiques).* Louvain: Le Muséon.

Holt, John Clifford. 1991. *Buddha in the Crown: Avalokiteśvara in the Buddhist Traditions of Sri Lanka.* New York: Oxford University Press.

———. 1996. *The Religious World of Kīrti Śrī.* New York: Oxford University Press.

Horner, I. B. 1938–52. *The Book of the Discipline.* 6 vols. London: Pali Text Society.

———. 1954–59. *The Collection of the Middle Length Sayings.* 3 vols. London: Pali Text Society.

———. 1975. *The Minor Anthologies of the Pali Canon, Part III.* London: Pali Text Society.

———. 1978. *The Clarifier of the Sweet Meaning (Madhuratthavilāsinī).* London: Pali Text Society.

Hou Ching-lang. 1984. "La cérémonie du Yin-cha-fa d'après les manuscrits de Touen-houang." *Contributions aux études de Touen-houang.* Paris: Ecole Française d'Extrême-Orient. 3:205–33.

Huang Chi-chiang. 1998. "Consecrating the Buddha: Legend, Lore, and History of the Imperial Relic-Veneration Ritual in the T'ang Dynasty." *Chung-Hwa Buddhist Journal* 11:483–533.

Huber, Edouard. 1908. *Açvaghoṣa Sūtrālaṃkāra.* Paris: Ernest Leroux.

Hubert, Henri, and Marcel Mauss. 1964. *Sacrifice, Its Nature and Function.* Translated by W. D. Halls. Chicago: University of Chicago Press.

Hudson, D. Dennis. 1997. "The Courtesan and Her Bowl: An Esoteric Buddhist Reading of the *Maṇimēkalai.*" In *A Buddhist Woman's Path to Enlightenment.* Edited by Peter Schalk. Uppsala: Uppsala University. Pp. 151–90.

Hummel, Siegfried. 1971. "Die Fusspur des Gautama-Buddha auf dem Wu-t'ai shan." *Asiatische Studien/ Etudes asiatiques* 25:389–406.

Huntington, John C. 1986. "Sowing the Seeds of the Lotus. A Journey to the Great Pilgrimage Sites of Buddhism, Part III." *Orientations* 17, 3:32–46.

Huntington, Susan L. 1990. "Early Buddhist Art and the Theory of Aniconism." *The Art Journal* 49:401–8.

———. 1992. "Aniconism and the Multivalence of Emblems: Another Look." *Ars Orientalis* 22:111–56.

Hurvitz, Leon. 1976. *Scripture of the Lotus Blossom of the Fine Dharma.* New York: Columbia University Press.

Hussein, Mahdi. 1976. *The Reḥla of Ibn Battūta (India, Maldive Islands and Ceylon).* Baroda: Oriental Institute.

Irwin, John. 1973. "'Aśokan' Pillars: A Reassessment of the Evidence." *The Burlington Magazine* 115:706–20.

Itivuttaka. 1890. Edited by E. Windisch. London: Pali Text Society.

Iwamoto Yutaka. 1968. *Sumāgadhāvadāna.* Studien zur buddhistischen Erzählungsliteratur, 2. Kyoto: Hōzōkan.

Jacobs, Alfred. 1860. "Le bouddhisme et son législateur." *Revue des deux mondes* 26:108–32.

Jaini, Padmanabh S. 1979. *The Jaina Path of Purification.* Berkeley: University of California Press.

———. 1986. *Apocryphal Birth-Stories.* 2 vols. London: Pali Text Society.

———. 1988. "Stages in the Bodhisattva Career of the Tathāgata Maitreya." In *Maitreya, the Future Buddha.* Edited by Alan Sponberg and Helen Hardacre. Cambridge: Cambridge University Press. Pp. 54–90.

Jan Yün-hua. 1964. "Buddhist Self-Immolation in Medieval China." *History of Religions* 4:243–68.

———. 1966. *A Chronicle of Buddhism in China 581–960 A.D.* Santiniketan: Visvabharati.

Jātaka Together with Its Commentary. 1877–96. 6 vols. Edited by V. Fausboll. London: Pali Text Society.

Jātakamālā by Ārya Śūra. 1959. Edited by P. L. Vaidya. Darbhanga: Mithila Institute.

Jayaswal, K. P. 1934. *An Imperial History of India in a Sanskrit Text.* Lahore: Motilal Banarsidass.

Jayawickrama, N. A. 1962. *The Inception of Discipline and the Vinaya Nidāna.* London: Luzac.

———. 1968. *The Sheaf of Garlands of the Epochs of the Conqueror.* London: Pali Text Society.

———. 1971. *The Chronicle of the Thūpa and the Thūpavaṃsa.* London: Pali Text Society.

———. 1990. *The Story of Gotama Buddha (Jātaka-nidāna).* London: Pali Text Society.

Jinakālamālī. 1962. Edited by A. P. Buddhadatta. London: Pali Text Society.

Johnston, E. H. [1936] 1972. *The Buddhacarita or Acts of the Buddha.* Delhi: Motilal Banarsidass.

———. 1937. "The Buddha's Mission and Last Journey (Buddhacarita xv to xxviii)." *Acta Orientalia* 15:26–62, 85–111, 231–92.

Jones, J. J. 1949–56. *The Mahāvastu.* 3 vols. London: Pali Text Society.

U Kala. 1960. *Mahāyazawingyi* . Vol. 1. Edited by U. Pwa. Rangoon: Burma Research Society.

Kaltenmark, Max. 1960. "Ling-pao: Note sur un terme du Taoïsme religieux." In *Mélanges publiés par l'Institut des Hautes Etudes Chinoises.* Paris: Presses Universitaires de France. 2:559–88.

Kane, Pandurang Vaman. 1973. *History of Dharmaśāstra.* Vol. 4. 2nd. ed. Poona: Bhandarkar Oriental Research Institute.

Karunaratne, Indumathie. 1984. "Daḷadā." In *Encyclopaedia of Buddhism.* Edited by Jotiya Dhirasekera. Colombo: Government of Sri Lanka Printing Press. 4:282–87.

Karunaratne, T. B. 1976. "The Significance of the Signs and Symbols on the Footprints of the Buddha." *Journal of the Sri Lanka Branch of the Royal Asiatic Society* n.s. 20:47–63.

Kemper, Steven E. G. 1991. *The Presence of the Past: Chronicles, Politics, and Culture in Sinhala Life.* Ithaca: Cornell University Press.

Kern, Hendrik. 1884. *Saddharma-Puṇḍarīka or the Lotus of the True Law.* Oxford: Clarendon.

Khantipālo (Bhikkhu). 1980. *Bag of Bones: A Miscellany on the Body.* The Wheel, no. 271–272. Kandy: Buddhist Publication Society.

Khoroche, Peter. 1989. *Once the Buddha Was a Monkey: Ārya Śūra's Jātakamālā.* Chicago: University of Chicago Press.

Khuddaka-Pāṭha Together with Its Commentary, Paramatthajotikā I. [1915] 1978. Edited by Helmer Smith. London: Pali Text Society.

Kidder, J. Edward. 1992. "Busshari and Fukuzō: Buddhist Relics and Hidden Repositories of Hōryū-ji." *Japanese Journal of Religious Studies* 19: 217–44.

Kieschnick, John. 1997. *The Eminent Monk: Buddhist Ideals in Medieval Chinese Hagiography.* Honolulu: Kuroda Institute.

———. 2003. *The Impact of Buddhism on Chinese Material Culture.* Princeton: Princeton University Press.

U Kin. 1957. *Maha-win wutthu.* Vol. 1. Rangoon: Hathawaddy.

———. 1981. *Jinathapakāsini.* Rangoon: Kayasukha.

Kinnard, Jacob N. 1999. *Imaging Wisdom: Seeing and Knowing in the Art of Indian Buddhism.* Delhi: Motilal Banarsidass.

———. 2000. "The Polyvalent Pādas of Viṣṇu and the Buddha." *History of Religions* 40:32–57.

Kloppenborg, Ria. 1973. *The Sūtra on the Foundation of the Buddhist Order.* Leiden: E. J. Brill.

———. 1974. *The Paccekabuddha: A Buddhist Ascetic.* Leiden: E. J. Brill.

Knox, Robert. 1958. *An Historical Relation of Ceylon.* Dehiwala: Tisara Prakasakayo.

U Ko Ko. 1983. [Untitled translations]. 2 vols. Mandalay, unpublished manuscript.

Konow, Sten. [1929] 1991. *Kharoshṭhī Inscriptions.* New Delhi: Archaeological Survey of India.

———. 1941. *The Two First Chapters of the Daśasāhasrikā Prajñāpāramitā.* Oslo: Jacob Dybwad.

Kottkamp, Heino. 1992. *Der Stūpa als Repräsentation des buddhistischen Heilsweges.* Wiesbaden: Otto Harrassowitz.

Krishnarao, Bhavaraj V. 1929. "The Identification of Kalinganagara." *Journal of the Bihar and Orissa Research Society* 15:105–15.

Kuwayama, Shoshin. 1982. "Kāpiśī and Gandhāra according to Chinese Buddhist Sources." *Orient* [Tokyo] 18:135–39.

———. 1990. "The Buddha's Bowl in Gandhāra and Relevant Problems." In *South Asian Archaeology, 1987.* Edited by M. Taddei. Rome: Istituto Italiano per il Medio ed Estremo Oriente. Pp. 945–78.

Lafont, Pierre Bernard. 1957. "Le That de Muong-Sing." *Bulletin de la Société des Études Indochinoises.* n.s. 32:39–57.

Lagerwey, John. 1998. "Dingguang Gufo: Oral and Written Sources in the Study of a Saint." *Cahiers d'Extrême-Asie* 10:77–129.

Lagirarde, François. 2000. "Gavampati et la tradition des quatre-vingts disciples du Buddha." *Bulletin de l'Ecole Française d'Extrême-Orient* 87:57–78.

Lahiri, Latika. 1986. *Chinese Monks in India: Biography of Eminent Monks Who Went to the Western World in Search of the Law During the Great T'ang Dynasty by I-ching.* Delhi: Motilal Banarsidass.

Lalitavistara. 1902. Edited by Salomon Lefmann. Halle: Verlag der Buchhandlung des Waisenhauses.

Lamotte, Etienne. 1949–80. *Le traité de la grande vertu de sagesse.* 5 vols. Louvain: Institut Orientaliste.

———. 1965. "Le suicide religieux dans le bouddhisme ancien." *Bulletin de la Classe des Lettres et Sciences Morales et Politiques, Académie de Belgique.* 51:156–68.

———. 1975. *La concentration de la marche héroïque (Śūraṃgamasamādhisūtra).* Brussels: Institut Belge des Hautes Etudes Chinoises.

———. 1988. *History of Indian Buddhism.* Translated by Sara Webb-Boin. Louvain-la-Neuve: Institut Orientaliste.

Lancaster, Lewis R. 1974. "An Early Mahāyāna Sermon about the Body of the Buddha and the Making of Images." *Artibus Asize* 36:287–91.

———. 1979. *The Korean Buddhist Canon: A Descriptive Catalogue*. Berkeley: University of California Press.

Lang, Karen. 1995. "Shaven Heads and Loose Hair: Buddhist Attitudes towards Hair and Sexuality." In *Off with Her Head*. Edited by Howard Eilberg-Schwartz and Wendy Doniger. Berkeley: University of California Press. Pp. 32–52.

La Vallée Poussin, Louis de. 1919. "Quelques observations sur le suicide dans le bouddhisme ancien." *Bulletin de la classe des lettres et sciences morales et politiques, Académie de Belgique*. Pp. 692ff.

———. [1923–31] 1980. *L'Abhidharmakośa de Vasubandhu*. 6 vols. Brussels: Institut Belge des Hautes Etudes Chinoises.

———. 1928. "Les neuf kalpas qu'a franchis Śākyamuni pour devancer Maitreya." *T'oung pao* 26:17–24.

Law, Bimala Churn. 1925. *The Dāṭhāvaṃsa (A History of the Tooth-relic of the Buddha)*. Lahore: Punjab Sanskrit Book Depot.

———. 1952. *The History of the Buddha's Religion (Sāsanavaṃsa)*. Delhi: Sri Satguru.

———. 1960–61. "A Chronicle of the Buddha's Six Hair Relics." *Ceylon Historical Journal* 10:31–42.

Leach, E. R. 1958. "Magical Hair." *Journal of the Royal Anthropological Institute* 88:147–68.

Leclère, Adhémard. 1899. *Le Buddhisme au Cambodge*. Paris: E. Leroux.

Lee, Peter H. 1969. *Lives of Eminent Monks*. Cambridge: Harvard University Press.

Legge, James. [1886] 1965. *A Record of Buddhistic Kingdoms*. New York: Paragon.

Leksukhum, Santi. 2000. *Temples of Gold. Seven Centuries of Thai Buddhist Paintings*. Translated by Kenneth D. Whitehead. New York: George Braziller.

Leumann, Ernst. 1919. *Maitreya-samiti, das Zukunftsideal der Buddhisten*. Strassburg: Trübner.

Lévi, Sylvain. 1907–11. *Mahāyāna-Sūtrālaṃkāra: Exposé de la doctrine du grand véhicule selon le système Yogācāra*. 2 vols. Paris: Honoré Champion.

———. 1910. "Textes sanskrits de Touen-houang." *Journal asiatique* 16:433–56.

———. 1930. "Manimekhalā, a Divinity of the Sea." *Indian Historical Quarterly* 6:597–614.

———. 1932. "Maitreya le consolateur." In *Etudes d'orientalisme publiées par le Musée Guimet à la mémoire de Raymonde Linossier*. Paris: E. Leroux. Pp. 355–402.

Lévi, Sylvain, and Edouard Chavannes. 1916. "Les seize arhats protecteurs de la loi." *Journal Asiatique* 8:5–48, 189–304.

Lévy-Bruhl, Lucien. 1926. *How Natives Think*. Translated by Lilian A. Clare. London: George Allen and Unwin.

Lewis, Todd T. 1994. "Contributions to the History of Buddhist Ritualism: A Mahāyāna Avadāna on Caitya Veneration from the Kathmandu Valley." *Journal of Asian History* 28:1–38.

Ling, Trevor. 1973. *The Buddha. Buddhist Civilization in India and Ceylon*. London: Temple Smith.

Lingat, Robert. 1930. "History of Wat Mahādhātu." *Journal of the Siam Society* 24:1–27.

———. 1965. "Les suicides religieux au Siam." *Felicitation Volume of Southeast Asian Studies Presented to His Highness Prince Dhanninivat Kromanmany Bidyalabh Bridyatorn.* Bangkok: Siam Society. 1:71–75.

Li Rongxi. 1961. *The Sixteen Arhats and the Eighteen Arhats.* Beijing: The Buddhist Association of China.

———. 1993. *The Biographical Scripture of King Aśoka.* Berkeley: Numata Center for Buddhist Translation and Research.

———. 1995. *A Biography of the Tripiṭaka Master of the Great Ci'en Monastery of the Great Tang Dynasty.* Berkeley: Numata Center for Buddhist Translation and Research.

———. 1996. *The Great Tang Dynasty Record of the Western Regions.* Berkeley: Numata Center for Buddhist Translation and Research.

———. 2000. *Buddhist Monastic Traditions of Southern Asia. A Record of the Inner Law Sent Home from the South Seas by Śramaṇa Yijing.* Berkeley: Numata Center for Buddhist Translation and Research.

———. 2002. "The Journey of the Eminent Monk Faxian." In *Lives of Great Monks and Nuns.* Berkeley: Numata Center for Buddhist Translation and Research. Pp. 155–214.

———. 2002a. "The Life of Aśvaghoṣa Bodhisattva." In *Lives of Great Monks and Nuns.* Berkeley: Numata Center for Buddhist Translation and Research. Pp. 3–13.

Liu Xinru. 1996. *Silk and Religion.* New Delhi: Oxford University Press.

Liyanaratne, Jinadasa. 1983. "La Jinabodhāvalī de Devarakkhita Jayabāhu Dhammakitti." *Bulletin de l'Ecole Française d'Extrême-Orient* 72: 49–80.

Lopez, Donald S. 1995. *Curators of the Buddha: The Study of Buddhism under Colonialism.* Chicago: University of Chicago Press.

Lorillard, Michel. 2000. "Aux origines du bouddhisme siamois. Le cas des buddhapāda." *Bulletin de l'Ecole Française d'Extrême-Orient* 87:23–55.

Low, James. 1848. "Gleanings in Buddhism; or translations of Passages from a Siamese version of a Pali work, termed in Siamese 'Phrâ Pat'hom,' with passing observations on Buddhism and Brahmanism." *Journal of the Royal Asiatic Society of Bengal* 17:72–98.

Lüders, Heinrich. [1912] 1973. *A List of Brahmi Inscriptions from the Earliest Times to about* A.D. *400 with the Exception of those of Asoka.* Varanasi: Indological Book House.

———. 1963. *Bharhut Inscriptions.* Rev. ed. Ooctacamund: Government Epigraphist for India.

Ludowyk, E.F.C. 1958. *The Footprint of the Buddha.* London: George Allen and Unwin.

MacCulloch, J. A. 1921. "Teeth." *Encyclopaedia of Religion and Ethics.* Edited by James Hastings. Edinburgh: T. and T. Clark. 12:215.

Madhuratthavilāsinī nāma Buddhavaṃsaṭṭhakathā of Bhadantācariya Buddhadatta Mahāthera. 1978. Edited by I. B. Horner. London: Pali Text Society.

Mahā-Bodhi-Vaṃsa. 1891. Edited by S. Arthur Strong. London: Pali Text Society.

Mahāvaṃsa. 1908. Edited by Wilhelm Geiger. London: Pali Text Society.

Mahāvastu. 1882–97. 3 vols. Edited by Emile Sénart. Paris: Imprimerie Nationale.

Majjhima Nikāya. 1888–99. 3 vols. Edited by V. Trenckner and R. Chalmers. London: Pali Text Society.

Makransky, John J. 1997. *Buddhahood Embodied*. Albany: State University of New York Press.

Malalasekera, G. P. 1928. *The Pali Literature of Ceylon*. London: Royal Asiatic Society.

———. [1938] 1960. *Dictionary of Pali Proper Names*. 2 vols. London: Pali Text Society.

Malalgoda, Kitsiri. 1976. *Buddhism in Sinhalese Society 1750–1900*. Berkeley: University of California Press.

Manorathapūraṇī: Buddhaghosa's Commentary on the Anguttara Nikāya. 1924–57. 5 vols. Edited by M. Walleser and H. Kopf. London: Pali Text Society.

Manowattanan, Kan. 1995. "The Saraburi Footprint: Buddhist Symbolism and Political Legitimation in Thailand." Paper presented at the seminar on "Buddhist Relics: Myths, Legends and Rituals," University of Chicago.

Marshall, John. 1902–3. "Buddhist Gold Jewellery." *Annual Report of the Archaeological Survey of India*. Pp. 185–94.

———. 1910–11. "Excavations at Sahēṭh-Mahēṭh." *Annual Report of the Archaeological Survey of India*. pp. 1–24.

———. 1936. *A Guide to Taxila*. 3rd. ed. Delhi: Manager of Publications.

———. 1953. *A Guide to Sanchi*. 3rd. ed. Calcutta: Government of India Press.

Martin, Dan. 1992. "Crystals and Images from Bodies, Hearts and Tongues from Fire: Points of Relic Controversy from Tibetan History." *Tibetan Studies: Proceedings of the Fifth Seminar of the International Association for Tibetan Studies, 1989*. Narita: Naritasan Shinshoji. Pp. 183–91.

———. 1994. "Pearls from Bones: Relics, Chortens, Tertons and the Signs of Saintly Death in Tibet." *Numen* 41:273–324.

Martini, Ginette. 1969. "Pañcabuddhabyākaraṇa." *Bulletin de l'Ecole Française d'Extrême-Orient* 55:125–44.

———. 1973. "*Brapaṃsukūlānisaṃsam.*" *Bulletin de l'Ecole Française d'Extrême-Orient* 60:55–76.

Masefield, Peter. 1986. *Divine Revelation in Pali Buddhism*. London: George Allen and Unwin.

———. 1994–95. *The Udāna Commentary*. 2 vols. Oxford: Pali Text Society.

Maspero, Henri. 1914. "Rapport sommaire sur une mission archéologique au Tchö-kiang." *Bulletin de l'Ecole Française d'Extrême-Orient* 14:1–75.

Maung Kin. 1903. "The Legend of Upagutta." *Buddhism* (Rangoon) 1:219–42.

Mauss. Marcel. 1972. *A General Theory of Magic*. Translated by Robert Brain. New York: W. W. Norton.

Mayer, Robert. 1997. "Caskets of Treasures and Visions of Buddhas: Indian Antecedents of the Tibetan gTer-ma Tradition." In *Indian Insights: Buddhism, Brahmanism and Bhakti*. Edited by Peter Connolly and Sue Hamilton. London: Luzac Oriental. Pp. 137–51.

McCallum, Donald F. 1994. *Zenkōji and its Icon: A Study in Medieval Japanese Religious Art*. Princeton: Princeton University Press.

McCullough, Helen Craig. 1979. *The Taiheiki: A Chronicle of Medieval Japan.* Rutland: Charles E. Tuttle.

Meddegama, Udaya, and John Clifford Holt. 1993. *Anāgatavaṃsa Desanā: The Sermon of the Chronicle-to-be.* Delhi: Motilal Banarsidass.

Michaelson, Carol. 1999. *Gilded Dragons: Buried Treasures from China's Golden Ages.* London: British Museum Press.

Migot, André. 1954. "Un grand disciple du Bouddha, Śāriputra." *Bulletin de l'Ecole Française d'Extrême-Orient 46:405–554.*

Milindapañho. 1880. Edited by V. Trenckner. London: Williams and Norgate.

Miller, Roy Andrew. 1975. *"The Footprints of the Buddha": An Eighth-Century Old Japanese Poetic Sequence.* New Haven: American Oriental Society.

Mills, Douglas E. 1960. "The Buddha's Footprint Stone Poems." *Journal of the American Oriental Society* 80:229–42.

Mingun Sayadaw. 1990–98. *The Great Chronicle of Buddhas.* 6 vols. Translated by U Tin Lwin and U Tin Oo (Myaung). Yangon: Ti-Ni Publishing Center.

Mitchiner, John E. 1982. *Traditions of the Seven Ṛṣis.* Delhi: Motilal Banarsidass.

Mitomo Ryōjun. 1984. "An Aspect of Dharma-śarīra." *Indogaku bukkyōgaku kenkyū / Journal of Indian and Buddhist Studies* 32:1120–15 (*sic*).

Mitra, Debala. 1971. *Buddhist Monuments.* Calcutta: Sahitya Samsad.

Mitra, Rajendralala. 1881. *The Lalita-Vistara or Memoirs of the Early Life of Śākya Siñha.* Calcutta: Asiatic Society.

———. 1972. *Buddha Gaya: The Great Buddhist Temple.* Reprint edition. Delhi: Indological Book House.

Monier-Williams, Monier. [1889] 1964. *Buddhism in its Connexion with Brāhmanism and Hindūism and in Its Contrast with Christianity.* Reprint edition. Varanasi: Chowkhamba Sanskrit Series Office.

———. 1899. *Sanskrit-English Dictionary.* Oxford: Clarendon.

Monius, Anne E. 2001. *Imagining a Place for Buddhism: Literary Culture and Religious Community in Tamil-Speaking South India.* Oxford: Oxford University Press.

Mukherjee, Biswadeb. 1966. *Die Überlieferung von Devadatta, dem Widersacher des Buddha in den kanonischen Schriften.* Munich: J. Kitzinger.

Mus, Paul. 1928. "Le Buddha paré. Son origine indienne. Śākyamuni dans le Mahāyānisme moyen." *Bulletin de l'Ecole Française d'Extrême-Orient* 28: 153–85.

———. 1934. "Barabuḍur, Sixième partie: Genèse de la bouddhologie mahāyāniste." *Bulletin de l'Ecole Française d'Extrême-Orient* 34:175–400.

———. 1935. *Barabuḍur: Esquisse d'une histoire du bouddhisme fondée sur la critique archéologique des textes.* 2 vols. Hanoi: Imprimerie d'Extrême-Orient.

———. 1937. "La tombe vivante." *La terre et la vie* 4:117–27.

———. 1938. "Hiuan-tsang et ses stūpas d'Açoka." *Atti del XIX Congresso Internazionale degli Orientalisti, Roma 1935.* Rome.

———. 1964. "Un cinéma solide." *Arts asiatiques* 10:21–34.

———. 1964a. "Thousand-Armed Kannon: A Mystery or a Problem?" *Indogaku bukkyōgaku kenkyū / Journal of Indian and Buddhist Studies* 12:1–33.

———. 1998. *Barabuḍur: Sketch of a History of Buddhism Based on Archaeological Criticism of Texts.* Translated by Alexander W. MacDonald. Delhi: Indira Gandhi National Centre for the Arts.

Mutsu Iso. 1918. *Kamakura, Fact and Legend.* Tokyo: Times Publishing Co.

U Mya. 1936. "A Note on the Buddha's Foot-Prints in Burma." *Annual Reports of the Archaeological Survey Of India for the Years 1930–31, 1931–32, 1932–33 & 1933–34.* Delhi: Manager of Publications. Part 2, pp. 320–31.

Nakamura Hajime. 2000. *Gotama Buddha: A Biography Based on the Most Reliable Texts.* Translated by Gaynor Sekimori. Vol. 1. Tokyo: Kosei.

Ñāṇamoli Bhikkhu. See also Ñyaṇamoli Bhikkhu.

———. 1996. *The Dispeller of Delusion (Sammohavinodanī).* 2 vols. Revised for publication by L. S. Cousins, Nyanaponika Mahāthera, and C.M.M. Shaw. Oxford: Pali Text Society.

———. 1997. *The Minor Readings.* Oxford: Pali Text Society.

Nantakumār, Pirēmā. 1997. "The Magic Bowl in the *Maṇimēkalai.*" In *A Buddhist Woman's Path to Enlightenment.* Edited by Peter Schalk. Uppsala: Uppsala University. Pp. 133–50.

Narada Thera. 1953. "Ma visite au Vietnam et au Cambodge." Translated by René de Berval. *France-Asie* 87:665–71.

Nattier, Jan. 1991. *Once upon a Future Time: Studies in a Buddhist Prophecy of Decline.* Berkeley: Asian Humanities Press.

———. Forthcoming. "Buddha(s)." In *Encyclopedia of Buddhism.* Edited by Robert Buswell. New York: MacMillan.

Naudou, Jean. 1968. *Les bouddhistes kaśmīriens au moyen age.* Paris: Presses Universitaires de France.

Nikam, N. A., and Richard McKeon. 1959. *The Edicts of Asoka.* Chicago: University of Chicago Press.

Nishiwaki, Tsuneki. 1992. "Die Reliquienverehrung (Śarīra) und ihre Beschreibung in den Mönchbiographien." *Monumenta Serica* 40:87–120.

Nissanka, H.S.S. 1994. *Maha Bodhi Tree in Anuradhapura, Sri Lanka.* New Delhi: Vikas.

Niwa Motoji. 1992. *Sekai no bussokuseki: bussokuseki kara mita Bukkyō / Buddha's Footprints: Pictures and Explanations: Buddhism as Seen Through the Footprints of Buddha.* Tokyo: Meicho Shuppan.

Nobel, Johannes. 1958. *Suvarṇaprabhāsottamasūtra. Das Goldglanz-Sūtra. Ein Sanskrittext des Mahāyāna-Buddhismus.* Leiden: Brill.

Norman, K. R. 1969–71. *The Elders' Verses.* 2 vols. London: Pali Text Society.

———. 1983. "The Pratyeka-Buddha in Buddhism and Jainism." *Buddhist Studies Ancient and Modern.* Edited by Philip Denwood and Alexander Piatigorsky. London: Curzon.

———. 1990–92. *Collected Papers.* 3 vols. Oxford: Pali Text Society.

———. 1996. *The Rhinoceros Horn and Other Early Buddhist Poems.* Oxford: Pali Text Society.

Notton, Camille. 1926–32. *Annales du Siam.* 3 vols. Paris: Charles Lavauzelle.

Nouth Oun. 1953. "Arrivée d'une relique du Bouddha à Phnom-Penh." *France-Asie* 90:1025–28.

Ñyāṇamoli Bhikkhu. See also Ñāṇamoli Bhikkhu.

———. 1976. *The Path of Purification*. 2 vols. Berkeley: Shambhala.

Nyanaponika Thera and Hellmuth Hecker. 1997. *Great Disciples of the Buddha*. Boston: Wisdom.

Obermiller, E. 1931–32. *History of Buddhism (Chos-hbyung) by Bu-ston*. 2 vols. Heidelberg: O. Harrassowitz.

Obeyesekere, Gananath. 1966. "The Buddhist Pantheon in Ceylon and Its Extensions." In *Anthropological Studies in Theravada Buddhism*. Edited by Manning Nash. New Haven: Yale University Southeast Asia Studies. Pp. 1--26.

———. 1981. *Medusa's Hair*. Chicago: University of Chicago Press.

———. 1984. *The Cult of the Goddess Pattini*. Chicago: University of Chicago Press.

Obeyesekere, Ranjini. 2001. *Portraits of Buddhist Women: Stories from the Saddharmaratnāvaliya*. Albany: State University of New York Press.

[O'Flaherty], Wendy Doniger. 1988. *Other Peoples' Myths*. New York: MacMillan.

Ohnuki-Tierney, Emiko. 1994. "The Power of Absence: Zero Signifiers and Their Transgressions." *L'homme* 130:57–75.

Ohnuma, Reiko. 1998. "The Gift of the Body and the Gift of Dharma." *History of Religions* 37:323–59.

Oldenberg, Hermann. [1886] 1981. *The Gṛhya-sūtras: Rules of Vedic Domestic Ceremonies*. Delhi: Motilal Banarsidass.

———. [1879] 1982. *The Dīpavaṃsa: An Ancient Buddhist Historical Record*. Reprint edition. New Delhi: Asian Educational Services.

———. 1928. *Buddha: His Life, His Doctrine, His Order*. Translated by William Hoey. London: Luzac.

Olivelle, Patrick. 1996. *Upanishads*. New York: Oxford University Press.

———. 1998. "Hair and Society: Social Significance of Hair in South Asian Traditions." In *Hair: Its Power and Meaning in Asian Cultures*. Edited by Alf Hiltebeitel and Barbara D. Miller. Albany: State University of New York Press. Pp. 11–50.

Olshki, Leonardo. 1950. "The Crib of Christ and the Bowl of the Buddha." *Journal of the American Oriental Society* 70:161–64.

Ono Katsutoshi. 1964–69. *Nittō guhō junrei kōki no kenkyū*. 4 vols. Tokyo: Suzuki gakujutsu zaidan.

Pal, Pratapaditya. 1971–72. "The *Aiḍūka* of the *Viṣṇudharmottarapurāṇa* and Certain Aspects of Stūpa Symbolism." *Jounal of the Indian Society of Oriental Art,* n.s. 4:49–62.

Pandit, Ranjit Sitaram. 1968. *Rājataraṅgiṇī: The Saga of the Kings of Kaśmīr*. New Delhi: Sahitya Akademi.

Paññāsa-jātaka or Zimme Paṇṇāsa. 1983. 2 vols. Edited by Padmanabh S. Jaini. London: Pali Text Society.

Papañcasūdanī Majjhimanikāyaṭṭhakathā of Buddhaghosācariya. 1922–1938. 5 vols. Edited by I. B. Horner. London: Pali Text Society.

Paramaṭṭha-dīpanī: Theragāthā-aṭṭhakathā. 1940–59. 3 vols. Edited by F. L. Woodward. London: Pali Text Society.

Paranavitana, S. 1934–43. "Tiriyāy Rock-Inscription." *Epigraphia Zeylanica* 4:151–60.

———. 1940–47. "Recent Discoveries at the Ruvanvāli Dāgäba (Mahāthūpa) of Anurādhapura." *Annual Bibliography of Indian Archaeology* 15:xlii–xlv.

———. 1946. *The Stūpa in Ceylon.* Colombo: Government Press.

———. 1958. *The God of Adam's Peak.* Ascona: Artibus Asiae.

Parlier, Edith. 1991. "La légende du roi des Śibi: du sacrifice brahmanique au don du corps bouddhique." *Bulletin d'Études Indiennes* 9:133–60.

Parry, Jonathan. 1982. "Sacrificial Death and the Necrophagous Ascetic." In *Death and the Regeneration of Life.* Edited by Maurice Bloch and Jonathan Parry. Cambridge: Cambridge University Press. Pp. 74–110.

———. 1994. *Death in Banaras.* Cambridge: Cambridge University Press.

Patrul Rinpoche. 1994. *Words of My Perfect Teacher.* Translated by the Padmakara Translation Group. Walnut Creek, Calif.: Altamira.

Pearn, B. R. 1939. *A History of Rangoon.* Rangoon: American Baptist Mission Press.

Pelliot, Paul. 1907. "Une bibliothèque médiévale retrouvée au Kan-sou." *Bulletin de l'Ecole Française d'Extrême-Orient* 7:501–29.

———. 1936. "A propos du Tokharien." *T'oung pao* 32:259–84.

Pe Maung Tin. 1934. "The Shwe Dagon Pagoda." *Journal of the Burma Research Society* 24:1–91.

Peppé, William Claxton. 1898. "The Piprāhwā Stūpa, Containing Relics of Buddha." *Journal of the Royal Asiatic Society.* Pp. 573–88.

Perera, H. R. 1971. "Buddhapāda." In *Encyclopedia of Buddhism.* Edited by G. P. Malalasekera. Colombo: Government Press. 3:450–58.

Péri, Noël. 1916. "Le dieu wei-t'o." *Bulletin de l'Ecole Française d'Extrême-Orient* 16:41–56.

Petech, Luciano. 1966–74. "La description des pays d'occident de Che Taongan." In *Mélanges de sinologie offerts à Monsieur Paul Demiéville.* Paris: Institut des Hautes Etudes Chinoises. 1:167–90.

Pichard, Pierre. 1993. "Sous les voûtes de Pagan." *Arts asiatiques* 48:86–109.

Pieris, Aloysius. 1985. "The Cult of the Sacred Tooth Relic—Its Origin and Meaning." *Dialogue* (Colombo), n.s. 10:63–72.

Pieris, Paul E. 1909. *Ribeiro's History of Ceilão.* 2nd ed. Colombo: Colombo Apothecaries.

Pieris, Ralph. 1956. *Sinhalese Social Organization.* Colombo: University of Ceylon Press Board.

Pollock, Sheldon I. 1986. *The Rāmāyaṇa of Vālmīki: An Epic of Ancient India. Volume II: Ayodhyākāṇḍa.* Princeton: Princeton University Press.

Porée-Maspero, Eveline. 1962–69. *Etude sur les rites agraires des Cambodgiens.* 3 vols. Paris: Mouton.

Pragnasara, Kiriwaththuduwe. 1994. "Bodhi Literature in Sri Lanka." In *Maha Bodhi Tree in Anuradhapura, Sri Lanka.* Edited by H.S.S. Nissanka. New Delhi: Vikas. Pp. 169–84.

Prasad, Dharmendra. 1981. "Riddles about the Relics of Sariputra and Mahamodggalana." *Indian Cultures* 36:72–79.

Pratt, James Bissett. 1928. *The Pilgrimage of Buddhism and a Buddhist Pilgrimage*. New York: MacMillan.

Prematilleke, Leelananda. 1966. "Vāhalkaḍas of the Sinhalese Dāgäbas." *The Ceylon Journal of Historical and Social Studies* 9:67–72.

Pridham, Charles. 1849. *An Historical, Political, and Statistical Account of Ceylon and Its Dependencies*. London: T. and W. Boone.

Prip-Moller, Johannes. 1967. *Chinese Buddhist Monasteries: Their Plan and Its Function as a Setting for Buddhist Monastic Life*. 2nd ed. Hongkong: Hongkong University Press.

Pruess, James B. 1976. *The Thāt Phanom Chronicle: A Shrine History and Its Interpretation*. Ithaca: Cornell University Department of Asian Studies.

———. 1976a. "Merit-Seeking in Public: Buddhist Pilgrimage in Northeastern Thailand." *Journal of the Siam Society* 64:169–206.

Przyluski, Jean. 1914. "Le Nord-ouest de l'Inde dans le Vinaya des Mūlasarvāstivādin et les textes apparentés." *Journal asiatique* 4:493–568.

———. 1920. *Le parinirvāṇa et les funérailles du Buddha*. Paris: Imprimerie Nationale.

———. 1923. *La légende de l'empereur Açoka (Açokāvadāna) dans les textes indiens et chinois*. Paris: Paul Geuthner.

———. 1926. *Le concile de Rājagṛha*. Paris: Paul Geuthner.

———. 1927. "La ville du cakravartin: Influences babyloniennes sur la civilisation de l'Inde." *Rocznik Orjentalistyczny* 5:165–85.

———. 1935–36. "Le partage des reliques du Buddha." *Mélanges chinois et bouddhiques* 4:341–67.

Quagliotti, Anna Maria. 1998. *Buddhapadas*. Kamakura: Institute of the Silk Road Studies.

Raghavan, V. 1952 "Yantras or Mechanical Devices in Ancient India." *Transactions of the Indian Institute of Culture* 10:1–31.

Rahula, Walpola. 1956. *History of Buddhism in Ceylon*. Colombo: M. D. Gunasena.

———. 1974. *The Heritage of the Bhikkhu*. New York: Oxford University Press.

Rawlinson, Andrew. 1986. "Nāgas and the Magical Cosmology of Buddhism." *Religion* 16:135–53.

Ray, Reginald A. 1994. *Buddhist Saints in India*. New York: Oxford University Press.

Rea, A. 1908–9. "Excavations at Amaravati." *Annual Report of the Archaeological Survey of India*. Pp. 88–91.

Reat, N. Ross. 1993. *The Śālistamba Sūtra*. Delhi: Motilal Banarsidass.

Reinders, Eric. 1997. "Ritual Topography: Embodiment and Vertical Space in Buddhist Monastic Practice." *History of Religions* 36:244–64.

Reischauer, Edwin O. 1955. *Ennin's Diary: The Record of a Pilrimage to China in Search of the Law*. New York: Ronald.

Reynolds, Frank E. 1976. "The Many Lives of Buddha: A Study of Sacred Biography and Theravada Tradition." In *The Biographical Process*. Edited by Frank E. Reynolds and Donald Capps. The Hague: Mouton. Pp. 37–61.

———. 1977. "The Several Bodies of the Buddha: Reflections on a Neglected Aspect of Theravāda Tradition." *History of Religions* 16:374–89.

Reynolds, Frank E., and Mani B. Reynolds. 1982. *Three Worlds According to King Ruang*. Berkeley: Asian Humanities Press.

Rhum, Michael R. 1994. *The Ancestral Lords*. DeKalb: Northern Illinois University Center for Southeast Asian Studies.

Richman, Paula. 1988. *Women, Branch Stories, and Religious Rhetoric in a Tamil Buddhist Text*. Syracuse: Syracuse University Press.

Robinson, Marguerite. 1968. "'The House of the Mighty Hero' or 'The House of Enough Paddy?' Some Implications of a Sinhalese Myth." In *Dialectic in Practical Religion*. Edited by Edmund R. Leach. Papers in Social Anthropology, no. 5. Cambridge: Cambridge University Press.

Rockhill, W. Woodville. 1907. *The Life of the Buddha*. London: Kegan Paul, Trench, Trübner.

Rosenthal, Franz. 1989. *The History of al-Ṭabarī. Vol. 1: General Introduction and From the Creation to the Flood*. Albany: State University of New York Press.

Roth, Gustav. 1987. "The Physical Presence of the Buddha and Its Representation in Buddhist Literature." In *Investigating Indian Art*. Edited by Marianne Yaldiz and Wibke Lobo. Berlin: Museum für Indische Kunst. Pp. 291–312.

Ruegg, David Seyfort. 1969. *La théorie du tathāgatagarbha et du gotra*. Paris: Ecole Française d'Extrême-Orient.

Ruelius, Hans. 1978. "Netrapratiṣṭhāpana—Eine singhalesische Zeremonie zur Weihe von Kultbildern." In *Buddhism in Ceylon and Studies on Religious Syncretism in Buddhist Countries*. Edited by Heinz Bechert. Göttingen: Vandenhoeck and Ruprecht. Pp. 304–34.

Ruppert, Brian K. 1997. "Buddha Relics and Power in Early Medieval Japan." Princeton University, Ph.D. diss.

———. 2000. *Jewel in the Ashes: Buddha Relics and Power in Early Medieval Japan*. Cambridge: Harvard University Press.

———. 2002a. "Buddhist Rainmaking in Early Japan: The Dragon King and Ritual Careers of Esoteric Monks." *History of Religions* 42:143–74.

———. 2002b. "Pearl in the Shrine: A Genealogy of the Buddhist Jewel of the Japanese Sovereign." *Japanese Journal of Religious Studies* 29:1–33.

Sadakata, Akira. 1997. *Buddhist Cosmology*. Tokyo: Kōsei.

Saddharmapuṇḍarīka Sūtra. 1912. Edited by Hendrik Kern and Bunyo Nanjo. St. Petersburg: Imprimerie de l'Académie Impériale des Sciences.

Saddhatissa, H. 1975. *The Birth-Stories of the Ten Bodhisattas and the Dasabodhisattuppattikathā*. London: Pali Text Society.

Sailer, Waldemar C. 1994. "The Buddha Footprint Tradition." *Lahore Museum Bulletin* 7:65–68.

Sainson, Camille. 1904. *Nan-tchao Ye-che: histoire particulière du Nan-tchao*. Paris.

Salomon, Richard. 1996. "An Inscribed Silver Buddhist Reliquary of the Time of King Kharaosta and Prince Indravarman." *Journal of the American Oriental Society* 116:418–52.

———. 1999. *Ancient Buddhist Scrolls from Gandhāra*. Seattle: University of Washington Press.

Salomon, Richard, and Gregory Schopen. 1984. "The Indravarman (Avaca) Casket Inscription Reconsidered: Further Evidence for Canonical Passages in Buddhist Inscriptions." *The Journal of the International Association of Buddhist Studies* 7:107–23.

Samantakūṭavaṇṇanā of Veheda Thera. 1958. Edited by C. E. Godakumbura. London: Pali Text Society.

Samantapāsādika: Buddhaghosa's Commentary on the Vinaya Piṭaka. 1968. 7 vols. Edited by J. Takakusu and M. Naigai. London: Pali Text Society.

Samyutta Nikāya. 1884–98. 5 vols. Edited by Léon Feer. London: Pali Text Society.

Sāratthappakāsinī. 1929–37. 3 vols. Edited by F. L. Woodward. London: Pali Text Society.

Sāsanavaṃsa. [1897] 1996. Edited by Mabel Bode. London: Pali Text Society.

Śāstri, Hirnananda. 1910–11. "Excavations at Kasiā." *Annual Report of the Archaeological Survey of India*. Pp. 63–72.

Schlingloff, Dieter. 1987. *Studies in the Ajantā Paintings: Identifications and Interpretations*. Delhi: Ajanta Publications.

Schmidt, I. J. 1843. *ḥDsangs bluṅ oder der Weise und der Thor*. St. Petersburg: W. Gräff.

Schober, Juliane. 1996. "Religious Merit and Social Status among Burmese Lay Associations." *Merit and Blessing in Mainland Southeast Asia in Comparative Perspective*. Edited by Cornelia Ann Kammerer and Nicola Tannenbaum. New Haven: Yale University Southeast Asia Studies. Pp. 197–211.

———. 1997. "Buddhist Just Rule and Burmese National Culture: State Patronage of the Chinese Tooth Relic in Myanma." *History of Religions* 36:218–43.

———. 1997a. "In the Presence of the Buddha: Ritual Veneration of the Burmese Mahāmuni Image." In *Sacred Biography in the Buddhist Traditions of South and Southeast Asia*. Edited by Juliane Schober. Honolulu: University of Hawai'i Press. Pp. 259–88.

———. 2000. "State Rituals and Ceremonies (Myanma)." In *The Life of Buddhism*. Edited by Frank E. Reynolds and Jason A. Carbine. Berkeley: University of California Press. Pp. 45–59.

———. 2001. "Venerating the Buddha's Remains in Burma: From Solitary Practice to the Cultural Hegemony of Communities." *Journal of Burma Studies* 6:111–39.

Schopen, Gregory. 1975. "The Phrase '*sa pṛthivīpradeśaś caityabhūto bhavet*' in the *Vajracchedikā:* Notes on the Cult of the Book in Mahāyāna." *Indo-Iranian Journal* 17: 147–81.

———. 1987. "Burial Ad Sanctos and the Physical Presence of the Buddha in Early Indian Buddhism." *Religion* 17:193–225.

———. 1988. "On the Buddha and his Bones: The Conception of a Relic in the Inscriptions of Nāgārjunikoṇḍa." *Journal of the American Oriental Society* 108:527–37.

———. 1991. "Archaeology and Protestant Presuppositions in the Study of Buddhism." *History of Religions* 31:1–23.

———. 1994. "Ritual Rights and Bones of Contention: More on Monastic Funerals and Relics in the *Mūlasarvāstivāda-Vinaya*." *Journal of Indian Philosophy* 22:31–80.

———. 1994a. "Stūpa and Tīrtha: Tibetan Mortuary Practices and an Unrecognized Form of Burial Ad Sanctos at Buddhist Sites in India." *The Buddhist Forum* 3:273–93.

———. 1995. "Immigrant Monks and the Proto-historical Dead: The Buddhist Occupation of Early Burial Sites in India." In *Festschrift Dieter Schlingloff*. Reinbek: Dr. Inge Wezler Verlag. Pp. 215–38.

———. 1996a. "The Suppression of Nuns and the Ritual Murder of Their Special Dead in Two Buddhist Monastic Texts." *Journal of Indian Philosophy* 24:563–92.

———. 1997. *Bones, Stones, and Buddhist Monks: Collected Papers on the Archaeology, Epigraphy, and Texts of Monastic Buddhism in India*. Honolulu: University of Hawai'i Press.

———. 1998. "Relic." In *Critical Terms for Religious Studies*. Edited by Mark C. Taylor. Chicago: The University of Chicago Press. Pp. 256–68.

———. 1999. "The Bones of a Buddha and the Business of a Monk: Conservative Monastic Values in an Early Mahāyāna Polemical Tract." *Journal of Indian Philosophy* 27:279–324.

Schrift, Melissa. 2001. *Biography of a Chairman Mao Badge: The Creation and Mass Consumption of a Personality Cult*. New Brunswick: Rutgers University Press.

Seidel, Anna. 1983. "Dabi." In *Hōbōgirin*. Paris: Adrien Maisonneuve. 6:573–85.

———. 1983a. "Dynastic Treasures and Taoist Sacraments: Taoist Roots in the Apocrypha." In *Tantric and Taoist Studies in Honour of R. A. Stein*. Edited by Michel Strickmann. Brussels: Institut Belge des Hautes Etudes Chinoises. 2:291–371.

Sen, Tansen. 2003. *Buddhism, Diplomacy, and Trade*. Honolulu: University of Hawai'i Press.

Seneviratne, Anuradha. 1994. "Customs, Rituals and Traditions Grown Around the Maha Bodhi Tree in Anuradhapura." In *Maha Bodhi Tree in Anuradhapura, Sri Lanka*. Edited by H.S.S. Nissanka. New Delhi: Vikas. Pp. 194–216.

Seneviratne, H. L. 1973. "L'ordination bouddhique à Ceylan." *Social Compass* 20:251–56.

———. 1978. *Rituals of the Kandyan State*. London: Cambridge University Press.

———. 1992. "Food Essence and the Essence of Experience." In *The Eternal Food: Gastronomic Ideas and Experiences of Hindus and Buddhists*. Edited by R. S. Khare. Albany: State University of New York Press. Pp. 179–200.

Shah, Priyabala. 1952. "Aiḍūka." *Journal of the Oriental Institute (Baroda)* 1:278–85.

Shah, U. P. 1970. "A Note on Aiḍūka." *Neue Indienkunde / New Indology. Festschrift Walter Ruben zum 70. Geburtstag*. Berlin: Akademie Verlag. Pp. 353–56.

Sharf, Robert H. 1992. "The Idolization of Enlightenment: On the Mummification of Ch'an Masters in Medieval China." *History of Religions* 32:1–31.

———. 1999. "On the Allure of Buddhist Relics." *Representations* 66:75–99.

Shaw, Julia. 2000. "The Sacred Landscape." *Buddhist Reliquaries from Ancient India*. Edited by Michael Willis. London: British Museum Press. Pp. 27–38.

Shinohara, Koichi. 1988. "Two Sources of Chinese Buddhist Biographies: Stupa Inscriptions and Miracle Stories." In *Monks and Magicians: Religious Biographies in Asia*. Edited by Phyllis Granoff and Koichi Shinohara. Oakville: Mosaic. Pp. 119–228.

———. 1992. "Guanding's Biography of Zhiyi, the Fourth Patriarch of the Tiantai Tradition." In *Speaking of Monks*. Edited by Phyllis Granoff and Koichi Shinohara. Oakville: Mosaic. Pp. 97–218.

———. 1999. "Literary Construction of Buddhist Sacred Places: *The Record of Mt. Lu* by Chen Shunyu." *Asiatische Studien / Etudes asiatiques* 53:937–64.

———. 2000. "The Kaṣāya Robe of the Past Buddha Kāśyapa in the Miraculous Instruction Given to the Vinaya Master Daoxuan (596–667)." *Chung-Hwa Buddhist Journal* 13:299–367.

———. 2001. "Contact Relics in the Heavenly Scripture Revealed to Daoxuan: 'Translocalizing' Buddhism in Medieval China." Paper presented to the conference "Absence Made Tangible: The Relics of the Buddha in India, China, and Japan," UCLA Center for Buddhist Studies, Los Angeles, January.

———. 2003. "The Story of the Buddha's Begging Bowl: Imagining a Biography and Sacred Places." In *Pilgrims, Patrons, and Place: Localizing Sanctity in Asian Religions*. Vancouver: University of British Columbia Press. Pp. 68–107.

Shorto, H. L. 1963. "The 32 *Myos* in the Medieval Mon Kingdom." *Bulletin of the School of Oriental and African Studies* 26:572–91.

———. 1970. "The Gavampati Tradition in Burma." In *R.C. Majumdar Felicitation Volume*. Edited by Himansu Bhusan Sarkar. Calcutta: K.L. Mukhopadhyay. Pp. 15–30.

———. 1971. "The Stupa as Buddha Icon in South East Asia." *Mahayanist Art after A.D. 900*. Edited by William Watson. London: School of Oriental and African Studies. Pp. 75–81.

Shway Yoe (James George Scott). 1882. *The Burman: His Life and Notions*. London: MacMillan.

Śikṣāsamuccaya. 1961. Edited by P. L. Vaidya. Darbhanga: Mithila Institute.

Silvestre, Hubert. 1952. "Commerce et vol de reliques au Moyen age." *Revue belge de philologie et d'histoire* 30:721–39.

Singer, Noel F. 1995. *Old Rangoon: City of the Shwedagon*. Gartmore, Scotland: Kiscadale.

Sinha, Bindeshwari Prasad. 1991. "The Earliest Buddhist Stūpas and Railings." *The Indian Journal of Buddhist Studies* 3, no. 2:1–7.

Sinha, Bindeshwari Prasad, and Sita Ram Roy. 1969. *Vaiśālī Excavations, 1958–62*. Patna.

Sircar, D. C. 1953. "Eḍūka." *Indian Historical Quarterly* 29:302–3.

Sirisoma, M. H. 1988. "Temples for the Tooth Relic in Sri Lanka—Their History." *The Buddhist Vesak Annual*. Pp. 43–47

Skeen, William. 1870. *Adam's Peak: Legendary, Traditional, and Historic Notices of the Samanala and Srī-Pāda*. Colombo: W.L.H. Skeen.

Skilling, Peter. 1992. "Symbols on the Body, Feet, and Hands of a Buddha. Part I—Lists." *Journal of the Siam Society*. 80:67–79.

———. 1996. "Symbols on the Body, Feet, and Hands of a Buddha. Part II—Short Lists." *Journal of the Siam Society.* 84:5–28.

Smith, Vincent. 1918. "Relics (Eastern)." *Encyclopaedia of Religion and Ethics.* Edited by James Hastings. Edinburgh: T and T. Clark. 10:658–62.

Smith, William Robertson. [1889] 1972. *The Religion of the Semites: The Fundamental Institutions.* New York: Schocken.

Snellgrove, David L. 1973. "Śākyamuni's Final *Nirvāṇa.*" *Bulletin of the School of Oriental and African Studies* 36:399–411.

———. 1987. *Indo-Tibetan Buddhism.* 2 vols. Boston: Shambhala.

Snellgrove, David L., ed. 1978. *The Image of the Buddha.* Tokyo: Kodansha International.

Snoek, G.J.C. 1995. *Medieval Piety from Relics to the Eucharist.* Leiden: E. J. Brill.

Soper, Alexander. 1940. "Japanese Evidence for the History of the Architecture and Iconography of Chinese Buddhism." *Monumenta Serica* 4:638–78.

———. 1948. "Hsiang-kuo-ssu, an Imperial Temple of Northern Sung." *Journal of the American Oriental Society* 68:19–45.

———. 1949–50. "Aspects of Light Symbolism in Gandhāran Sculpture." *Artibus Asiae* 12:252–83, 314–30; 13:63–85.

———. 1959. *Literary Evidence for Early Buddhist Art in China.* Ascona: Artibus Asiae.

———. 1959a. "A T'ang Parinirvāṇa Stele." *Artibus Asiae* 20:159–69.

Soymié, Michel. 1984. "Quelques représentations de statues miraculeuses dans les grottes de Touen-houang." In *Contributions aux études de Touen-houang.* Paris: Ecole Française d'Extrême-Orient. 3:77–102.

Spooner, D. B. 1908–09. "Excavations at Shāh-jī-kī-dherī." *Annual Report of the Archaeological Survey of India.* Pp. 38–59.

Srivastava, A. L. 1983. *Life in Sanchi Sculpture.* Atlantic Highlands: Humanities.

Srivastava, K. M. 1986. *Buddha's Relics from Kapilavastu.* Delhi: Agam Kala Prakashan.

Stevenson, Margaret. 1915. *The Heart of Jainism.* London: Oxford University Press.

Stone, Elizabeth Rosen. 1994. *The Buddhist Art of Nāgārjunakoṇḍa.* Delhi: Motilal Banarsidass.

Strachan, Paul. 1989. *Imperial Pagan: Art and Architecture of Burma.* Honolulu: University of Hawai'i Press.

Strickmann, Michel. 1996. *Mantras et mandarins: Le bouddhisme tantrique en Chine.* Paris: Gallimard.

———. 2002. *Chinese Magical Medicine.* Stanford: Stanford University Press.

Strong, John S. 1973. "Buddhism in China." *The Atlantic Monthly* 231:16–22.

———. 1979. "The Transforming Gift: An Analysis of Devotional Acts of Offering in Buddhist Avadāna Literature." *History of Religions* 18:221–37.

———. 1983. *The Legend of King Aśoka.* Princeton: Princeton University Press.

———. 1987. "Relics." In *The Encyclopedia of Religion.* Edited by Mircea Eliade. New York: MacMillan. 12:275–82.

———. 1992. *The Legend and Cult of Upagupta.* Princeton: Princeton University Press.

———. 1995. "Tooth and Cross: Buddhist and Christian Relics and the Interaction of Traditions." The 1995 Numata Lecture, The University of Chicago, 17 May. Unpublished manuscript.

———. 1997. "Mortarized Molar or Canonized Canine? The Portuguese Destruction of the Buddha's Tooth Relic in the Sixteenth Century." Stewart Lecture, Princeton University, 3 December. Unpublished manuscript.

———. 1998. "Les reliques des cheveux du Bouddha au Shwe Dagon de Rangoon." *Aséanie* 2:79–107.

———. 2001. *The Buddha: A Short Biography.* Oxford: OneWorld.

———. 2002. *The Experience of Buddhism: Sources and Interpretations.* 2nd. ed. Belmont: Wadsworth.

———. 2002a. "The Legend and Cult of Gavāṃpati in South and Southeast Asia." Paper presented to the "Asian Gods and Demons" Lecture Series, Stanford University, 25 February.

———. Forthcoming. "Buddhist Relics in Comparative Perspective: Beyond the Parallels." In *Embodying the Dharma: Buddhist Relic Veneration in Asia.* Edited by David Germano and Kevin Trainor. Albany: State University of New York Press.

Strong, John S., and Sarah M. Strong. 1973. "A Post-Cultural Revolution Look at Buddhism." *The China Quarterly* 54:321–30.

———. 1995. "A Tooth Relic of the Buddha in Japan: An Essay on the Sennyūji Tradition and a Translation of Zeami's Nō Play 'Shari.'" *Japanese Religions* 20:1–33.

Subrahmanyam, B. 1998. *Buddhist Relic Caskets in South India.* Delhi: Bharatiya Kala Prakashan.

Sumangalavilāsinī: Buddhaghosa's Commentary on the Dīgha Nikāya. 1971. 2d. ed. 3 vols. Edited by William Stede. London: Pali Text Society.

Sutta-Nipāta. 1997. Edited by Dines Andersen and Helmer Smith. Oxford: Pali Text Society.

Suvarṇaprabhāsasūtra. 1967. Edited by S. Bagchi. Darbhanga: Mithila Institute.

Swearer, Donald K. 1976. *Wat Haripuñjaya. A Study of the Royal Temple of the Buddha's Relic, Lamphun, Thailand.* Missoula: Scholars.

———. 1982. "The Kataragama and Kandy Äsaḷa Perahäras: Juxtaposing Religious Elements in Sri Lanka." In *Religious Festivals in South India and Sri Lanka.* Edited by Guy R. Welbon and Glenn E. Yocum. New Delhi: Manohar. Pp. 295–312.

———. 1995. "Hypostasizing the Buddha: Buddha Image Consecration in Northern Thailand." *History of Religions* 34:263–80.

———. Forthcoming. *Becoming the Buddha: The Ritual of Image Consecration in Thailand.* Princeton: Princeton University Press.

———. Forthcoming A. "Signs of the Buddha in Northern Thai Chronicles." Paper presented to the American Academy of Religion Seminar on Buddhist Relics, Chicago.

Swearer, Donald K. and Sommai Premchit. 1998. *The Legend of Queen Cāma.* Albany: State University of New York Press.

Tachard, Guy. [1688] 1981. *A Relation of the Voyage to Siam Performed by Six Jesuits Sent by the French King, to the Indies and China in the Year 1685.* Facsmile reprint. Bangkok: White Orchid.

Taishō shinshū daizōkyō [new Taishō era edition of the Buddhist canon] 1924–29. 55 vols. Edited by J. Takakusu and K. Watanabe. Tokyo: Taishō issaikyō kankōkai.

Tambiah, Stanley J. 1970. *Buddhism and the Spirit Cults in North-East Thailand.* Cambridge: Cambridge University Press.

———. 1976. *World Conqueror and World Renouncer.* Cambridge: Cambridge University Press.

———. 1984. *The Buddhist Saints of the Forest and the Cult of Amulets.* Cambridge: Cambridge University Press.

———. 1990. *Magic, Science, Religion and the Scope of Rationality.* Cambridge: Cambridge University Press.

Tamura Kōyū. 1967. "Aśoka Temple." In *Encyclopaedia of Buddhism.* Edited by G. P. Malalasekera. Colombo: Government of Ceylon Press. 2:198.

Tatelman, Joel. 2000. *The Glorious Deeds of Pūrṇa.* Delhi: Motilal Banarsidass.

Taw Sein Ko. 1903–4. "Ancient Relics Found at Shwebo." *Annual Report of the Archaeological Survey of India.* Pp. 145–57.

Taylor, J. L. 1993. *Forest Monks and the Nation-State.* Singapore: Institute of Southeast Asian Studies.

Tennent, James Emerson. 1859. *Ceylon: An Account of the Island.* 2 vols. London: Longman, Green, Longman and Roberts.

Thera and Therī-gāthā. 1883. Edited by Hermann Oldenberg and Richard Pischel. London: Pali Text Society.

Trainor, Kevin. 1992. "When Is a Theft Not a Theft? Relic Theft and the Cult of the Buddha's Relics in Sri Lanka." *Numen* 39:1–26.

———. 1996. "Constructing a Buddhist Ritual Site: Stūpa and Monastery Architecture." In *Unseen Presence: The Buddha and Sanchi.* Mumbai: Marg. Pp. 18–35.

———. 1997. *Relics, Ritual, and Representation in Buddhism: Rematerializing the Sri Lankan Theravāda Tradition.* Cambridge: Cambridge University Press.

Tsukamoto Zenryū. 1985. *A History of Early Chinese Buddhism: From Its Introduction to the Death of Hui-yüan.* 2 vols. Translated by Leon Hurvitz. Tokyo: Kodansha International.

Tucci, Giuseppe. [1932] 1988. *Stupa: Art, Architectonics, and Symbolism.* Translated by Uma Marina Vesci. New Delhi: Aditya Prakashan.

Turnour, George. 1837. "Account of the Tooth Relic of Ceylon, supposed to be alluded to in the opening passage of the Feroz lât inscription." *Journal of the Asiatic Society of Bengal* 6:856–68.

Vajirañāṇavarorasa [Prince]. 1973. *Ordination Procedure.* Bangkok: Mahāmakut Educational Council.

Van Buitenen, J.A.B. 1973–75. *The Mahābhārata.* Vols. 1–2. Chicago: University of Chicago Press.

Van den Heuvel, Theodorus Jacobus. 1997. *In the King's Trail: An 18th Century Dutch Journey to the Buddha's Footprint.* Edited by Remco Raben and Dhravat na Pombejra. Bangkok: The Royal Netherlands Embassy.

Van Gennep, Arnold. 1960. *The Rites of Passage.* Translated by Monika Vizedom and Gabrielle Caffee. Chicago: University of Chicago Press.

Vaudeville, Charlotte. 1964. "La légende de Sundara et les funérailles du Buddha." *Bulletin de l'Ecole Française d'Extrême-Orient* 52:73–91.

Vergati, Anne. 1982. "Le culte et l'iconographie du Buddha Dīpankara dans la vallée de Kathmandou." *Arts asiatiques* 37:22–27.

Vetch, Hélène. 1981. "Lieou Sa-ho et les grottes de Mo-kao." In *Nouvelles contributions aux études de Touen-houang*. Edited by Michel Soymié. Geneva: Droz. Pp. 137–48.

Vickery, Michael. 1976. "The Lion Prince and Related Remarks on Northern History." *Journal of the Siam Society* 64:326–77.

Viennot, Odette. 1954. *Le culte de l'arbre dans l'Inde ancienne*. Paris: Presses Universitaires de France.

Vinaya piṭakam. [1879–83] 1969–84. 5 vols. Edited by Hermann Oldenberg. London: Pali Text Society.

Visuddhajanavilāsinī nāma Apadānaṭṭhakathā. 1954. Edited by C. E. Godakumbura. London: Pali Text Society.

Visuddhimagga. 1920–21. 2 vols. Edited by C.A.F. Rhys Davids. London: Pali Text Society.

Vogel, J. Ph. 1925. "The Earliest Sanskrit Inscriptions of Java." *Publicaties van den oudheidkundigen dienst in Nederlandsch-Indië* (Batavia) 1:15–35.

———. 1954. "The Past Buddhas and Kāśyapa in Indian Art and Epigraphy." *Asiatica: Festschrift F. Weller*. Leipzig: Otto Harrassowitz.

Von Simson, Georg. 1981. "Die Buddhas der Vorzeit: Versuch einer astralmythologischen Deutung." *Studien zur Indologie und Iranistik* 7:77–91.

Voragine, Jacobus de. 1993. *The Golden Legend: Readings on the Saints*. 2 vols. Translated by William Granger Ryan. Princeton: Princeton University Press.

Waldschmidt, Ernst. 1944–48. *Die Überlieferung vom Lebensende des Buddha: Eine vergleichende Analyse des Mahāparinirvāṇasūtra und seiner Textentsprechungen*. 2 vols. Abhandlungen der Akademie der Wissenschaften in Göttingen, philologish-historische Klasse, nos. 29–30. Göttingen: Vandenhoeck and Ruprecht.

———. 1950–51. *Das Mahāparinirvāṇasūtra*. 3 parts. Abhandlungen der deutschen Akademie der Wissenschaften zu Berlin, Philosophisch-historische Klasse, 1949, no. 1 and 1950, nos. 2–3. Berlin: Akademie.

———. 1953–56. *Das Mahāvadānasūtra: Ein kanonischer Text über die sieben letzten Buddhas*. Abhandlungen der deutschen Akademie der Wissenschaften zu Berlin, Klasse für Sprachen, Literatur und Kunst, 1952, nr. 8. Berlin: Akademie.

———. 1962. *Das Catuṣpariṣatsūtra, eine kanonische Lehrschrift über die Begründung der buddhistischen Gemeinde*. Abhandlungen der deutschen Akademie der Wissenschaften zu Berlin, Klasse für Sprachen, Literatur und Kunst, 1960, nr. 1. Berlin: Akademie.

———. 1967. "Der Buddha preist die Verehrungswürdigkeit seiner Reliquien." *Vom Ceylon bis Turfan*. Göttingen: Vandenhoeck und Reprecht. Pp. 417–27.

Wallis, Glenn. 2001. "The Buddha's Remains: *Mantra* in the *Mañjuśrīmūlakalpa*." *Journal of the International Association of Buddhist Studies* 24:89–125.

Walshe, Maurice. 1987. *Thus Have I Heard: The Long Discourses of the Buddha*. London: Wisdom.

Wang, Eugene. 2003. "Biography and Spatiality: Visual Logic of Medieval Chinese Representation of Buddha's Life Stories." Paper presented to the Conference on "The Life of the Buddha: New Directions of Research." McMaster University, October.

Wang Yi-t'ung. 1984. *A Record of Buddhist Monasteries in Lo-Yang by Yang Hsüan-chih*. Princeton: Princeton University Press.

Wang Zhaolin and Xiong Lei. 1989. "Report from China: Discovery of Rare Buddhist Relics." *Oriental Art* 35:61–65.

Wang-Toutain, Françoise. 1994. "Le bol du Buddha: Propagation du bouddhisme et légitimité politique." *Bulletin de l'Ecole Française d'Extrême-Orient* 81:59–82.

Warren, Henry Clarke. 1896. *Buddhism in Translations*. Cambridge: Harvard University Press.

Watson, Burton. 1993. *The Lotus Sutra*. New York: Columbia University Press.

Watters, Thomas. [1904] 1961. *On Yuan Chwang's Travels in India*. 2 vols. Delhi: Munshiram Manohar Lal.

Weerasinghe, G. D. 1969. "The Alms Bowl of the Buddha—What Happened to This Relic Brought to Lanka?" *Buddhist Annual* (Colombo). Pp. 62–65.

Weinstein, Stanley. 1987. *Buddhism under the T'ang*. Cambridge: Cambridge University Press.

Welch, Holmes. 1972. *Buddhism under Mao*. Cambridge: Harvard University Press.

Weller, Friedrich. 1939–40. "Buddhas letzte Wanderung." *Monumenta Serica* 4:40–84, 406–40; 5:141–207.

Whitfield, Roderick. 1989. "Buddhist Monuments in China: Some Recent Finds of Śarīra Deposits." In *The Buddhist Heritage* . Edited by Tadeusz Skorupski. Tring: Institute of Buddhist Studies. Pp. 128–41.

———. 1990. "Esoteric Buddhist Elements in the Famensi Reliquary Deposit." *Asiatische Studien / Etudes asiatiques* 44:247–66.

Wickremasinghe, Don Martino De Zilva. 1928. *Epigraphia Zeylanica being Lithic and Other Inscriptions of Ceylon*. London: Humphrey Milford.

Wickremeratne, Ananda. 1987. "Shifting Metaphors of Sacrality: The Mythic Dimensions of Anurādhapura." *The City as a Sacred Center.* Edited by Bardwell Smith and Holly Baker Reynolds. Leiden: E. J. Brill. Pp. 45–59.

Wieger, Léon. 1913. "Les vies chinoises du Buddha: Récit de l'apparition sur terre du Buddha des Sakya." In *Buddhisme,* vol. 2. Sien-Hsien: Imprimerie de la Mission Catholique.

Wiesner, U. 1977. "Zur Frage der vier sogennanten Asoka-stūpas in Patan, Nepal." In *Zur Kunstgeschichte Asiens: 50 Jahre Lehre und Forschung an der Universität Köln*. Wiesbaden: Franz Steiner. Pp. 189–98.

Wijayaratna, Mohan. 1990. *Buddhist Monastic Life*. Translated by Claude Grangier and Steven Collins. Cambridge: Cambridge University Press.

Willemen, Charles. 1994. *The Storehouse of Sundry Valuables*. Berkeley: Numata Center for Buddhist Translation and Research.

Williams, Paul. 1997. "Some Mahāyāna Buddhist Perspectives on the Body." In *Religion and the Body.* Edited by Sarah Coakley. Cambridge: Cambridge University Press. Pp. 205–30.

Willis, Michael. 2000. "Relics and Reliquaries." *Buddhist Reliquaries from Ancient India*. Edited by Michael Willis. London: British Museum Press. Pp. 12–23.

Wilson, Liz. 1996. *Charming Cadavers: Horrific Figurations of the Feminine in Indian Buddhist Hagiographic Literature*. Chicago: University of Chicago Press.

Wiltshire, Martin G. 1990. *Ascetic Figures before and in Early Buddhism*. Berlin: Mouton de Gruyter.

Winternitz, Maurice. [1933] 1972. *A History of Indian Literature*. Vol. 2. Translated by S. Ketkar and H. Kohn. New Delhi: Oriental Books Reprint Corporation.

Wirz, Paul. 1948. "Buddhas Füsse und Fussabdrücke." *Jahrbuch des bernischen historischen Museum in Bern* 27:59–66.

Witanachchi, C. 1976. "Upagutta and Indagutta." In *Malalasekera Commemoration Volume*. Edited by O. H. DeA. Wijesekera. Colombo: Malalasekera Commemoration Volume Editorial Committee. Pp. 353–62.

Wood, W.A.R. [1924] 1982. *History of Siam*. Bangkok: Chalermnit.

Woodward, F. L. 1948. *The Minor Anthologies of the Pali Canon II: Udāna—Verses of Uplift and Itivuttaka—As It Was Said*. London: Pali Text Society.

Woodward, F. L., and E. M. Hare. 1932–36. *The Book of the Gradual Sayings*. 5 vols. London: Pali Text Society.

Wray, Elizabeth, Clare Rosenfield, and Dorothy Bailey. 1972. *Ten Lives of the Buddha: Siamese Temple Painting and Jātaka Tales*. Tokyo: Weatherhill.

Wright, Arthur F. 1957. "The Formation of Sui Ideology, 581–604." In *Chinese Thought and Institutions*. Edited by John K. Fairbank. Chicago: University of Chicago Press. Pp. 71–104.

Wyatt, David K. 2001. "Relics, Oaths and Politics in Thirteenth-Century Siam." *Journal of Southeast Asian Studies* 32:3–66.

Wylie, Alexander. [1897] 1966. *Chinese Researches*. Taipei: Ch'eng Wen.

Yamada, Isshi. 1968. *Karuṇāpuṇḍarīka*. 2 vols. London: School of Oriental and African Studies.

Yampolsky, Philip B. 1967. *The Platform Sūtra of the Sixth Patriarch*. New York: Columbia University Press.

Yiengpruksawan, Mimi Hall. 1987. "One Millionth of a Buddha: The *Hyakumantō Darani* in the Scheide Library." *Princeton University Library Chronicle* 48:225–38.

Yü, Chün-fang. 2001. *Kuan-yin. The Chinese Transformation of Avalokiteśvara*. New York: Columbia University Press.

Yule, Henry, and A. C. Burnell. [1903] 1994. *Hobson-Jobson*. Edited by William Crooke. New Delhi: Munshiram Manoharlal.

Yule, Henry, and Henri Cordier. [1903] 1993. *The Travels of Marco Polo*. 2 vols. New York: Dover.

Zhang Tinghao. 1990. *Fa-men si / Famen Temple / Homon-ji*. Xian: Shanxi Tourist Publishing House.

Zhu Qixin. 1990. "Buddhist Treasures from Famensi." *Orientations* May 1990:77–83.

Zimmer, Heinrich. 1925. *Karman: Ein buddhistischer Legendenkranz*. Munich: Verlag F. Bruckmann.

Zürcher, Erik. [1959] 1972. *The Buddhist Conquest of China*. Leiden: E. J. Brill.

———. 1982. "Prince Moonlight: Messianism and Eschatology in Early Medieval Chinese Buddhism." *T'oung pao* 68:1–75.

Zwalf, W. 1985. *Buddhism: Art and Faith*. New York: MacMillan.

INDEX

BUDDHISMS:

A PRINCETON UNIVERSITY PRESS SERIES

Relics of the Buddha, by John S. Strong

Becoming the Buddha: The Ritual of Image Consecreation in Thailand,
by Donald K. Swearer

The Impact of Buddhism on Chinese Material Culture,
by John Kieschnick

The Power of Denial: Buddhism, Purity, and Gender,
by Bernard Faure

Neither Monk nor Layman: Clerical Marriage in Modern Japanese Buddhism,
by Richard M. Jaffe

Buddhist Learning and Textual Practice in Eighteenth-Century Lankan Monastic Culture,
by Anne M. Blackburn

The Red Thread: Buddhist Approaches to Sexuality,
by Bernard Faure